LAW
&
MENTAL
HEALTH
PROFESSIONALS

MINNESOTA

LAW & MENTAL HEALTH PROFESSIONALS SERIES

Bruce D. Sales and Michael Owen Miller, Series Editors

LAW & MENTAL HEALTH PROFESSIONALS

MINNESOTA

Eric S. Janus
Ruth Mickelsen
Sheva Sanders

American Psychological Association
Washington, DC

Published by
American Psychological Association
750 First Street, NE
Washington, DC 20002

Copies may be ordered from
APA Order Department
P.O. Box 2710
Hyattsville, MD 20784

In the UK and Europe, copies may be ordered from
American Psychological Association
3 Henrietta Street
Covent Garden, London
WC2E 8LU England

This book was typeset in Palatino by General Graphic Services, York, PA

Text and cover designer: Rubin Krassner, Silver Spring, MD
Printer: Edwards Brothers, Inc., Ann Arbor, MI
Technical/production editor: Olin J. Nettles

Library of Congress Cataloging-in-Publication Data
Janus, Eric S.
    Law and mental health professionals,   Minnesota / Eric
S. Janus, Ruth Mickelson, Sheva Sanders.
        p.   cm. — (Law & mental health professionals series)
    Includes index.
    ISBN 1-55798-230-9 (acid-free paper)
    1. Mental health personnel—Legal status, laws, etc.—
Minnesota.   2. Forsenic psychiatry—Minnesota
    3. Psychology, Forsenic.   I. Mickelson, Ruth.   II. Sanders,
Sheva.   III. Title.   IV. Series.
KFM5726.5.P73J36   1994
344.776′044—dc20
[347.760444]   93-46108
                                                                        CIP

British Library Cataloguing-in-Publication Data
A CIP record is available from the British Library.

Printed in the United States of America
First edition

Contents

Editors' Preface

The Need to Know the Law

For years, providers of mental health services (hereinafter mental health professionals, or MHPs) have been directly affected by the law. At one end of the continuum, their practice has been controlled by laws covering such matters as licensure and certification, third-party reimbursement, and professional incorporation. At the other end, they have been courted by the legal system to aid in its administration, providing such services as evaluating the mental status of litigants, providing expert testimony in court, and engaging in therapy with court-referred juveniles and adults. Even when not directly affected, MHPs find themselves indirectly affected by the law because their clients sometimes become involved in legal entanglements that involve mental status issues (e.g., divorce proceedings or termination of parental rights hearings).

Despite this pervasive influence, most professionals do not know about, much less understand, most of the laws that affect their practice, the services they render, and the clients they serve. This state of affairs is particularly troubling for several reasons. First, not knowing about the laws that affect one's practice typically results in the MHP's not gaining the benefits that the law may provide. Consider the law relating to the incorporation of professionals. It confers significant benefit, but only if it is known about and applied. The fact that it has been enacted by the state legislature does not help the MHP, any more than an MHP will be of help to a distressed person who refuses to contact the MHP.

Second, not knowing about the laws that affect the services they render can result in incompetent performance of, and liability for, the MHP either through the civil law (e.g., malpractice law) or through criminal sanctions. A brief example may help underscore this point. When an MHP is asked to evaluate a party to a lawsuit and testify in court, the court (the law's term for the judge) is asking the professional to assess and testify about whether that litigant meets some legal standard. The court is often not concerned with the defendant's mental health per se, although this may be relevant to the MHP's evaluation of the person. Rather, the court wants to know if the person meets the legal standard as it is set down by the law. Not knowing the legal standard means that the MHP is most likely evaluating the person for the wrong goal and providing the court with irrelevant information, at least from the court's point of view. Regretfully, there are too many cases in which this has occurred.

Third, not knowing the law that affects the clients that MHPs serve may significantly diminish their capability for handling their clients' distress. For example, a client who is undergoing a divorce and child custody dispute may have distorted beliefs about what may happen during the legal proceedings. A basic understanding of the controlling law in this area will allow the therapist to be more sensitive in rendering therapy.

The Problem in Accessing Legal Information

Given the need for this information, why have MHPs not systematically sought it out? Part of the reason lies in the concern over their ability to understand legal doctrines. Indeed, this is a legitimate worry, especially if they had to read original legal materials that were not collected, organized, and described with an MHP audience in mind. This is of particular concern because laws are written in terms and phrases of "art" that do not always share the common law definition or usage, whereas some terms and phrases are left ambiguous and undefined or are used differently for different legal topics. Another part of the reason is that the law affecting MHPs and their clients is not readily available—even to lawyers. There are no compendiums that identify the topics that these laws cover or present an analysis of each topic for easy reference.

To compound the difficulty, the law does not treat the different mental health professional disciplines uniformly or always specify the particular disciplines as being covered by it. Nor does the law emanate from a single legal forum. Each state enacts its own rules and regulations, often resulting in wide variations in the way a topic is handled across the United States. Multiply this confusion times the one hundred or so topics that relate to mental health practice. In addition, the law within a state does not come from one legal source. Rather, there are five primary ones: the state constitution; state legislative enactments (statutes); state agency administrative rules and regulations; rules of court promulgated by the state supreme court; and state and federal court cases that apply, interpret, and construe this existing state law. To know about one of these sources without knowing how its pronouncements on a given topic have been modified by these other sources can result in one's making erroneous conclusions about the operation of the law. Finally, mental health practice also comes under the purview of federal law (constitutional and statutory law, administrative rules and regulations, and case law). Federal law authorizes direct payments to MHPs for their services to some clients, sets standards for delivery of services in federal facilities (e.g., Veterans Administration hospitals), and articulates the law that guides cases that are tried in federal courts under federal law.

Purposes of This Series

What is needed, therefore, is a book for each state, the District of Columbia, and the federal jurisdictions that comprehensively and accurately reviews and integrates all of the law that affects MHPs in that jurisdiction (hereinafter state). To ensure currency, regular supplements to these books will also need to be drafted. These materials should be written so that they are completely understandable to MHPs, as well as to lawyers. To accomplish these goals, the editors have tried to identify every legal topic that affects mental health practice, making each one the subject of a chapter. Each chapter, in turn, describes the legal standards that the MHP will be operating under and the relevant legal process that the MHP will be operating within. If a state does not have relevant law on an issue, then a brief explanation of how this law works in other states will be presented while noting the lack of regulation in this area within the state under consideration.

This type of coverage facilitates other purposes of the series. Although each chapter is written in order to state exactly what is the present state of the law and not argue for or against any particular approach, it is hoped that the comprehensiveness of the coverage will encourage MHPs to question the desirability of their states' approach to each topic. Such information and concern should provide the impetus for initiating legislation and litigation on the part of state mental health associations to ensure that the law reflects the scientific knowledge and professional values to the greatest extent possible.

In some measure, states will initially be hampered in this proactivity because they will not know what legal alternatives are available and how desirable each alternative actually is. When a significant number of books in this series is available, however, it will allow for nationally oriented policy studies to identify the variety of legal approaches that are currently in use and to assess the validity of the behavioral assumptions underlying each variant, and ultimately lead to a conclusion as to the relative desirability of alternate approaches.[1] Thus, two other purposes of this book are to foster comprehensive analyses of the laws affecting

---

1. Sales, B. D. (1983). The legal regulation of psychology: Professional and scientific interactions. In C. J. Scheirer & B. L. Hammonds (Eds.), *The master lecture series: Vol. 2. Psychology and law* (pp. 5–36). Washington, DC: American Psychological Association.

MHPs across all states and of the validity of the behavioral assumptions underlying these laws, and to promote political, legislative, and legal action to change laws that are inappropriate and impede the effective delivery of services. Legal change may be required because of gaps in legal regulation, overregulation, and regulation based on invalid behavioral and social assumptions. We hope this process will increase the rationality of future laws in this area and improve the effectiveness and quality of mental health service delivery nationally.

There are three remaining purposes for this series. First, although it will not replace the need for legal counsel, this series will make the MHP an intelligent consumer of legal services. This ability is gaining importance in an era of increasing professionalization and litigiousness. Second, it will ensure that MHPs are aware of the law's mandates when providing expert services (e.g., evaluation and testimony) within the legal system. Although chapters will not address how to clinically assess for the legal standard, provider competency will increase because providers now will be sure of the goals of their service (e.g., the legal standard that they are to assess for) as well as their roles and responsibilities within the legal system as to the particular topic in issue. Third and finally, each book will make clear that the legal standards that MHPs are asked to assess for by the law have typically not been translated into behavioral correlates. Nor are there discussions of tests, scales, and procedures for MHPs to use in assessing for the behavioral correlates of the legal standards in most cases. This series will provide the impetus for such research and writing.

Content and Organization of Volumes

Each book in this series is organized into six sections. Section 1 addresses the legal credentialing of MHPs. Section 2 deals with the different business forms for conducting one's practice. Section 3 then addresses insurance reimbursement and tax deductions that clients can receive for utilizing mental health services. With the business matters covered, the book then turns to the law directly affecting service delivery. Section 4 starts by covering the law that affects the maintenance and privacy of professional information. Section 5 then considers each area of law that may require the services of MHPs. It is subdivided into five parts: families and juveniles, other civil matters, topics that apply similarly in both civil and criminal cases, criminal matters, and voluntary and involuntary receipt of state services by the clients of mental health services. The last section of the book, section 6, discusses the law that limits service delivery and that sets liability for unethical and illegal behavior as a service provider.

Collectively, the chapters in these sections represent all topics pertaining to the law as it affects MHPs in their practices. Two caveats are in order, however. First, the law changes slowly over time. Thus, a supplement service will update all chapters on a regular basis. Second, as MHPs become more involved in the legal system, new opportunities for involvement are likely to arise. To be responsive to these developments, the supplements will also contain additional chapters reflecting these new roles and responsibilities.

Some final points about the content of this book are in order. The exact terms that the law chooses are used in the book even if they are a poor choice from an MHP's point of view. And where terms are defined by the law, that information is presented. The reader will often be frustrated, however, because, as has already been noted, the law does not always define terms or provide detailed guidance. This does not mean that legal words and phrases can be taken lightly. The law sets the rules that MHPs and their clients must operate by; thus, the chapters must be read carefully. This should not be too arduous a task because chapters are relatively short. On the other hand, such brevity will leave some readers frustrated because chapters appear not to go far enough in answering their questions. Note that all of the law is covered. If there is no law, however, there is no coverage. If a question is not answered in the text, it is because Minnesota law has not addressed the issue. Relatedly, if an obligation or benefit is created by a professional regulation (i.e., a rule of a professional organization) but is not directly recognized by the law, it is not covered. Thus, for example, professional credentials are not addressed in these volumes.

Bruce D. Sales
Michael Owen Miller
Series Editors

Authors' Preface

The work of Minnesota mental health professionals (MHPs) is governed by an interrelated web of state and federal law. In many areas of concern to MHPs, state law predominates. Examples of such areas are family law,[1] juvenile law,[2] guardianship law,[3] and much of contract, tort, and business law.[4] In other areas, federal and state laws operate in largely separate spheres. For example, civil and criminal procedures are governed by federal rules in federal court and by state rules in state court.[5] In yet other areas, federal and state law have a more complex relationship. For example, much of Minnesota tax law is based on federal tax rules.[6] Many state benefit programs are governed by both federal and state rules.[7] And the outer limits of state activity are often set by the U.S. Constitution.[8]

This book is principally a treatment of state law applicable to MHPs practicing in Minnesota. We have not hesitated, however, to make liberal reference to federal law where, in our judgment, such references are necessary to an understanding of how Minnesota law and Minnesota programs work. However, where federal law is truly separable from Minnesota law, our focus is on Minnesota law alone.

Minnesota law has several sources. These include the Minnesota Constitution, state statutory law, state administrative rules, decisions of state courts, and the rules of state courts.

The Minnesota Constitution establishes the framework for state government and guarantees various individual rights. Citations to the Minnesota Constitution appear in the following form: Minn. Const. Art. 1, § 1. This reference indicates that the citation is to the first paragraph of the first article in the Minnesota Constitution.

Citations to state statutes, which result from legislation passed by the Minnesota State Legislature, appear in the following forms: M.S.A. § 595.02, subd. 1 (West 1988), or M.S.A. § 626.556, subd. 2 (West Supp. 1992). "M.S.A." stands for *Minnesota Statutes Annotated*, published by West Publishing Com-

---

1. *See* chapter 5A.5.
2. *See* chapters 5A.8 through 5A.23.
3. *See* chapter 5A.2.
4. *See* section 5B.
5. *See* sections 5C and 5D.
6. *See* chapter 3.3.
7. *See, e.g.,* chapters 5A.20 and 5E.1.
8. *See, e.g.,* chapter 5E.3.

pany. The date in parentheses is the date of publication of the volume. The "Supp." notation means that the cited provision is found in the supplemental pocket part of the volume. M.S.A. is the unofficial source for Minnesota statutory law. The official source is Minnesota Statutes, published by the state of Minnesota. We have chosen to cite M.S.A. because, unlike the official source, it contains extensive annotations about each statutory section. These annotations show the historical development of the law, summarize court decisions interpreting the law, and contain references to other statutory sections and to secondary material. Thus, the annotated version of the laws is a useful starting point for further research.

State administrative rules are created by state agencies operating under the authority delegated to them by the legislature to carry out specific agency functions. For example, the legislation creating the State Board of Psychology does not list all types of professional misconduct, but rather gives the Board the authority to make administrative rules delineating specific types of misconduct that can result in the suspension or revocation of a license.[9] These administrative rules are published in the State Register and are codified in a series of volumes titled *Minnesota Rules*. References to the codified rules appear in the following form: Minn. R. 3525.2750 (1991).

State court decisions report on the judicial dispositions of individual cases. Such decisions help define the interpretation of statutes and administrative rules. Court decisions are also the vehicle for the articulation of judge-made law, often called "common law." The Minnesota court system has three levels of courts. District courts, the lowest level, are the courts in which cases are initially brought, tried, and adjudicated. The decisions of district court judges are not published and are therefore not an authoritative source of law.

The middle level of the Minnesota system is the Minnesota Court of Appeals. This court hears appeals from the district courts. Appeals are heard and decided by panels of three judges. Some Court of Appeals opinions are published and (unless overruled by the Minnesota Supreme Court) are authoritative statements of Minnesota law. Court of Appeals decisions are published in *Northwestern Reporter 2nd*, published by West Publishing Company. They are cited in the following format: Andrew v. White-Rodgers, 465 N.W.2d 102 (Minn. Ct. App. 1991). This case, known by the names of the plaintiff and defendant, begins at page 102 of volume 465 of *Northwestern Reporter 2nd*. It was decided in 1991.

---

9. *See* chapter 1.3.

The highest authority on Minnesota law is the Minnesota Supreme Court. This seven-member court reviews a small number of Court of Appeals decisions. Generally, its consideration is reserved for cases presenting important questions of public policy. Minnesota Supreme Court opinions are published in West's *Northwestern Reporter 2nd*, and are cited as follows: Holm v. Sponco Mfg., Inc., 324 N.W.2d 207 (Minn. 1982). Prior to 1977, Minnesota Supreme Court opinions were published in an official reporter called *Minnesota Reports*, as well as in the *Northwestern Reporter 2nd*. These older cases are cited with references to both reporters: for example, Magnuson v. Rupp Mfg., 285 Minn. 32, 171 N.W.2d 201 (1969).

At times, we have provided citations to a particular page of a case. For example, the citation "Holm v. Sponco Mfg., Inc., 324 N.W. 2d 207, 212" refers to page 212 of the case, which begins on page 207 of volume 324 of *Northwestern Reporter 2nd*.

State court rules, in contrast with judicial decisions, are the products of judges acting in a legislative rather than a judicial capacity. In this role, judges make procedural rules of general application in the courts. The Minnesota Supreme Court promulgates court rules that relate to civil procedure, criminal procedure, civil appellate procedure, and practice in other specified courts. Most rules can be found in *Minnesota Rules of Court* (West Publishing Company).

Citations to federal court decisions are from the United States District Court (F. Supp.), the United States Court of Appeals (F. or F.2d), and the United States Supreme Court (U.S., S.Ct., or L.Ed.). As is the case with the reports of state decisions, the number preceding the reporter is the volume number and the number following is the page. References to federal legislation appear in the form 26 U.S.C. § 213(a) (1992). This particular citation to the United States Code, the repository of federal legislation, is from title 26, section 213(a), current as of 1992. References to federal administrative regulations are to the Code of Federal Regulations, as follows: 34 CFR § 300.5 (1991). In addition, there are citations to treatises and law review articles. These references may provide a fuller background of an issue of interest to MHPs.

Although some chapters were updated until the manuscript went to press, the reader should consider the entire volume current as of September 1993.

This volume is the work of three coauthors. Ruth Mickelson, JD, is Associate General Counsel of Medica. She authored the chapters of the book dealing with insurance and the regulation of forms of practice (chapters 2.4, 2.5, 2.6, 2.7, 3.1, and 3.2). Sheva Sanders, JD, an attorney in private practice, authored the chapters on taxes, professional liability, and the organization of MHPs' businesses (chapters 2.0–2.3, 3.3, 6.0, 6.4–6.9). Eric S. Janus, professor of law at William Mitchell College of Law, wrote the remainder of the book and served as editor for the entire volume.

Eric S. Janus
Ruth Mickelsen
Sheva Sanders

Acknowledgments

Many people contributed to the preparation of this book. Professors Ken Kirwin, Mike Steenson, and Carl Moy reviewed chapters in their areas of expertise and provided valuable suggestions. Many student research assistants worked on the book; among these were Tim Becker, Ann Bray, Karin Chedister, Michael Fleming, Margaret Truesdell Hall, David Hunt, Jessica Lipsky, Lee Scholder, and Tom Williams. Also contributing were Mike Brose, Chris Chilstrom, Brad Fisher, Susan Hallenbeck, Pam Hester, Katie Fashant Leifur, Troy Wolf, and Jeff Zick. Cal Bonde, of the William Mitchell College of Law Word Processing Department, showed high professionalism and skill in putting together the manuscript for this project. And my administrative assistant, Deb Aanestad Long, provided skillful and efficient support.

Eric S. Janus

Legal
Credentialing

1.1

Licensure and Regulation of Psychiatrists

The licensure and regulation of psychiatrists is governed by statutory law[1] that establishes a Board of Medical Examiners, defines the practice of medicine, establishes qualifications and procedures for the licensure of physicians, establishes exceptions to licensure, regulates the conduct of physicians, establishes grounds for disciplinary action, and prescribes criminal sanctions for violations of the licensure requirements. There is no separate licensure provision pertaining to the practice of psychiatry; the law is a generic one that regulates the practice of medicine without regard to specialty.[2] Portions of the statute that do not apply to psychiatrists are omitted from this discussion.

Board of Medical Examiners

The Board of Medical Examiners is the primary administrative body that licenses and regulates psychiatrists.[3] By law, it consists of 16 residents of the state of Minnesota appointed by the governor. Ten of the members must be licensed doctors of medicine, one must be a licensed doctor of osteopathy, and five must be public members. The Board's duties include

---

1. Minn. Stat. Chapter 147.
2. The references to psychiatrists therefore apply generally to physicians. State law does not address the prescription of drugs, which is governed by federal law.
3. M.S.A. § 147.01 (West 1989 & Supp. 1991).

1. issuing,[4] suspending, revoking, limiting, restoring, and re-issuing[5] licenses to practice medicine;
2. disciplining physicians;[6]
3. determining whether to approve a school of medicine that will enable its graduates to qualify for licensure in the state of Minnesota;[7]
4. adopting rules to carry out its duties,[8] including rules determining what constitutes a passing score on the examination for licensure;[9]
5. adopting a written statement of internal operating procedures for complaints and disciplinary matters;[10] and
6. publishing at least annually a description of all disciplinary measures taken by the Board.[11]

Licensure

Applicability

Persons who practice medicine[12] must be licensed by the Board.[13] A person practices medicine if he or she holds out to the public that he or she is authorized to practice medicine; offers to, or does, prescribe or administer any drug or medicine; diagnoses or treats diseases, wounds, infirmities, and so forth; performs any surgery; uses hypnosis for treatment;[14] or uses the designation "doctor of medicine," "medical doctor," or so forth in connection with any diagnosis.[15]

Basic Requirements

The consent of the Board is required for the issuance of a license to practice medicine. Applicants must satisfy several requirements to be licensed.[16] The burden of proof is on the applicant to demonstrate satisfaction of the following requirements:[17]

---

4. M.S.A. § 147.02 (West 1989).
5. M.S.A. § 147.091 (West 1989).
6. M.S.A. § 147.091 (West 1989); § 147.141 (West 1989 & Supp. 1991).
7. M.S.A. § 147.02 (West 1989); § 147.037 (West 1989 & Supp. 1991).
8. M.S.A. § 147.01, subd. 3 (West 1989 & Supp. 1991).
9. M.S.A. § 147.02, subd. 1(c) (West 1989).
10. M.S.A. § 147.02, subd. 5 (West 1989).
11. M.S.A. § 147.02, subd. 6 (West 1989).
12. Exceptions are listed below. See M.S.A. § 147.09 (West 1989).
13. M.S.A. § 147.081 (West 1989).
14. See chapter 1.9.
15. M.S.A. § 147.081 (West 1989).
16. M.S.A. § 147.02, subd. 1 (West Supp. 1993).
17. M.S.A. § 147.091, subd. 1(a) (West 1989).

1. filing a written application showing that the applicant is of good moral character and satisfies the other requirements for licensure;

2. graduation from a medical school approved by the Board, or current enrollment in the final year of study at the school;

3. passing an examination prepared and graded by the National Board of Medical Examiners or the Federation of State Medical Boards;[18]

4. completing a one-year program of graduate, clinical medical training in an approved[19] program;

5. making a personal appearance before the Board;

6. paying a nonrefundable fee;

7. not being under license suspension or revocation in another state or jurisdiction; and

8. not having engaged in conduct warranting disciplinary action (see below).[20]

Alternate Licensure Requirements

In addition to the basic requirements, two alternate routes to licensure exist. Applicants licensed to practice medicine in another state or in a province of Canada may be licensed on the basis of reciprocity. The requirements are identical to the basic requirements listed above.[21]

Graduates of approved[22] foreign medical schools may be licensed if they satisfy relevant basic requirements and, in addition, have a certificate from the educational council for foreign medical graduates, have a working knowledge of English, have an additional two years of graduate clinical medical training,[23] and have passed an examination of the Federation of State Medical Boards or the Medical Council of Canada.[24]

---

18. The Board determines what constitutes a passing score on the examination. M.S.A. § 147.02, subd. 1(c) (West Supp. 1993). Under some circumstances, passage of the United States Medical Licensing Examination may suffice. *Id.*

19. The program must either be accredited by a national accrediting organization approved by the Board or be approved in advance by the Board itself. M.S.A. § 147.02, subd. 1(d) (West Supp. 1993).

20. The Board may issue a conditional or limited license to persons who do not meet this requirement only if the applicant demonstrates that the public will be protected. M.S.A. § 147.02, subd. 1(g) (West Supp. 1993).

21. M.S.A. § 147.037 (West 1989 & Supp. 1991).

22. The Board approves foreign medical schools that are equivalent to accredited U.S. or Canadian schools. M.S.A. § 147.037, subd. 1(b) (West 1989 & Supp. 1991).

23. This requirement is not applicable to persons admitted as permanent immigrants by reason of exceptional ability in the sciences. M.S.A. § 147.037, subd. 1(d) (West 1989 & Supp. 1991).

24. M.S.A. § 147.037, subd. 1(e) (West 1989 & Supp. 1991).

The Board may issue temporary certificates for graduate training to graduates of foreign medical schools.[25] Holders of temporary certificates may perform services incidental to the training prescribed by the institution while acting under the direction of a person licensed to practice medicine and surgery in Minnesota. No fee or remuneration of any kind may be collected by the holder of the certificate.

Exceptions to Licensing

The licensing law[26] does not apply to[27] persons who are commissioned medical officers of, members of, or employees of the armed forces, the United States Public Health Service, the Veterans Administration, or any federal institution; physicians licensed elsewhere in actual consultation in Minnesota; physicians licensed elsewhere treating coparticipants in outdoor recreation programs[28] in Minnesota; students of a recognized medical school under the direct supervision of a preceptor; students performing the duties of an intern or resident or engaged in equivalent postgraduate work in an approved hospital or institution; persons employed by the state university, the state Department of Education, any public or private educational institution, or the state Department of Health engaged in duties that are of a public health or educational character; registered physicians' assistants; persons licensed as doctors of osteopathy or by health-related licensing boards[29] or registered by the commissioner of health,[30] provided the activities are confined to the scope of the license; Christian Scientists or others who endeavor to prevent or cure disease exclusively by mental or spiritual means or who practice ritual circumcision; or physicians licensed in other states who are in Minnesota for the sole purpose of providing medical services at athletic competitions.

---

25. Minn. R. 5600.0800 (1991).
26. M.S.A. § 147.081 (West 1989).
27. M.S.A. § 147.09 (West 1989).
28. Defined at M.S.A. § 86A.03, subd. 3 (West 1989).
29. Defined at M.S.A. § 214.01 (West 1989).
30. *See* M.S.A. § 214.13 (West 1989).

Regulation

Disciplinary Actions Against a Licensed Physician

A physician may be subjected to disciplinary action by the Board[31] for the following reasons:

1. obtaining a license improperly;

2. conviction, during the previous five years, of a felony reasonably related to the practice of medicine;[32]

3. disciplinary action against the person's medical license in another jurisdiction, or failure to report to the Board that charges regarding the person's license have been brought in another jurisdiction;

4. improper advertising;

5. violating a federal or state rule relating to the practice of medicine, or a federal or state controlled substance law;

6. engaging in unethical, deceitful conduct; conduct demonstrating a willful or careless disregard for the health or welfare of a patient; or medical practice that is professionally incompetent;

7. failure to supervise a physician's assistant or a physician under an agreement with the Board;

8. aiding or abetting an unlicensed person in the practice of medicine;[33]

9. adjudication as mentally incompetent, mentally ill, or mentally retarded, or as a chemically dependent person, a person dangerous to the public, or a person with a psychopathic personality;[34]

10. engaging in unprofessional conduct, which includes any departure from minimal standards of acceptable and prevailing medical practice. Actual injury need not be shown;

---

31. M.S.A. § 147.091 (West 1989). Revocation and suspension of the physician's license are among the disciplinary measures possible. *See* below and M.S.A. § 147.141 (West 1989 & Supp. 1991) for descriptions of the other types of disciplinary action possible.

32. *See* chapter 6.7.

33. It is not grounds for discipline to delegate properly to qualified persons the provision of health services. M.S.A. § 147.091, subd. 1(i) (West 1989).

34. *See generally* M.S.A. § 525.55 (appointment of guardian for incapacitated persons); § 253B.02 (definitions of mentally ill, mentally retarded, chemically dependent); § 526.09 (West 1989) (psychopathic personality). Adjudication by a court under these provisions results in the automatic suspension of the physician's license, unless the Board directs otherwise. M.S.A. § 147.091, subd. 1(j) (West 1989). *See* chapters 5A.2, 5A.3, 5B.1, 5D.25, 5E.4, 5E.5, 5E.6.

11. inability to practice medicine with reasonable skill and safety by reason of some impairment of mental or physical condition;[35]

12. improperly revealing a privileged communication from or relating to a patient;[36]

13. improper management or maintenance of medical records, including failing to furnish medical records as required by law;[37]

14. fee splitting, including paying or receiving payment for the referral of patients or the prescription of drugs; dividing fees with another physician not in proportion to the services provided, unless disclosure is made; referring patients to a health care provider where the physician has a financial interest in the provider, unless disclosure is made; or dispensing for profit drugs or devices, unless disclosure is made. Where disclosure is required, the disclosure must be made in advance, in writing to the patient. The writing must disclose that the patient is free to choose another health care provider;

15. engaging in fraudulent or abusive billing practices;

16. becoming addicted or habituated to a drug or intoxicant;

17. prescribing a drug or referring a patient to a health care provider for other than accepted medical purposes;

18. engaging in any conduct with a patient that is sexual, reasonably interpreted as sexual, seductive, or sexually demeaning;[38]

19. failing to make any mandatory report to the Board.[39] This obligation includes reporting personal knowledge that the physician reasonably believes constitutes grounds for disci-

---

35. *See* chapter 5B.1.
36. *See* chapters 4.1, 4.2, 4.3. Privilege is defined at M.S.A. § 595.02(d) (West 1989). Regulations of the Department of Health require physicians to report certain information about communicable disease. Minn. R. 4605.7030 (1991). Physicians are required to report information from or about patients where they suspect abuse or neglect. M.S.A. § 626.557 (West 1989 & Supp. 1991) (vulnerable adults); § 626.556 (West 1989 & Supp. 1991) (children). *See* below in this chapter and chapters 5A.7 and 5A.8.
37. For example, M.S.A. § 144.335 (West 1989 & Supp. 1991) requires physicians to furnish medical records to patients, with some exceptions, on request of the patient. *See* chapter 4.1.
38. Sexual contact with psychotherapy patients or former patients may result in civil and criminal liability as well. *See* M.S.A. § 148A.01 et seq. (civil liability) and § 603.341 et seq. (criminal liability). *See* chapters 6.6 and 6.7.
39. *See* the section on Reporting Obligations below.

plinary action against a physician, including him- or herself; or

20. failing to cooperate with an investigation of the Board.[40]

Also, the Board may not issue or renew a license[41] if the applicant or licensee owes the state delinquent taxes in the amount of $500 or more.[42]

Upon receiving a complaint, the Board forwards the information to a designee of the attorney general's office. The designee reviews the information and consults with the executive secretary and/or members of the Board and determines whether the complaint alleges illegal or unauthorized activities warranting Board action.[43] The Board may, with some exceptions, attempt to correct the complaint through nonadversarial, nondisciplinary means.[44]

Penalties for Violations

The Board may revoke, suspend, limit, or condition a person's license to practice medicine; impose a civil penalty not exceeding $10,000 for each violation; order the physician to provide uncompensated professional service; or censure or reprimand the physician.[45]

Any person practicing medicine without a license is guilty of a gross misdemeanor.[46]

Reporting Obligations

The law imposes on physicians a number of reporting obligations:

1. Licensed health professionals (including physicians) must report to the Board of Medical Examiners any "personal knowledge" of any physician's conduct that the person "reasonably believes" constitutes grounds for disciplinary action.[47]

---

40. M.S.A. § 147.131 (West 1989) describes the required cooperation, which includes responding fully and promptly to questions raised and providing copies of patient medical records reasonably requested by the Board.
41. Licenses must be renewed annually. Minn. R. 5600.0605 (1991).
42. M.S.A. § 147.091, subd. 7 (West 1989). There are exceptions for certain tax delinquencies that are contested or subject to a payment agreement.
43. M.S.A. § 214.10, subds. 1, 2 (West 1989 & Supp. 1991).
44. M.S.A. § 214.10, subd. 2 (West 1989 & Supp. 1991). Exceptions involve complaints alleging a violation of a statute or rule that involves sexual contact with a patient. M.S.A. § 214.10, subd. 8(a) (West 1989 & Supp. 1991).
45. M.S.A. § 147.141 (West 1989 & Supp. 1991).
46. M.S.A. § 147.081 (West 1989).
47. M.S.A. § 147.111, subd. 4 (West 1989 & Supp. 1991).

2. Institutions (hospitals and clinics) must report to the Board any action taken by the institution restricting a physician's privilege to practice or disciplining the physician.

3. A physician has an obligation to report any of his or her own actions that are reportable to the Board.

The reporting requirements described in the three paragraphs above must be accomplished no later than 30 days after the occurrence of the reportable event.[48] Reporters under these provisions are immune from civil liability or criminal prosecution for submitting a report. All reports are confidential and privileged.[49]

4. A physician has an obligation to report suspected abuse or neglect of a child or of a vulnerable adult.[50]

---

48. M.S.A. § 147.111, subd. 8 (West 1989 & Supp. 1991).
49. M.S.A. § 147.121, subd. 1 (West 1989 & Supp. 1991).
50. M.S.A. § 626.556 (West 1989 & Supp. 1991) (children); § 626.557 (West 1989 & Supp. 1991) (vulnerable adults). *See* chapters 5A.7 and 5A.8 for additional information on these duties.

Licensure and Regulation of Psychiatric Nurses

The licensure and regulation of psychiatric nurses is governed by statutory law[1] that establishes a Board of Nursing, defines terms contained within the law, establishes exceptions to licensure, and prescribes sanctions for violations of the statute. Because the law does not distinguish the specialty of psychiatric nursing, there is no separate license pertaining to the practice of psychiatric nursing.[2]

Board of Nursing

The Board of Nursing is the primary administrative body that licenses and regulates nurses. The Board consists of 16 members appointed for four-year terms by the governor. The Board is composed of eight registered nurses,[3] four licensed practical nurses,[4] and four public members.[5] The Board has the power

---

1. M.S.A. §§ 148.171 to 148.283 (West Supp. 1993).
2. The statute distinguishes between professional or registered nurses (RNs) and practical or licensed practical nurses (LPNs). This discussion will be limited to professional nursing because psychiatric nurses will have the additional education required by the former category.
3. The statute sets qualifications regarding the type and length of experience required of professional nurses serving on the Board. M.S.A. § 148.181 (West 1988 & Supp. 1993).
4. Practical nurses must be licensed by and residents of the state of Minnesota, be graduates of an approved school of practical nursing, and have had at least five years of experience in practical nursing. M.S.A. § 148.181(1) (West Supp. 1992).
5. A public member is a person who is not, and never was, a member of the nursing profession or a spouse of a member of the profession, or who has not had a financial interest in the profession. M.S.A. § 214.02 (West 1992).

and/or duty to

1. regulate the granting, denial, revocation, restriction, and suspension of licenses;[6]

2. establish standards for schools of nursing and determine which schools meet the standards necessary for Board approval;[7]

3. keep a record of all proceedings and make a biannual report to the governor, the legislature, and the commissioner of health;[8] and

4. initiate the prosecution of persons violating provisions of the laws pertaining to the licensing and regulation of nurses.[9]

Licensure

Applicants will be licensed as professional nurses in Minnesota if they[10]

1. have not engaged in conduct warranting disciplinary action;[11]

2. have satisfactorily met secondary education requirements;

3. have completed a course of study in a professional nursing program approved by the Board, another United States nursing board, or a Canadian province;

4. have passed a written examination administered by the Board;[12]

5. have verified that they are of good moral character and in good mental health;[13] and

6. have paid the necessary licensing fee.

Under the following circumstances a nonrenewable temporary permit to practice professional nursing may be issued to persons who are not the subject of any disciplinary investigation:[14]

1. The applicant has graduated from an accredited nursing program and has been authorized to take the licensure examination;

---

6. M.S.A. § 148.261 (West Supp. 1992).
7. M.S.A. § 148.251 (West Supp. 1992).
8. M.S.A. § 214.07 (West 1992).
9. M.S.A. § 148.191 (West 1989 & Supp. 1992).
10. M.S.A. § 148.211, subd. 1 (West Supp. 1993).
11. M.S.A. § 148.261, subd. 1 (West Supp. 1992).
12. The written examination may be supplemented by an oral or practical examination. M.S.A. § 148.211, subd. 1 (West Supp. 1992).
13. Minn. R. 6315.0400, subp. 3 (1991). *See* chapter 5B.1.
14. M.S.A. § 148.212 (West Supp. 1992).

2. the applicant is currently licensed to practice nursing in another state; and

3. the applicant is presently in a formal refresher course for nurses that includes clinical practice.[15]

Licensing Renewal

After the initial licensing period has expired, registration for renewal of the license with the Board takes place every two years.[16] Both professional and practical nurses are required to obtain 30 hours of continuing education during each two years preceding licensing renewal.[17] Licenses expire on the last day of the licensee's month of birth in either an even- or odd-numbered year according to the licensee's year of birth.[18] A renewal application must be received before the last day of the month preceding the month in which the license expires.[19] Failure to make timely renewal will result in a late fee.[20] Licensees who do not complete the renewal process by the registration expiration date may be removed from the list of individuals authorized to practice.[21]

Allowable Unlicensed Practices

The provisions of this law do not prohibit unlicensed individuals from engaging in the following:[22]

1. the deliverance of nursing assistance in an emergency;

2. the practice of nursing by a legally qualified nurse from another state who is employed by the United States government;

3. the practice of any profession licensed by the state, other than nursing;

4. the practice of nursing or a nursing-related service by a nurse's aide under the direction and supervision of a registered nurse;

5. the care of the sick in nursing homes conducted in accordance with the teachings of the Church of Christ, Scientist;[23]

15. M.S.A. § 148.231 (West 1989 & Supp. 1993).
16. Minn. R. 6310.2600, subp. 15 (1991).
17. Minn. R. 6310.2800, subp. 1 (1991).
18. Minn. R. 6310.2600, subp. 15 (1991).
19. Minn. R. 6310.2800, subp. 4 (1991).
20. Minn. R. 6310.2800, subp. 5 (1991).
21. M.S.A. § 148.271 (West Supp. 1992).
22. M.S.A. § 148.271 (West Supp. 1992).
23. M.S.A. § 144A.09, subd. 1 (West 1989).

6. the practice of nursing by registered nurses or licensed practical nurses licensed in another state who are in Minnesota as students enrolled in formal education; and

7. the practice of nursing by a student under the direction of an instructor while the student is enrolled in a nursing program approved by the Board.[24]

Regulation

Disciplinary Actions Against a Licensed Nurse

A nurse's license may be denied, restricted, suspended, or revoked upon proof that the person[25]

1. has failed to satisfy the necessary requirements for licensure;[26]

2. has engaged in fraud to procure a license, permit, or registration certificate;

3. has been convicted of a felony or gross misdemeanor within the previous five years;

4. has had his or her license suspended or revoked in another state or country;

5. has engaged in unprofessional conduct as defined by the Board's rules of professional nursing practice;

6. has delegated or assumed responsibilities that could reasonably be expected to result in harm to a client;

7. has been adjudicated as mentally incompetent, mentally ill, mentally retarded, chemically dependant, or dangerous to the public;[27]

8. has engaged in sexual conduct with a client or former client;

9. has obtained money or services from a client through undue influence, duress, or harassment;

10. has disclosed confidential communications relating to a client, not otherwise permitted by law;[28]

11. has engaged in fraudulent billing practices;

12. has failed to maintain satisfactory client records;

---

24. M.S.A. § 148.251 (West Supp. 1992).
25. M.S.A. § 148.261, subd. 1 (West Supp. 1993).
26. M.S.A. §§ 148.171 to 148.285 (West 1989 & Supp. 1992).
27. *See generally* M.S.A. § 525.55 (appointment of guardian for incapacitated persons); § 253B.02 (definitions of mentally ill, mentally retarded, chemically dependent, dangerous to the public). *See* chapters 5A.2, 5A.3, 5B.1, 5D.25, 5E.4, 5E.5, 5E.6.
28. *See* chapters 4.1, 4.2, 4.3, 5A.7, 5A.8.

13. has knowingly assisted an unlicensed person to engage in the unlawful practice of nursing;

14. has knowingly provided false or misleading information directly related to the case of a patient;

15. has aided a suicide or an attempted suicide;

16. has practiced outside the scope authorized by law;

17. has provided false information to the Board or has failed to provide required information to the Board; or

18. has engaged in deceptive advertising.

Investigations by the Board[29]

The Board must investigate complaints alleging violations of statutes or rules the Board is empowered to enforce. The attorney general provides legal services to the Board and may, in conjunction with the Board, investigate complaints. If an initial investigation suggests illegal or unauthorized activities, the Board will schedule a disciplinary hearing. The Board has the power to issue subpoenas and compel the attendance of witnesses and the production of documents. Hearings are conducted by an administrative law judge whose decisions are subject to review by the Court of Appeals.

Penalties for Violations[30]

In addition to the penalties listed previously under "Disciplinary Actions," persons engaged in the following acts may be found guilty of a misdemeanor:

1. selling, fraudulently obtaining, or furnishing nursing diplomas, licenses, or records;

2. practicing professional nursing without a license;

3. using a designation that indicates or implies that the person is licensed when the person is not;

4. practicing nursing under cover of a fraudulently obtained license;

5. practicing nursing in a manner prohibited under a restricted license, or practicing nursing while a license is suspended or revoked;

6. conducting nursing education programs for nurses to become registered, unless the program has been approved by the Board; or

---

29. M.S.A. § 214.10 (West 1992).
30. M.S.A. § 148.281, subd. 1 (West Supp. 1992).

7. hiring persons to practice nursing knowing they have not been issued a current permit or license in this state.

Duty to Report or Warn and Civil Liability

When a patient or other person has communicated to a licensed nurse a specific and serious threat of physical violence against a clearly identified or identifiable potential victim, that nurse has a statutory duty to make reasonable efforts to communicate the threat to the potential victim or the appropriate authorities. Failure to make such efforts exposes the nurse to potential civil liability.[31] Additionally, nurses are required by law to report known or suspected acts of child neglect, physical or sexual abuse of a child,[32] and the abuse or neglect of vulnerable adults.[33] The failure to report such abuse or neglect is a misdemeanor[34] and may expose the nurse to civil liability.[35]

---

31. M.S.A. § 148.975 (West 1989). *See* chapter 4.2.
32. M.S.A. § 626.556, subd. 3 (West Supp. 1992). *See* chapter 5A.8.
33. M.S.A. § 626.557, subd. 3 (West Supp. 1992). *See* chapter 5A.7.
34. M.S.A. § 626.556, subd. 6 (West Supp. 1992), and § 626.557, subd. 7 (West 1983).
35. *See* chapters 5A.7 and 5A.8.

1.3

Licensure and Regulation of Psychologists and Psychological Practitioners

The licensure and regulation of licensed psychologists and psychological practitioners is governed by statutory law[1] that establishes a Board of Psychology. The Board establishes qualifications and procedures for examination and licensure and regulates professional conduct. In addition, the Board promulgates rules[2] to carry out the provisions of the statutes.

The Board of Psychology

The Board is the primary administrative body that licenses and regulates psychologists. It consists of 11 Minnesota residents appointed to not more than two consecutive four-year terms by the governor. Membership includes three licensed psychologists with doctoral degrees, two licensed psychologists with master's degrees, two psychologists not necessarily licensed, one licensed psychological practitioner, and three public members.[3] The Board has the duty to

1. regulate the granting, denial, revocation, renewal, suspension, and restoration of licenses;[4]

2. prescribe the fees, forms, and timetables for the examination and licensing process;[5]

---

1. M.S.A. Chapter 214 (West 1992); M.S.A. §§ 148.88 to 148.98 (West Supp. 1992).
2. Minn. R. 7200.0100 to 7200.6100 (1991).
3. M.S.A. § 148.90, subds. 1, 2 (West Supp. 1992).
4. M.S.A. § 148.91 (West Supp. 1992); M.S.A. § 148.95 (West Supp. 1992).
5. M.S.A. § 148.91 (West Supp. 1992).

3. maintain records[6] and establish procedures for the collection and dissemination of regulatory information;[7]

4. establish rules and investigate charges of violations of the rules and applicable statutes;[8]

5. adopt rules that provide for examinations and create a code of professional ethics and requirements for continuing education;[9]

6. educate the public about the requirements for licensure and its code of professional ethics;[10] and

7. create and implement a method for certifying psychologists' competencies in specialty areas.[11]

Licensure and Renewal

The statutes pertaining to licensure recite the qualifications needed for the Board to grant a license for each of two levels of psychological practice: (a) licensed psychologist and (b) psychological practitioner. Both forms of licensure require that an applicant[12]

1. pass a skills assessment and an examination in psychology;[13]

2. pay an application fee; and

3. have attained the age of majority and be of good moral character.[14]

In addition, both forms of licensure have educational requirements. A *licensed psychologist* must have[15]

1. received a doctoral degree with a major in psychology from an accredited educational institution; and

2. completed at least two full years of supervised postdoctorate employment in the practice of psychology.

---

6. M.S.A. § 214.04, subd. 3 (West 1992).
7. M.S.A. § 214.10, subd. 8 (West 1992), which stipulates that such procedures shall comply with the confidentiality requirements of M.S.A. § 13.39 (West 1988) and M.S.A. § 13.41 (West 1988 & Supp. 1992).
8. M.S.A. § 214.10, subds. 1 to 4 (West 1992).
9. M.S.A. § 148.905, subd. 1 (West Supp. 1993).
10. *Id.*
11. *Id.*
12. M.S.A. § 148.91 (West Supp. 1992).
13. Minn. R. 7200.0300 to 7200.0500 and 7200.3000 (1991).
14. Minn. R. 7200.0600 and 7200.4500 to 7200.5500 (1991); M.S.A. § 148.98 (West Supp. 1992).
15. M.S.A. § 148.91 (West Supp. 1992).

A *psychological practitioner* must have either a doctorate or master's degree in psychology from an accredited educational program.[16]

Licensing categories were substantially changed in 1991. People licensed as of August 1, 1991, as either licensed consulting psychologists or licensed psychologists qualify for licensure as licensed psychologists under the new law.[17]

A license is valid for the period beginning with the date on which the license is granted or reissued and ending two years later on the last day of the month in which the license was granted or reissued. Thereafter, the license is renewable every two years.[18]

Practice of Psychology Defined

The practice of psychology is defined to mean

> the observation, description, evaluation, interpretation, and modification of human behavior by the application of psychological principles, methods, and procedures, to prevent or eliminate symptomatic, maladaptive, or undesired behavior and to enhance interpersonal relationships, work and life adjustment, personal and organizational effectiveness, behavioral health, and mental health.[19]

Independent and Supervised Practice of Psychology

The key distinction between licensed psychologists and licensed psychological practitioners is that the former, but not the later, are permitted to engage in the independent, unsupervised practice of psychology.[20]

Psychological practitioners may practice psychology only while employed by either a licensed psychologist or a health care or social services agency that employs or contracts with a supervising licensed psychologist. The supervising psychologist must share clinical responsibility for the care provided by the practitioners.[21] In addition, psychological practitioners may practice psychology only if properly "supervised."[22] Supervision means "face-to-face documented consultation" between the practitioner

---

16. *Id.*
17. M.S.A. § 148.921, subd. 1 (West Supp. 1992). The law permits licensure as a licensed psychologist for certain persons who entered master's degree programs prior to November 1, 1991. *See id.*, subd. 2.
18. Minn. R. 7200.3200 (1991).
19. M.S.A. § 148.89, subd. 5 (West Supp. 1992). The law specifically exempts from regulation by the Board of Psychology the work of clergy, physicians, social workers, alcohol or drug counselors, optometrists, attorneys, and teachers, despite the fact that they all may, from time to time, do work that would technically fall within the definition of the practice of psychology. M.S.A. § 148.97 (West 1989).
20. M.S.A. § 148.93, subd. 2 (West Supp. 1992).
21. M.S.A. § 148.93, subd. 3 (West Supp. 1992).
22. *Id.*

and a licensed psychologist.[23] Supervisory consultation must be on a one-to-one basis at a ratio of at least 1 hour of supervision for the initial 20 or fewer hours of psychological services per month, and not less than 1 hour per month. The consultations must include discussions of the nature and content of the practitioner's practice, including a review of a representative sample of psychological services rendered.[24] Requirements for the supervision of applicants for licensure as licensed psychologists are more stringent.[25]

Rules of Professional Conduct

The Board of Psychology, in compliance with the law, has promulgated a set of Rules of Professional Conduct for its applicants and licensees.[26] These rules constitute the "standards against which the professional conduct of a psychologist is measured."[27] Violation of the rules constitutes unprofessional or unethical conduct and is sufficient reason for disciplinary action or denial of licensure.[28] The following is a summary of the code of rules (the term psychologist refers both to licensed psychologists and to licensed psychological practitioners):

1. Psychologists may not violate any law while providing psychological services.[29]
2. Psychologists must limit their practices to their areas of competence, accurately represent their education and training, consult with other professionals about newly developing areas of specialty, and refer their clients to other professional services when appropriate.[30]
3. Psychologists must respect their clients' privacy and protect the private information obtained during therapy or research.[31]

---

23. M.S.A. § 148.89, subd. 8 (West Supp. 1992).
24. M.S.A. § 148.925, subd. 2 (West Supp. 1993).
25. *Id.*, subds. 1 and 2.
26. M.S.A. § 148.98 (West Supp. 1993) requires the establishment of a "code of ethics"to govern the practice of psychology. The Board's Rules of Professional Conduct constitute that code of ethics. Minn. R. 7200.4500, subp. 1 (1991). The code for the most part refers to psychologists. Under the Rules of the Board, the term *psychologist* includes all licensees of the Board. Minn. R. 7200.0100, subp. 9 (1991).
27. Minn. R. 7200.4500, subp. 2 (1991).
28. *Id.*, subp. 3.
29. Minn. R. 7200.5500 (1991).
30. Minn. R. 7200.4600 (1991).
31. Minn. R. 7200.4700 (1991). *See* chapters 4.1, 4.2, and 4.3 for more information on the rules governing private client information. *See* chapters 5A.7 and 5A.8 for information on psychologists' duties to report suspected abuse or neglect.

4. Psychologists may not provide psychological services when they are unable to remain objective because of personal or interpersonal factors.[32]

5. Psychologists must provide an explanation of the nature and purpose of any psychological procedures and results of tests administered to the client. The explanation must be given in such a way that a lay person could understand. Clients may access their records upon request, provided it would not be to their detriment.[33]

6. Psychologists must adequately explain the purpose, logic, and scoring of any psychological tests given to a client.[34]

7. Psychologists may not misrepresent to the public their professional qualifications, such as education, experience, or areas of expertise.[35]

8. Psychologists must disclose to the client the cost of services provided and make an itemized statement available to the client.[36]

9. Psychologists may not assist an unlicensed individual in engaging in the unauthorized practice of psychology.[37]

10. Psychologists must safeguard the well-being of psychology students, supervisees, and research subjects.[38]

11. Psychologists must safeguard client welfare by[39]

   a. not stereotyping clients;

   b. disclosing to the client the psychologist's treatment or outcome preferences, presenting other options as well;

   c. terminating the professional relationship when the client is no longer likely to benefit from the psychologist's services;

   d. informing the client when the psychologist becomes aware of divergent values, attitudes, or interests sufficient to impair the relationship;

   e. making prompt, appropriate referrals when requested;

   f. not engaging in sexual intimacies or behavior with a client;

   g. coordinating services with other professionals;

---

32. Minn. R. 7200.4800, subp. 1 (1991).
33. Minn. R. 7200.4900 (1991); M.S.A. § 144.335, subd. 1(c) (West Supp. 1992). *See* chapter 4.1.
34. Minn. R. 7200.5000 (1991).
35. Minn. R. 7200.5100 and 7200.5600 (1991).
36. Minn. R. 7200.5200 (1991).
37. Minn. R. 7200.5300 (1991).
38. Minn. R. 7200.5400 (1991).
39. Minn. R. 7200.4900, subps. 3 to 12 (1991).

h. filing a complaint with the board when the psychologist has reason to believe that another psychologist is engaged in improper conduct; and

i. providing information to the client on procedures for filing a complaint with the Board.

Disciplinary Procedures

Investigation of Complaints[40]

Upon receipt of a complaint, the Board will forward a summary of the complaint to the lawyer in the attorney general's office assigned to the Board (the "designee") and to any other government agency that is appropriate, given the nature of the complaint. The designee will evaluate the complaint and, as the Board's legal counsel and chief investigator, may investigate the complaint if it alleges a violation of a Board statute or rule.[41]

In the process of his or her investigation, the designee may conduct interviews and obtain relevant records and documents.[42] The designee will then present his or her findings to the Board. If dismissal of the complaint is not recommended, the licensee will be requested to attend an informal conference with the Board's Ethics Panel to discuss the allegations.

Disciplinary Conferences with the Board's Ethics Panel

The two Board members composing the Ethics Panel will conduct the conference along with the Board's executive director and the attorney general's designee. The licensee may attend with or without counsel. Once the licensee has had an opportunity to present his or her version of the facts, the Panel will propose a settlement to the licensee. Settlement may be a reprimand, conditional or restricted license, stayed suspension, suspension, or revocation. If the licensee accepts the recommendation, the matter will be presented to the full Board for approval.

If the licensee declines to accept the recommendation, the matter may result in a contested case hearing before an administrative law judge. The judge will make findings of fact and conclusions of law and submit any recommendation to the Board.[43] The Board may or may not follow the judge's recommen-

---

40. The information in this section is based in part on M.S.A. § 214.10, which sets out the general procedures to be followed by the Board in dealing with a complaint against a psychologist, and in part on unpublished procedures of the Board in effect at the time this was written.
41. M.S.A. § 214.10, subds. 1, 2 (West 1992).
42. M.S.A. § 214.10, subd. 4 (West 1992). Although such investigative data are generally nonpublic, wholly inactive data are generally public. M.S.A. § 13.39 (West 1988). *See* chapter 4.5.
43. M.S.A. §§ 14.48 to 14.69 (West 1988).

dation and will ultimately resolve the complaint at its own discretion. In any event, the Board may not dismiss a complaint unless at least two Board members have reviewed the matter. Additional procedures apply to violations involving alleged sexual contact with a client.[44]

Penalties for Violations

Any person who violates the licensing laws is guilty of a misdemeanor.[45] In addition, the Board may bring an action for injunctive relief if continued practice by the person would create an imminent risk of harm to others.[46] Violations may also form the basis for a civil suit against the psychologist.[47]

---

44. M.S.A. § 214.10, subd. 8 (West 1992).
45. M.S.A. § 148.97, subd. 1 (West Supp. 1992).
46. M.S.A. § 214.11 (West 1992).
47. *See* chapters 6.5 and 6.6.

1.4

Unlicensed Psychologists

As noted in chapter 1.3, the law provides that a person must be licensed by the Board of Psychology as a licensed psychologist in order to engage in the independent practice of psychology.[1] The law prohibits all persons from presenting themselves to the public as psychologists unless they are licensed by the Board of Psychology as either a licensed psychologist or a licensed psychological practitioner.[2] However, the law provides the following exceptions to these licensure limitations:

1. Psychologically trained employees of accredited educational institutions or governmental facilities may use the title of psychologist if it is the title designated by their organization;[3]

2. school psychologists employed by a school for grades prekindergarten to 12 may use the title of psychologist (and practice psychology) if licensed by the Minnesota Board of Teaching;[4]

3. students of psychology preparing for the profession of psychologist under qualified supervision in a recognized training institution may use the title of psychologist if it includes the word "trainee," "intern," or other indication of training status;[5] and

4. psychologists who reside out of state may use the title of psychologist if currently licensed or certified as a psychologist in that state. Persons who reside in a state that does not grant

1. M.S.A. § 148.93, subd. 2 (West Supp. 1992).
2. M.S.A. § 148.96, subd. 3 (West Supp. 1992).
3. *Id.*
4. *Id.* at subd. 3(d); Minn. R. 8700.6310 (1991); *see also* chapter 1.6.
5. M.S.A. § 148.96 (West Supp. 1992).

such licensure or certification may use the title if they meet the requirements set out in chapter 1.3 All out-of-state psychologists must restrict their Minnesota activities to 60 days per year and must inform the Board of Psychology if they practice in Minnesota more than 12 days per year.[6]

Rights and responsibilities of unlicensed mental health practitioners (including unlicensed psychologists) are discussed in chapter 1.12.

---

6. M.S.A. § 148.97, subd. 5 (West 1989).

1.5

Licensure and Regulation of Social Workers

The licensure and regulation of social workers is governed by statutory law.[1] It establishes a Board of Social Work, defines terms contained within the statute, defines the practice of social work, establishes qualifications and procedures for the licensure of social workers, establishes exceptions to licensure, and prescribes sanctions for violations of the statute.

Social Work Practice Defined

The practice of social work involves applying psychosocial theory and methods in treating, resolving, and preventing social and psychological dysfunction caused by environmental stress, interpersonal or intrapersonal conflict, physical or mental disorders, or combinations of these causes. Social work practice includes but is not limited to psychotherapy.[2]

Board of Social Work

The Board of Social Work is the primary administrative body that licenses and regulates social workers. The Board consists of 10 members, each appointed by the governor to a four-year term.[3]

---

1. M.S.A. §§ 148B.01 to 148B.28 (West 1989 & Supp. 1992).
2. M.S.A. § 148B.18, subd. 11 (West 1989).
3. M.S.A. § 214.09 (West 1992); § 148B.19, subd. 1 (West 1989).

The Board is composed of six licensed social workers,[4] three public members,[5] and one social worker licensed by the Board of Teaching. The duties of the Board include[6]

1. adopting and enforcing rules for the licensure of social workers and for the regulation of their professional conduct;
2. adopting rules, standards, and methods to determine whether applicants and licensees are qualified to practice social work;
3. holding examinations at least twice a year to ascertain applicants' knowledge and skill;
4. implementing a disciplinary process for violation of Board rules;
5. overseeing the application and licensing process; and
6. educating the public about the licensing of social workers.

Licensure

Categories of Licenses and Licensure Requirements

The Board issues licenses in the following four categories to practice social work:

1. *Social worker:*[7] To become a licensed social worker, an applicant must

   (a) have a baccalaureate degree from an accredited program of social work;

   (b) pass an examination administered by the Board;

   (c) agree to practice social work under supervision for at least two years of full-time employment or 4,000 hours; and

   (d) agree to comply with the Board's standards of professional conduct.

2. *Graduate social worker:*[8] To become a licensed graduate social worker, an applicant must

   (a) have a master's degree from an accredited program of social work or a doctoral degree in social work;

---

4. The statute requires that the Board consist of a mixture of public and private social workers. The statute also requires minority and rural representation. M.S.A. § 148B.19, subd. 2 (West 1989).
5. A public member is a person not a member of the profession, not the spouse of a member of the profession, and not with a financial interest in the profession. M.S.A. § 214.02 (West 1992).
6. M.S.A. § 148B.20 (West 1989).
7. M.S.A. § 148B.21, subd. 3 (West 1989).
8. M.S.A. § 148B.21, subd. 4 (West 1989).

(b) pass an examination administered by the Board;

(c) engage in social work practice only under supervision; and

(d) agree to comply with the Board's standards of professional conduct.

3. *Independent social worker:*[9] To become a licensed independent social worker, an applicant must

(a) have a master's degree from an accredited program of social work or a doctoral degree in social work;

(b) pass an examination administered by the Board;

(c) have practiced social work for at least two years in full-time employment or for 4,000 hours under supervision; and

(d) agree to comply with the Board's standards of professional conduct.

4. *Independent clinical social worker:*[10] To become a licensed independent clinical social worker, an applicant must

(a) have a master's degree from an accredited program of social work or a doctoral degree in social work that included advanced clinically oriented course work and a supervised clinical field placement at the graduate level;

(b) have practiced clinical social work for at least two years full-time or for 4,000 hours under supervision;

(c) pass an examination administered by the Board; and

(d) agree to comply with the Board's standards of professional conduct.

Licensing Renewal

All licenses must be renewed every two years.[11] For a license to be renewed, a licensee must pay the necessary renewal fee and provide evidence that the licensee has completed during each three-year period at least 45 hours of continuing professional postdegree education in programs accredited by the Board.[12]

Exceptions to Licensing

Licensing requirements do not apply to the following:[13]

1. students or interns in an accredited program of social work practicing social work under supervision;

---

9. M.S.A. § 148B.21, subd. 5 (West 1989).
10. M.S.A. § 148B.21, subd. 6 (West 1989).
11. Minn. R. 8740.0190 (1991).
12. M.S.A. § 148B.22 (West 1989).
13. M.S.A. § 148B.28 (West 1989).

2. members of other licensed occupations performing functions for which they are qualified or licensed;[14]

3. social workers employed by city, county, or state agencies;

4. social workers employed by federally recognized tribes;

5. social workers employed by private nonprofit agencies serving primarily ethnic populations when the social workers are themselves members of the ethnic minority population; and

6. social workers employed by hospitals and licensed nursing homes.

Regulation

Disciplinary Actions[15]

The Board may refuse to grant or renew a license, or may restrict, suspend, or revoke a license, if after a hearing the Board determines that the individual

1. is incompetent to engage in the practice of social work or engages in the practice of social work in a manner that is harmful or dangerous to a client or the public;[16]

2. has violated rules or statutes the Board is empowered to enforce;

3. has knowingly made a false statement on a license or license renewal application;

4. has obtained or attempted to obtain a license or license renewal by bribery or fraudulent misrepresentation; or

5. has violated the Code of Ethics (see below).[17]

Investigations by the Board[18]

Upon receipt of a complaint alleging a violation of a statute or rule that the Board is empowered to enforce, a designee of the attorney general's office is authorized to investigate the allegations. The Board has the power to issue subpoenas and compel

---

14. This includes licensed physicians (chapter 1.1); registered nurses (chapter 1.2); practical nurses; licensed psychologists (chapter 1.3); probation officers; members of the clergy; attorneys; marriage and family therapists (chapter 1.8); chemical dependency counselors; professional counselors; school counselors (chapter 1.7); and registered occupational therapists or certified occupational therapist assistants. These persons must not represent themselves as licensed social workers. M.S.A. § 148B.28, subd. 1 (West 1989).

15. M.S.A. § 148B.26 (West 1989).

16. *See* chapter 5B.1.

17. Minn. R. 8740.0300 and 8740.0310 (1991).

18. M.S.A. § 214.10, subds. 2, 3 (West 1992).

the attendance of witnesses and the production of documents. If an initial investigation suggests illegal or unauthorized activities, the Board may schedule a disciplinary hearing.

Hearings are conducted by an administrative law judge.[19] Administrative proceedings are not bound by the strict procedural rules that circumscribe the actions of a court,[20] nor are they bound by the rules of evidence.[21] The parties or agencies involved have the right to cross-examine witnesses and submit rebuttal evidence.[22] Decisions of the administrative law judge are subject to judicial review by the Minnesota Court of Appeals.[23]

Code of Ethics[24]

The Code of Ethics establishes professional standards of conduct to measure the behavior of social workers. Violating the Code of Ethics constitutes unprofessional and unethical conduct and is sufficient cause for denying a license to or taking disciplinary action against a licensed social worker. The Code of Ethics requires that all social workers

1. not discriminate in providing professional services;
2. not engage in any type of sexual activity with a current client, student, or trainee, or engage in sexual activity with a former client, for at least two years after the termination of the professional relationship;
3. not offer to or receive from a client any controlled substance or alcoholic beverages;
4. not use any drug, controlled substance, alcoholic beverage, or medication in a manner that impairs the licensee's ability to practice;
5. avoid dual relationships that impair the licensee's professional judgment;
6. not use a professional relationship to advance personal, religious, political, or business interests;
7. not wrongfully disparage the character or qualifications of any professional colleague;
8. not treat, diagnose, or advise a client on problems outside of the licensee's area of competence;

---

19. M.S.A. § 14.50 (West 1988).
20. Hagen v. Civil Service Bd., 282 Minn. 296, 164 N.W.2d 629 (1969).
21. Padilla v. Minnesota State Bd. of Medical Examiners, 382 N.W.2d 876 (Minn. Ct. App. 1986).
22. M.S.A. § 14.60, subd. 3 (West 1988).
23. M.S.A. § 14.63 (West 1988).
24. Minn. R. 8740.0310 (1991).

9. terminate services when no longer required or when in the client's best interests;

10. keep all client records accurate and up-to-date;

11. conduct research practices with respect for the rights and dignity of participants involved; and

12. not use fraudulent or misleading means of advertising in marketing their services.

Duty to Warn; Confidentiality

When a licensed social worker has reason to believe that a client presents clear and immediate danger to an individual or society, he or she has the duty to warn the potential victim and the appropriate authorities.[25] Failure to warn is sufficient reason for disciplinary action or denial of a license to practice social work.[26]

A licensed social worker must also inform clients of the limits on confidentiality. Client records are generally confidential[27] and must not be released unless

1. the client consents in writing;

2. a court authorizes the records' release;

3. the records are disclosable under the Minnesota Government Data Practices Act;[28]

4. the information released does not compromise the confidentiality of any other individuals; or

5. the Board of Social Work subpoenas the records.[29]

Duty to Report

Social workers must report suspected abuse and neglect of children[30] and vulnerable adults.[31] Failure to report such abuse or neglect is a misdemeanor.[32]

As licensed health care providers, social workers are also required to report certain communicable diseases.[33] Conduct of other licensed health care professionals that may constitute

---

25. Minn. R. 8740.0310, subp. 5 (1991). *See* chapter 4.2.
26. Minn. R. 8740.0300 (1991).
27. *See* chapters 4.1, 4.2, 4.3.
28. Minn. Stat. Chapter 13. *See* chapter 4.5.
29. Minn. R. 8740.0310, subp. 5 (1991). The provisions of this rule, as reflected in the text, are somewhat ambiguous. In the authors' opinion, items 1 and 4 should be read together. The client's consent is sufficient only if the information does not compromise the confidentiality of others.
30. M.S.A. § 626.556 (West 1990 & Supp. 1991). *See* chapter 5A.8.
31. M.S.A. § 626.557 (West 1990 & Supp. 1991). *See* chapter 5A.7.
32. M.S.A. § 626.556, subd. 6 (West 1990 & Supp. 1991); § 626.557, subd. 7 (West 1990 & Supp. 1991).
33. Minn. R. 4605.7030, subp. 6 (1991).

grounds for a disciplinary action must also be reported.[34] All reports must be submitted in a timely manner so that the client's well-being is not adversely affected.[35]

No criminal or civil liability may be imposed for good faith reporting under any of the foregoing duties.[36]

---

34. M.S.A. § 148B.07, subd. 4 (West 1990 & Supp. 1991).
35. Minn. R. 8740.0310, subp. 5 (1991).
36. M.S.A. § 148B.08 (West 1990 & Supp. 1991). *See also* M.S.A. § 144.4175, subd. 2 (West 1990); § 626.556, subd. 4 (West 1990 & Supp. 1991); § 626.557, subd. 5 (West 1990 & Supp. 1991).

1.6

Licensure and Regulation of School Psychologists

The Minnesota Board of Teaching licenses persons in school psychology who are employed in primary and secondary school settings.[1] The licensure is entirely independent of the Board of Psychology because these school psychologists are specifically exempted from the regular licensure procedures.[2]

To become a school psychologist, the Board of Teaching requires an applicant to

1. hold an education specialist degree or its equivalent;

2. satisfactorily complete the special education core skill requirements[3] ; and

3. satisfactorily complete a Board-approved[4] preparation program in school psychology consisting of a minimum of 90 graduate-quarter credits.[5]

---

1. Minn. R. 8700.6310 (1991).
2. M.S.A. § 148.96, subd. 3 (West Supp. 1992); § 148.97, subd. 3 (West 1989). *See* chapter 1.3.
3. As enumerated in Minn. R. 8700.5500 (1991).
4. *See* Beaty v. Minnesota Bd. of Teaching, 354 N.W.2d 466 (Minn. Ct. App. 1984) (under some circumstances, the Board's arbitrary failure to approve a program will be overridden by the courts).
5. Minn. R. 8700.6310 (1991).

1.7

Licensure of School Counselors

The state Board of Education licenses school counselors who are employed in elementary, middle, and secondary school settings.[1]

Licensure

The rules governing the licensure of school counselors set out three types of licensure: elementary, secondary, and middle school counselors.[2]

Elementary and Secondary School Counselors

Before granting a license to an elementary[3] or secondary[4] school counselor, the Board requires an applicant to

1. have at least 2,000 hours of noneducation-related work experience;

2. have a master's degree in school guidance and counseling, including at least 54 quarter credit hours in an approved elementary or secondary preparation program; and

3. satisfactorily complete a 400-hour school guidance and counseling practicum at the elementary or secondary level.

In addition, an applicant must either

---

1. As authorized by M.S.A. § 125.05 (West 1979 & Supp. 1992).
2. Minn. R. 8700.8000 to 8700.8190 (1991 & Supp. 1992).
3. Minn. R. 8700.8090 to 8700.8170 (1991 & Supp. 1992).
4. Minn. R. 8700.8000 to 8700.8080 (1991 & Supp. 1992).

4a. have a valid Minnesota elementary or secondary classroom teaching license; and

4b. complete one year of (i) elementary or secondary teaching experience or (ii) an internship in elementary or secondary counseling; or

5a. have a baccalaureate degree from an accredited teacher preparation institution; and

5b. satisfactorily complete an approved internship in elementary or secondary counseling.

Middle School Counselors

Before granting a license to a middle school counselor[5], the Board requires an applicant to

1. hold either an elementary or secondary school counselor's license; and

2. complete an approved training program for middle school counselors consisting of at least 10 quarter hours or the equivalent.

Middle school licensure is unnecessary if the licensee counsels at grade levels for which a valid Minnesota school counselor's license is held.

---

5. Minn. R. 8700.8180 (1991).

1.8

Licensure and Regulation of Marriage and Family Therapists

The licensure and regulation of marriage and family therapy is governed by statutory law.[1] The law establishes a Board of Marriage and Family Therapy, defines the practice of marriage and family therapy, establishes exceptions to licensure, and prescribes sanctions for violations of the law.

Marriage and Family Therapy Defined

Marriage and family therapy consists of providing individuals and family groups with professional marriage and family psychotherapy. Marriage and family therapy includes premarital, marital, divorce, and family therapy. The practice consists of recognizing, treating, and resolving mental and emotional dysfunction on an individual and familial level.[2] Individuals are prohibited from practicing marriage and family therapy or representing themselves as marriage and family therapists unless licensed.[3]

---

1. M.S.A. §§ 148B.29 to 148B.39 (West 1989 & Supp. 1992).
2. M.S.A. § 148B.29, subd. 3 (West 1989).
3. M.S.A. § 148B.32, subd. 2 (West Supp. 1992).

Board of Marriage and Family Therapy

The Board of Marriage and Family Therapy is the administrative body that licenses and regulates marriage and family therapists. The Board consists of seven members appointed by the governor for terms of four years. The Board is composed of four licensed marriage and family therapists,[4] one professional engaged in the teaching and research of marriage and family therapy,[5] and two members of the general public.[6] The duties of the Board include[7]

1. creating and implementing rules for marriage and family therapy licensing;
2. developing techniques for determining whether licensees and applicants are qualified for licensure;
3. issuing licenses;
4. establishing and enforcing procedures to assure that licensed marriage and family therapists comply with the Board's guidelines;
5. working to improve the standards for licensure;
6. formulating a code of ethics for all licensed marriage and family therapists;
7. establishing continuing education requirements for marriage and family therapists; and
8. submitting a biannual report to the governor, the legislature, and the commissioner of health.[8]

Licensure

Applicants can be licensed as marriage and family therapists in Minnesota if they[9]

1. have a master's or doctoral degree in marriage and family therapy from an accredited institution;[10]

---

4. Each must have at least five years of experience as a marriage and family therapist immediately preceding appointment. M.S.A. § 148B.30 (West 1989).
5. M.S.A. § 148B.30, subd. 1 (West 1989).
6. Public members must have no direct affiliation with the practice of marriage and family therapy. M.S.A. § 148B.30, subd. 1 (West 1989).
7. M.S.A. § 148B.31 (West 1989).
8. M.S.A. § 214.07 (West 1992).
9. M.S.A. § 148B.33 (West 1989 & Supp. 1992).
10. A master's or doctoral degree in a related field will satisfy this requirement if the Board determines that the course work is equivalent to the course work in marriage and family therapy. Minn. R. 5300.0140 (Supp. 1991).

2. have at least two years of supervised postgraduate experience in marriage and family counseling;

3. are of good moral character;[11]

4. agree to comply with the Code of Ethics (see below);

5. pass a written and oral examination administered by the Board;

6. have attained the age of majority; and

7. are citizens of the United States.

Licensing Renewal[12]

All licenses are valid for one year and must be renewed annually prior to December 31. Each licensee is required to complete at least 30 hours of continuing education every two years.

Exceptions to Licensing

The licensing law does not prohibit[13]

1. students or interns, clearly designated as such, from practicing marriage and family therapy under the supervision of a licensed professional;

2. qualified members of other licensed or certified professions[14] from doing work of a marriage and family nature in the course of their work;

3. the unlicensed practice of marriage and family therapy by therapists employed by federally recognized tribes;[15] or

4. the unlicensed practice of marriage and family therapy by therapists employed by private nonprofit marriage and family therapy agencies whose primary service is to ethnic minority populations, when the therapists are themselves members of the ethnic minority population.[16]

---

11. The applicant must submit two letters of endorsement attesting to the applicant's good moral character. Minn. R. 5300.0200(1)(e) (Supp. 1991). The letters must be from individuals who are licensed to practice marriage and family therapy in this or another state or who have education and experience that meets the Minnesota licensing standard. Minn. R. 5300.0230 (Supp. 1991).
12. Minn. R. 5300.0280 (Supp. 1991) and 530.0320 (Supp. 1991).
13. M.S.A. § 148B.38 (West 1989 & Supp. 1992).
14. This includes licensed physicians (chapter 1.1), professional and practical nurses (chapter 1.2), licensed psychologists (chapter 1.3), social workers (chapter 1.5), probation officers, clergy, attorneys, school counselors (chapter 1.7), and registered occupational therapists. M.S.A. § 148B.38, subd. 1 (West 1989).
15. M.S.A. § 148B.38, subd. 3 (West Supp. 1992).
16. *Id.*

Regulation[17]

The Board may deny an individual a license or may restrict, suspend, or revoke an individual's license if after a hearing the Board determines that the individual

1. is incompetent[18] to practice or has engaged in the practice of marriage and family therapy in a manner that is harmful or dangerous to clients or the public;
2. has been convicted of a crime that renders the person unfit to practice marriage and family therapy;
3. has knowingly made a false statement in a license or license renewal application;
4. has obtained or attempted to obtain a license fraudulently;
5. has failed to obtain the required continuing education requirements; or
6. has violated any provision of statutes or rules governing marriage and family therapists or has violated any of the rules of the Board.[19]

Privileged Communications[20]

Licensed marriage and family therapists and their employees or professional associates cannot be required to disclose information they have acquired in providing marriage and family therapy services, unless

1. disclosure is required by law;[21]
2. the therapist, employee, or associate is a defendant in a civil, criminal, or disciplinary action arising from therapy;
3. the client is a defendant in a criminal proceeding, and the use of the privilege of confidentiality would violate the defendant's right to present testimony and witnesses on his or her behalf;
4. failure to disclose the information presents a clear and present danger to the health and safety of an individual; or
5. the client has agreed to a waiver.

---

17. M.S.A. § 148B.37 (West 1989).
18. *See* chapter 5B.1.
19. M.S.A. §§ 148B.29 to 148B.39 (West 1989).
20. M.S.A. § 148B.39 (West 1989).
21. *See* Duty to Warn/Duty to Report section below.

Confidentiality[22]

Information obtained in the course of providing marriage and family therapy is private, and therapists must safeguard the confidences of their clients. Access to client records is therefore permitted only to the therapist. A therapist must obtain written consent before recording or permitting third-party observation of a therapy session. A therapist must also inform any individuals who pay for the client's therapy that all information obtained is private. Also, a therapist must protect the identity of clients when using material from counseling sessions for training, research, or publication.

Duty to Warn/Duty to Report

As professionals engaged in the practice of psychological treatment, marriage and family therapists are required by law to report any known or suspected acts of child neglect or the physical or sexual abuse of a child.[23] Marriage and family therapists are also required by law to report the abuse or neglect of vulnerable adults.[24] The failure to report such suspected abuse or neglect constitutes a misdemeanor offense[25] and may subject the therapist to civil liability.[26]

Minnesota law requires that certain professionals, upon receiving a serious threat of violence against a specific and identifiable person, report that threat to the proper authorities or make reasonable efforts to warn the potential victim.[27] Failure to do so exposes the professional to potential civil liability.[28] Although marriage and family therapists are not one of the groups specifically listed within the statute, the principles articulated in the statute could conceivably apply to them as well, given the confidential nature of the counseling involved in the practice of marriage and family therapy.

Code of Ethics[29]

The Code of Ethics establishes professional standards of conduct against which the behavior of a marriage and family therapist is measured. Violating the Code of Ethics constitutes unprofessional and unethical conduct and is sufficient cause for denying a license

---

22. Minn. R. 5300.0350, subp. 6 (Supp. 1991).
23. M.S.A. § 626.556, subd. 3 (West Supp. 1992). *See* chapter 5A.8.
24. M.S.A. § 626.557, subd. 3 (West Supp. 1992). *See* chapter 5A.7.
25. M.S.A. § 626.556, subd. 6 (West Supp. 1992); § 626.557, subd. 7 (West 1983).
26. M.S.A. § 626.557, subd. 7 (West 1983) (for negligent failure to make vulnerable adult report). *See* chapter 6.6.
27. M.S.A. § 148.975 (West 1989). *See* chapter 4.2.
28. M.S.A. § 148.975 (West 1989).
29. Minn. R. 5300.0350 (Supp. 1991).

or taking disciplinary action against a licensed therapist. The Code of Ethics requires that therapists

1. not engage in conduct that is deceitful or fraudulent, nor advertise in a false or misleading manner;
2. not perform services beyond their competence, and refer clients when it is in the client's best interest to do so;
3. not disparage the qualifications of colleagues;
4. not engage in sexual intimacy with a current client, trainee, or student, nor engage in sexual intimacy with former clients for at least two years following the termination of the professional relationship;
5. not engage in sexual or other forms of harassment or exploitation of clients, students, or employees;
6. not discriminate in providing professional services;
7. not use counseling relationships to further personal, religious, political, sexual, or financial interests;
8. not practice under the influence of alcohol or nonprescription controlled substances;
9. not exploit the trust and dependency of clients, nor use any confidence of a client to the client's disadvantage;
10. terminate services when no longer necessary or in the client's best interest or when the therapist's objectivity has been impaired;
11. display or make available to clients a copy of the clients bill of rights as specified in the Rules;
12. avoid dual relationships that impair the therapist's professional judgment;
13. hold in confidence all information obtained in the course of professional services, except where disclosure is required by law;[30] and
14. seek professional help for the therapist's own personal problems that may impair work performance.

---

30. *See* chapters 4.1, 4.2, 4.3.

1.9

Licensure and Regulation of Hypnotists

In some states, the law regulates hypnosis and the professional title "hypnotist" by prescribing education, experience, and skills. MHPs in these states must obtain licensure to use the title of hypnotist. Minnesota has no law requiring such licensure and no restriction on the use of the title "hypnotist." However, the use of hypnosis is not entirely unregulated.

The use of hypnosis for the treatment or relief of any "wound, fracture, or bodily injury, infirmity, or disease" is, by statutory definition, deemed to be "practicing medicine."[1] In general, the practice of medicine is restricted to persons licensed to practice medicine under Minnesota Statutes Chapter 147.[2] However, persons licensed by a health-related licensing board,[3] or in human services occupations registered by the commissioner of health,[4] are not restricted by this prohibition, to the extent that the use of hypnosis for physically manifested conditions is permitted by their licensure.[5] In particular, the permissible practice of psychology includes the use of hypnosis in the diagnosis and treatment of

---

1. M.S.A. § 147.081, subd. 3 (West Supp. 1993). *See* chapter 1.1.
2. M.S.A. § 147.081, subd. 1.
3. *See* M.S.A. § 214.01, subd. 2. This term includes nursing home administrators, nurses, chiropractors, optometrists, psychologists, social workers, marriage and family therapists, unlicensed mental health service providers, dentists, pharmacists, and podiatrists.
4. *See* M.S.A. § 214.13 (West 1992). Examples of such occupations are speech and language pathologists, audiologists (see Minn. R. 4750.0100 et seq.), physician assistants (Minn. R. 5600.2600), occupational therapist practitioners (in the process of being registered), and respiratory care therapists (Minn. R. 4762.0100).
5. M.S.A. § 147.09(9) (West Supp. 1993). It is not clear how this provision applies to persons in occupations that are registered with the commissioner of health but are not subject to licensure.

the psychological aspects of physical illness, accident, injury, or disability.[6]

The practice of psychology also includes the use of hypnosis in the diagnosis and treatment of mental and emotional disorder or disability, alcoholism and substance abuse, and disorders of habit or conduct.[7] With certain limitations, only licensed psychologists can engage in the unsupervised practice of psychology.[8] It is not clear how far this prohibition extends regarding the use of hypnosis by nonpsychologists.

Unlicensed persons who provide "mental health services" are regulated by the Office of Mental Health Practice.[9] Although hypnosis is not specifically mentioned in the definition of mental health services, the definition is broad enough to cover some uses of hypnosis.[10]

Hypnotically induced testimony is not ordinarily allowed in a criminal trial because such evidence is considered too unreliable to have probative value.[11] However, the courts do recognize that "the use of hypnotic evidence can be an extremely useful investigative tool."[12]

---

6. M.S.A. § 148.89, subd. 5 (West Supp. 1992). *See* chapter 1.3.
7. M.S.A. § 148.89, subd. 5.
8. *See* chapters 1.3 and 1.4.
9. *See generally* M.S.A. § 148B.60 et seq. (West Supp. 1992).
10. *See* chapter 1.12.
11. State v. Mack, 292 N.W.2d 764, 771 (Minn. 1980).
12. *Id. See* chapter 5D.2.

1.10

Licensure and Regulation of Polygraph Examiners

In some states, the law regulates the administration of polygraph examinations and the professional title "polygraph examiner" by prescribing education, experience, and skills. MHPs in these states must obtain licensure to use the title of polygraph examiner. Because Minnesota does not have such a law, use of the title "polygraph examiner" is unregulated.

However, the use of polygraph examinations in an employment setting is prohibited,[1] as is disclosure to a third party that another person has taken a polygraph examination.[2] In addition, Minnesota courts do not allow the admission of polygraph test results in civil or criminal cases because they are too unreliable to have probative value.[3]

---

1. M.S.A. § 181.75 (West Supp. 1992) (except where the employee requests such an examination). *See* chapter 5C.3.
2. M.S.A. § 181.76 (West Supp. 1992) (except where the subject requests such disclosure). *See* chapter 5C.3.
3. State v. Michaeloff, 324 N.W.2d 926, 927 (Minn. 1982). *See* chapter 5C.3.

1.11

Sunset of Regulatory Agencies

A sunset law specifies that a designated provision of law expires on a given date, in the absence of action by the legislature to extend the law. Sunset laws function to assure that creations of law (for example, administrative boards or agencies) are reviewed and revised periodically.

Although some states make extensive use of sunset provisions,[1] Minnesota uses this technique only occasionally. For example, the 1987 law establishing the Board of Unlicensed Mental Health Service Providers[2] provided that the authority for the Board would be repealed in 1991.[3]

1. Miller, M. O., & Sales, B. D. (1986). *Law & mental health professionals:* Arizona (chap. 1.11). Washington, DC: American Psychological Association.
2. *See* chapter 1.12.
3. Minn. Laws 1987, c. 347, art. 4, §§ 1, 11.

1.12

Regulation of Unlicensed Mental Health Practitioners

Established in 1991, the Office of Mental Health Practice in the Department of Health[1] receives and investigates consumer complaints and enforces disciplinary action against unlicensed mental health practitioners who engage in any prohibited conduct.[2]

Unlicensed Mental Health Practitioner Defined

An *unlicensed mental health practitioner* is a person who provides mental health services, including psychotherapy and the professional assessment, treatment, or counseling of persons with cognitive, behavioral, emotional, social, or mental disabilities.[3] The term includes[4]

1. hospital and nursing home social workers exempt from licensure by the Board of Social Work;[5]

2. persons employed by a program licensed by the commissioner of human services who provide mental health services within the scope of their employment;

3. persons who are employed by a program licensed by the commissioner of human services and who counsel chemically dependent persons; and

---

1. M.S.A. §§ 148B.60 to 148B.72 (West Supp. 1992).
2. M.S.A. § 148B.61 (West Supp. 1992); § 148B.68 (West Supp. 1992).
3. M.S.A. § 148B.60, subd. 4 (West Supp. 1992).
4. M.S.A. § 148B.60, subd. 3 (West Supp. 1992).
5. M.S.A. § 148B.28, subd. 6 (West Supp. 1992).

4. clergy who provide mental health services.

The following are excluded from the term *unlicensed mental health practitioner:*

1. persons licensed by the Board of Medical Examiners;[6]
2. persons licensed by the Board of Nursing;[7]
3. persons licensed by the Board of Social Work;[8]
4. persons licensed by the Board of Marriage and Family Therapy;[9]
5. persons licensed by any other licensing board if the person is working within the scope of the license; and
6. members of the clergy engaged in their duties as clergy by a religious congregation.

Mental Health Practitioner Advisory Council

The Mental Health Practitioner Advisory Council acts in an advisory capacity to the commissioner of health and the Office of Mental Health Practice. Together, they work toward the advancement of rules and procedures having to do with the regulation of practitioners and the enforcement of disciplinary action. The Council consists of nine members appointed to serve terms of four years by the commissioner of health. Membership includes six mental health service providers and three public members.[10]

Regulation

Mental Health Client Bill of Rights

Unlicensed mental health practitioners are not required to register with the state of Minnesota. However, these practitioners are required to provide their clients with a "Mental Health Client Bill of Rights," which includes the following:[11]

---

6. M.S.A. § 148B.60 (West 1989 & Supp. 1992). *See also* M.S.A. § 147 et seq. (West 1989 & Supp. 1992). *See* chapter 1.1.
7. M.S.A. §§ 148.171 to 148.285 (West 1989 & Supp. 1992). *See* chapter 1.2.
8. M.S.A. §§ 148B.18 to 148B.28 (West 1989 & Supp. 1992). *See* chapter 1.5.
9. M.S.A. §§ 148B.29 to 148B.39 (West 1989 & Supp. 1992). *See* chapter 1.8.
10. M.S.A. § 148B.41, subd. 2 (West Supp. 1992).
11. M.S.A. § 148B.71 (West Supp. 1992). Unlicensed MHPs who provide services at a licensed or government facility are exempt. The Bill of Rights must be posted in the MHP's office. The MHP must make reasonable accommodations to make the Bill of Rights accessible to clients who have impaired English reading ability.

1. the name and business address of the practitioner;
2. the degrees and qualifications of the practitioner;
3. the names and addresses of the practitioner's supervisor and of the Office of Mental Health Practice;
4. the practitioner's method of billing;
5. the practitioner's psychological orientation in treating clients;
6. a statement that the client has a right to current information regarding the practitioner's assessment and recommended course of treatment;
7. a statement that all records and tests are confidential without the client's signed release of those documents;[12]
8. a statement that the client has a right to access his or her medical records, provided that to do so would not be to the client's detriment;[13]
9. a statement that the client has a right to change practitioners after services have begun and may refuse services or treatment, unless otherwise provided by law;[14] and
10. a statement that the client may assert these rights unconditionally and without retaliation.

Prohibited Conduct; Disciplinary Action

The commissioner of health may revoke, suspend, or limit an unlicensed practitioner's right to practice when the practitioner has engaged in any prohibited conduct.[15] The following conduct is prohibited and is grounds for disciplinary action:[16]

1. conviction of a crime that is reasonably related to the provision of mental health services or that is against a person;
2. failure to report knowledge of conduct constituting grounds for disciplinary action relating to an unlicensed practitioner;
3. engaging in sexual activity with a client or former client;
4. advertising in a way that is misleading or deceptive;
5. adjudication as mentally incompetent or as a person who is mentally retarded, chemically dependant, or psychopathic;[17]
6. being incapable of providing client services with reasonable safety;

---

12. *See* chapters 4.1, 4.2, 4.3.
13. M.S.A. § 144.335 (West 1989 & Supp. 1992). *See* chapter 4.1.
14. *See* chapter 6.2.
15. M.S.A. § 148B.69 (West Supp. 1992).
16. M.S.A. § 148B.68 (West Supp. 1992).
17. M.S.A. § 526.09 (West 1975). *See* chapters 5B.1, 5E.4, 5E.5, 5E.7, 5D.5.

7. disclosing a client-related communication, unless otherwise permitted by law;[18]

8. refusal to furnish a client with medical records, as required by law;[19]

9. splitting fees;

10. engaging in fraudulent billing practices;

11. violating an order issued by the commissioner; and

12. continuing a professional relationship with a client in which the practitioner is unable to remain objective.

When the Council determines that a practitioner has engaged in prohibited conduct, the Council may revoke, suspend, restrict, or limit the practitioner's right to practice; impose a maximum civil of penalty of $10,000 per violation; require the practitioner to donate his or her services to a designated organization; or censure or reprimand the practitioner.[20]

Revocation or suspension of the practitioner's right to practice is mandatory for violations of prohibited conduct that involve crimes related to the provision of mental health services, crimes against persons, or crimes that involve sexual contact with a current or former client.[21]

As an aid to a disciplinary action involving the MHP's right to practice, the commissioner may issue cease and desist orders and seek injunctive relief from the courts.[22]

Reporting Obligations[23]

The law requires institutions, professional societies, licensed professionals, insurers, courts, and unlicensed MHPs to report to the Office of Mental Health Practice prohibited conduct by, and any adverse action taken in other contexts against, unlicensed MHPs.

Professional Cooperation[24]

Any unlicensed MHP who is the subject of an investigation or who is questioned in connection with an investigation has an obligation to cooperate fully with the investigation. Cooperation includes responding to questions, giving testimony, and producing any documents, books, records, or correspondence deemed necessary. If the Office of Mental Health Practice does not have

---

18. *See* chapters 4.1, 4.2, and 4.3 for a more extensive discussion of the law regarding disclosure of client information.
19. M.S.A. § 144.335 (West Supp. 1992). *See* chapter 4.1.
20. M.S.A. § 148B.69 (West Supp. 1992).
21. M.S.A. § 148B.69, subd. 5 (West Supp. 1992).
22. M.S.A. § 148B.70 (West Supp. 1992).
23. M.S.A. § 148B.63, subd. 7 (West Supp. 1992).
24. M.S.A. § 148B.66 (West Supp. 1992).

the client's written consent to access the client's records, the unlicensed MHP must omit any data in the record that would identify the client, before providing it to the Office.

Forms of Business Practice

2.0

Choice of Operational Form

A professional practice may take any one of a variety of legal forms. Among the most common choices are a sole proprietorship, a partnership, and a professional corporation.[1] The choice of operational form should be made by matching the features of the various forms against the current and future needs of your practice.[2] Of primary concern are features relating to operational and organizational flexibility and the availability of limited liability. The tax treatment of the various forms may also influence the choice of form.

---

1. As of January 1, 1993, a new type of entity, a Minnesota limited liability company, also became available as a choice through which to organize a professional practice. M.S.A. §§ 322.01 to 322.31; §§ 322A.01 to 322A.87 (West 1981 & Supp. 1992). *See* Bishop & Kleinberger, *Beyond Subchapter 5: The New Limited Liability Company,* 49 Bench & Bar of Minnesota 18 (1992). The limited liability organization combines attractive features of both the corporation and the partnership. For example, like a corporation, it provides limited liability to its owners, and like a partnership, it provides for the pass-through of losses and gains to its owners.

   However, there are several major questions about the limited liability organization that are still to be resolved. For example, it is unclear both whether a professional practice would be required to report its income on an accrual rather than a cash basis and whether all states will recognize the limited liability bestowed by the Minnesota statute. Until these ambiguities are resolved, it is unlikely that the limited liability organization will be a common choice for professional practices.

2. Because of the complexity of the law pertaining to the selection of an entity, this choice should be made with the advice of a qualified professional such as a lawyer or an accountant.

2.1

Sole Proprietorships

If an MHP chooses not to adopt a formal legal structure for his or
her practice, he or she operates as a sole proprietorship. Choosing
not to organize as a corporation,[1] a partnership,[2] or a limited
liability company[3] has both legal and practical implications. This
chapter discusses those implications.

If an MHP commences to practice on her or his own without
electing to establish her or his practice as a partnership or corporation, she or he is likely to be considered self-employed and
doing business in the form of a sole proprietorship.[4] Unlike
corporations and partnerships, sole proprietorships are not considered separate legal entities from their owners and accordingly
have no rights and obligations of their own. Any legal right or
obligation is that of the sole proprietor. The law does not provide
a structural form for the operation of a sole proprietorship. Any
income from the practice is reported on the proprietor's personal
tax returns and will be taxed at individual rates.[5] Any liability
that is incurred in the course of operating the proprietorship (for
example, as the result of either a malpractice judgment or a
business obligation) will be a personal liability that must be satisfied out of the proprietor's personal assets.

The potential for personal exposure to liability and the lack of
a prescribed operational structure may be problematic in some

---

1. *See* chapter 2.2.
2. *See* chapter 2.3.
3. *See* chapter 2.2.
4. If the practice is operated under a name other than that of the MHP, she or
   he must make an assumed name filing with the secretary of state. M.S.A.
   § 33.01 (West 1981 & Supp. 1992).
5. Note that it will also be necessary to pay any applicable self-employment
   taxes.

circumstances. Any practice involving more than one MHP or employing ancillary personnel, and any practice contemplating the assumption of significant business obligations, should consider choosing an organizational form that provides both some insulation from liability and an operational framework.[6] Likewise, tax planning considerations may favor electing to organize in a different form.

Practitioners who practice with others, whether it be pursuant to an office-sharing relationship or otherwise, should be aware that multiple separate solo practitioners may sometimes unwittingly create a partnership, with the consequent implications for attribution of liability.[7] Proper planning can reduce the potential for this problem.

---

6. For a discussion of these forms, *see* chapters 2.2 and 2.3.
7. For further discussion of this possibility, *see* chapter 2.3.

2.2

Corporations

An MHP or group of MHPs may find it useful to practice in the corporate form. The corporate form provides both insulation from many types of liability (contrast the treatment of partners[1]) and a convenient operational structure. This chapter will review the most pertinent features of corporations and will discuss the implications of incorporating for purposes of limited liability, organizational and operational structure, and taxation.

The services of most licensed health care professionals may be rendered through a professional corporation organized either as a business corporation or as a nonprofit corporation.[2] A corporation is a separate legal entity and as such has certain rights and responsibilities. A corporation is owned by one or more shareholders whose ownership is represented by stock in the corporation. The shareholders have ultimate control of the corporation but generally delegate the responsibility for day-to-day management to a board of directors. The board is appointed or elected by the shareholders. The board may consist of all or a subset of the shareholders and may have members who are not shareholders but who have some special expertise to offer the corporation. In turn, the board may appoint committees to oversee and explore particular aspects of corporate concern.

---

1. *See* chapter 2.3.
2. M.S.A. § 319A.03 (West Supp. 1992).

Limited Liability

By electing the corporate form, the individuals associated with the practice may achieve substantial insulation from legal liability.[3] Each practitioner will still be personally liable for his or her own acts and omissions. However, any liability arising as a result of the acts or omissions of one party associated with the corporation cannot be attributed to another party who had no involvement in the matter from which the liability arises.[4] Thus, the malpractice of one MHP-shareholder should not result in personal liability for another, unless the second had personally participated in the malpractice.

The corporate form also insulates shareholders from personal liability for corporate obligations. With a few exceptions, if proper corporate formalities are followed, the individuals associated with a corporation cannot be required to pay corporate debts or to make good on corporate contracts.[5] It should be noted, however, that voluntarily assuming personal responsibility, as when personally guaranteeing a loan or lease, negates this protection and allows creditors and aggrieved parties to look to personal assets to satisfy claims that they may have against the corporation.

Corporate Structure

The process of incorporation is initiated by filing Articles of Incorporation with the secretary of state. The Articles, together with the Bylaws, set forth the basic rules for operation of the corporation. For example, these documents set forth the number of persons to serve on the board of directors and stipulate the manner of selecting directors.[6] The Articles and Bylaws also set forth the circumstances under which shares of stock may be issued and may set forth the process for holding corporate meetings of the board of directors and of the shareholders.

In order to preserve the protection from liability noted above, it is imperative that the MHP observe the corporate "formalities" described in the organizational and operational documents. Corporate and personal bank accounts and funds should be kept separate, and a separate set of corporate records, including minutes of meetings, should be maintained. The failure to keep the affairs of the corporation separate from the personal affairs of its

---

3. M.S.A. § 319A.10 (West Supp. 1992).
4. *Id.*
5. *Id.*
6. *See, e.g.,* M.S.A. § 302A.111 (West 1985 & Supp. 1992).

principals can result in the "piercing of the corporate veil" and the consequent ability of creditors to reach the personal assets of its shareholders.

The relatively straightforward and well-established set of rules for the operation and organization of a corporation provides a useful structure for the operation of a practice. Furthermore, the simplicity and familiarity of the corporate form to accountants, lawyers, and other professionals can often help limit the professional fees associated with running a practice. Partnerships, for example, can often be more complicated, and hence more costly, to establish and to operate.[7]

The law governing professional corporations requires that the corporation be organized to provide only one type of professional service and services ancillary thereto.[8] Only licensed members of the chosen profession may be shareholders of the corporation.[9] Likewise, with the exception of the treasurer and the secretary, every officer and director must be licensed in the applicable field.[10]

It is permissible to place restrictions on the transferability of a professional corporation's stock,[11] and it is advisable to carefully consider the circumstances under which a shareholder will be allowed to transfer stock to another individual. Otherwise, there is the prospect that stock will be transferred to shareholders who are not acceptable to the other shareholders. Similarly, there may be instances (for example, the death of a shareholder) in which it might be appropriate to agree that the corporation will have the option or obligation to purchase a shareholder's stock. The terms of any restrictions on the transfer of shares, or of any options to purchase shares, may be incorporated into the Articles of Incorporation, the Bylaws, or a written agreement among the shareholders and the corporation.

---

7. *See* chapter 2.3.
8. The corporation may be organized to provide two or more types of professional services together only when the licensing laws of each professional service specifically authorize the professions to be practiced in combination. M.S.A. § 319A.04 (West Supp. 1992).
9. M.S.A. § 319A.8 (West Supp. 1992) provides that shares also may be issued to professional corporations and partnerships rendering the same kind of professional service as the issuer.
10. If the corporation is organized as a nonprofit corporation, a majority of the board of directors need not be professionals.
11. M.S.A. § 319A.13 (West Supp. 1992).

Taxation

In making the choice to incorporate, one must carefully consider the tax implications.[12] Among the most significant tax implications are the existence of a corporate level tax, the differences between corporate and personal rates of taxation, and the availability of certain tax-free benefits to corporate employees.

Corporations are treated as separate legal entities for the purpose of taxation. Thus, in most cases, corporate income is subject to taxation wholly apart from the income of its shareholders.[13] If income is retained in the corporation (for example, for the purpose of purchasing equipment), that income will be taxed to the corporation, not the shareholders, and that rate may be different than that imposed on individuals.[14] If the income is subsequently distributed to shareholders as a dividend or pursuant to a liquidation, it may be subject to a second layer of taxation as it is reported on the shareholders' returns. In a professional corporation, however, corporate expenses, in the form of salary and supplies, together with other deductions and depreciations, often approximate corporate income, so that there is often very little corporate taxable income.

Certain tax-free fringe benefits are available through the corporate form that are not generally available through other forms of operation. For example, group life, group health, and group disability plans are fully deductible and excludable only if offered by a corporate employer.[15]

---

12. The tax implications of entity choice are so varied and complex that it is impossible to address them in a book of this scope. Although we will briefly set forth some of the major tax considerations bearing on entity choice, we cannot overstress the importance of consulting a qualified tax advisor with regard to particular tax planning questions.
13. There is an exception to this rule for corporations that make a timely Subchapter S election. If the corporation makes such an election and otherwise qualifies under Subchapter S, it may qualify for taxation on terms similar to a partnership. Note that the favorable treatment of fringe benefits detailed here is limited in the case of owners with a greater than 2% interest in a Subchapter S corporation. I.R.C. § 1372 (1988).
14. Personal service corporations providing health care services are currently taxed at a flat rate of 34% of their taxable income. I.R.C. § 11(b)(2).
15. I.R.C. §§ 79, 105(b), 104(a).

2.3

Partnerships

Two or more MHPs who practice together may organize as a partnership. Becoming a partner in a partnership can greatly increase exposure to liability (contrast the treatment of shareholders in a corporation[1]). Electing to practice in a partnership may also influence the operational and organizational structure of the practice, and it will dictate the method of taxation.

Relationship Between the Partners

The characterization of a relationship as a partnership has significant implications for the partners. The partnership form contemplates the sharing of profits and losses from the venture and accordingly is distinct from a typical office expense-sharing arrangement. As with profits and losses, authority and responsibility for the partnership's business are also shared by the partners. Each partner has the authority to bind the partnership to a variety of commitments.[2] Likewise, any liability incurred by a partner as a result of a wrongful act or omission, occurring either while acting in the ordinary course of the business (for example, rendering professional services) or with the authority of other partners, is considered a partnership liability.[3] Because each partner is

---

1. *See* chapter 2.2.
2. M.S.A. § 323.08 (West 1981). There are exceptions to the general rule, however. *Id.*
3. M.S.A. § 323.12 (West 1981). Contrast the treatment of shareholders in a corporation. *See* chapter 2.2.

personally liable,[4] jointly and severally,[5] for partnership liabilities,[6] the decision to join a partnership can result in significant additional exposure to personal liability.[7]

Characteristics of a Partnership

A partnership is defined as an association of two or more persons to carry on as co-owners a business for profit.[8] Despite the seeming clarity of this definition, it is not always apparent when a partnership exists. An MHP, because of his or her involvement in an arrangement such as a joint venture or office-sharing agreement, may find him- or herself unwittingly involved in a partnership.

A court will look at a variety of factors to determine whether a partnership exists. Evidence that a person receives a share of the profits of a business is considered to be indicative of the existence of a partnership, unless the amounts were paid on account of a debt, as wages, as rent, or on account of one of a number of other specified obligations.[9] One must carefully structure any financial relationship so as to assure that it does not inadvertently become a partnership.

Choosing to Organize as a Partnership: The Partnership Agreement

Notwithstanding the foregoing cautions, there may be situations in which the partnership form is attractive. For example, tax planning may, depending on the circumstances, support the organization of a particular venture as a partnership. The taxation of

---

4. Because of the limited utility of the limited partnership for professional practices, this discussion deals solely with general partnerships. However, it should be noted that some protection from liability can be obtained by the limited partners of a limited partnership. See M.S.A. §§ 322.01 to 322.31; §§ 322A.01 to 322A.87 (West 1987 & Supp. 1992).
5. This means that an individual partner can be held liable for either a pro rata share or all of the partnership liability. A partner who is held liable for all of a liability may normally seek reimbursement from the other partners.
6. M.S.A. § 323.14 (West 1981).
7. Characterization of an arrangement as a partnership can also result in the forced sharing of property and profits. See, e.g., M.S.A. §§ 323.07, 323.17 (West 1981).
8. M.S.A. § 323.02, subd. 8 (West 1981).
9. M.S.A. § 323.06(4) (West 1981).

corporations and partnerships is radically different. Corporations pay corporate taxes on corporate income, and corporate losses are generally only available for use by the corporation. In contrast, items of partnership income and loss are generally "passed-through" to the individual partners.[10]

If it is determined that a partnership should be formed, the MHP should seek professional assistance for the purpose of developing a written partnership agreement. This agreement should, among other things, set forth the goals of the partnership, the terms and conditions on which partners may join and leave the partnership, the conditions on which a partner can be called on to make additional capital contributions, the share of any partnership profits or losses to be allocated to each partner, the authority of the individual partners to prosecute the partnership's business independently of the partnership, and the terms and conditions on which the partnership can be dissolved.

---

10. Similar results, without the resulting exposure to liability, can often be obtained by choosing to organize as a Subchapter S corporation or as a limited liability company. *See* chapters 2.0 and 2.1 for further discussion of this issue.

2.4

Health Maintenance Organizations

Minnesota has a high rate of health maintenance organization (HMO) enrollment. More than 25% of the population is enrolled in an HMO. As a result, all health care providers should be generally familiar with HMO administrative requirements and the general legal and regulatory framework within which HMOs operate.

A health maintenance organization (HMO) is a nonprofit corporation that agrees to provide a defined package of inpatient and outpatient benefits, without regard to the frequency or extent of services provided, in return for a fixed, prepaid sum.[1] Minnesota is the only state that requires that HMOs be organized as nonprofit corporations. The HMO provides health care services directly or through contractual arrangements with providers. Providers may be salaried, or paid on a discounted fee-for-service or capitated basis. All HMOs limit the number and types of providers that an enrollee may see without a referral. The majority of HMOs contract with a limited number of mental health professionals and utilize a "closed-panel" approach to the delivery of mental health services.

All HMOs are licensed and regulated by the Minnesota Department of Health. Some HMOs may also be federally qualified. These organizations will be licensed and regulated by the Health Care Financing Administration.

---

1. M.S.A. § 62D.02, subd. 4 (West Supp. 1993).

Benefits for Mental Health and Chemical Dependency Services

HMOs are required to provide a specific array of mental health services. They must provide at least 30 days per contract year of inpatient mental health treatment.[2] In all group contracts, HMOs must provide a minimum of 10 hours of outpatient mental health treatment in a 12-month benefit period. Copayments for these initial 10 hours of outpatient treatment are limited to $10 or 20% of the usual and customary charge. The law does not mandate an outpatient mental health benefit in nongroup or individual benefit contracts.[3]

If a mental or nervous disorder is "serious or persistent," the HMO must cover at least 75% of the usual and customary charges for the additional treatment. The HMO may require prior authorization for all outpatient mental health treatment beyond 10 hours and may limit such extended treatment to 30 "visit hours" in any 12-month benefit period.[4] Visit hours or hours of treatment for group therapy are calculated using a ratio of not less than two group treatment sessions to one individual treatment hour.

Minnesota law also provides that family therapy must be covered by an HMO if it is recommended as part of a plan of therapy for a minor.[5] An HMO must also provide for coverage of residential facility care for emotionally disturbed children. This coverage must be at the same level as inpatient medical care. Like outpatient mental health services, this benefit is only mandated for group contracts.[6]

An HMO must also provide inpatient chemical dependency treatment in a licensed residential facility or hospital for up to the greater of 28 days or a number equal to 20% of the standard inpatient hospital benefit.[7]

HMOs are required to promptly evaluate the needs of enrollees seeking mental health or chemical dependency treatment. If the HMO concludes that structured treatment is not necessary, the enrollee may request a second opinion by a qualified health care professional. This second opinion must be paid for by the HMO. The HMO is obligated to consider the second opinion but is not required to accept it.[8]

---

2. Minn. R. 4685.0700 (1991).
3. M.S.A. § 62D.102 (West Supp. 1993).
4. Id.
5. Id.
6. M.S.A. § 62A.151 (1992) (West 1986).
7. Minn. R. 4685.0700 (1991).
8. M.S.A. § 62D.103 (1992) (West 1986).

Mental health benefits may be administered by a variety of providers, including hospitals, community mental health centers, licensed psychologists and licensed consulting psychologists, marriage and family therapists, social workers, psychiatric nurses, and psychiatrists. Unlike commercial insurers or Blue Cross and Blue Shield, HMOs are not required to accept direct reimbursement from psychologists, licensed consulting psychologists, and other nonphysician providers, except in the context of "combination" or "wrap-around" insurance products.[9]

---

9. M.S.A. § 62A.152, subds. 2, 3 (West Supp. 1993).

2.5

Preferred Provider Arrangements

A preferred provider arrangement (PPA) or preferred provider organization (PPO) is a health care benefit program that is designed to control costs by giving members incentives to use health care providers designated as preferred but that also provides substantial coverage for services from nonpreferred providers. A PPA or PPO may be a nonprofit or for-profit corporation or a separate line of business of a commercial insurer, third-party administrator, or other entity. PPAs and PPOs may be formed by employers, unions, provider groups, hospitals, insurers, and third-party administrators.

Providers are selected for participation in a PPA or PPO on the basis of a variety of factors including geographic location, specialty, outcomes data, and cost effectiveness. Preferred providers are usually paid on a discounted fee-for-service basis and agree to cooperate with utilization review protocols and other administrative procedures. The primary advantage to a provider of participating in a PPA or PPO is a potential increase in the number of patients requesting care from the provider.

Minnesota does not separately regulate PPOs. Commercial insurers, Blue Cross and Blue Shield, and HMOs may create preferred provider panels under their respective licenses. Minnesota law expressly permits the payment by commercial insurers and health service plans of different amounts of reimbursement to preferred providers. In many cases, preferred providers may receive a lower-level reimbursement than nonpreferred providers, in exchange for the higher volume of patients associated with designation as a preferrred provider.[1]

---

1. M.S.A. § 72A.20, subd. 15(4) (West Supp. 1993).

PPOs and PPAs must frequently carefully analyze the application of state and federal antitrust laws to their business practices. Other laws that may apply to these arrangements include state licensing laws, tax laws, negligence and contract law, and the Employee Retirement Income Security Act of 1974.[2]

The laws governing the direct reimbursement of mental health professionals or the type and extent of mental health and chemical dependency benefits that must be provided by a PPA or PPO are determined by the type of licensed entity creating or sponsoring the arrangement. For example, a commercial insurer creating a PPA will be required to directly reimburse psychologists and licensed consulting psychologists, whereas an HMO developing a PPA option will not be required to offer direct reimbursement to such providers. PPOs and PPAs that are part of self-insured arrangements will generally be exempt from all state regulation regarding mandated benefits and the direct reimbursement of providers.[3] The third-party administrators who often administer such arrangements are subject to minimal regulation by the Department of Commerce.

2. 29 U.S.C. § 1144(a).
3. 29 U.S.C. § 1144(a). *See* Metropolitan Life Ins. Co. v. Mass., 471 U.S. 724 (1985); Rapp v. Travelers Ins. Co., 869 F.2d (9th Cir. 1989).

2.6

Individual Practice Associations

An individual practice association (IPA) is often defined as an integrated group of health care providers that contracts with third-party payers to provide health care services to the payer's members or enrollees. The IPA also contracts with individual providers to participate in the IPA and provide the medical care required by enrollees or insureds. As a result, most IPAs involve the establishment and maintenance of multifaceted contractual arrangements.

An IPA may be organized as a for-profit or nonprofit corporation and is often viewed as a joint venture among groups of providers. Members of the IPA practice in their own offices but are compensated by the organization on a fee-for-service or fee-per-patient basis. The providers may be loosely affiliated through the IPA, or the IPA may function like a "clinic without walls" and closely oversee the practices of an integrated group of providers.

Minnesota law does not contain any special statutory provisions specific to IPAs.

2.7

Hospital, Administrative, and Staff Privileges

Some states specify which classes of MHPs are eligible for hospital staff and administrative privileges. Minnesota law does not closely regulate general hospital staff and administrative privileges. As in many other states, Minnesota relies heavily on private accreditation bodies such as the Joint Commission on the Accreditation of Healthcare Organizations (JCAHO) and the Medicare participation standards.[1]

Staff privileges at hospitals and other acute and residential treatment facilities are governed by rules and regulations of the Department of Health, the hospital or facility bylaws, and common law principles. These rules, regulations, and principles generally establish the legal responsibility of the medical staff to properly credential, supervise, and discipline hospital personnel and health care professionals with staff privileges. Facilities accepting Medicare or Medicaid reimbursement must comply with the Medicare Conditions of Participation.[2] Many facilities are also accredited by the JCAHO. Staff privileges granted by these accredited facilities will be governed by JCAHO standards.

JCAHO standards permit health care professionals other than physicians to be granted staff and/or clinical privileges.[3] Such persons may be granted clinical privileges consistent with their scope of practice as articulated by local licensure law and the individual's training, experience, and demonstrated competence.

---

1. M.S.A. § 144.55, subd. 3 (West Supp. 1993); Minn. R. 4640.0700, subp. 1 (1991).
2. 42 U.S.C. § 1395 (1991).
3. Joint Commission on Accreditation of Hospitals, *Accreditation Manual for Hospitals*, p. 109 (1990).

Unlike other states, Minnesota law does not require that allied or limited practitioners be granted medical staff memberships.

Department of Health rules recommend that all hospitals adopt the JCAHO standards.[4] In addition, Minnesota law separately regulates mental and psychiatric hospitals. These regulations specify the qualifications of the hospital medical director and the director of nursing and require the provision of qualified physical and occupational therapists.[5] The chief of staff or medical director of a mental or psychiatric hospital must be a licensed physician with training and experience in psychiatry.[6] The qualifications of other staff are not specified.

---

4. Minn. R. 4640.0700, subp. 1 (1991).
5. *Id.*
6. *Id.*

2.8

Zoning for Residential Programs

Zoning laws, which control the type of use to which land in a political subdivision may be put, are important and legitimate tools for controlling the growth and development of urban areas. In the past, these laws have sometimes been used to exclude group living facilities for mentally disabled people from residential areas.[1] Such exclusionary use of zoning laws has been sharply curtailed in Minnesota since at least 1976.[2] Current Minnesota law reflects a policy that no person[3] shall be "excluded by municipal zoning ordinances or other land use regulations from the benefits of normal residential surroundings."[4]

The law carries out this policy by mandating that zoning codes treat residential programs just as they do other residential uses of property. Residential programs with six or fewer persons must be treated just as "single-family" residential uses of property are treated.[5] The law also prohibits neighbors from excluding

---

1. *See* City of Cleburne, Texas v. Cleburne Living Center, 473 U.S. 432 (1985); Northwest Residence, Inc. v. City of Brooklyn Center, 352 N.W.2d 764 (Minn. Ct. App. 1984); Costley v. Caromin House, Inc., 313 N.W.2d 21 (Minn. 1981).
2. Minn. Laws 1976, c. 243, § 12, codified at M.S.A. § 245.812 (repealed by Minn. Laws 1987, c. 333, § 20).
3. "Person" is defined here to mean a child under age 18 or an adult who has a mental illness, mental retardation or a related condition, a physical handicap, or a functional impairment. It also includes people who are chemically dependent or abuse chemicals. "Functional impairment" means substantial difficulty in carrying out a major activity of daily living, or a mental disorder that significantly impairs a person's ability to cope with the ordinary demands of life and that requires support to maintain independence in the community. M.S.A. § 245A.02, subds. 2, 4, 7, 11 (West Supp. 1992).
4. M.S.A. § 462.357, subd. 6a; § 245A.11, subd. 1 (West 1991 & Supp. 1992).
5. M.S.A. § 462.357, subd. 7; § 245A.11, subd. 2 (West 1991 & Supp. 1992).

such a program by use of "restrictive covenants."[6] Residential programs licensed for 7 to 16 persons are to be treated the same as multifamily residential uses of property. A municipality may impose additional conditions on the zoning of these larger programs, but only if the conditions are necessary to protect the health and safety of the clients of the program.[7]

To foster the integration of persons with handicaps into the mainstream, Minnesota law imposes density restrictions on the location of residential programs.[8] These restrictions are carried out as part of the licensing process and are thus under the control of the commissioner of human services rather than local zoning officials. The commissioner may not grant a license to any residential program if it will be within 1,320 feet of an existing program, with certain exceptions.[9] Each county is required to develop plans to promote the dispersal of group residential programs. The plans are submitted to the Department of Human Services, which must determine whether they are acceptable. The commissioner of human services may reduce grants to counties that do not have acceptable dispersal plans.

---

6. M.S.A. § 245A.11, subd. 1 (West Supp. 1992). "Restrictive covenants" are contractual provisions governing land use. Prohibited are provisions, for example, that require that all of a home's occupants be related or that homes be owner-occupied. *See, e.g.,* Costley v. Caromin House, Inc., 313 N.W.2d 21 (Minn. 1981).
7. Scott County Lumber Co., Inc. v. City of Shakopee, 417 N.W.2d (Minn. Ct. App. 1988), pet. for rev. denied (March 23, 1988).
8. These density restrictions do not violate the Fair Housing Act, 42 U.S.C. §§ 3604(f)(1,3), 3615, by discriminating against handicapped persons, because they further the proper governmental interest of integrating handicapped persons in the mainstream of society. Familystyle of St. Paul, Inc. v. City of St. Paul, 923 F.2d 91, reh. denied. (8th Cir. 1991).
9. M.S.A. § 245A.11, subd. 4 (West Supp. 1992). The limitation does not apply if the existing program is located in a hospital, if the municipality grants the program permission to locate, if the program services six or fewer people and is not located in a city of the first class, or if the program is foster care.

Insurance Reimbursement and Deductions for Services

Insurance Reimbursement for Professional Services

The majority of individuals seeking mental health or chemical dependency treatment will wish to maximize their insurance coverage for such treatment. Patients are often ignorant of or confused by the various insurance entities and products currently offered in the marketplace. It is therefore important that mental health professionals possess a rudimentary understanding of the types of insurance available and the type and extent of coverage mandated by state law.

Types of Insurance Affected

Insurance policies are issued by accident and health insurers licensed under Chapter 62A. Subscriber contracts are issued by nonprofit health service plans licensed under Chapter 62C. Blue Cross and Blue Shield of Minnesota is an example of a nonprofit health service plan. Health maintenance contracts are issued by health maintenance organizations (HMOs) licensed under Chapter 62D. The mental health benefits offered by HMOs are discussed in chapter 2.4.

Mental Health Services

Statutory mandates regarding the insurance reimbursement for mental health benefits do not apply to nongroup or individual contracts. Specific mandates apply to large groups (defined as 100 or more certificate holders), and different mandates apply to employers electing to purchase a small employer plan (defined as 2 to 29 employees).[1] Technically, there are no mental health mandates for groups of between 30 and 99 contract holders. However, third-party payers generally treat any group over 29 employees as a large group for purposes of mental health benefits.

The large-group mandate requires coverage of inpatient mental health benefits at the same level as other inpatient services. Benefits for outpatient mental health services must be at least 80% of the usual and customary charge for the first 10 hours of treatment during a 12-month benefit period. If a condition is a "serious or persistent mental or nervous disorder," coverage must equal or exceed 75% of the usual and customary charges for a maximum of 30 additional hours of treatment.[2] The insurer or health service plan may institute a prior authorization process for any outpatient treatment in excess of 10 hours. If treatment is provided on a group basis, two group sessions are counted as a single individual session for the purpose of determining compliance with statutory mandates.[3]

This statutory mandate is only applicable if the services are furnished by specific types of mental health providers. Those provider types are (a) a licensed or accredited hospital, (b) a community mental health center or mental health clinic approved or licensed by the commissioner of human services or other authorized state agency, and (c) a licensed psychologist, licensed consulting psychologist, or licensed psychiatrist.[4]

In 1992 and 1993, Minnesota enacted a number of insurance reforms.[5] This insurance reform and cost containment initiative is popularly known as MinnesotaCare. Some of the reforms focused on the small-group insurance market, defined as employers with between 2 and 29 employees. These reforms became effective on July 1, 1993, and are commonly referred to as the Minnesota Small Employer Health Benefit Act. With respect to mental health benefits, health carriers participating in the small-group market may offer a reduced mental health benefit to small employers purchasing group health insurance. This benefit is restricted to inpatient treatment and 10 hours of outpatient treatment for a limited number of mental illnesses or conditions.[6]

---

1. M.S.A. § 62A.152 (1992); §§ 62L.01 to 62L.23 (West 1992 & West Supp. 1993).
2. M.S.A. § 62A.152, subd. 2 (West Supp. 1993).
3. M.S.A. § 62A.152, subd. 2 (West Supp. 1993).
4. Id.
5. Minn. Sess. Laws Chapter 569, art. 2.
6. Only those illnesses and conditions classified as ICD-9 codes 295 to 299 by the International Classification of Diseases–Clinical Modification (7th ed. ; 1990), will be covered. M.S.A. § 62L.05, subd. 4 (1992).

Chemical Dependency Services

All group insurance policies and subscriber contracts must include benefits for the treatment of chemical dependency.[7] This benefit may be waived in individually underwritten contracts if the individual provides a written refusal to elect coverage and if the premium is appropriately reduced to reflect the absence of such coverage. Treatment may be rendered by licensed hospitals, licensed residential treatment programs if such treatment is recommended by a physician, and nonresidential treatment programs licensed by the state or approved by the state.

Policies that provide benefits for treatment in licensed hospitals and residential treatment programs must cover at least 20% of the total patient days allowed by the policy.[8] Coverage must not be for less than 28 days in each 12-month benefit year. Insurance coverage of nonresidential treatment programs must extend for at least 130 hours in a 12-month benefit year.

The law does not require chemical dependency coverage by any policy designed primarily to provide coverage that is payable on a per diem, fixed-indemnity, or nonexpense-incurred basis. Policies that provide coverage for accidents only are likewise not required to provide benefits for treatment of alcoholism, chemical dependency, or drug addiction.

If a small employer elects to purchase a small-employer plan under the Minnesota Small Employer Health Benefit Act, the chemical dependency benefit may be limited to 60 hours of outpatient treatment per year.[9] Inpatient chemical dependency treatment is not a covered benefit under the Minnesota Small Employer Health Benefit Act.[10]

MinnesotaCare

In 1992 and 1993, Minnesota enacted a complex and comprehensive health care reform initiative designed to improve access to health care and control escalating health care costs. Several provisions of the MinnesotaCare legislation are of interest to mental health professionals. The legislation was controversial and is expected to be repeatedly amended in the future. As a result, a limited number of sections of interest to mental health professionals are only briefly highlighted here.

---

7. M.S.A. § 62A.149, subd. 2 (West 1992).
8. *Id.*
9. M.S.A. § 62L.05, subd. 4 (West Supp. 1993).
10. M.S.A. § 62L.05, subd. 4 (West Supp. 1993).

In addition to reforming the small-employer insurance market, MinnesotaCare establishes a Private Employer Insurance Program (PEIP). This program is designed to provide small private employers with the same advantages of a large employer when purchasing health insurance by allowing groups of unrelated employers to participate in a large purchasing pool administered by the state of Minnesota.[11] The benefits available under the pooled plan must be equivalent to the current level of mandated benefits for insurers, nonprofit health service plans, and HMOs. It is anticipated that the PEIP may increase the number of individuals with access to insurance plans that include all mandated mental health and chemical dependency benefits.

MinnesotaCare also expands a previous state program known as the Children's Health Plan. Under the new program, low income state residents who are not eligible for Medical Assistance will be eligible to participate in a state-subsidized health insurance program. Eligibility for the program will be phased in from July 1992 to July 1994. The program is targeted at the currently uninsured. Coverage includes inpatient and outpatient mental health services and inpatient and residential chemical dependency services. The inpatient hospital benefit for adult enrollees is subject to an annual benefit limit of $10,000. Outpatient mental health services are limited to diagnostic assessments; psychological testing; explanation of findings; mediation management by a physician; day treatment; partial hospitalization; and individual, family, and group psychotherapy.

Chemical dependency services must be provided by a qualified health professional or outpatient program. Individuals seeking chemical dependency treatment must be assessed by a local social service agency, and treatment must be coordinated with other state chemical dependency programs.

This health care access program is financed with a 5% cigarette tax increase, a 2% tax on hospital gross revenues, a 2% tax on the gross revenues of health care providers, and a 1% tax on third-party payers. The hospital tax is scheduled to become effective on January 1, 1993; the provider tax on January 1, 1994; and the third-party payer tax on January 1, 1996. Providers who are subject to the tax include all providers who are eligible for reimbursement under the Minnesota medical assistance program. This includes psychiatrists, licensed consulting psychologists, psychologists, marriage and family therapists, and chemical dependency counselors.

The 1993 Minnesota legislature also called for the creation of integrated service networks (ISNs) and the establishment of an

---

11. M.S.A. § 43A.317 (West Supp. 1993).

all-payer system for health care services delivered outside of an ISN system. These reforms are scheduled to become effective in July 1994 and will be the subject of extensive administrative rule making. These reforms are exceedingly complex and are expected to have an impact on all health care providers. As of this writing, few details are known as to how such a system will actually operate. Mental health professionals will need to be constantly attuned to new developments in this area.

3.2

Mental Health Benefits in State Insurance Plans

The state of Minnesota provides its eligible employees with hospital and medical benefits.[1] A number of different plan designs are made available to eligible employees, and each provides certain minimum benefits.[2] Because state employees are a self-insured group operating under unique statutory authority, many mandated benefits, including mental health benefits, do not technically apply to state employees. However, the Minnesota Department of Employee Relations and the various labor unions representing public employees have historically incorporated all mental health mandates in state benefit contracts.[3] Because mandated benefits differ slightly among insurance plans, HMOs, and health service plans, the mental health mandate applicable to a state-sponsored benefit plan will depend on which type of third-party payer is offering the plan.

State-sponsored plans will generally provide for a minimum of 30 days of inpatient coverage and coverage for at least 80% of the usual and customary charges for the first 10 hours of outpatient treatment during a 12-month benefit period.[4] Coverage may be extended beyond 10 hours of outpatient treatment when required to treat "serious or persistent" mental or nervous disorders.[5] This coverage must include at least 75% of the usual and customary charges. However, prior authorization from the third-party payer may be required before extending coverage beyond

---

1. M.S.A. § 43A.22 (West 1988).
2. M.S.A. § 62E.06 (West 1986 & Supp. 1993).
3. M.S.A. § 62A.152, subd. 2 (West Supp. 1993).
4. *Id.*
5. *Id.*

the initial 10 hours.[6] This extension of outpatient coverage may be limited to a maximum of 30 hours during any 12-month benefit period.[7]

6. *Id.*
7. *Id.*

3.3

Tax Deductions for Services

There are certain limited circumstances in which an individual taxpayer may take a deduction on her or his federal and state tax returns for the cost of mental health services incurred by the taxpayer or his or her spouse or dependents.[1] There may be other circumstances in which the cost of mental health services may be taken as a legitimate business expense. This chapter will provide an overview of the tax treatment of mental health expenses.

Mental Health Expenses as an Individual Deduction

An individual taxpayer may deduct qualified medical expenses on her or his personal return.[2] To qualify, the expenses must

1. not be reimbursed by insurance;[3]
2. in aggregate, for the year, exceed 7.5% of the taxpayer's adjusted gross income[4] (i.e., the taxpayer must have substantial medical expenses to be eligible for this deduction); and

---

1. In the interest of avoiding liability and other complications, the MHP should refrain from offering tax planning advice to patients and instead refer interested patients to a qualified tax adviser.
2. The discussion that follows deals only with the federal law. However, a Minnesota taxpayer's tax liability is determined with reference to his or her federal taxable income (M.S.A. § 290.01, subds. 19, 29 [West 1989 & Supp. 1992]), and accordingly, the rules set forth in the federal law operate to determine the deductibility of medical expenses for purposes of state law.
3. Treas. Reg. § 1.213-1(a)(3)(i).
4. I.R.C. § 213(a) (1992).

3. be for services that meet the definition of "medical care."[5]

To qualify as "medical care," the services must be for "the diagnosis, cure, mitigation, treatment or prevention of disease or for the purpose of affecting any structure or function of the body. . . ."[6] Expenses are considered to be for medical care only if they are "incurred primarily for the prevention or alleviation of a physical or mental defect or illness."[7]

Some mental health services clearly qualify as "medical care," whereas the treatment of others is ambiguous or unfavorable. Hospital, surgical, and laboratory services will generally qualify.[8] Likewise, treatment for sexual dysfunction has been held to be deductible.[9] On the other hand, expenses for marriage counseling have been disallowed,[10] and programs offering services to stop smoking or lose weight are generally nondeductible.[11]

The ability to qualify is not, however, dependant on the qualifications, or lack thereof, of the practitioner.[12] Services of psychiatrists, psychologists,[13] psychotherapists,[14] and a variety of other practitioners are eligible if they meet the definition of medical care.

Mental Health Expenses as a Business Deduction

In certain circumstances, it may be possible for a taxpayer to take the expenses of mental health services as a business deduction. The general rule is that a taxpayer may take a deduction for any "ordinary and necessary expenses [incurred in the course of] carrying on a trade or business."[15] Thus, for example, a seminar on the reduction of stress in the workplace, offered to employees, may be deductible to the employer.

---

5. I.R.C. § 213(d)(1)(A) (1992).
6. I.R.C. § 213(a) (1992).
7. Treas. Reg. 1.213-1(e)(ii).
8. Treas. Reg. 1.213-1(e)(1).
9. Rev. Rul. 75-187, 1975-CB 92.
10. Rev. Rul. 1975-2 CB 88.
11. Rev. Rul. 55-261, 1955-1-CB307; Pr. Ltr. Rul. 82-51-045 (Sept. 17, 1982).
12. See, e.g., Rev. Rul. 63-91, 1963-1 CB.
13. Rev. Rul. 143, 1953-2 CB 129.
14. Rev. Rul. 91, 1963-1 CB 54.
15. I.R.C. § 162(a) (1992).

Privacy of Professional Information

4.1

Extensiveness, Ownership, Maintenance, and Access to Records

Records are a central and required feature of an MHP's practice. The records and information that the MHP accumulates about patients or clients are highly regulated.

Because Minnesota statutes do not state otherwise, it is presumed that MHPs have a substantial ownership interest in the records that they create. Patients, clients, and the public have substantial interests, as well, in these records and the information they contain. This chapter discusses the laws and rules governing those records.

Psychologists

Extensiveness of Records

Minnesota rules regarding psychologist licensure and ethics provide that a psychologist must maintain an accurate record for each client. Each record must minimally contain[1]

1. an accurate chronological listing of all client visits, together with fees charged to the client or a third-party payer;

2. copies of all correspondence relevant to the client;

3. a personal data sheet; and

4. copies of all client authorizations for release of information and any other legal forms pertaining to the client.

---

1. Minn. R. 7200.4900, subp. 1a (1991).

Maintenance of Records

Although no minimum length of time is provided by rule or statute for a psychologist to maintain records, a rule does provide that a psychologist must continue to maintain as private information the records of a client after the professional relationship between the psychologist and the client has ceased.[2] Hospital records may be destroyed after three years provided that they are first transferred onto photographic film.[3]

Client Access

Rights of a client to have access to his or her psychological records are governed by statute and rule.

Rules governing psychologists provide that the client "who is the direct recipient of psychological services has the right of access to the records relating to psychological services maintained by the psychologists on that client . . . provided the records are not classified as confidential. . . ."[4] Although the rule does not itself define "access," it specifies that access must be provided in accordance with the Access to Health Records law.[5] Under this law, upon the client's[6] request, the psychologist must provide complete and current information regarding the client's diagnosis, treatment, and prognosis in terms the client can understand. Upon request, the psychologist must furnish to the client a copy of the client's record, or portions of the record relating to a condition specified by the client. If the client consents, the psychologist may provide the information in summary form. If the psychologist believes that the information may be detrimental to

---

2. Minn. R. 7200.4700, subp. 9 (1991).
3. M.S.A. § 145.32, subd. 1 (West 1989). However, portions of the file that include miscellaneous documents, correspondence, and papers may be destroyed after seven years without those portions being transferred to photographic film.
4. Minn. R. 7200.4900, subp. 1a (1991). The "confidential" data referred to by the rule are "court services" data, as specified by M.S.A. § 13.84, subd. 3, gathered by a psychologist at the direction of a court, where the source of the data requests that the data be held confidential. The data may be released to the subject of the data only under limited circumstances, including with written permission from the source of the data, and pursuant to a court order. M.S.A. § 13.84, subd. 5 (West 1988).
5. M.S.A. § 144.335, subd. 2 (West Supp. 1992).
6. The right to access records applies only to "clients" or "patients" of the psychologist. The Access to Health Records law defines "patient" as one who has "received health care services . . . for a treatment of a . . . psychiatric, or mental condition . . . or a person the patient designated in writing as a representative." The parents of most minors have the same rights to have access to the records of their children as do the children themselves. The rights of access do not extend to people who have seen psychologists not for treatment, but rather for "adverse" examinations in connection with insurance claims or litigation. Saari v. Litman, 486 N.W.2d 813 (Minn. Ct. App. 1992).

the client's mental health or is likely to cause the client to harm him- or herself or someone else, the psychologist may instead supply the information to an appropriate third party, who may then convey the information to the client.[7] In general, the psychologist may charge the client a fee for copying the record.[8] However, the law provides that no fee may be charged "when a patient requests a copy of the patient's record for purposes of reviewing current medical care."[9]

Protecting the Privacy of Clients

The psychologist must safeguard private information about a client that is obtained in the course of teaching, practice, or research.[10] In general, the information obtained may not be disclosed to others without the informed written consent of the client.[11] Under state law, there are a number of exceptions to the prohibition of disclosure without consent. In limited circumstances, these state law provisions that permit unconsented-to disclosure of information may be superseded by stricter federal privacy provisions, particularly those governing information gathered in connection with chemical dependency treatment programs, that prohibit disclosure.[12] Under state law, consent is not required to release private information about a client in the following circumstances:

1. In general, a psychologist may disclose records and information about a client to conform with state or federal law, rule, or regulation, and upon order of a court.[13]

2. Under certain circumstances, a psychologist is required or permitted to warn of the violent or dangerous behavior of his or her client. Clearly, such warnings can be given without the client's consent. Provisions concerning such warnings are found in the rules and statutes. Under the rules, a psychologist

---

7. M.S.A. § 144.335, subd. 2 (West Supp. 1992).
8. M.S.A. § 144.335, subd. 5 (West Supp. 1992). The law sets a ceiling of 75 cents per page, plus $10 for time spent retrieving and copying the records, or the actual cost of copying and retrieval, whichever is less. A formula, based on the change in the consumer price index for all urban consumers in Minneapolis–St. Paul, published by the Department of Labor, is provided for calculating the ceiling after calendar year 1992.
9. Id.
10. Minn. R. 7200.4700 (1991).
11. Id.; M.S.A. § 144.335, subd. 3a (West Supp. 1992). With certain exceptions, written consents are valid for one year at most. Exceptions include consents to provide information to a health care provider who is currently being consulted or is currently providing services to the client.
12. See, e.g., 42 U.S.C. §§ 290ee-2, 290dd-2, 290dd-3. See chapter 5E.6.
13. Minn. R. 7200.4700, subp. 10 (1991); M.S.A. 144.335, subd. 3a (West Supp. 1992) (consent not required where release is "specifically authorized by law").

is *permitted* to make unconsented-to disclosures when he or she determines that disclosure is necessary to protect against a "clear and substantial risk of imminent serious harm" to the client or a third party.[14] Disclosure under this provision is permitted only to "appropriate professional workers, public authorities, the potential victim, or the family of the client."[15] Minnesota statutory law imposes on psychologists a duty to warn only where the psychologist's client (or another person) has communicated to the psychologist a "specific, serious threat [by the client] of physical violence against a specific, clearly identified or identifiable potential victim."[16] A psychologist is *permitted* to disclose confidences to third parties "in a good faith effort to warn against or take precautions against a patient's violent behavior" even if the statutory duty to warn does not arise.[17]

3. In connection with a disciplinary proceeding, a psychologist must disclose to the Board of Psychology and its agents client records that the Board or its agents consider to be germane to the proceeding. This disclosure may be made without the client's consent.[18]

4. Psychological records may be disclosed to hospital medical review boards in connection with their reviews of admissions and the medical necessity of professional services furnished.[19]

5. Psychologists are required to report suspected maltreatment of minors and vulnerable adults.[20] Such reports may be made without the consent of the patient.[21]

---

14. Minn. R. 7200.4700, subp. 2 (1991).
15. *Id.*
16. M.S.A. § 148.975 (West 1989).
17. M.S.A. § 148.976 (West 1989).
18. Minn. R. 7200.4700, subps. 1, 12 (1991).
19. *See* M.S.A. § 144.55, subd. 3 (West 1989), which requires that hospitals meet standards set out in 42 U.S.C. § 1395 et seq. establishing a "hospital utilization review plan." *See* 42 U.S.C. § 1395x(k) (1983).
20. M.S.A. § 626.556, subd. 3 (West Supp. 1992); § 626.557, subd. 3 (West Supp. 1992). *See* chapters 5A.7 and 5A.8 for a fuller discussion of these reporting requirements.
21. Minn. R. 7200.4700, subp. 11 (1989). However, for some clients who are receiving chemical dependency services, stricter disclosure rules may apply. *See* 21 U.S.C. § 1175 (1981); 42 U.S.C. §§ 290dd.2, 290dd.3 (1981); 42 CFR 2.1 to 2.67-1 (1991). *See* chapter 5E.6.

6. Psychologists are probably permitted to furnish information without consent to the proper authorities in connection with civil commitment proceedings.[22]

7. Records of minors may be furnished to their parents without the consent of the minor, except in certain circumstances.[23] At the beginning of the professional relationship, the psychologist must inform the minor of this limit on the privacy of the minor.[24]

Liability for Violation

Liability for improper maintenance and handling of client information can take several forms.[25] Violation of the rules governing the maintenance and privacy of and access to client records is a sufficient basis for disciplinary action or denial of a license by the Board of Psychology.[26] In addition, negligent or intentional release of records in violation of the law can subject the psychologist to liability for compensatory damages caused by the unauthorized release, plus reasonable attorney's fees.[27] Failure to make "reasonable efforts" to warn of threats, as defined by law, may also result in civil liability.[28] Failure to report suspected maltreatment of minors can result in disciplinary action and criminal prosecution.[29] Failure to report suspected maltreatment of a vulnerable adult can result in disciplinary action, criminal prosecution, and/or civil liability.[30] Violation of federal laws and regu-

---

22. The Minnesota Commitment Act is not free from ambiguity on this point. *See* M.S.A. § 253B.23, subd. 4 (West 1982) (providing for the "waiver" of the privilege with respect to any "examiner" who "provides information with respect to a patient pursuant to any provision" of the act). The Minnesota Court of Appeals has generally given this provision an expansive reading. *See, e.g.,* In re D.M.C., 331 N.W.2d 236 (Minn. Ct. App. 1983). *See generally* Janus, E. S. (1991). *Civil commitment in Minnesota* (2nd ed.). St. Paul, MN: Butterworth.

23. M.S.A. § 144.335, subd. 2 (West Supp. 1992). The excepted circumstances are those set forth in M.S.A. §§ 144.341 to 144.347 (West 1989), which define when a minor has the capacity to consent to treatment. These circumstances are the following: (a) The minor is emancipated, (b) the minor is married or has borne a child, or (c) any minor can give consent to services to determine the presence of or treat alcohol and other abuse. Presumably, where the minor has given competent consent pursuant to these sections, his or her parents may not have unconsented-to access to the minor's records. *See* chapter 5A.21.

24. Minn. R. 7200.4700, subp. 4 (1991).

25. *See* chapter 6.6.

26. Minn. R. 7200.4500, subp. 3 (1991). *See* chapter 1.3.

27. M.S.A. § 144.335, subd. 3a(e) (West Supp. 1992).

28. M.S.A. § 148.975 (West 1989). "Reasonable efforts" to warn means communicating the threat to the potential victim or, if that is impossible, to the law enforcement agency "closest to" the potential victim. *Id.*, subd. 1(e).

29. M.S.A. § 626.556, subd. 6 (West Supp. 1992). *See* chapter 5A.8.

30. M.S.A. § 626.557, subds. 7(a), 7(b) (West 1983). *See* chapter 5A.7.

lations protecting the confidentiality of chemical dependency treatment records is a crime punishable by a fine.[31]

Psychiatrists

Extensiveness of Records

Improper management of medical records, including failure to maintain adequate records, is grounds for disciplinary action, according to the physician licensing statute.[32] The statute does not define "improper management" or what constitutes an "adequate record," but presumably these terms refer to an orderly record system with sufficient information to conduct the practice of medicine.

Maintenance of Records

The law does not address the issue of the length of time records should be maintained.

Client Access

In Minnesota, all health care providers, including psychiatrists, are subject to the Access to Health Records law. This law was discussed earlier in connection with psychologists.

Protecting the Privacy of Clients

In general, information obtained from a patient may not be disclosed to others without the informed written consent of the patient.[33] Under state law, there are a number of exceptions to the prohibition of disclosure without consent. In limited circumstances, these provisions that permit unconsented-to disclosure of information may be superseded by stricter federal privacy provisions, particularly those governing information gathered in connection with chemical dependency treatment programs.[34] Under state law, consent is not required to release private information on the patient in the following circumstances:

---

31. 42 U.S.C. § 290ee-3(f); 42 U.S.C. § 290dd-3(f); 42 CFR § 2.4. *See* chapter 5E.7.
32. M.S.A. § 147.091, subd. 1(o) (West 1989). *See* chapter 1.1.
33. M.S.A. § 147.091, subd. 1(o) (West 1989); § 144.335, subd. 3a (West Supp. 1992). With certain exceptions, written consents are valid for one year at most. Exceptions include consents to provide information to a health care provider who is currently being consulted or who is currently providing services to the client.
34. *See, e.g.,* 42 U.S.C. §§ 290ee-2, 290dd-2, 290dd-3. *See* chapter 5E.6.

1. In general, a psychiatrist may disclose records and information about a patient to conform with state or federal law, rule, or regulation, and upon order of a court.[35]

2. The Board of Medical Examiners may obtain access to hospital and medical records of a patient treated by a physician under review if the patient signs a written consent permitting such access. If no consent form has been signed, the hospital or physician must first delete data in the record that identify the patient, before providing it to the Board.[36]

3. Medical records may be disclosed to hospital medical review boards in connection with their reviews of admissions and the medical necessity of professional services furnished.[37]

4. Psychiatrists are required to report suspected maltreatment of minors and vulnerable adults.[38] Such reports may be made without the consent of the patient.[39]

5. Physicians are required by rules of the Department of Health to report certain information about communicable diseases.[40] The Minnesota Health Threat Procedures Act authorizes physicians (and others) to provide information to the commissioner of health without patient consent, where the physician has "knowledge or reasonable cause to believe that an individual is a health threat to others."[41]

6. Psychiatrists are probably permitted to furnish information without consent to the proper authorities in connection with civil commitment proceedings.[42]

---

35. The Access to Health Records law requires written consent for the release of records "unless the release is specifically authorized by law." M.S.A. § 144.335, subd. 3a(a) (West Supp. 1992).
36. M.S.A. § 147.161, subd. 3 (West 1989).
37. See M.S.A. § 144.55, subd. 3 (West 1989), which requires that hospitals meet standards set out in 42 U.S.C. § 1395 et seq. establishing a "hospital utilization review plan." See 42 U.S.C. § 1395x(k) (1983).
38. M.S.A. § 626.556, subd. 3 (West Supp. 1992); § 626.557, subd. 3 (West Supp. 1992). See chapters 5A.7, 5A.8.
39. M.S.A. § 626.556, subd. 3; § 626.557, subd. 3 (West 1992). However, for some patients who are receiving chemical dependency services, stricter disclosure rules may apply. See footnote 12 above and chapter 5E.6.
40. Minn. R. 4605.7030 (1991).
41. M.S.A. § 144.4175, subd. 1 (West 1989).
42. The Minnesota Commitment Act is not free from ambiguity on this point. See M.S.A. § 253B.23, subd. 4 (West 1982) (providing for the "waiver" of the privilege with respect to any "examiner" who "provides information with respect to a patient pursuant to any provision" of the act). The Minnesota Court of Appeals has generally given this provision an expansive reading. See, e.g., In re D.M.C., 331 N.W.2d 236 (Minn. Ct. App. 1983). See generally Janus, E. S. (1991). Civil commitment in Minnesota (2nd ed.). St. Paul, MN: Butterworth.

7. Records of minors may be furnished to their parents without the consent of the minor, except in certain circumstances.[43]

Liability for Violation

Psychiatrists may be disciplined by the Board of Medical Examiners for improperly revealing privileged communications and for improper management or maintenance of medical records, including failing to furnish medical records as required by law.[44] Violation of federal laws and regulations protecting the confidentiality of chemical dependency treatment records is a crime punishable by a fine.[45]

In addition, negligent or intentional release of records in violation of the law can subject the psychiatrist to liability for compensatory damages caused by the unauthorized release, plus reasonable attorneys fees.[46] Failure to make reasonable efforts to warn of patient threats to others may also result in civil liability.[47] Failure to report suspected maltreatment of minors can result in disciplinary action and criminal prosecution.[48] Failure to report suspected maltreatment of a vulnerable adult can result in disciplinary action, criminal prosecution, and/or civil liability.[49]

---

43. M.S.A. § 144.335, subd. 2 (West Supp. 1992). The excepted circumstances are those set forth in M.S.A. §§ 144.341 to 144.347 (West 1989), which define when a minor has the capacity to consent to treatment. These circumstances are the following: (a) The minor is emancipated, (b) the minor is married or has borne a child, or (c) any minor can give consent to services to determine the presence of or treat alcohol and other abuse. Presumably, where the minor has given competent consent pursuant to these sections, his or her parents may not have unconsented-to access to the minor's records. *See* chapter 5A.21.
44. M.S.A. § 147.091 subd. 4 (West 1989). *See* chapter 1.1.
45. 42 U.S.C. § 290ee-3(f); 42 U.S.C. § 290dd-3(f); 42 CFR § 2.4 (1991). *See* chapter 5E.6.
46. M.S.A. § 144.335, subd. 3a(e) (West Supp. 1992). *See* chapter 6.6.
47. *See* chapter 4.2.
48. M.S.A. § 626.556, subd. 6 (West Supp. 1992). M.S.A. § 147.091 (West 1989) provides for discipline if a physician violates a federal or state "rule relating to the practice of medicine." *See* chapter 5A.8.
49. M.S.A. § 626.557, subds. 7(a), 7(b) (West 1989). *See* chapter 5A.7.

4.2

Confidential Relations and Communications

As a general matter, MHPs have a duty to maintain the confidentiality of all information made by or to a client or patient within the scope of the professional relationship. There are several broad statements of that duty. The Patients and Residents Bill of Rights states that "patients and residents shall be assured confidential treatment of personal and medical records, and may approve or refuse their release to any individual. . . ."[1] The Access to Health Records law[2] provides, as a general rule, that health records may not be released to third persons in the absence of informed written consent of the patient or client.[3] The law also provides for an evidentiary privilege for physicians, registered nurses, psychologists, sexual assault counselors, licensed chemical dependency counselors,[4] and licensed family therapists.[5]

Many of the rules and codes governing individual professions have specific provisions dealing with confidential information.[6]

Violations of the duty to maintain confidences can be the basis for disciplinary action by licensing boards[7] and may be the

---

1. M.S.A. § 144.651, subd. 16 (West 1989).
2. M.S.A. § 144.335 (West Supp. 1992).
3. *Id.*, subd. 3a (West Supp. 1992).
4. M.S.A. § 595.02, subd. 1(d), (g), (i), (j) (West 1988 & Supp. 1992). *See* chapter 4.3.
5. M.S.A. § 148B.39 (West 1989). *See* chapter 4.3.
6. *See generally* section 1 of this book for a further discussion of those provisions.
7. *See* chapters in section 1 of this book on individual professions for more detail.

basis for civil damages on the principle of breach of contract or invasion of privacy.[8]

Limitations on the Duty to Maintain Confidences: Major Mandatory and Permissive Reporting Provisions

The MHP's duty to maintain client or patient confidences is subject to several important exceptions. The major exceptions involve permissive or mandatory reporting and warning provisions of the law. These provisions generally apply to MHPs. The most important provisions are the Reporting of Maltreatment of Minors Act[9] and the Reporting of Maltreatment of Vulnerable Adults Act.[10] Other exceptions, which are of applicability only in specific situations (e.g., civil commitment,[11] criminal cases,[12] access to records[13]), are discussed elsewhere in this volume.

Duty to Warn

In its 1976 *Tarasoff* decision, the California Supreme Court held a psychiatrist liable for damages for failing to warn the victim of his patient's violence.[14] Minnesota appellate courts have apparently adopted the *Tarasoff* rule.[15]

The Minnesota legislature codified this liability for mental health professionals other than psychiatrists in its Duty to Warn statute. Although not altogether free from ambiguity, the main thrust of this statute is to clarify the duties and liabilities of treatment professionals concerning the violent behavior of their patients. The statute applies to "practitioners," which is defined to include psychologists, school psychologists, nurses, and chemical dependency counselors who are licensed by the state or who

---

8. *See generally* 48 ALR 4th 668. *See* chapters 4.1, 4.3, 6.6.
9. Discussed in chapter 5A.8.
10. Discussed in chapter 5A.7.
11. *See* chapter 5E.4.
12. *See* chapter 5D.9.
13. *See* chapters 4.1 and 4.3.
14. Tarasoff v. Regents of Univ. of California, 17 Cal.3d 425, 551 P. 2d 334 (1976).
15. In McElwain v. Van Beek, 447 N.W.2d 442 (Minn. Ct. App. 1989), the court stated, "The Minnesota Supreme Court has . . . limited a physician's duty to warn to cases where the patient makes specific threats against identifiable third parties."

perform psychotherapy services within licensed programs or facilities.[16]

The Duty to Warn statute clearly limits the liability of a practitioner (as defined above) for failure to predict, warn of, or take reasonable precautions to protect against a patient's violent behavior. No such liability can arise unless the patient, or another person, has communicated to the practitioner a specific, serious threat of physical violence against a specific, clearly identified or identifiable potential victim. Only under those limited circumstances (i.e., where such a threat is communicated to the practitioner) does a duty to warn the potential victim arise. The statute provides that the duty to warn is discharged if the threat is communicated (a) to the potential victim or (b) to the law enforcement agency closest to the potential victim or the patient, if the practitioner is unable to make contact with the victim.[17]

No monetary liability may be imposed, and no disciplinary action may be taken, against a practitioner for complying with this duty. Furthermore, there can be no such consequences against a practitioner for disclosing confidences of a client or patient in a good faith effort to take precautions against the patient's violent behavior, even where no duty to warn arises under this law. In other words, a practitioner may warn a potential victim about his or her client, disclosing client confidences in the process, even where there has been no specific threat communicated.

---

16. Or in programs or facilities established pursuant to rules adopted under M.S.A. § 245.69, subd. 2. With respect to licensed chemical dependency counselors, see M.S.A. § 595.02, subd. 1(i) (West 1992) (creating the duty to maintain client confidences, and the exception in order to warn of clear and imminent harm).

17. The provisions of this law do not apply to threats by a patient against him- or herself or to threats by patients who have been adjudicated mentally ill and dangerous in the civil commitment process. This exception apparently leaves it to the courts to develop the rules for practitioner liability for patient self-injury and for injuries caused by those adjudicated "mentally ill and dangerous."

Privileged
Communications

Privileged communications are those that are protected from disclosure in a court of law. The concept of privilege is related to, but not the same as, the notion of confidentiality. Most communications between an MHP and a client are confidential.[1] The MHP, in most circumstances, is under an obligation to the client not to disclose the information without the client's consent. But even the obligation of confidentiality must yield to the power of courts to compel testimony by subpoena. Only information that is *privileged* is exempt from such coerced production. Thus, whereas confidentiality measures the MHP's duty to the client, privilege is a measure of the client's right to protect information from unconsented-to disclosure in legal proceedings. This evidentiary privilege protects the client's information both against in-court disclosure and against disclosure in pretrial discovery proceedings, such as depositions.[2]

The privilege protects most confidential communications between MHP and client. However, there are significant limitations on the coverage of the privilege, hence the possibility that client information may not be protected against forced disclosure. The major limitations on the privilege involve waiver by the client, information regarding maltreatment of minors or vulnerable adults, information relevant to civil commitment or health-threat proceedings, and information gained in nontreatment examinations. These are explored in more detail in this and other chapters.[3] Because clients generally expect their communications with

1. *See* chapter 4.2.
2. Minn. R. Civ. P. 26.
3. *See* chapters 5A.7 and 5A.8 for discussion of the laws requiring reports of maltreatment of vulnerable adults and minors.

MHPs to be confidential, good practice requires MHPs to inform their clients of limitations on the privilege that appear to be applicable.

In Minnesota, MHPs who are covered by the privilege statute include psychiatrists, psychologists, registered nurses, sexual assault counselors, licensed chemical dependency counselors, and clergy.[4] Licensed family therapists are covered by a separate provision of the law,[5] which is discussed in detail in chapter 1.8.

Privilege for Psychologists and Registered Nurses

The Minnesota statute provides that a "registered nurse [or] psychologist . . . shall not, without the consent of the professional's client, be allowed to disclose any information or opinion based thereon which the professional has acquired in attending the client in a professional capacity, and which was necessary to enable the professional to act in that capacity."[6]

Privilege for Psychiatrists

The Minnesota statute states that "a licensed physician . . . shall not, without the consent of the patient, be allowed to disclose any information or any opinion based thereon which the professional acquired in attending the patient in a professional capacity, and which was necessary to enable the professional to act in that capacity."[7]

Privilege for Sexual Assault Counselors

The privilege for sexual assault counselors is as follows:[8]

Sexual assault counselors may not be compelled to testify about any opinion or information received from or about the victim without the consent of the victim. However, a counselor may be compelled to identify or disclose information in investigations

---

4. *See generally* M.S.A. § 595.02 (West 1988 & Supp. 1992).
5. M.S.A. § 148B.29 (West 1989).
6. M.S.A. § 595.02, subd. 1(g) (West 1988).
7. *Id.*, subd. 1(d).
8. *Id.*, subd. 1(j).

or proceedings related to neglect or termination of parental rights if the court determines good cause exists. . . .

Privilege for Licensed Chemical Dependency Counselors

The privilege for licensed chemical dependency counselors is as follows:[9]

Licensed chemical dependency counselors shall not disclose information or an opinion based on the information which they acquire from persons consulting them in their professional capacities, and which was necessary to enable them to act in that capacity. . . .

Assertion and Waiver of the Privilege

The privilege is for the benefit of the patient or client; thus, the patient or client may either assert or waive the privilege.[10] Once waived, the privilege may not be reasserted by the patient or client,[11] nor may the MHP assert the privilege.[12]

The party who invokes the privilege must prove the facts necessary to establish its existence.[13] Thus, the court must determine "1) that an [MHP]-patient relationship existed; 2) that the 'information' acquired by the [MHP] was of the type contemplated by the statute; 3) that such information was acquired by the [MHP] in attending the patient; and 4) that the information was necessary to enable [the MHP] to act in a professional capacity."[14]

Information may become nonprivileged in three ways: (a) It may fall into a statutory exception, (b) the privilege may be expressly waived, or (c) the privilege may be waived by implication.

Statutory exceptions to the privilege include disclosure of information relating to the abuse or neglect of minors[15] or vulnerable adults,[16] or to the revocation of a day-care or foster care

---

9. *Id.*, subd. 1(j). These provisions create both a privilege and a duty of confidentiality for chemical dependency counselors. Exceptions to the duty are created where there is written, informed consent; where there is "clear and imminent danger" to the client or to others; to report the contemplation of or ongoing commission of a crime; and in connection with a malpractice suit brought against the counselor by the client.
10. Recent Case, *Privileged Communications—Physician and Patient—Waiver of Privilege in Will Contest*, 39 Minn. L. Rev. 800, 801 (1955) [hereinafter *Privileged Communications*].
11. Maas v. Laursen, 219 Minn. 461, 464, 18 N.W.2d 233, 235 (1945).
12. 8 Wigmore, Evidence § 2386 (McNaughton rev. 1961).
13. Staat v. Staat, 291 Minn. 394, 398, 192 N.W.2d 192, 197 (1971).
14. Staat v. Staat, 291 Minn. at 399, 192 N.W.2d at 196 (1971).
15. M.S.A. § 626.556, subd. 8 (West Supp. 1992). *See* chapter 5A.8.
16. M.S.A. § 626.557, subd. 8 (West 1983). *See* chapter 5A.7.

license.[17] Privilege does not apply to criminal proceedings arising out of the neglect or physical or sexual abuse of a minor if the court finds that (a) there is a reasonable likelihood that the records in question will disclose material information in connection with the prosecution, (b) there is no other practicable way of obtaining the information or evidence, and (c) the actual or potential injury to the patient–health professional relationship is outweighed by the public interest in authorizing the disclosure sought.[18] Under this statute, privilege is waived only with respect to information required for the investigation, and the information can be obtained only with a court order.[19]

In general, a person who puts his or her mental or physical condition "in controversy" in a lawsuit waives, in that action, any privilege respecting that condition.[20] Express waiver of the privilege occurs when the patient agrees verbally or in writing to waive the privilege.[21] Express waiver of the privilege may also occur as a term of a contract.[22]

In addition to statutory and express waiver, a privileged communication may be waived by implication in the following ways: (a) The client voluntarily testifies about his or her communications with an MHP.[23] (The privilege is not waived, however, merely because the client testifies as to his or her own condition at trial.)[24] (b) Waiver at a former trial bars the privilege at a later trial.[25] (c) Calling the MHP to testify is a waiver as to all of her or his knowledge of the condition asked about[26] and as to knowledge acquired by other MHPs of the same condition.[27] (d) Failure to object to an MHP's testimony is a waiver to that MHP and to other MHPs for the same condition.[28]

---

17. M.S.A. § 245.781 (West 1982). *See* chapter 5A.13.
18. M.S.A. § 595.02, subd. 2 (West 1988).
19. *Id.* State v. Odenbrett, 349 N.W.2d 265 (Minn. 1984); State v. Andring, 342 N.W.2d 128 (Minn. 1984); Matter of Schroeder, 415 N.W.2d 436 (Minn. Ct. App. 1987) (applying and upholding the no-privilege provisions of the Maltreatment of Minors Act).
20. Minn. R. Civ. P. 35.03 (1992) (general rule of waiver in civil actions); M.S.A. § 595.02, subd. 5 (West 1988) (actions against health care providers).
21. Wigmore, *supra* note 12, §§ 2388 to 2389.
22. *Id.*
23. *Id.*, § 2389.
24. Roeder v. North Am. Life Ins. Co. of Chicago, 259 Minn. 168, 106 N.W.2d 624 (1961).
25. Wigmore, *supra* note 12, § 2389.
26. *Id.*
27. *Id.*, § 2390. Maas v. Laursen, 219 Minn. at 463, 18 N.W.2d at 234 (1945) (citing 8 Wigmore, Evidence § 2390(2) [McNaughton rev. 1961]).
28. Wigmore, *supra* note 12, § 2390; Tweith v. Duluth, M. & I.R. Ry., 66 F. Supp. 427, 431 (D. Minn. 1946) ("A patient may impliedly waive [the privilege] by failing to object to the proffered testimony").

Extent of and Limitations on the Scope of the Privilege

The privilege extends only to those communications necessary to develop and maintain the MHP–patient relationship, which the patient can reasonably expect to remain confidential. Thus, the privilege (a) covers the MHP's observations as well as verbal communication,[29] (b) "extends by implication to . . . attendants who are employees or acting under the direction of the [MHP] examining or treating the patient,"[30] and (c) includes "confidential group psychotherapy sessions where such sessions are an integral and necessary part of a patient's diagnosis and treatment."[31]

In addition to the noted exceptions to the privilege, the privilege does not "exempt a third person who overheard the conversation or gained the information, with or without the knowledge of the patient, from testifying unless the third person is an agent of the [MHP]."[32] Conversations between the MHP and the client in which there is not the usual expectation of privacy may not be protected by the privilege. For example, the presence of a third person at the consultation who is not an employee of the MHP and not part of the therapy may destroy the privilege.[33] Furthermore, "communications concerning non-professional matters, or manifestations which would be discernible to a layman are not privileged."[34]

In general, statements made to MHPs in connection with court-ordered examinations are not considered privileged.[35]

Liability for Violation

MHPs who improperly testify may face civil suits brought by clients who have been injured by the MHP's statements.[36] In general, if the client is a party in the proceeding at which the MHP

---

29. Staat v. Staat, 291 Minn. 394, 401, 192 N.W.2d 192, 198 (1971).
30. *Id.*
31. State v. Kunz, 457 N.W.2d 266, 267 (Minn. Ct. App. 1990), rev. denied (1990); State v. Andring, 342 N.W.2d 128, 132 (Minn. 1984).
32. Staat v. Staat, 291 Minn. 394, 401, 192 N.W.2d 192, 197 (1971).
33. State v. Kunz, 457 N.W.2d 265, 267 (Minn. Ct. App. 1990).
34. *Privileged Communications, supra* note 10.
35. Minn. R. Crim. P. 20.02, subs. 1, 4, 5, 6 (1992) (criminal proceedings) (see chapter 5D.9); M.S.A. § 253B.23, subd. 4 (West 1992) (civil commitment proceedings) (see chapter 5E.4). *Compare* M.S.A. § 144.4175, subd. 4 (West 1989) (Health Threat Procedures Act; "waiver" of privilege for health care providers who "voluntarily" provide information).
36. *See generally* 20 ALR 3d 1112–14 (1968). *See* chapter 6.6.

is called to testify, the MHP may rely on the client to take steps to protect the privilege. For example, during depositions, the client's lawyer may "instruct" the testifying MHP not to answer questions that may violate the privilege. During trial, the client's lawyer asserts the privilege by making appropriate and timely objections or by making a motion *in limine* prior to the commencement of the trial. If the court rules against the assertion of the privilege, the MHP will be required to testify and will generally be protected from liability by the court's order, even if the trial court's ruling is subsequently held to be erroneous. However, both the client (if a party) and the testifying MHP can seek immediate review of the court's ruling from an appellate court. Such review is discretionary and would rarely be granted.

An MHP who is testifying in an action in which his or her client is not a party is in a somewhat different position. Under these circumstances, the obligation to protect the privilege may fall on the MHP. In a deposition, the MHP can seek a protective order from the court,[37] whereas in a courtroom situation, the MHP should assert the privilege prior to or during his or her testimony.

---

37. *See generally* Minn. R. Civ. P. 26.

Search, Seizure, and Subpoena of Records

An MHP's office may be searched and his or her records seized or subpoenaed in the course of investigations of either the MHP or the MHP's client. A court's demand for information obtained in the course of the MHP–client relationship will usually be carried out by subpoena. However, both search and subpoena threaten a client's right to confidentiality.[1] It is important to note that although records may be obtained by a search or subpoena, the ultimate ruling on their admissibility will be made by the court. Thus, although records may be taken, MHP–client privilege and confidentiality remain intact until the court rules otherwise.

Search and Seizure

The law in this area concerns the exercise of the government's power to search for and seize evidence to be used in a court of law. This governmental power is a limited power. Citizens of Minnesota are protected from unreasonable governmental searches and seizures by both the 4th and the 14th amendments to the United States Constitution[2] and by Article I, section 10 of the Constitution of the State of Minnesota.[3]

The power to "search and seize" discussed in this section is a governmental power limited by constitutional provisions. Non-

---

1. *See* chapters 4.2 and 4.3.
2. U.S. Const. amends. IV and XIV § 1.
3. "The right of the people to be secure in their persons, houses, papers, and effects against unreasonable searches and seizures shall not be violated; and no warrant shall issue but on probable cause, supported by oath or affirmation, and particularly describing the place to be searched and the person or things to be seized." Minn. Const. Art. 1, § 10.

governmental parties are constrained by the laws of private property from searching for and seizing an MHP's records. In civil litigation, however, the rules of "discovery" give private parties substantial rights to force disclosure of information held by adverse litigants and by nonlitigant third parties.[4]

In general, before a search and seizure may legally occur, a search warrant must be issued. A warrantless search is authorized only in exigent circumstances, such as an "emergency threatening life or limb."[5] "A search warrant is an order in writing in the name of the state, signed by a court . . . directed to a peace officer, commanding the peace officer to make a search as authorized by law and hold any item seized, subject to the order of a court."[6] A search warrant can be issued only for probable cause and must describe in detail the place or thing to be searched.[7] Prior to issuing the warrant, the court may examine under oath both the person seeking the warrant and any witness.[8] Issuance must be based on written affidavits that must set forth the facts tending to establish the grounds for the application.[9]

A search warrant may be issued for any of the following grounds:[10]

1. The property or things were stolen or embezzled;
2. the property or things were used as the means of committing a crime;
3. the possession of the property or things constitutes a crime;
4. the property or things are in the possession of any person with the intent to use them as a means of committing a crime, or the property or things so intended to be used are in the possession of another to whom they have been delivered for the purpose of concealing them or preventing their being discovered; or
5. the property or things to be seized consist of any item or constitute any evidence that tends to show that a crime has been committed or tends to show that a particular person has committed a crime.

The property or things described in this section may be taken pursuant to the warrant from any place, or from any person in whose possession they may be.[11]

---

4. The rules governing such discovery are discussed in this chapter under the heading "Subpoena" and in chapters 4.1 and 4.3.
5. Mincy v. Arizona, 437 U.S. 385, 392 (1978).
6. M.S.A. § 626.05, subd. 1 (West Supp. 1992).
7. M.S.A. § 626.08 (West 1983).
8. M.S.A. § 626.09 (West Supp. 1992).
9. M.S.A. § 626.10 (West 1983).
10. M.S.A. § 626.07 (West 1983).
11. Id.

A search warrant may be served only in the daytime, unless the court determines that a nighttime search is necessary to prevent the loss, destruction, or removal of the object of the search.[12] Unless a search warrant is executed and returned to the court that issued it within 10 days, the warrant becomes void.[13] The officer conducting the search must give a copy of the warrant to the person whose premises are searched, and if property or things are taken, a detailed receipt must also be given. If no person is present, the officer must leave a copy of the warrant in the place where the property taken was found. The delivery of the warrant constitutes "service."[14] Immediately after the search and seizure, the officer must return the warrant to the court and deliver a written inventory of the things taken.[15]

Furthermore, if the warrant provides for the arrest of an individual, the officer may use force to make the arrest. After the officer gives notice of the authority and purpose of the entry, an officer may break open a door or window to execute a warrant if (a) the officer is refused admittance, (b) the entry is necessary for the officer's own liberation, or (c) entry is necessary for liberating another person who is being detained.[16] Therefore, an MHP should both cooperate with a warrant-bearing officer and contact his or her attorney as soon as possible if questions about the warrant exist.

The Minnesota Supreme Court has held that a warrant authorizing the search of an attorney's office is unreasonable and invalid when the attorney is not suspected of wrongdoing and no threat exists that documents sought will be destroyed.[17] Because this holding was based in part on the attorney–client privilege, it is reasonable to assume that a warrant authorizing the search of a nonsuspect MHP's office would be equally unreasonable and invalid, on the basis of the MHP–client privilege. The court further held that documents sought from an attorney's office should be obtained by subpoena.[18]

Subpoena

A subpoena is an order from a court that "commands" the person to whom it is directed to attend and give testimony at the time

---

12. M.S.A. § 626.14 (West Supp. 1992).
13. M.S.A. § 626.15 (West Supp. 1992).
14. M.S.A. § 626.16 (West 1983).
15. M.S.A. § 626.17 (West Supp. 1992)
16. M.S.A. § 629.33 (West Supp. 1992).
17. O'Conner v. Johnson, 287 N.W.2d 400 (Minn. 1979).
18. *Id*. at 405.

and place specified.[19] A subpoena may also "command" the person to produce designated books, papers, documents, or other tangible items.[20] The subpoena must also state the name of the court and the title of the action.[21] A subpoena is issued only in connection with a duly noticed deposition, hearing, or trial.[22]

Service of a subpoena is accomplished by delivering a copy to the named individual or leaving a copy at his or her residence (with a person of suitable age) and by tendering the fees for one day's attendance and mileage allowed by law.[23] Furthermore, a witness who is not a party to the action and who is required to give testimony or produce documents is entitled to reasonable compensation for the time and expense involved in preparing and giving testimony or producing documents.[24] A criminal defendant is guaranteed compulsory process to obtain a witness in his or her favor.[25]

If the subpoena is unreasonable or oppressive, the court, upon a promptly made motion by the subpoenaed witness, may either (a) quash (invalidate) the subpoena or (b) condition the denial of the motion upon the advancement of the reasonable cost to produce the documents by the party on whose behalf the subpoena is issued.[26] The fact that a subpoena for privileged information has been issued by the clerk of court does not determine that the MHP–client privilege is invalidated. The MHP is required to assert the privilege until the client expressly waives the privilege or the judge rules that the privilege is waived (e.g., where the client has in some way disclosed the confidential information to a third party, thus extinguishing his or her expectation of privilege).[27] Failure of the MHP to assert the privilege may result in civil liability.[28]

Failure to obey a subpoena without adequate excuse is a contempt of court[29] that is punishable by fine, imprisonment, or both.[30]

---

19. Minn. R. Civ. P. 45.01(a) (1992).
20. Minn. R. Civ. P. 45.02 (1992).
21. Id.
22. Minn. R. Civ. P. 45.04, 45.05 (1992).
23. Minn. R. Civ. P. 45.03 (1992).
24. Minn. R. Civ. P. 45.06 (1992).
25. Minn. Const. Art. 1, § 6. (It is unclear whether the state must pay reasonable costs to the witness.)
26. Minn. R. Civ. P. 45.02 (1992).
27. See chapter 4.3.
28. See chapter 4.3.
29. Minn. R. Civ. P. 45.07 (1992).
30. M.S.A. § 588.02 (West 1988).

4.5

State Government
Data Practices

The law governing access to government information is complex, but it can be simplified into two discrete steps. First, the law creates a series of data-access categories. Each category is characterized by particular access rights. Second, the law places each particular type of government information into one of these data-access categories.

MHPs create and handle government information that is often of a sensitive nature. There are legal penalties for mishandling government information. MHPs thus need to be aware of the guidelines for handling government data and the penalties for their violation. This chapter summarizes the law concerning these subjects.

Data-Access Categories

The Minnesota Government Data Practices Act governs public and individual access to government data.[1] The act applies to all "government data," which are defined expansively to include all data collected, created, received, maintained, or disseminated by any state agency, political subdivision, or statewide system.[2] In general, persons or agencies contracting with the government must treat data received from the government according to the rules set forth in the act.[3]

---

1. M.S.A. § 13.02, subd. 12 (West 1988).
2. M.S.A. § 13.02, subd. 7 (West 1988).
3. M.S.A. § 13.05, subd. 6 (West 1988).

The act divides government data into a number of categories. Access rights are determined by this categorization. The major categories are as follows:

Public data. All government data are "public data" unless otherwise classified by statute, by temporary classification, or by federal law.[4] Public data are accessible to the public, upon request, at reasonable times and places. Upon request, the government agency must explain the meaning of the data.[5]

Private data on individuals means data that are made by statute or federal law (a) not public and (b) accessible to the individual subject of the data.[6] An individual who is the subject of private data must, upon request, be informed of the existence of the data, shown the data without any charge, and informed of their content and meaning. Upon payment of the actual costs of making copies, the subject must be given copies of the data.[7]

Most data collected by MHPs are private data on individuals. An "individual" means any natural person. However, in the case of a minor or an individual adjudged incompetent, "individual" includes a parent or a guardian. Such information may be withheld from the parents or guardians upon the minor's request if the responsible authority determines that withholding data would be in the best interests of the minor.[8]

Confidential data on individuals means data that statute or federal law make not public and not accessible to the individual subject of the data.

Protected nonpublic data means information not on individuals that statute or federal law makes not public and not accessible to the subject of the data.[9]

Nonpublic data means data not on individuals that statute or federal law makes not public but accessible to the subject of the data.[10]

Investigative data include data collected as part of an active investigation undertaken for the purpose of the commencement or defense of a pending civil legal action.[11] Investigative data are classified as protected nonpublic data or as confidential data. Inactive civil investigative data are public, with some exceptions.[12]

---

4. M.S.A. § 13.03, subd. 1 (West 1988).
5. M.S.A. § 13.02, subds. 14, 15; § 13.03, subd. 3 (West 1988).
6. M.S.A. § 13.02, subd. 14 (West 1988).
7. M.S.A. § 13.04, subd. 3 (West 1988).
8. M.S.A. § 13.02, subd. 8 (West 1988).
9. M.S.A. § 13.02, subd. 13 (West 1988).
10. M.S.A. § 13.02, subd. 19 (West 1988).
11. M.S.A. § 13.39, subd. 1 (West 1988).
12. *Id.*, subd. 2 (West 1988).

Access Rights to Particular Types of Information

Minnesota law classifies a wide variety of data. Among the classifications that may be of interest to MHPs are the following:

Medical data in the welfare system are data relating to the medical, psychiatric, or mental health of any individual, including diagnosis, progress charts, treatment received, case histories, and opinions of health care providers. These are classified as private data on individuals. Thus, they are available to the data subject unless they were furnished by a private health care provider who has clearly requested in writing that the data be withheld pursuant to section 144.335.[13] This rule applies both to state agencies and to any provider under contract with a state agency.[14]

Mental health center data are private data on individuals.[15]

Employment and training data are private data on individuals.[16]

Medical data means data collected because a person is or was a patient or client of a hospital, nursing home, medical center, clinic, or health or nursing agency.[17] "Directory information" is public, unless the patient requests otherwise. Otherwise, medical data are private data on individuals.[18]

Licensing data refers to information gathered by government agencies on persons who are, were, or have applied to be licensed or registered. These data are subject to a more complex classification. Much of the data are public, including the nature and content of resolved complaints about licensees, and findings in final disciplinary actions.[19] Some of the data are private data on individuals. Included in the private classification are the identities of persons who have made reports concerning licensees, and personal and financial data on family day-care program and family foster-care program applicants.[20]

---

13. M.S.A. § 13.46, subd. 5 (West Supp. 1992). M.S.A. § 144.335, subd. 2(c) allows an MHP to withhold information from a client when the MHP reasonably determines that the information is detrimental to the physical or mental health of the patient. *See* chapter 4.1.
14. M.S.A. § 13.46, subd. 5 (West Supp. 1992). *See also* M.S.A. § 13.05, subd. 6 (West 1988).
15. M.S.A. § 13.46, subd. 7 (West 1988).
16. M.S.A. § 13.47 (West 1988).
17. M.S.A. § 13.42 (West Supp. 1992).
18. M.S.A. § 13.42 (West Supp. 1992). Medical data can be communicated to a patient's or client's family member or other appropriate person in accordance with acceptable medical practice, unless the patient or client directs otherwise.
19. M.S.A. § 13.46, subd. 4 (West Supp. 1993).
20. The public category includes information about any waiver of disqualifications for child and adult day- and foster-care providers. *Id.*

Rights of Subjects of Data

Individuals have the right to have access to public and private data of which they are the subject.[21] Most information about MHPs falls into one of these categories and thus is accessible to the MHP. There are some exceptions. Investigative data (see above) are classified as confidential, at least while a government investigation is active. Special provisions govern access to the names of people who report suspected abuse or neglect of vulnerable adults or minors.[22] Finally, the names of individuals who have filed complaints against licensees are classified as private. The law does not clarify whether the licensee has access to these names.[23]

An individual asked to supply private or confidential data concerning that individual must be informed of the purpose and intended use of the data, whether the individual may refuse or is legally required to supply the data, any known consequences arising from supplying or refusing to supply private or confidential data, and the identity of other persons or entities authorized to receive the data.[24]

Private or confidential data on individuals may not be disseminated for any purposes other than those disclosed to the individual at the time of collection.[25] However, the commissioner of administration may approve of dissemination for other purposes, if necessary to carry out the law.[26]

In addition, private data may be disseminated if the individual subject of the data has given informed consent. A signed statement authorizing disclosure of the information constitutes "informed consent" only if the statement is

1. in plain language;

2. dated;

3. specific in designating the particular persons or agencies the data subject is authorizing to disclose information about him- or herself;

4. specific as to the nature of the information the subject is authorizing to be disclosed;

5. specific as to the persons or agencies to whom the subject is authorizing disclosure;

---

21. M.S.A. § 13.04, subd. 3 (West 1988).
22. *See* chapters 5A.7 and 5A.8.
23. M.S.A. § 13.46, subd. 4(d) (West 1988).
24. *Id.*, subd. 2 (West 1988). This does not apply to persons asked to supply investigative data.
25. Generally, the purposes disclosed will include dissemination pursuant to a court order. *See, e.g.,* M.S.A. § 13.46, subd. 7 (West 1988).
26. M.S.A. § 13.05, subd. 4(c) (West 1988).

6. specific as to the purpose or purposes for which the information may be used by any parties named, both at the time of the disclosure and at any time in the future; and

7. specific as to its expiration date, which should be in a reasonable period of time, not to exceed one year.[27]

In addition to the above guidelines, "medical data" may be disclosed

1. to the surviving spouse, parents, children, and siblings of a deceased patient or client or, if there are no such relatives, to the surviving heirs of the nearest degree of kindred;

2. to communicate a patient's or client's condition to a family member or other appropriate person in accordance with acceptable medical practice, unless the patient or client directs otherwise; or

3. as otherwise required by law.[28]

Data on Decedents

Upon the death of the MHP's patient, the private data become known as "private data on decedents." Private data on decedents become public when 10 years have elapsed from the actual or presumed death of the individual and 30 years have elapsed from the creation of the data.[29] The rights of the deceased individual may be exercised by the representative of the deceased.[30]

Liability for Violations

Any individual who has been damaged as a result of a violation of the Data Practices Act may bring an action against the state agency involved and may recover monetary damages or cause the agency to be enjoined from practices that violate the act.[31] An

---

27. M.S.A. § 13.05, subd. 4(d) (West 1988).
28. M.S.A. § 13.42, subds. 3(d), (e), (f) (West Supp. 1992). Instances in which the law requires dissemination of medical information without consent include reporting maltreatment of minors and vulnerable adults, warning of potential violence of a patient or client, and providing information in a commitment or health threat procedures matter. These are discussed in chapters 4.1 and 4.2.
29. M.S.A. § 13.10, subd. 2 (West 1988). An individual is presumed to be dead if either 90 years has elapsed since the creation of the data or 90 years has elapsed since the individual's birth, whichever is earlier, unless readily available data indicate that the individual is still living. *Id.*
30. M.S.A. § 13.10, subd. 3 (West Supp. 1992).
31. M.S.A. § 13.08, subds. 1, 2 (West 1988).

MHP who willfully violates the act is guilty of a misdemeanor. Furthermore, a willful violation by a public employee constitutes just cause for suspension without pay or dismissal.[32]

Procedure When Data Are Not Accurate or Complete

An individual who is the subject of data may contest the accuracy or completeness of the data. To begin the process, the individual notifies the authority responsible for the data, describing in writing the nature of the disagreement.[33]

---

32. M.S.A. § 13.09 (West 1988).
33. M.S.A. § 13.04, subd. 4.

Practice Related to the Law

Section 5A

Families and Juveniles

5A.1

Competency to Marry

In Minnesota, persons who are at least 18 years of age are capable of marriage if they are otherwise "competent." People ages 16 and 17 may marry with their parents' consent or with the consent of the court.[1]

Mentally retarded persons under guardianship of the commissioner of human services[2] must receive the consent of the commissioner prior to marriage.[3] The commissioner, upon application for her or his consent to marry, must conduct an investigation to determine if the proposed marriage is in the best interests of the ward and the public.[4] Although the law does not specifically detail the commissioner's decision-making process, it presumably might involve consultation with an MHP in an effort to determine the best interests of the ward and the public.

Appointment of a guardian is evidence of incompetence to marry.[5] A court may appoint a conservator with the power to give or withhold consent for the marriage of the conservatee.[6] If a marriage has been celebrated, the fact that one of the parties was under guardianship may not automatically render the marriage void.[7]

---

1. M.S.A. § 517.02 (West 1990).
2. *See* chapter 5E.7.
3. M.S.A. § 517.03(c) (West 1990); § 246.01 (West 1982). The same rule applies to persons who are under conservatorship of the commissioner of human services.
4. M.S.A. § 246.01; § 517.03(c) (West 1990). *See* chapter 5A.2.
5. M.S.A. § 525.54, subd. 5 (West Supp. 1992). *See* chapter 5A.3.
6. In re Guardianship of Mikulanec, 356 N.W. 2d 683 (Minn. 1984).
7. Johnson v. Johnson, 214 Minn. 462, 8 N.W. 2d 620 (1943). *See* chapter 5A.4.

5A.2

Guardianship for Adults

An individual who is unable to conduct his or her day-to-day affairs because of impaired abilities to meet personal or financial needs may have a surrogate decision maker appointed.[1] Depending on the needs and condition of the person, the surrogate decision maker may be designated as the guardian or as the conservator. This chapter discusses the law generally applicable to the appointment of guardians for adults. Chapter 5A.3 discusses the closely related topic of the appointment of conservators for adults.

The type of guardianship discussed in this chapter is generally known as "private" guardianship.[2] There are separate provi-

---

1. M.S.A. § 525.54, subds. 2, 3 (West 1988).
2. In general, private individuals, rather than government officials or employees, initiate these proceedings and serve as guardians and conservators. The expenses of the guardian or conservator are paid out of the ward's or conservatee's estate. M.S.A. § 525.703 (West Supp. 1992). Under some circumstances, the county has an obligation to take the initiative and to provide the funds necessary to have a guardian or conservator appointed. Under the Maltreatment of Vulnerable Adults Act, M.S.A. § 626.557 (West 1983 & Supp. 1992), the county itself may be required to prosecute the guardianship or conservatorship petition in the absence of another interested person. The county must "contract with or arrange for" a suitable person or organization to provide ongoing guardianship services. The guardianship law provides for compensation for attorneys, health professionals, and guardians and conservators. M.S.A. § 525.703 (West Supp. 1992) provides that lawyers and health professionals rendering necessary services with regard to the appointment of a guardian or conservator are entitled to reasonable compensation from the estate or, if the ward or conservatee is indigent, from the county. Furthermore, the court may, or in certain circumstances must, order reimbursement or reasonable compensation to the guardian or conservator. If the ward is indigent, the court may appoint a guardian under contract with the county. M.S.A. § 525.544, subd. 2 (West Supp. 1993).

sions governing the appointment of the commissioner of human services as guardian or conservator of adults who are mentally retarded.[3] These provisions are generally referred to as "public" guardianship and conservatorship and are discussed in chapter 5E.7. Guardianship and conservatorship for minors[4] are discussed in chapters 5A.11 and 5A.12.

The two forms of surrogate decision making, conservatorship and guardianship, both provide for a surrogate to exercise the legal powers of an individual who is incapable of acting on his or her own. Guardianship is appropriate where an individual's needs and mental condition are such that he or she needs a surrogate decision maker to undertake substantially all of his or her legal powers. Where the person's condition requires more limited protection, a conservator is appropriate. Guardians have broad powers to act on behalf of the ward, whereas conservators have only those powers specifically granted by the court.[5]

The law specifies that those under guardianship are, for most purposes, "incompetent'; that is, they lose their rights to vote, enter into most contracts, transfer property, and so forth.[6] Those under conservatorship lose those rights only if the court explicitly specifies.[7]

Guardians and conservators may be *of the estate, of the person,* or both. The "estate" designation is appropriate where the individual is unable to manage his or her money and property. The "person" designation is appropriate where the individual is unable to manage other matters of day-to-day life. These designations and their implications are discussed in more detail below.

MHPs interact professionally with the guardianship system in two major ways: First, they may be called on to evaluate the capacity of an individual, to determine whether he or she meets the statutory criteria for guardianship, or to determine whether the court should give consent for certain medical procedures for a person under guardianship.[8] Second, in the therapist–client context, the MHP must determine whether his or her client has given adequate consent for treatment. If the client is under guardianship, the power to consent to the treatment may rest with the guardian, or it may be reserved for the court.[9]

A person for whom a guardian has been appointed is known as the *ward* of the guardian.

---

3. M.S.A. § 252A.01, subd. 1(b) (West Supp. 1992).
4. M.S.A. § 525.615 et seq. (West Supp. 1992).
5. M.S.A. § 525.56, subd. 3 (West Supp. 1992).
6. M.S.A. § 525.54, subd. 5 (West Supp. 1992).
7. *Id.*; M.S.A. § 525.56, subd. 3 (West Supp. 1992).
8. M.S.A. § 525.56, subd. 3(4)(a) (West Supp. 1992). *See* below for a further discussion of these provisions.
9. *Id.*

Substantive Standards for Appointment of a Guardian

This section discusses the criteria courts apply to determine whether to appoint a guardian. See below for a discussion of the procedures involved in making these determinations.

To appoint a guardian of the person, the court must find that the proposed ward is an *incapacitated person*. In this context, the term means that the person is "impaired to the extent of lacking sufficient understanding or capacity to make or communicate responsible personal decisions, and who has demonstrated deficits in behavior which evidence an inability to meet personal needs for medical care, nutrition, clothing, shelter, or safety."[10] Note that the definition has two parts. The first refers to "understanding or capacity" and clearly calls for an assessment of mental functioning. The second, in contrast, focuses on objectively manifested behavior connected with managing life's basic needs. The court must also find that the person "needs" supervision and protection and that there are no appropriate alternatives to the appointment that are "less restrictive of the person's civil rights and liberties. . . ."[11]

Appointment of a guardian of the estate is authorized either *voluntarily* or *involuntarily*. The court may make the appointment voluntarily if the individual her- or himself petitions the court or consents in writing and if the court determines that there is a need for the appointment.[12] Under the involuntary condition, the court must find that the person is an *incapacitated person*. In this context, the term means that the person "lacks sufficient understanding or capacity to make or communicate responsible decisions concerning the person's estate or financial affairs, and who has demonstrated deficits in behavior which evidence an inability to manage the estate. . . ."[13] In addition, the court must find that the person has property that will be dissipated, that the funds are needed for the support of the person or others, and that appointment of a guardian is necessary to adequately protect the person's estate or

---

10. M.S.A. § 525.54, subd. 2 (West Supp. 1992).
11. M.S.A. § 525.551, subd. 5 (West Supp. 1992). Appointment of a conservator would be "less restrictive" in general than appointment of a guardian. The law provides for some "protective arrangements" as alternatives to the appointment of a guardian or conservator. *See* M.S.A. § 525.54, subd. 7 (West Supp. 1992). Under such arrangements, instead of appointing a guardian or conservator, the court itself grants authorization for a contract, service, transfer of property, etc.
12. M.S.A. § 525.54, subd. 3 (West Supp. 1993).
13. *Id.* Incapacity can also be shown if the person is detained by a foreign power or has disappeared.

financial affairs.[14] Alternatively, the court may appoint a guardian of the estate if the person is indigent and institutionalized and has a need for financial services beyond those provided by the institution or the county human services agency.[15]

Procedures

Anyone, including an incapacitated person, may petition the court for the appointment of a guardian. The petition must specify the grounds for the appointment and the nature of the powers sought for the guardian.

Upon receiving the petition, the probate court sets a time and place for a hearing.[16] The county human services agency may establish a screening committee to review petitions involving indigent persons. The committee is to explore less restrictive alternatives.[17] At least 14 days prior to the hearing, the proposed ward must be personally informed about the upcoming hearing. The notice and petition may, at the court's discretion, be delivered to the person by a "visitor," who is to explain the papers to the person.[18] A visitor is a person trained in law, health care, or social work with no personal interest in the proceedings.[19] The papers are also served on the spouse, parents, adult children, siblings, and any other person the court finds appropriate.[20] At the hearing, the person alleged to be incapacitated has the right to be present,[21] to be represented by counsel,[22] and to summon and cross-examine witnesses.[23]

The law contains provisions for the appointment of a "special" guardian.[24] This procedure is generally used in emergency situations, such as where there is a need to provide consent to emergency surgery for an individual who is refusing to give consent. It provides shortened notice and time requirements that allow the court to move promptly to protect an incapacitated individual. Special guardianships are of limited duration.

---

14. *Id.*
15. *Id.*
16. M.S.A. § 525.55, subd. 1 (West Supp. 1992).
17. M.S.A. § 525.54, subd. 1 (West Supp. 1993).
18. M.S.A. § 525.55, subd. 2 (West Supp. 1992).
19. M.S.A. § 525.539, subd. 6 (West Supp. 1992).
20. M.S.A. § 525.55, subd. 1 (West Supp. 1992).
21. M.S.A. § 525.551, subd. 1 (West Supp. 1992).
22. M.S.A. § 525.55, subd. 2 (West Supp. 1992).
23. M.S.A. § 525.551, subd. 3 (West Supp. 1992).
24. M.S.A. § 525.591 (West Supp. 1992).

Appointment of the Guardian

An individual may nominate her or his own guardian or may leave instructions for the guardian. The nomination or instructions must be in writing and must have been made when the person had the capacity to form an intelligent preference.[25] The court is to appoint the nominated person unless it finds that the appointment is not in the best interests of the proposed ward.[26] In the absence of an appropriate designated candidate, the court may appoint a person qualified to meet the best interests of the proposed ward or conservatee. Minnesota does not require that kinship be a conclusive factor[27] when appointing a guardian. The appointee need not reside in Minnesota.[28]

In connection with selecting and appointing a guardian, the court's best-interest determination is to include, but not be limited to,

1. the reasonable preference of the individual;
2. the interaction between the individual and the proposed appointee; and
3. the proposed appointee's interest in and commitment to the individual's welfare, and her or his ability to maintain a current understanding of the individual's physical and mental status and needs.[29]

Duties and Powers of a Guardian

Although guardians exercise legal power of and over the individual, the guardian is subject to court control and direction at all times and in all matters.[30] When a petition for guardianship is filed, the court determines which powers and duties are "necessary to provide for the demonstrated needs" of the individual. The court appoints a guardian only if it determines that all of the possible powers are necessary. If the evidence has shown that the individual has incapacities in some areas but not in others, the court may, at most, appoint a conservator with enumerated powers and duties corresponding to the demonstrated incapacities of the conservatee.[31] In the next sections, the powers and duties of a guardian are summarized.

---

25. M.S.A. § 525.544, subd. 1 (West Supp. 1992).
26. M.S.A. § 525.544, subd. 1 (West Supp. 1992).
27. M.S.A. § 525.539, subd. 7 (West Supp. 1992).
28. M.S.A. § 525.544, subd. 2 (West Supp. 1992).
29. M.S.A. § 525.539, subd. 7 (West Supp. 1992).
30. M.S.A. § 525.56, subd. 1 (West Supp. 1992).
31. *Id.* at subd. 3. *See* chapter 5A.3.

Duties of a Guardian

A guardian's duties include providing for care, comfort, and maintenance needs such as food, clothing, shelter, health care, social and recreational requirements, and, whenever appropriate, training, education, and habilitation and rehabilitation.[32] A guardian also has a duty to take reasonable care of the ward's clothing, furniture, vehicle, and other personal effects.[33]

Except when expressly waived by the court, a guardian of the person shall file with the court an annual report containing the guardian's good-faith evaluation of the following information from the preceding year:

1. changes in the ward's medical condition;
2. changes in the ward's living conditions;
3. changes in the ward's mental and emotional condition;
4. a listing of hospitalizations of the ward;
5. if the ward is institutionalized, an evaluation of the care and treatment received by the ward;[34] and
6. if the ward is indigent, a review of the continued need for guardian services beyond those provided by the institution or the county human services agency.

Each year, the guardian of a person's estate and finances shall file a verified annual account of

1. property received and dispensed;
2. the property on hand;
3. the present addresses of the ward and the guardian;
4. the amount of the bond; and
5. the names and addresses of all sureties, as well as their ability to meet their obligations.[35]

Each year, except when expressly waived by the court, the guardian shall give notice to the ward of the right to petition for restoration to capacity, discharge of the guardian, or modification of the orders of guardianship. The notice must have an understandable description of the petition procedure and must inform the ward that after a petition is filed the court will hold a hearing on the matter. The ward has the right to be present and represented by counsel.[36]

---

32. M.S.A. § 525.56, subd. 3(2) (West Supp. 1992).
33. M.S.A. § 525.56, subd. 3(3) (West Supp. 1992).
34. M.S.A. § 525.58, subd. 4 (West Supp. 1993).
35. M.S.A. § 525.58, subd. 1 (West Supp. 1992).
36. M.S.A. § 525.58, subd. 2 (West Supp. 1992).

A guardian has a duty and the power to exercise supervisory authority over the ward, limiting civil rights and restricting personal freedom, but only to the extent necessary to provide needed care and services.[37] A guardian has custody of the ward and power to establish an in- or out-of-state abode.[38] The guardian has the power to give legally sufficient consent for the ward to receive necessary medical or professional care, counsel, treatment, or service.[39] Additionally, a guardian has the power to approve or withhold approval of any contract (except for necessities) the ward may make or wish to make.[40]

Along with delegating certain powers to the guardian, the law imposes specific limitations. Except for outpatient services, or for the purpose of receiving temporary care for no more than 90 days, a ward may not be admitted to a regional treatment center (state hospital) without a court hearing pursuant to the civil commitment laws.[41]

Similarly, although a guardian may consent to medical treatment, she or he may not consent to psychosurgery, electroshock, sterilization, or experimental treatment of any kind without an approving court order.[42] Neither may the guardian consent to medical care that violates the known conscientious, religious, or moral beliefs of the ward.[43]

Termination of Guardianship– Restoration to Capacity

A guardianship ends if the ward dies[44] or if the ward is "restored to capacity" by the court.[45] If any person, including the ward, believes the ward is no longer incapacitated, she or he may, by filing a petition, ask the court to order the ward "restored to

---

37. M.S.A. § 525.56, subd. 3(6) (West Supp. 1992).
38. M.S.A. § 525.56, subd. 3(1) (West Supp. 1992). *See* below for limitations on this power.
39. M.S.A. § 525.56, subd. 3(4)(a) (West Supp. 1992). *See* below for limitations on this power.
40. M.S.A. § 525.56, subd. 3(5) (West Supp. 1992).
41. M.S.A. § 525.56, subd. 3(1) (West Supp. 1992). *See generally* M.S.A. Chapter 253B and section 5 of this book.
42. M.S.A. § 525.56, subd. 3(4)(a) (West Supp. 1992). The law sets out procedures for court approval, including, for sterilization of a mentally retarded ward, the appointment of a panel of experts, including a physician, a psychologist, and a social worker, to examine or evaluate the ward or conservatee and make reports to the court. *Id.* at subds. 3(a)–(d).
43. M.S.A. § 525.56, subd. 3(4)(a) (West Supp. 1992).
44. M.S.A. § 525.60, subd. 1 (West Supp. 1992).
45. M.S.A. § 525.61, subd. 1 (West Supp. 1992).

capacity."[46] The court may appoint a person licensed by a health-related licensing board and a social worker to assist with determining the ward's mental condition and ability to care for her or his self or property.[47] The court must restore the ward to capacity, thereby terminating the guardianship, if the ward is no longer incapacitated (as defined above) and is able to make provisions for personal care or self-management of property.[48] The court is also authorized to transform a guardianship into a conservatorship if the ward, although not entirely restored to capacity, is no longer in need of the full protections of guardianship. See chapter 5A.3 for a discussion of conservatorship.

---

46. *Id.*
47. M.S.A. § 525.61, subd. 2 (West Supp. 1992).
48. *Id.*

5A.3

Conservatorship for Adults

Conservatorship is a limited form of guardianship. It is used where an individual is incapacitated from performing some, but not all, functions of daily living, and needs a surrogate to exercise some of his or her legal powers and provide some forms of supervision and protection.[1]

Where an individual needs all of the potential powers of a guardianship, the court may appoint a guardian. Persons under guardianship are considered to be legally incompetent. See chapter 5A.2 for a complete discussion of guardianship.

However, when an incapacitated individual needs only some of the potential powers that a guardian could exercise, the court may not appoint a guardian, but may, at most, appoint a conservator. A person subject to conservatorship is call the *conservatee*.

Conservatorship for adults is discussed in this chapter. The type of conservatorship discussed in this chapter is generally

---

1. *See generally* M.S.A. § 525.539 et seq.

known as *private* conservatorship.[2] Public conservatorship for mentally retarded persons is discussed in chapter 5E.7. Conservatorship for minors is discussed in chapter 5A.11.

Conservators may be *of the estate, of the person,* or both. The "estate" designation is appropriate where the individual is unable to manage his or her money and property. The "person" designation is appropriate where the individual is unable to manage other matters of day-to-day life. These designations and their implications are discussed in more detail below.

MHPs interact professionally with the conservatorship system in two major ways: First, they may be called on to evaluate the capacity of an individual, to determine whether he or she meets the statutory criteria for conservatorship, or to determine whether the court should give consent for certain medical procedures for a person under conservatorship.[3] Second, in the therapist–client context, the MHP must determine whether his or her client has given adequate consent for treatment. If the client is under conservatorship, the power to consent to the treatment may rest with the conservator or the client, or it may be reserved for the court, depending on the type of treatment and the terms of the conservatorship.[4]

Substantive Standards for Appointment of a Conservator

To appoint a conservator, the court must find that the proposed conservatee is an *incapacitated person.* This term has the same

---

2. In general, private individuals, rather than government officials or employees, initiate these proceedings and serve as conservators. The expenses of the conservator are paid out of the conservatee's estate. M.S.A. § 525.703 (West Supp. 1992). Under some circumstances, the county has an obligation to take the initiative and to provide the funds necessary to have a conservator appointed. Under the Maltreatment of Vulnerable Adults Act, M.S.A. § 626.557 (West 1983 & Supp. 1992), the county itself may be required to prosecute the conservatorship petition in the absence of another interested person. The county must "contract with or arrange for" a suitable person or organization to provide ongoing conservatorship services. The law provides for compensation for attorneys, health professionals, and conservators. M.S.A. § 525.703 (West Supp. 1992) provides that lawyers and health professionals rendering necessary services with regard to the appointment of a conservator are entitled to reasonable compensation from the estate or, if the conservatee is indigent, from the county. Furthermore, the court may, or in certain circumstances must, order reimbursement or reasonable compensation to the conservator.
3. M.S.A. § 525.56, subd. 3(4)(a) (West Supp. 1992). *See* below for a further discussion of these provisions.
4. *Id.*

meaning in the conservatorship context as it does in the guardianship context, and is discussed fully in chapter 5A.2.

Procedures

The procedures followed by the court in connection with a proposed conservatorship are identical with those involved in guardianship proceedings. These procedures are discussed in chapter 5A.2.

Appointment of the Conservator

The factors taken into account in selecting and appointing the conservator are the same as those in connection with guardianships. These factors are discussed in chapter 5A.2.

Duties and Powers of a Conservator

Although conservators exercise legal power of and over their conservatees, the conservator is subject to court control and direction at all times and in all matters.[5] At the time of appointment (and thereafter, if necessary), the court determines which powers and duties are "necessary to provide for the demonstrated needs" of the conservatee. The court is to grant to the conservator only those powers.[6] Only if the court determines that all of the possible powers are necessary is it to appoint a guardian. If the evidence establishes that the individual has incapacities in some areas but not in others, the court may, at most, appoint a conservator with enumerated powers and duties corresponding to the demonstrated incapacities of the conservatee.[7]

Duties of a Conservator

The court selects from among a list of potential duties in appointing a conservator. Depending on the needs and condition of the conservatee, a conservator's duties may include providing for care, comfort, and maintenance needs like food, clothing, shelter, health care, social and recreational requirements, and, whenever appropriate, training, education, and habilitation and rehabilita-

---

5. M.S.A. § 525.56, subd. 1 (West Supp. 1992).
6. M.S.A. § 525.56, subd. 2 (West Supp. 1992).
7. *Id.*, subd. 3.

tion.[8] A conservator may also be given the duty to take reasonable care of the conservatee's clothing, furniture, vehicle, and other personal effects.[9]

Except when expressly waived by the court, a conservator of the person shall file with the court an annual report containing the conservator's good-faith evaluation of the following information from the preceding year:

1. changes in the conservatee's medical condition;
2. changes in the conservatee's living conditions;
3. changes in the conservatee's mental and emotional condition;
4. a listing of hospitalizations of the conservatee;
5. if the conservatee is institutionalized, an evaluation of the care and treatment received by the conservatee;[10] and
6. if the conservatee is indigent, a review of the continued need for conservator services beyond those provided by the institution or the county human services agency.

Each year, the conservator of a person's estate and finances shall file a verified annual account of

1. property received and dispensed;
2. the property on hand;
3. the present addresses of the conservatee and the conservator;
4. the amount of the bond; and
5. the names and addresses of all sureties, as well as their ability to meet their obligations.[11]

Each year, except when expressly waived by the court, the conservator shall give notice to the conservatee of the right to petition for restoration to capacity, discharge of the conservator, or modification of the orders of conservatorship. The notice must have an understandable description of the petition procedure and must inform the conservatee that after a petition is filed the court will hold a hearing on the matter. The conservatee has the right to be present and represented by counsel.[12]

Powers of a Conservator

The court may grant a conservator only such powers as are necessary to provide for the needs of the conservatee. In assigning powers, the court can choose from the following:

---

8. M.S.A. § 525.56, subd. 3(2) (West Supp. 1992).
9. M.S.A. § 525.56, subd. 3(3) (West Supp. 1992).
10. M.S.A. § 525.58, subd. 4 (West Supp. 1992).
11. M.S.A. § 525.58, subd. 1 (West Supp. 1992).
12. M.S.A. § 525.58, subd. 2 (West Supp. 1992).

1. the power to exercise supervisory authority over the conservatee, limiting civil rights and restricting personal freedom, but only to the extent necessary to provide needed care and services;[13]

2. custody of the conservatee and power to establish an in- or out-of-state abode;[14]

3. the power to give legally sufficient consent for the conservatee to receive necessary medical or professional care, counsel, treatment, or service;[15] and

4. the power to approve or withhold approval of any contract (except for necessities) the conservatee may make or wish to make.[16]

The law imposes specific limitations on the powers that the court may grant to the conservator. Except for outpatient services, or for the purpose of receiving temporary care for no more than 90 days, a conservatee may not be admitted to a regional treatment center (state hospital) without a court hearing pursuant to the civil commitment laws.[17]

Similarly, although a conservator may be given the power to consent to medical treatment, she or he may not consent to psychosurgery, electroshock, sterilization, or experimental treatment of any kind without an approving court order.[18] Neither may the conservator consent to medical care that violates the known conscientious, religious, or moral beliefs of the conservatee.[19]

---

13. M.S.A. § 525.56, subd. 3(6) (West Supp. 1992).
14. M.S.A. § 525.56, subd. 3(1) (West Supp. 1992). *See* below for limitations on this power.
15. M.S.A. § 525.56, subd. 3(4)(a) (West Supp. 1992). *See* below for limitations on this power.
16. M.S.A. § 525.56, subd. 3(5) (West Supp. 1992).
17. M.S.A. § 525.56, subd. 3(1) (West Supp. 1992). *See generally* M.S.A. Chapter 253B and section 5 of this book.
18. M.S.A. § 525.56, subd. 3(4)(a) (West Supp. 1992). The law sets out procedures for court approval, including, for sterilization of a mentally retarded ward, the appointment of a panel of experts, including a physician, a psychologist, and a social worker, to examine or evaluate the conservatee and make reports to the court. *Id.*, subds. 3(a)–(d). Conservatees whose right to consent to sterilization has not been given to the conservator may be sterilized only upon the written consent of the conservatee or upon the sworn acknowledgment by an interested person of a nonwritten consent by the conservatee. The consent must certify that the conservatee has received a full explanation of the nature and irreversible consequences of the sterilization operation. *Id.* at subd. 3(4)(d).
19. M.S.A. § 525.56, subd. 3(4)(a) (West Supp. 1992).

Termination of Conservatorship–Restoration to Capacity

A conservatorship ends if the conservatee dies[20] or if the conservatee is "restored to capacity" by the court.[21] If any person, including the conservatee, believes the conservatee is no longer incapacitated, she or he may, by filing a petition, ask the court to order the conservatee "restored to capacity."[22] The court may appoint a person licensed by a health-related licensing board and a social worker to assist with determining the conservatee's mental condition and ability to care for her or his self or property.[23] The court is to restore the conservatee to capacity, thereby terminating the conservatorship, if the conservatee is no longer incapacitated (as defined above) and is able to make provisions for personal care or self-management of property.[24] The court is also authorized to modify the terms of the conservatorship if the conservatee's needs dictate.

---

20. M.S.A. § 525.60, subd. 1 (West Supp. 1992).
21. M.S.A. § 525.61, subd. 1 (West Supp. 1992).
22. Id.
23. M.S.A. § 525.61, subd. 2 (West Supp. 1992).
24. Id.

5A.4

Annulment

Divorce is the process by which a valid marriage is dissolved. Annulment, on the other hand, is the process by which a marriage is declared void and legally held to never have existed.[1] Because lack of capacity to consent to marriage is one ground for annulment, MHPs may be called on to assess competency in connection with an annulment proceeding.

Certain marriages are considered legally voidable, and an annulment of such marriages may be sought. A marriage may be declared a nullity under the following circumstances:[2]

1. where a party to the marriage was under the age of marriage established by law;[3]
2. where a party lacked the capacity[4] to consent to marriage at the time the marriage was solemnized, because of mental incapacity, infirmity, or the influence of drugs or alcohol, and the other party at the time the marriage was solemnized did not know of the incapacity;[5] or

---

1. Even though a marriage was, and has been declared, void, a person cohabitating with another in a good-faith belief that she or he is married to the other may acquire the rights conferred on a legal spouse. M.S.A. § 518.055 (West Supp. 1992).
2. M.S.A. § 518.02 (West 1990).
3. In Minnesota, the legal age of marriage is 18 without parental consent and 16 with parental consent. M.S.A. § 517.02 (West 1990).
4. *See* chapter 5A.1.
5. Either party or the legal representative of the party who lacked the capacity to consent must seek annulment no later than 90 days after obtaining knowledge of the particular incapacity. M.S.A. § 518.05(a) (West 1990).

3. where a party was unable to physically consummate the marriage by sexual intercourse and the other party did not know of the incapacity at the time of the marriage.[6]

---

6. Either party must seek annulment no later than one year after the person seeking annulment obtained knowledge of the incapacity. M.S.A. § 518.05(b) (West 1990).

5A.5

Divorce

In Minnesota, as in many other states, divorce or dissolution[1] of marriage is based on "no fault" principles. The sole substantive criterion for granting a marriage dissolution is whether the marriage has suffered an "irretrievable breakdown."[2] Contests over the existence of such a breakdown, although theoretically possible, are rare. Most contests surrounding the breakup of marriages arise from the division of property, the obligation to pay spousal or child support, and issues of custody and visitation of the children of the marriage. Some spouses do not wish to be divorced but need court intervention in declaring their respective rights and obligations. These individuals may seek a decree of legal separation, following many of the same procedures applicable to dissolution.[3] Custody and visitation issues are discussed in chapter 5A.6. This chapter summarizes the procedures followed in divorce proceedings.

MHPs play several key roles in divorce proceedings. When child custody or visitation is at issue, MHPs often provide evaluations and testimony about the best interests of the child and the capabilities of the parents.[4] MHPs often serve as mediators to assist the parties in determining whether they want a divorce or separation and in resolving their disputes without court intervention.[5] On rare occasions, MHPs may be asked to evaluate and testify about whether the marriage breakdown is irretrievable.

---

1. Under Minnesota law, the terms *divorce* and *dissolution* are used interchangeably. M.S.A. § 518.002 (West 1990).
2. M.S.A. § 518.10 (West 1990).
3. M.S.A. § 518.06, subd. 1 (West 1990).
4. *See* chapter 5A.6.
5. *See* chapter 5A.6.

Upon petition to the court by either spouse, the process of dissolution of the marriage begins. The petition must allege that there has been an irretrievable breakdown in the marriage.[6] If both parties agree that the marriage is irretrievably broken, a decree of dissolution is granted.[7] If one party denies that the marriage is irretrievably broken, the court must consider all relevant factors in determining if the marriage is irretrievably broken.[8] No dissolution will be granted unless at least one of the parties has resided in the state for at least 180 days immediately preceding the filing of the dissolution petition.[9]

During a proceeding for the dissolution of a marriage, the court may grant a temporary order, pending final disposition, regarding[10]

1. temporary custody and visitation rights;[11]
2. temporary spousal maintenance and child support;
3. temporary use and possession of home and personal property;
4. prohibiting the transfer, encumbrance, concealment, or disposition of property;
5. prohibiting a spouse from harassing or disturbing the children or other spouse;
6. prohibiting a spouse from removing children from the jurisdiction of the court; or
7. excluding a party from the family or home of the other party.

A temporary order will continue in force until it is modified, the action has been dismissed, or a final decree of dissolution has been granted.[12] The issues in a proceeding may be resolved by agreement of the parties (a "stipulation") or by the judge on the basis of a full trial. The final decree of the court defines the respective rights and obligations of the parties, divides the marital property, and may order one party to pay spousal maintenance and/or child support.

A decree of dissolution is final when entered, subject to the right of appeal.[13] A party may remarry before the time for appeal has run out if the appeal does not contest that the marriage is irretrievably broken.[14]

---

6. M.S.A. § 518.10 (West 1990).
7. M.S.A. § 518.13, subd. 3; § 518.06, subd. 2 (West 1990).
8. M.S.A. § 518.13, subd. 2 (West 1990).
9. M.S.A. § 518.07 (West 1990).
10. M.S.A. § 518.131 (West Supp. 1992).
11. *See* chapter 5A.6.
12. M.S.A. § 518.131, subd. 5 (West Supp. 1992).
13. M.S.A. § 518.145 (West 1990).
14. *Id.*

The law sets out the factors to be considered by the court in making temporary or permanent orders regarding property, maintenance, support, visitation, and custody.[15]

---

15. *See* M.S.A. § 518.551 (child support), § 518.552 (spousal maintenance), §§ 518.17 to 518.175 (child custody and visitation), § 518.58 (division of marital property). *See* chapter 5A.6 for a full discussion of child custody and visitation determinations.

5A.6

Child Custody and Visitation Determinations

Issues of child custody and visitation can arise for judicial determination in a number of ways. Most often, these issues are raised by parents in marriage dissolution proceedings. Custody and visitation can be addressed in temporary rulings, which govern affairs during the pendency of the proceeding, and in final decrees. Final decrees can be modified to fit changing circumstances. In addition, child custody and visitation matters are raised by petitions for legal separation. Finally, persons other than the parents of a child can seek custody of the child by filing a petition or a motion with the proper court.[1] MHPs play central roles in helping parents and courts decide what is best for the children who are the subjects of these proceedings. Their roles may be therapeutic or evaluative, or they may act as mediators in these disputes. The evaluative and mediational roles are discussed in this chapter.

Court Jurisdiction

To make a valid ruling on a child custody matter, a court must have jurisdiction over the matter. A rather complex set of rules governs child custody jurisdiction, designed to provide some national uniformity in the determinations as well as to reduce the incentive for parents to remove their children from one state to another to establish jurisdiction. Generally, Minnesota courts have jurisdiction if Minnesota is the child's "home state." In

---

1. Grandparents may seek court-ordered visitation. M.S.A. § 257.022 (West Supp. 1993).

addition, courts can apply a "best interests" test of jurisdiction if the child and at least one of the custody contestants have "significant connections" to this state.[2]

Standard in Custody Determinations: Best Interests of the Child

The court determines custody in accordance with the best interests of the child.[3] In determining the "best interests" of the child, the court considers

1. the wishes of the parent(s);
2. the preference of the child, if of a sufficient age to express a preference;
3. the child's primary caretaker;
4. the interaction and interrelationship of the child with the parent(s), siblings, and any other person who may significantly affect the child's best interests;
5. the child's adjustment to the home, school, and community;
6. the length of time the child has lived in a stable, satisfactory environment and the desire to maintain continuity;
7. the permanence, as a family unit, of the proposed custodial home;
8. the mental and physical health of all individuals involved;
9. the capacity and disposition of the parties to give the child love, affection, and guidance and to continue educating and raising the child in his or her culture, religion, or creed, if any;
10. the child's cultural background; and
11. the effect on a child of domestic abuse that has occurred between the parents.

No one factor can be used to the exclusion of the others. The court may not consider conduct of the proposed custodian that does not affect the custodian's relationship with the child. Furthermore, the court may not prefer one parent over the other solely on the basis of the sex of the parent.[4]

---

2. M.S.A. § 518A.03, subd. 1 (West 1990). Other provisions permit the state to take jurisdiction of custody matters in an emergency if the child is physically present in the state.
3. M.S.A. § 518.17 (West Supp. 1992).
4. M.S.A. § 518.15, subd. 3(3) (West 1990).

The custody determination will be reflected in an order establishing the legal custody of the child (either sole or joint), physical custody and residence, visitation rights and obligations, and child support obligations.[5] Legal custody gives the custodian the right to determine the child's upbringing, including education, health care, and religious training.[6] Physical custody concerns where the child lives and with whom.[7]

When joint custody is sought, the court will also consider the following relevant factors:[8]

1. the ability of the parents to cooperate in the rearing of their children;

2. methods for resolving disputes regarding major decisions concerning the child's life;

3. whether domestic abuse[9] has occurred between the parents; and

4. whether it would be detrimental to a child if one parent were to have sole authority over the child's upbringing.

Generally, if both parents request joint legal custody, the court will order it, unless there has been domestic abuse between the parties.

In determining visitation rights for the parent not granted custody, the court will aim to enable the child and parent to maintain a parent–child relationship that will be in the best interests of the child.[10] Visitation may be restricted or even denied if the court finds, after a hearing, that visitation is likely to endanger the child's physical or emotional health or impair the child's emotional development.

Mediation[11]

When it appears to the court that an issue involving child custody or visitation is contested, the court may set the matter for mediation of the contested issue. Mediation is an informal process by which an impartial third party attempts to facilitate an agreement

---

5. M.S.A. § 518.17, subd. 3 (West 1990).
6. M.S.A. § 518.003, subd. 3(a) (West Supp. 1992); § 518.176, subd. 1 (West 1990). *See* chapter 5A.23.
7. M.S.A. § 518.003, subd. 3(c) (West Supp. 1992).
8. M.S.A. § 518.17, subd. 2 (West Supp. 1992).
9. *See* M.S.A. § 518B.01 (West 1990 & Supp. 1992).
10. M.S.A. § 518.175 (West 1990 & Supp. 1992).
11. M.S.A. § 518.619 (West 1990). Each district court adopts its own rules governing mediation.

between the parents.[12] Mediators have no coercive authority. If the court has probable cause to believe that one of the parties has been abused by the other, the court is not permitted to require mediation.[13]

To participate in custody mediation, a mediator must be appointed by the court;[14] know the court system and custody procedures; know the resources in the community that might assist in contested custody matters; know child development, clinical issues relating to children, the effects of marriage dissolution on children, and child custody research; and have had 40 hours of certified mediation training.

Custody mediation proceedings are conducted in private, and records are unavailable to be used as evidence. If an agreement is not reached by the parties, the mediator may recommend that a custody investigation be conducted or that other steps be taken to assist the parties in resolving the issue. Generally, the mediator does not conduct the investigation or make recommendations concerning custody or visitation.

Custody and Visitation Evaluations

In contested custody proceedings, and in other custody proceedings if the parent or custodian requests, the court may seek the recommendations of MHPs, whether or not they are employed on a regular basis by the court. The court also may order an investigation and report concerning custody to be made by the county welfare agency or the department of court services.[15] With parental consent, the investigator obtains information from medical, psychiatric, and school personnel or other experts who have worked with the child in the past. Upon court order, the investigator may also refer the child to an MHP for diagnosis. The investigator prepares a written report to the court. The report is admissible as evidence in the custody hearing. The investigator and any person consulted may be called for cross-examination at the hearing by either party.[16]

Information gathered by MHPs in connection with court-ordered custody evaluations is not protected by the usual thera-

---

12. M.S.A. § 518.003, subd. 4 (West Supp. 1992).
13. M.S.A. § 518.619, subd. 2 (West 1990). This prohibition is designed to minimize the chance that the informal setting of mediation will be used by a stronger, dominant party to bully the other into a custody or visitation agreement.
14. Each court is to maintain a list of mediators.
15. M.S.A. §§ 518.166, 518.167 (West 1990 & Supp. 1992).
16. M.S.A. § 518.167 (West 1990 & Supp. 1992).

pist–client privilege.[17] Information gathered in the course of mediation is not accessible to the court, the parties, or the investigation except upon consent of all parties thereto.[18] Information gathered by MHPs in connection with providing counseling or therapy to parents or children around issues generated by the dissolution or custody dispute retains its privileged status.[19]

---

17. *See* chapter 4.3.
18. M.S.A. § 518.167, subds. 2, 3 (West 1990 & Supp. 1992).
19. Joint counseling of husband and wife may, as well, be privileged. Although the presence of "third parties" generally destroys a privilege, this may not be the case for "group therapy." State v. Andring, 342 N.W.2d 128 (Minn. 1984). *See* chapter 4.3.

5A.7

Reporting of Adult Abuse and Neglect

The Reporting of Maltreatment of Vulnerable Adults Act[1] aims to facilitate the transmission of information about abuse and neglect of vulnerable adults[2] to the proper authorities, so that steps can be taken to provide appropriate protective and social services to the adults. The law requires certain professionals to report known or suspected abuse or neglect of vulnerable adults. Abuse and neglect include not only behavior resulting in physical or emotional harm, but also mismanagement of property or finances. This is a mandatory law that carries criminal and civil sanctions for non-compliance.

The act defines a group of mandated reporters, the protected population (vulnerable adults), and the terms abuse and neglect. It establishes a duty to report and sanctions for failure to report.

---

1. M.S.A. § 626.557 (West 1983 & Supp. 1992). For a more complete analysis of the act, see Janus, *Minnesota Vulnerable Adults Protection Act: Analysis*, Revised November 1991, in Medical Decisionmaking (Minn. CLE 1991).
2. See chapter 5A.8 for a discussion of parallel provisions regarding minors.

Obligation to Report

The definition of *mandated reporter* includes most if not all MHPs who are engaged directly or indirectly in providing mental health or human services.[3]

Mandated reporters must report if they have knowledge or reasonable cause to believe that a vulnerable adult is or has been abused or neglected.[4] The report must be made "immediately" to the police, sheriff, local welfare agency, or appropriate licensing or certifying agency. The act provides limited exceptions to the reporting requirement where the incident has already been reported or federal law specifically prohibits the disclosure of the information.[5]

Abuse is defined to include

1. sexual abuse,
2. nontherapeutic conduct that produces or could reasonably be expected to produce pain or injury and that is not accidental,
3. repeated conduct that produces or could reasonably be expected to produce mental or emotional distress,
4. sexual contact between a facility staff person and a resident or client of the facility,
5. certain forms of economic exploitation, and
6. aversive or deprivation procedures that are not properly authorized.[6]

Neglect includes the absence or likelihood of absence of necessary financial management, food, clothing, shelter, health care, or supervision.[7]

Persons who are not required to report may voluntarily report suspected abuse or neglect. Reporters, whether voluntary or

---

3. The statutory definition includes professionals or their delegates who are engaged in the care of vulnerable adults, education, social services, or law enforcement; licensed psychologists (*see* chapter 1.3); physicians (*see* chapter 1.1); nurses (*see* chapter 1.2); any person licensed or credentialed by an agency responsible for credentialing human services occupations; employees of rehabilitation facilities; employees or persons providing services at hospitals, nursing homes, and licensed facilities serving adults; and home care providers. M.S.A. § 626.557, subd. 3 (West Supp. 1992).
4. M.S.A. § 626.557, subd. 3 (West Supp. 1992). Also, a mandated reporter must report if he or she has knowledge of a physical injury that is not reasonably explained by the caretaker.
5. *Id.*, subds. 3, 3a. *But see* State v. Andring, 342 N.W.2d 128 (Minn. 1984) (the Federal Comprehensive Alcohol Abuse and Alcoholism Prevention, Treatment, and Rehabilitation Act, 42 U.S.C. §§ 290dd, 290ee, does not prevent disclosure of records required by the Minnesota Maltreatment of Minors Reporting Act). *See* chapter 5E.5.
6. *See* chapter 6.3.
7. M.S.A. § 626.557, subd. 2(e) (West Supp. 1992).

mandated, are immune from civil or criminal liability arising from their actions, if they have acted in good faith.[8] Mandated reporters who fail to report may be guilty of a misdemeanor or held liable for damages arising from their failure to report.

The act provides a two-pronged definition of vulnerable adults. Satisfaction of either prong is sufficient. Under the functional prong, a person is a vulnerable adult if he or she is "unable or unlikely to report abuse or neglect without assistance because of impairment of mental or physical function or emotional status."[9] Under the categorical prong, a person is a vulnerable adult if he or she is a resident or inpatient of a licensed facility or receives services from a licensed facility or from a home care provider.

Confidentiality and Privilege

Most services provided by an MHP are confidential, through either the law or the ethics of the profession.[10] This confidentiality, however, is no bar if the MHP is required to report suspected adult abuse or neglect under the law.[11] Furthermore, no evidence regarding the abuse or neglect of a vulnerable adult may be excluded in any proceeding arising out of the alleged abuse or neglect on the grounds of privilege claimed by the following:[12] husband–wife, licensed physician or surgeon, dentist, chiropractor, registered nurse, psychologist, or consulting psychologist.

---

8. *Id.* at subd. 5 (West 1983). *See* chapter 6.6.
9. M.S.A. § 626.557, subd. 2(b) (West Supp. 1992).
10. *See* chapters 4.1, 4.2, 4.3, 5E.5.
11. *See* chapter 5E.5 for a discussion of federal and state rules on the confidentiality of alcohol and drug treatment information.
12. M.S.A. § 595.02, subd. 1 (West 1988). *See* chapter 4.3.

5A.7A

Protection From Domestic Abuse

The Minnesota Domestic Abuse Act[1] provides a simplified, summary procedure to protect victims of domestic abuse. These proceedings are often referred to as "order for protection" or "OFP" proceedings. MHPs should be aware of this procedure so that they can make appropriate referrals for clients who are subjected to domestic abuse.

Definitions

The act relies on two definitions. *Domestic abuse* is defined as physical or bodily harm, or the infliction of fear of imminent harm or injury, between family or household members. It includes criminal sexual conduct committed by a family or household member against a child of the family or household. It also includes "terroristic threats."

Family or household members is defined to include spouses, former spouses, parents and children, persons who are related by blood, and persons who are presently residing together or who have resided together in the past. It also includes persons who have a child in common regardless of whether they have lived together. It also includes a man and a woman if the woman is pregnant and the man is alleged to be the father, regardless of whether they have lived together.[2]

---

1. M.S.A. § 518B.01 (West Supp. 1993).
2. *Id.*, subd. 2.

Procedures

The act is designed to provide a simple, streamlined procedure by which a person suffering from domestic abuse can obtain protection from the abuse. The procedure is commenced by the filing of a petition alleging abuse. Any member of the family or household may file a petition. The petition may be filed on the person's own behalf or on behalf of a child member of the family or household.[3] Courts are required to provide simplified forms and clerical assistance to help with the writing and filing of petitions.[4] People who have few financial resources may be permitted to file and serve the petition *in forma pauperis* (i.e., without payment of the usual fees). When the petition is filed, the court sets a date for a hearing. The hearing must be held within 14 days of the filing. The petition must be served on the alleged abuser at least 5 days prior to the hearing.

After hearing the matter, the court may issue an "order for protection," providing some or all of the following relief:[5]

1. restrain the abusing party from committing further acts of domestic abuse;
2. require the abusing party to leave the dwelling;
3. award temporary custody, visitation, and support rights for minor children, giving primary consideration to the safety of the victim and the children;
4. provide counseling or other social services for the parties;
5. order the abusing party to participate in treatment or counseling;
6. make orders concerning use, possession, and disposition of property;
7. exclude the abusing party from the petitioner's place of employment;
8. order the abusing party to pay restitution to the petitioner;
9. order the continuation of currently existing insurance coverage; and
10. make any other suitable orders.

Court orders must be for a fixed period not exceeding one year. The act provides for police assistance in enforcing these

---

3. Public officials may seek orders for protection of minor children through juvenile court proceedings. *See* chapter 5A.9.
4. M.S.A. § 518A.01, subd. 4 (West Supp. 1993).
5. *Id.*, subd. 6.

orders.[6] It also provides for penalties for the violation of the orders.[7]

Where the petition alleges an immediate and present danger of domestic abuse, the court may grant an immediate order for protection.[8] This order may be granted on an *ex parte* basis (i.e., it may be granted without notice to the alleged abuser). *Ex parte* orders for protection may have an effective period not longer than 14 days. A full hearing, with notice to the alleged abuser, must be scheduled for no later than 7 days after the issuance of the *ex parte* order.

---

6. *Id.*, subd. 9
7. *Id.*, subd. 14.
8. *Id.*, subd. 7.

5A.8

Reporting of Maltreatment of Minors

The goal of the Reporting of Maltreatment of Minors Act[1] is to facilitate reports of suspected maltreatment of minors[2] to the proper authorities so that appropriate protective and social services[3] can be provided to the minors. The act requires that certain professionals (referred to in this chapter as "mandated reporters") must report any known or suspected neglect, physical abuse, sexual abuse, or deprivation of parental rights affecting or endangering a child. The act also permits voluntary reporting by providing immunity for nonmandated reports made in good faith. It also provides certain penalties for its violation. Its major provisions are summarized here.

Obligation to Report

Mandatory reporters include professionals and their "delegates" who are "engaged in the practice of the healing arts, social services, hospital administration, psychological or psychiatric treatment, child care, education, or law enforcement."[4] Also included are persons who are employed as members of the clergy who

---

1. M.S.A. § 626.556, subd. 3(1) (West Supp. 1992).
2. *See* chapter 5A.7 for a discussion of parallel provisions regarding vulnerable adults.
3. *See* chapter 5A.9.
4. M.S.A. § 626.556, subd. 3 (West Supp. 1992).

received information while engaged in ministerial duties.[5] Most MHPs involved in providing direct services or administration of treatment services are covered by this definition.[6]

A mandatory reporter must make a report if he or she knows or "has reason to believe" that a child is, or within the preceding three years has been, neglected or physically or sexually abused.

A child is *neglected* when the person responsible for its care has failed to supply necessary food, clothing, shelter, or medical care or has failed to protect the child from conditions that imminently and seriously endanger the child's health.[7] Neglect includes prenatal exposure of a fetus to a controlled substance[8] and the withholding of medically indicated treatment from a disabled infant with a life-threatening condition.[9]

Physical abuse means physical[10] or mental injury[11] inflicted other than accidentally by the person responsible for the child's care.[12] It also includes *threatened injury*, which means a "statement, overt act, condition, or status that represents a substantial risk of physical or sexual abuse or mental injury."[13] Also included are any "aversive" or "deprivation" procedures not authorized under Minn. Stat. § 245.825.[14]

---

5. M.S.A. § 626.556, subd. 3 (West Supp. 1992). However, members of the clergy are not mandated to report information that is "privileged." *See* chapter 4.3. This includes "confessions" and communications by or to persons seeking religious or spiritual advice, aid, or comfort. M.S.A. § 595.02, subd. 1(c) (West 1988).
6. The act specifically includes employee-assistance counseling and the provision of guardian *ad litem* services in the definition. M.S.A. § 626.556, subd. 2(j) (West Supp. 1992).
7. M.S.A. § 626.556, subd. 2(c) (West Supp. 1992).
8. *Id.* A number of circumstances could trigger a report of suspected exposure. It may be evidenced by withdrawal symptoms in the child at birth, toxicology tests, or medical effects or developmental delays during the child's first year of life. *See* M.S.A. § 253B.02, subd.2 (West Supp. 1992) (allowing commitment of the mother to curtail prenatal exposure of the fetus to a controlled substance). *See* chapter 5E.5. Mandated reporters are required to report knowledge or reason to believe that a woman is pregnant and has used a controlled substance for a nonmedical purpose during the pregnancy. M.S.A. § 626.5561, subd. 1 (West Supp. 1992).
9. M.S.A. § 260.015, subd. 2a(5) (West 1993).
10. Physical abuse includes injuries that are not reasonably explained by the caretaker. M.S.A. § 626.556, subd. 2(d) (West Supp. 1992).
11. *Mental injury* means "an injury to the psychological capacity or emotional stability of a child as evidenced by an observable or substantial impairment in the child's ability to function within a normal range of performance and behavior with due regard to the child's culture." M.S.A. § 626.556, subd. 2(k) (West Supp. 1992).
12. Persons responsible for the child's care include parents and guardians, as well as nonfamily members with either full-time or short-term care responsibilities. Counselors are included. M.S.A. § 626.556, subd. 2(b) (West Supp. 1992).
13. M.S.A. § 626.556, subd. 2(k) (West Supp. 1992).
14. *See* chapter 6.3.

Sexual abuse refers to the commission by persons responsible for the child's care, or by persons in positions of authority,[15] of sexual acts that violate the criminal law.[16] Threatened sexual abuse is also a reportable event.

Mandated reporters must also report, in certain circumstances, known or suspected deprivation of custodial or parental rights.[17] Reportable acts are those that violate the law. These include intentionally concealing a minor from the child's parent and taking or failing to return a minor child in violation of a court order and in certain other circumstances.[18]

Reports must be made "immediately" to the local welfare agency, police department, or county sheriff.[19] Reports may be made orally or in writing, although oral reports must be followed within 72 hours by a report in writing.[20] Any person may voluntarily report suspected child neglect or abuse.

Persons making good-faith voluntary or mandated reports are immune from any liability, civil or criminal, that otherwise might result from the reports.[21] Employers are prohibited from retaliating against employees for making good-faith reports of abuse or neglect.[22] A mandated reporter who fails to make a mandatory report is guilty of a misdemeanor.[23] Any person who knowingly or recklessly makes a false report is liable for actual and punitive damages.

Most evidentiary privileges[24] are abrogated in connection with reports and evidence under this act.[25]

---

15. As defined in M.S.A. § 609.341, subd. 10 (West 1987).
16. Included are sexual contact and sexual penetration. *See* M.S.A. § 609.342 (West 1987 & Supp. 1992); § 609.343 (West 1987 & Supp. 1992); § 609.344 (West 1987 & Supp. 1992); § 609.345 (West 1987 & Supp. 1992).
17. M.S.A. § 626.556, subd. 3a (West Supp. 1992); § 609.26 (West 1987 & Supp. 1992).
18. *See id.* for more detail.
19. Suspected abuse or neglect that occurs within a licensed facility must be reported by mandated reporters to the agency that licenses the facility. M.S.A. § 626.556, subd. 2(c). Where a child has died as a result of neglect or abuse, the report must be made to the medical examiner or coroner instead. *Id.*, subd. 9.
20. *Id.*, subd. 7.
21. *Id.*, subd. 4. Presumably, this immunity would protect reporters from liability for violations of otherwise-existing duties to maintain client confidences. *See* chapters 4.2, 4.3, 6.6.
22. M.S.A. § 626.556, subd. 4a (West Supp. 1992). Retaliation against the child with respect to whom the report is made is likewise prohibited. *Id.*
23. *Id.*, subd. 6.
24. *See* chapter 4.3.
25. M.S.A. § 626.556, subd. 8 (West Supp. 1992). Abrogated privileges include husband–wife, licensed physician or surgeon, dentist, chiropractor, registered nurse, and psychologist or consulting psychologist. Note that attorney–client, clergy–penitent, and sexual assault counselor privileges are not abrogated.

Investigation and Assessment

Upon receiving a report, welfare agencies are required to conduct an assessment[26] and offer protective social services to prevent further abuse and preserve family life, if possible.[27] Local law enforcement agencies are required to investigate if there is an allegation of violation of criminal laws. Where the child is a client of an agency or facility that provides services or treatment for mental illness, mental retardation, chemical dependency, or emotional disturbance, the ombudsman for mental health and mental retardation must be notified by the welfare agency.[28] Extensive provisions of the law govern the rights and duties of welfare and other agencies conducting assessments and investigations of suspected abuse or neglect.[29] Where the alleged abuse took place in a licensed facility, the commissioner of human services also has an obligation to investigate.

Where the report indicates "medical neglect" of a newborn infant, the act imposes special duties on the local welfare agency. These include consulting with hospital staff and parents, securing an independent medical review, and, if necessary, seeking a court order for an examination or medical intervention.[30]

The act contains provisions governing the release and retention of information and data generated from reports and from assessments and investigations.[31]

---

26. State law requires that a record be made of assessment or investigation interviews with child abuse victims. This requirement applies to interviews conducted by government employees and any person acting as an agent of the government. M.S.A. § 626.561 (West Supp. 1992). The record can be written, or on video- or audiotape. If in writing, it must contain identifying information and a summary of the information obtained during the interview. There are dual purposes to this requirement. One is to encourage accuracy in the documentation of interviews. The other is to help avoid interviews that are duplicative and therefore unnecessary.
27. *See* chapter 5A.9.
28. M.S.A. § 626.556, subd. 10(b) (West Supp. 1993). *See* M.S.A. §§ 245.91 to 245.97 (West Supp. 1992) (ombudsman for mental health and mental retardation). *See* chapter 5E.7.
29. M.S.A. § 626.556, subds. 10, 10a (West Supp. 1993).
30. M.S.A. § 626.556, subd. 10c (West Supp. 1992).
31. *See* M.S.A. § 626.556, subds. 10f, 10g, 10h, 11, 11a, 11b, 11c (West Supp. 1992).

5A.9

Abused and Neglected Children

Procedures for handling child abuse and neglect cases reflect a balance of conflicting societal values. Of paramount importance is the duty and right of the society to protect abused and neglected children. Thus, the procedures provide for prompt assessment and emergency intervention, where needed. Sometimes in tension with this protective function is the right of the family to be free from state interference. The law attempts to protect that value through both substantive principles (intervention should be as unobtrusive as possible) and procedural protections (right to notice, hearing, time limits, etc.). This chapter discusses the typical stages involved in a case of alleged abuse or neglect: assessment, emergency intervention, and disposition. MHPs are often involved at all stages of this process. They assess children and their families, recommend dispositions, and provide services.

Assessment

The law gives governmental agencies substantial powers to investigate reports[1] of child abuse or neglect in order to assess the child's need for protective services and intervention. The assessment must be done promptly, although the timing depends on the agency's initial determination as to the urgency of the child's need and the degree of risk posed to the child.[2] Reports alleging that the child is abandoned, life-threatened, or likely to experience physical injury due to abuse require an immediate, on-site

1. *See* chapter 5A.8.
2. Minn. R. 9560.0280 (1991).

investigation.[3] If the child is not in need of immediate care but is allegedly physically or sexually abused, the investigation must be undertaken within 72 hours.

The investigators determine whether there appears to be substance to the complaint and, if so, whether there is risk if the child remains in his or her current setting[4] and whether the child can safely remain at home if appropriate services are provided. In making these determinations, the agency may interview the child at school or at any facility or place he or she may be found. Such an interview may be conducted without the parents' consent and outside of their presence. Unless there is good reason shown, the parent will be notified at the conclusion of the investigation that the interview took place.[5] Investigators may seek a court order if their access to the child is impeded.[6]

Emergency Intervention

Having determined that there is a need for protective services, the welfare agency next determines whether the child must be removed from the home for his or her own protection. If it is possible consistent with the safety of the child, the agency seeks to keep the family unit intact by providing services to the family unit. The services may include case management,[7] family counseling, homemaking or other in-home services, respite care,[8] crisis nurseries,[9] and referral to parent support organizations for courses in parenting or child care.[10] If the family rejects such services, the agency can petition the juvenile court for authorization to intervene to provide the services.[11]

If the agency determines that the safety of the child requires emergency court intervention, several options are available. The agency may seek an *order for protection*.[12] This order, which may

---

3. *Id.*, subp. 2.
4. *Id.*
5. M.S.A. § 626.556, subd. 10(c) (West Supp. 1993). Where the alleged abuse or neglect took place in a facility, however, the parents are to be notified prior to the interview of the child. *Id.* at subd. 10(b).
6. *Id.*, subd. 10(e).
7. Child welfare case management services are available to children at risk of out-of-home placement. Case managers help plan for and coordinate services to the child. M.S.A. § 256B.094 (West Supp. 1993).
8. M.S.A. § 256F.12 (West Supp. 1993).
9. M.S.A. § 256F.11 (West Supp. 1993).
10. Minn. R. 9560.0280, subp. 3 (1991).
11. *See* chapter 5A.15.
12. M.S.A. § 260.132 (West 1992).

be issued on an *ex parte* basis pending a full hearing,[13] may grant such relief as the court deems proper, including an order restraining any person from abusing the child or an order excluding the alleged abuser from the home.[14] If the agency determines that the child should be removed from the home, it must first offer the parents the opportunity to place the child voluntarily out of the home.[15] If the parents are unwilling or unable to cooperate, the agency may petition the court for immediate custody of the child,[16] or seek the assistance of a peace officer in taking the child into custody.[17] In either case, if the child is detained outside of the home, he or she must be placed in a shelter facility,[18] and a hearing must generally be held within 72 hours to determine whether the out-of-home placement should continue.[19] A child placed out of the home as an alleged victim of child abuse may not be given mental health treatment for the alleged abuse until the parents consent, the court finds probable cause to believe that the abuse occurred, or the court specifically orders the treatment.[20]

Disposition

After a hearing, if the court finds that the child is in need of protection or services,[21] it orders a disposition of the matter. Possible dispositions include

1. placing the child under protective supervision in his or her own home,

2. transferring legal custody of the child,

3. ordering special treatment or care for the child,

4. restraining acts of abuse,

5. excluding the abusing party from the home,

6. providing counseling or other social services for the family, or

7. ordering the abusing party to participate in treatment.

---

13. *Id.*, subd. 2. "*Ex parte*" means without the presence or notification of the parents or other interested parties.
14. *See* chapter 5A.7A for a discussion of proceedings brought by family members to exclude an abuser from the home or otherwise protect a child from abuse.
15. Minn. R. 9560.0280, subp. 2(E) (1991).
16. M.S.A. § 260.135, subd. 5; § 260.165, subd. 1 (West 1992).
17. M.S.A. § 260.135, subd. 1(c) (West 1992).
18. M.S.A. § 260.173, subd. 2 (West 1992).
19. M.S.A. § 260.172, subd. 1 (West 1992). The time period excludes Saturdays, Sundays, and holidays.
20. M.S.A. § 260.172, subd. 2b (West 1992).
21. *See generally* chapter 5A.15.

Additionally, the court will order a written *case plan*.[22] The case plan sets out the actions to be taken by the various parties and the services to be offered and provided by the social services agency. Dispositional orders are limited in duration to one year. They may be extended or modified at any time.[23]

---

22. M.S.A. § 260.191, subd. 1e (West 1992). *See* chapter 5A.15.
23. M.S.A. § 260.191, subd. 2 (West 1992).

5A.10

Termination of Parental Rights

Termination of parental rights is the ultimate tool available to the state to provide for the best interests of the child. It is a drastic step, reserved, in theory, for the most grave and weighty reasons.[1] A full panoply of judicial procedural protections, including appointment of counsel, is available to all parties including the parent(s) and child. Often, the request for termination comes only after the child has been found to be in need of protection and services[2] and removed from his or her home to a foster placement.[3] However, such an antecedent is not required, and the state could, in theory, move to terminate parental rights without such a preliminary determination.

Termination of parental rights is viewed as a last resort. Thus the court will look closely at whether the conditions alleged to support termination are likely to continue and at whether the social services agency has made appropriate efforts to support the reuniting of the family.[4] Termination of parental rights cases often involve MHPs to evaluate the mental health of the child, the capabilities of the parent(s), and the need for, suitability of, and prognosis for various therapeutic and supportive interventions.

In any proceeding dealing with the termination of parental rights, the best interests of the child must be the paramount consideration.[5]

---

1. Matter of Welfare of K.T., 327 N.W.2d 13 (1982).
2. See chapter 5A.15.
3. See chapter 5A.13.
4. M.S.A. § 260.221 (1988).
5. M.S.A. § 260.221, subd. 4 (West Supp. 1992).

Initiating the Process

Any reputable person, including agents of the commissioner of human services, who has knowledge of circumstances that indicate that the rights of a parent to a child should be terminated, may petition the juvenile court.[6] The petition shall be drafted by the county attorney upon the showing of reasonable grounds to support it.[7] The petition must state the names and addresses of and relationships among the various parties, in addition to the facts that allegedly show that the parental rights should be terminated.

Grounds for Termination

The court may terminate parental rights if it finds by clear and convincing evidence,[8] after a hearing, that one or more of the following conditions exist:[9]

1. The parent consents in writing to the termination and has "good cause" for the consent.[10]

2. The parent has abandoned the child. This is presumed when the parent has no contact or merely incidental contact for 6 or 12 months, depending on the child's age, and social services have made reasonable efforts to facilitate contact. The parent can rebut the presumption under certain circumstances, and the court can find abandonment under other conditions.

3. The parent has substantially, continuously, or repeatedly refused or neglected to comply with his or her parental duties and responsibilities, including a failure to provide necessary food, clothing, shelter, or education or to otherwise provide for the child's physical, mental, or emotional health and development. This ground for termination is available only if the parent is physically and financially able to comply with those duties and the social service agency has failed, after reasonable efforts, to correct the conditions.

---

6. M.S.A. § 269.231, subd. 1 (West Supp. 1992).
7. M.S.A. § 260.131, subd. 2 (West 1982).
8. The standard is "beyond a reasonable doubt" in cases governed by the Indian Child Welfare Act, 25 U.S.C. § 1912(f). *See* chapter 5A.15.
9. M.S.A. § 260.241 (West 1982); § 260.221 (West 1988).
10. In Matter of Welfare of K.T., 327 N.W.2d 13 (Minn. 1982), the Minnesota Supreme Court upheld a finding of "good cause" on grounds of the parent's lack of contact with the child and a parental belief that he or she was unable to financially support the child.

4. The parent has continuously failed to contribute to the child's support without good cause, if ordered and financially able to make such support payments.

5. The parent is unfit because of a consistent pattern of conduct or conditions that renders the parent unable to care appropriately for the ongoing physical, mental, or emotional needs of the child for the reasonably foreseeable future.

6. The child had previously been determined to be neglected, dependent, or in need of protection or services,[11] and reasonable efforts, under the direction of the court, have failed to correct the conditions leading to a determination of a child's need for protection or services. Reasonable efforts may be presumed to have failed when a child under 12 has resided out of the home under court order for more than one year following the determination of dependency, neglect, or "neglected and in foster care."[12] The court will also look at whether reasonable efforts have been made by the social service agency to rehabilitate the parent and reunite the family. Reasonable efforts may also be presumed to have failed under certain circumstances where the parent has failed or refused appropriate chemical dependency treatment.[13]

7. The parent has been convicted of causing the death of another of the parent's children.

8. The child is neglected and in foster care.[14]

In the case of an action involving an American Indian child, other provisions of the law may govern.[15]

Effect of Termination

If the court terminates parental rights of both parents (or of the only known living parent), the court shall order the guardianship

---

11. *See* chapter 5A.15.
12. *See* chapter 5A.15.
13. *See* chapter 5E.5.
14. *See* chapter 5A.15.
15. M.S.A. § 260.221, subd. 1 (West 1992). The Minnesota Indian Family Preservation Act, M.S.A. §§ 257.35 to 257.3579, governs certain voluntary foster care placements and child placement proceedings involving Indian children. The Indian Child Welfare Act, 25 U.S.C. §§ 1901 to 1923, controls termination proceedings to the extent that its provisions are inconsistent with Minnesota laws. M.S.A. § 260.221, subd. 1 (West 1992). The Indian Child Welfare Act provides that the court may not terminate parental rights unless the evidence proves "beyond a reasonable doubt," with testimony by "qualified expert witnesses," that the child is likely to suffer serious emotional or physical damage if parental rights are not terminated. 25 U.S.C § 1912(f). *See* chapter 5A.15.

and the legal custody of the child transferred to the commissioner of human services, a licensed child placing agency, or an individual who is willing and capable of assuming the appropriate duties and responsibilities to the child.[16] Termination of parental rights severs all rights, powers, privileges, immunities, duties, and obligations, including any rights to custody, control, visitation, or support existing between parent and child.[17]

In ordering guardianship or transferring legal custody of a child with respect to whom parental rights have been terminated, the court must comply with the provisions of law designed to protect the heritage and ethnic background of the child.[18]

---

16. M.S.A. § 260.242, subd. 1 (West Supp. 1992).
17. M.S.A. § 260.241, subd. 1 (West 1982).
18. M.S.A. § 260.241, subd. 1a, referring to M.S.A. § 260.181, subd. 3. *See* discussion in chapter 5A.15. The Indian Child Welfare Act of 1978 governs the placement of Indian children. This is also discussed in chapter 5A.15.

5A.11

Guardianship for Minors

A guardian may be appointed for a minor when the minor is deprived of parental care by death or judicial action.[1] Guardianships may be created in three ways: through a "testamentary appointment" in the will of a parent, by appointment made by the probate court, or by appointment made by the juvenile court.[2] Guardianship of minors is of importance to MHPs in two ways. MHPs may be involved in the procedures leading up to the appointment of a guardian for a child, either in the process of terminating the child's parents' rights or in evaluating the suitability of candidates to become guardian. MHPs may also be in the position of providing services to a child who is under guardianship. In such circumstances, the MHP must be aware of issues surrounding the guardian's power to give or withhold consent to the minor's treatment.[3]

Guardianship for adults is discussed in chapters 5A.2 and 5E.7. The closely related concept of conservatorship for minors is discussed in chapter 5A.12.

Testamentary Appointment[4]

A parent may, in his or her will, appoint a guardian of his or her unmarried minor child. The appointment becomes effective upon the filing of the guardian's acceptance with the court probating

1. *See* chapter 5A.10.
2. *See* chapter 5A.10.
3. *See also* chapter 5A.19.
4. M.S.A. § 525.6155 (West Supp. 1992).

the will. The acceptance must take place after the death of both parents, or after the death of one parent where the surviving parent has been adjudged incapacitated. The appointment is blocked, however, if the minor (14 or more years of age) or an interested adult files a timely objection with the court.[5] If such an objection is filed, a guardian may be appointed, but only after a petition and hearing before the court.[6] Upon acceptance, the guardian must give notice within five days to the minor, the person previously caring for the minor, and the minor's adult siblings, grandparents, aunts, and uncles.[7] The appointment is finalized when the guardian files an acceptance in the court in which the will is probated.

Appointment by the Probate Court

The second method of appointment is by a formal court hearing that has been convened because a person interested in the child's welfare has petitioned the court requesting that a guardian be appointed.[8]

The court has jurisdiction to appoint a guardian if all parental rights of custody have been terminated or suspended by prior court order or if the appointment in a will has been nullified by objection, as discussed above.[9] Priority is given to any candidate nominated by the minor, if the minor is 14 years of age or older, unless the court finds that the appointment would be contrary to the best interests of the minor.[10]

Guardians of minors have the powers and responsibilities of parents, except that guardians are not legally obligated to provide their own funds for the children and are not liable to third persons for acts of the children.[11] The law further specifies that the guardian must

1. take reasonable care of the child's personal effects;
2. receive money payable for support of the child;[12]

---

5. M.S.A. § 525.616 (West Supp. 1992).
6. M.S.A. § 525.618 (West Supp. 1992). The court may, in such a proceeding, appoint the person named in the will despite the filed objections. M.S.A. § 525.616 (West Supp. 1992).
7. M.S.A. § 525.6155 (West Supp. 1992).
8. M.S.A. § 525.6165 et seq.
9. *Id.*
10. M.S.A. § 525.6175 (West Supp. 1992).
11. M.S.A. § 525.619 (West Supp. 1992).
12. Generally, a minor's guardian has charge of the finances of the child relative to his or her current support. Managing the child's estate, if there is one, is the work of a conservator, if there is one. *See* M.S.A. § 525.619(b) (West Supp. 1992) and chapter 5A.12.

3. facilitate the child's education and social and other activities;

4. authorize medical or other professional care, treatment, and advice;[13] and

5. report on the condition of the children as specified by court order.

A guardian's authority and responsibility terminate upon the death, resignation, or removal of the guardian; upon the child's death, adoption, or marriage; or when the child reaches 18 years of age.[14] A child over 14 years old, or an interested adult, may petition for removal of the guardian on the ground that removal would be in the best interests of the child. The court considers the matter in a hearing and may appoint a new guardian.

Appointment by the Juvenile Court

A juvenile court has the authority to appoint a guardian and transfer legal custody of a child under two circumstances: after it has terminated the parental rights of both parents,[15] or if, upon a petition, it finds that both of the parents are deceased and that no guardian has been appointed by the probate court, as described above.[16] In either case, the court may transfer guardianship and legal custody to the commissioner of human services,[17] a licensed placing agency, or an individual who is willing and able to assume the duties of a guardianship. In ordering a guardianship and transferring legal custody, the court must act to preserve the racial or ethnic heritage of the child and the expressed religious preference of the parents.[18]

---

13. A guardian may admit a ward under the age of 16 to a treatment facility as an informal patient for mental health, mental retardation, or chemical dependency treatment, but the ward may not be committed to any state institution except pursuant to the civil commitment laws. See chapter 5A.19 and section 5E. The guardian is not authorized to give consent to psychosurgery, electroshock, sterilization, or experimental treatment unless the procedure is first approved by court order. See chapter 5A.2 for a discussion of the procedures to be followed to obtain such an order. See M.S.A. § 525.56, subd. 3.

14. M.S.A. § 525.6192 (West Supp. 1992).

15. M.S.A. § 260.242, subd. 1 (West Supp. 1992). See chapter 5A.15.

16. M.S.A. § 260.242, subd. 1b (West Supp. 1992).

17. The commissioner may delegate his or her authority to the welfare board of the county in which the ward resides. M.S.A. § 260.242 (West Supp. 1992).

18. Id., subd. 1a. See M.S.A. § 260.181, subd. 3 (West 1992), which establishes an order of "preference" for the transfer of legal custody or the appointment of a guardian under the laws relating to juvenile courts. The order of preferences is (1) a relative of the child, (2) a person of the same racial or ethnic heritage as the child, and (3) a person who is knowledgeable and appreciative of the child's racial and ethnic heritage. The court is to attempt to follow any religious preferences expressed by the child's genetic parents.

A guardian appointed by the juvenile court has legal custody of the child unless the court awards custody to another person. *Legal custody* means the right to the "care, custody and control" of the child.[19] In addition to exercising legal custody, the guardian has the authority to make "major decisions affecting the person of the ward," including giving consent to marriage; enlistment in the armed forces; medical, surgical, or psychiatric treatment;[20] or adoption. A guardianship created by the juvenile court does not include guardianship of the estate of the ward.[21]

The guardian may be removed and a new guardian appointed by the court. The court may discharge the guardianship upon a showing that the minor is emancipated.[22] Under appropriate circumstances, the guardianship may be transferred to the minor's foster parents.[23]

---

19. M.S.A. § 260.015 (West 1992).
20. The juvenile court-appointed guardian's authority to consent to psychosurgery, electroshock, sterilization, or experimental treatment is not explicitly limited by the juvenile court act. Other provisions of the law impose such limitations on guardians, and it may be assumed that a juvenile court guardian's authority is similarly limited. *See* above and M.S.A. § 525.619 (West Supp. 1992). The guardian's authority to admit his or her minor ward for mental health treatment may also be limited. *See* chapter 5A.19.
21. M.S.A. § 260.242 (West 1992). *See* chapter 5A.12.
22. In general, a minor is emancipated if he or she is totally self-supporting. *See* Black's Law Dictionary 521 (6th ed. 1990). Under Minnesota law, emancipation is defined in a number of particular contexts. *See, e.g.*, M.S.A. § 256D.05 (West 1992) (in the context of eligibility for general assistance benefits); § 144.341 (West 1989) (in the context of consent for health care services). *See* chapter 5A.19.
23. *See* chapter 5A.13.

5A.12

Conservatorship for Minors

Conservators are appointed to manage and protect the estates (e.g., money, property, business affairs) of minors. Although the appointment depends primarily on a financial determination, MHPs may be asked to determine whether minors are capable of handling their own estates.[1]

Procedures

Application for Conservatorship

Any person may petition for appointment of a conservator.[2] The petition must include[3]

1. the name, date of birth, and address of the person to be protected;

2. the names and addresses of living parents, siblings, and nearest kindred;

3. the conservator's name, age, address, and occupation;

4. a statement of the powers that the petitioner believes to be necessary to protect and supervise the minor's property;

5. the value of the minor's property or debts; and

6. reasons why appointment of a conservatorship is necessary.

---

1. *See* chapter 5A.11 for a discussion of guardianship for minors.
2. M.S.A. § 525.541 (West Supp. 1992).
3. M.S.A. § 525.542, subd. 1 (West Supp. 1992).

After receiving a petition, the court will set a date for the hearing. Within 14 days, the petitioner must give notice to all persons who require notice in a guardianship hearing.[4]

First, the court will determine whether the minor owns money or property that requires management or protection. It will also consider any business affairs of the minor that may be jeopardized or prevented by that person's minority status. A conservator may also be required if the court finds a need to protect the funds necessary for the support or education of the minor.[5] If the court determines that the welfare and the best interests of the minor will be served, it will make the appointment.[6] If the minor's interests are not adequately represented in the proceeding, the court may appoint an attorney to represent the minor.[7]

Powers and Duties of the Conservator

The court may grant very broad authority to the conservator, including the following:[8]

1. the duty to pay the reasonable costs for the support, maintenance, and education of the minor. Wherever possible, the conservator should meet these requirements through government benefits or services to which the conservatee is entitled, rather than from the conservatee's estate. Conservators have no duty to pay money from their own funds;

2. the duty to pay all of the minor's debts from the minor's estate;

3. the duty collect all debts or claims in favor of the minor;

4. the duty to invest any extra funds; and

5. the duty to pay the minor a reasonable allowance for personal use.[9]

The conservator is also required to file an annual account concerning any financial transactions during that year.[10] The account should detail all property received and disbursed, the property on hand, the present address of the minor, the conserva-

---

4. M.S.A. § 525.55, subd. 1 (West Supp. 1992). *See* chapter 5A.11.
5. M.S.A. § 525.6198 (West Supp. 1992).
6. M.S.A. § 525.618, subd. 2 (West Supp. 1992).
7. *Id.*
8. M.S.A. §§ 525.6198(2), 525.56, subd. 4 (West Supp. 1992).
9. M.S.A. § 525.583 (West Supp. 1992) (upon court approval).
10. M.S.A. § 525.58, subd. 1 (West Supp. 1992).

tor's address, the names and addresses of any sureties, and the total amount of any investments.

If the court determines that there has been any mismanagement or misconduct by the conservator regarding the minor's funds, it may move to discharge the conservator.[11] Any interested person may also make a motion to discharge the conservator. The conservator will be held liable for any shortage of funds. A new conservator can be appointed according to the procedure described above.

---

11. M.S.A. § 525.582 (West Supp. 1992).

5A.13

Foster Care for Children

Foster care provides residential housing and support under the supervision of the Department of Human Services for children and adults who are unable to live in their own homes. MHPs may be involved in the licensing of a home, in the ongoing training provided to foster families, in the development and monitoring of the placement plan, and in providing assessments and therapeutic services to those placed in foster care.

This chapter discusses foster home services for children. There are three important aspects to the provision of these services to children: first, licensing requirements for the homes; second, the provision of services to children in foster placement; and third, the role of the courts in supervising foster placement.

Licensing Requirements[1]

A foster family home (FFH) must be licensed by the Department of Human Services. Licenses will not be issued to an applicant where any member of the household has been convicted of a felony or an offense involving moral turpitude within the past five years; where there is substantial evidence of or a conviction for assault, child abuse, or neglect; or where there are ongoing chemical dependency issues.

The personal qualities of FFH applicants are extremely important because children who are placed there are often emotionally, mentally, or physically handicapped and need stable and understanding families. The FFH applicants need to be kind,

---

1. Minn. R. 9545.0010–0190 (1991 and Supp. 1992).

mature, and responsible people with a genuine liking for children. To protect children in foster care and assure them the maximum opportunities for growth and development, each FFH will be evaluated on its ability to meet the emotional needs of the children placed there; to deal with its own emotions; to provide positive guidance, care, and training; to use discipline in a constructive way; to have good problem-solving abilities; and to work cooperatively with the foster child's own family and with community resources.

In addition, FFH applicants must be in good physical health and must provide a statement from their physicians verifying a physical examination within six months showing that they are physically able to provide care to children. The licensing agency may also require an evaluation of the applicant by a mental health specialist when anyone in the home exhibits a mental health problem.

FFHs may be specially licensed as emergency shelter homes or as special services homes. Regardless of the type of FFH, all foster care providers must participate in training to develop and enhance their skills and ability to provide the highest quality of services to children. Training opportunities can include child and adolescent development, methods of discipline, communication skills, home safety, and human sexuality. In addition, a foster family home must comply with the licensing agency's requirements as to appropriate and acceptable discipline in order to protect children from any potential physical or psychological abuse. Finally, FFH providers must maintain a clean and safe physical environment and are subject to the regulations of the licensing agency.

Services for Children in Foster Homes[2]

In all foster home placements, the local social service agency must prepare a written case plan for the child.[3] The case placement plan includes an assessment of the child's family, including the problems leading to the placement in foster care, and an agreement and plan by which the problems will be eliminated. Such planning usually includes the social service agency, the parents, the child, and the foster family.

---

2. Minn. R. 9560.0500–0670 (1991).
3. M.S.A. § 257.071, subd. 1 (West Supp. 1993).

Prior to placing a child in foster care, the local social service agency must obtain either the written consent of the parents (voluntary placement) or a court order (legal custody). All foster placements must be reviewed by an administrative panel at least once every six months.[4] The review must determine (a) whether the placement remains necessary and appropriate, (b) the extent of compliance with the case plan, (c) the progress made toward overcoming the problems which led to the placement, and (d) the likely date of return to the home or placement for legal adoption. In certain circumstances, a "dispositional hearing" by the juvenile court can take the place of the administrative review.[5]

The child-placing agency must ensure that the child's best interests are protected by giving due, but not sole, regard to the child's racial or ethnic heritage in making the placement.[6]

The placing agency is responsible for seeing that the health and dental needs of the child are met by ensuring that each child has had a health examination prior to the placement and that ongoing medical and dental needs are met. In all placements, the social service agency will provide at least one visit for the child to the foster home prior to placement. The agency will also provide help to the child in his or her initial adjustment to the foster home by visiting the child in the foster home, arranging for the parents to visit the child within a week of the placement, and providing ongoing visits and social services to the child throughout the placement. The social service agency will also provide assistance to the foster parents during the placement. Finally, upon the child's return home, the agency will provide follow-up services to the family and the child to help in the transition back home and to prevent the recurrence of the circumstances which led to the placement in foster care.

The social services agency must seek the written consent of the child's parents for major decisions affecting the child. It must coordinate with other agencies, including schools, in the planning for the child.

---

4. *Id.*, subd. 2.
5. M.S.A. § 257.071, subd. 2 (West Supp. 1993).
6. *Id.*, subd. 1a. Where a child of color is placed in a foster home with a different racial or ethnic background, the placement must be reviewed every 30 days. Placement of American Indian children in foster homes is governed by the Indian Child Act of 1978. This act, which reserves jurisdiction for tribal courts in some circumstances and mandates preference for placement of Indian children in Indian homes, 25 U.S.C. §§ 1911, 1915, is discussed more fully in chapter 5A.15.

Supervision By The Court

The nature of court supervision depends on whether the child has been placed in foster care voluntarily or pursuant to court order. If the placement was by order of the court, the social service agency must petition the court periodically for a dispositional hearing to review the appropriateness of the placement.[7]

If the child has been placed voluntarily by the parents, a more complicated set of rules governs court supervision of the placement. Embodied in these rules is the concern that children may be placed in foster homes and then forgotten or abandoned for long periods of time. Court supervision is necessary, even where the placement is voluntary, to ensure that the child's interests are adequately protected.

The general rule is that after 12 months of voluntary placement in a foster home, the social service agency must either return the child to his or her parents' home or file a petition with the court alleging either that the child is in need of protection or services[8] or that parental rights should be terminated.[9] If a petition is filed, the court reviews the child's situation and makes one of three dispositional orders: (a) If the court finds that the placement meets the child's needs and that the child will be returned home in six months, it approves of the placement and continues the matter for six months to assure the child's return home.[10] (b) If the court finds that the child's needs are not being met, it may order the social service agency or the parents to take steps to correct the situation.[11] (c) If the court finds that the child has been abandoned by his or her parents, it orders the social service agency to bring a petition alleging that the child is in need of protection or services or seeking to terminate parental rights.[12]

Different rules apply to children who are developmentally disabled or emotionally handicapped. If such a child has been placed voluntarily by the parents because of the child's handicapping condition or need for long-term residential treatment or supervision, the social service agency brings a petition to review

---

7. Minn. R. 9560.0610, subp. 5 (1991). The time period for review is, in general, every 12 months, M.S.A. § 260.191, subd. 2 (West Supp. 1992) (dispositional orders limited to one year in duration). For children whose parents' rights have been terminated (*see* chapter 5A.10), review must take place within 18 months of placement, and every two years thereafter. M.S.A. § 260.242, subd. 2(d) (West 1992). If the court determines that the special needs of the child in the latter circumstances are met through permanent or long-term foster care placement, no subsequent dispositional hearings are required.
8. *See* chapter 5A.15.
9. M.S.A. § 257.071 subd. 3 (West Supp. 1992). *See* chapter 5A.10.
10. M.S.A. § 260.192 (West Supp. 1993).
11. *Id.*
12. *Id.*

the foster placement (rather than a petition alleging that the child is neglected). This review must be sought within 18 months of the placement (for developmentally disabled children) or within 6 months of the placement (for emotionally handicapped children). Dispositions after this review are similar to those described above.

Adoption

The primary goal of the Minnesota adoption program is to ensure for children who are free to be legally adopted in the state suitable adoptive homes and agency services supportive of their integration into new families.[1] The adoptions law covers four major topics: (a) determining whether a child is properly available for adoption, (b) ensuring that the adoptive family is suitable, (c) providing subsidies to help support adopted children with special needs, and (d) specifying the types of information that are available after the adoption to the adopted child and his or her genetic parents.

The most direct contribution of MHPs to the process of adoption is in the assessment of the suitability of the adoptive family. MHPs may also be involved in determining whether the adoptive child has special needs and in assessing those needs. Other potential roles for MHPs include counseling those involved about the implications of adoption and assessing the competency of the biological parents to give consent to adoption.

Adoption Requirements—Adoptee

In general, no child may be adopted without the consent of the child's parents.[2] Where the adoptive child is over 14, his or her consent must be obtained as well. Where the commissioner of human services or an agency has authority to place the child for

---

1. Minn. R. 9560.0010–0180 (1991).
2. M.S.A. § 259.24 (West Supp. 1992). If the parent is an unmarried minor, the consent of the parent's parents or guardian is also required.

adoption, the consent of the commissioner or agency is required. Consents must satisfy certain formal requirements and may, under limited circumstances and time requirements, be withdrawn.[3] There are significant exceptions to this rule. No consent is required of parents who meet any of the following criteria:[4] (a) parents whose parental rights have been terminated;[5] (b) parents who have abandoned the child or who have lost custody of the child through a divorce decree, and who have been given notice of the adoption petition; or (3) parents whose names do not appear on the child's birth certificate, who have not substantially supported the child, who were neither married to the natural mother nor living openly with the child or the natural mother of the child, and who have not been adjudicated the child's parent nor have filed an affidavit stating an intention to retain parental rights.[6]

In dealing with situations involving minor parents, the agency overseeing the proceedings must ensure that the minor parent has the opportunity to consult with an attorney, a member of the clergy, or a physician before consenting to the adoption of the child.

In general, adoption can proceed only where the child has been placed by the commissioner, the commissioner's agent, or a licensed child-placing agency.[7]

Adoption Requirements–Adoptive Family

Once the child is legally free to be adopted, the commissioner, child-placing agency, or county welfare department must perform a suitability study on the potential adoptive home.[8]

The suitability study of the potential adoptive home includes preadoptive counseling and an evaluation to determine whether the home can adequately parent and meet the social, educational,

---

3. M.S.A. § 259.24, subd. 1 (West Supp. 1992). Consent may be withdrawn by a parent for any reason within 10 working days after the consent has been given. After the 10th day, the consent becomes irrevocable, except if the court finds that the consent was obtained by fraud.
4. M.S.A. § 259.24, subd. 1 (West Supp. 1992).
5. See chapter 5A.10 regarding termination of parental rights.
6. The affidavit is described in M.S.A. § 259.261 (West 1992).
7. M.S.A. § 259.22, subd. 2 (West Supp. 1992). There are exceptions to this requirement. See Minn. R. 9560.0120 (1991) for a discussion of procedures the Department of Human Resources follows where there has been a waiver by the court of this requirement or where the parties involved have made an independent placement.
8. M.S.A. § 259.27 (West Supp. 1992).

and health needs of a particular child. The minimum standards governing such suitability are[9] that the applicant be primarily motivated to meet the child's needs; be emotionally mature, with healthy interpersonal relationships; be in good physical and mental health; and be able to adequately support and parent a child in a healthy and secure environment. The applicant must also have the capacity to accept and incorporate into the applicant's family a child born to other parents and to assist the child in understanding his or her genetic background and adoption.

If desiring to adopt a child of minority race or ethnic heritage, the applicant must be able to demonstrate an understanding and appreciation of the heritage and be able to assist the child with it. It is the policy of the state to ensure that the best interests of the child are met by requiring due, not sole, consideration of the child's minority race or ethnic heritage in adoption placements.[10] Special effort must be made to recruit adoptive families of the same race or ethnic heritage as the child.[11]

Prospective adoptive parents deemed unsuitable by the local agency will be informed of that decision in writing. Notice is sent after the agency has counseled the family on the relevant facts upon which the decision was based. Such determinations may be further reviewed by the agency upon the written request of the applicant.[12]

Final Decree

Upon receipt of the final report and recommendations, if the court finds that it is in the best interests of the child that the petition be

---

9. Minn. R. 9560.0140 (1991). Where the potential adoptive home is the child's current foster home, additional criteria are applied. Minn. R. 9560.0050 (1991). Generally, foster homes will be considered only if the child has special needs, is older than an infant, has lived at least 12 consecutive months with the foster family, and is an integrated member of the foster family.
10. M.S.A. § 259.255 (West Supp. 1993). The child-placing agency must give preference, in the absence of good cause, to placing the child with a relative, a family with the same racial or ethnic heritage, or a family that is knowledgeable and appreciative of the child's racial or ethnic heritage. Where the child's genetic parents explicitly request that this preference list not be followed or that the religious background of the child be matched with adoptive parents, the agency is required to honor those requests, if they are consistent with the child's best interests. Placement of American Indian children for adoption is governed by the Indian Child Welfare Act of 1978. See M.S.A. § 260.157 (West Supp. 1993). This act, which reserves jurisdiction for tribal courts in some circumstances and mandates preference for placement of Indian children in Indian homes, 25 U.S.C. §§ 1911, 1915, is discussed more fully in chapter 5A.15.
11. M.S.A. § 259.455 (West Supp. 1993).
12. Minn. R. 9560.0140, subp. 3 (1991).

granted, a decree of adoption will be made and the court will order that the child shall from then on be the child of the petitioner(s). Upon legally adopting a child, adoptive parents become the legal parents of the child and assume all rights and responsibilities of birth parents.[13] The responsibilities include providing for the child's financial support and caring for health, emotional, and behavioral problems.

Subsidized Adoptions

Adoption subsidy is a program that provides financial assistance to the adoptive parents because of the special needs of a child who is certified as eligible for subsidy. A child can be eligible if[14] a placement agency has made reasonable efforts to place the child for adoption without subsidy but has been unsuccessful; or if the child's foster parents want to adopt the child and it is in the child's best interests, and because of the child's circumstances or characteristics it would be difficult to provide an adoptive home without such a subsidy. In addition, the child must be a Minnesota resident and a ward of the Department of Human Services or licensed child-placing agency. The placing agency may determine that a subsidy is needed for children placed as sibling groups; children entitled to placement with a family of similar ethnic background; or children with special needs, such as medical, dental, and surgical expenses, psychiatric and psychological expenses, maintenance costs, or other costs necessary for the child's care and well-being. In determining the amount of the subsidy, consideration is given to financial resources, social security and veteran benefits, health insurance coverage, medical assistance programs, and other resources that may be available to the child.

---

13. M.S.A. § 259.29 (West Supp. 1992). In particular, the child gains inheritance rights that are the same as if he or she were the "natural" child of the parents. The natural parents of the adopted child are relieved of all parental responsibilities and rights over the child and his or her property. *Id*. Different rules apply where the adoptive parent is a stepparent. *Id*., subd. 1a. Furthermore, the adoption of a child whose natural parents are enrolled in an American Indian tribe does not change the child's enrollment status. *Id*., subd. 2.
14. M.S.A. § 259.40 (West Supp. 1992).

Sharing of Information About Genetic Parents and Adopted Children

The law contains a number of provisions for the sharing of information about and between genetic parent and child, even after the finalization of the adoption. These rules modify the traditional approach, which was to sever that relationship permanently and entirely. They serve several purposes. They are designed to share information that may be of importance to the health of the child or parent. They are also designed to serve the emotional needs of some adopted children who, when they reach adulthood, have a desire to learn about their genetic heritage.[15]

---

15. M.S.A. § 259.253 (West Supp. 1992); § 259.49 (West Supp. 1992); Minn. R. 9560.0180 (1991). *See also* 25 U.S.C. § 1917 (American Indian individuals who were the subjects of adoption proceedings have the right to learn of the tribal affiliations of their biological parents).

5A.15

Children in Need of Protection or Services, Neglected and in Foster Care, and Delinquent

A core function of the juvenile court is to take jurisdiction over cases involving children that potentially require the intervention of the state. State intervention may be sought to protect the child, to protect the public, or both. This chapter discusses the role of the juvenile court where the child is brought before it because the child's needs or safety are not being assured or because the child has engaged in behavior that is considered undesirable.

Generally, the court is required to attempt to remedy these problems in a way that is consistent with the child's continuing connection with his or her family. Where the needs of the child seem inconsistent with the continued relationship with his or her parents, the court may consider terminating the parents' rights over the child. This procedure is discussed in chapter 5A.10. Other juvenile court proceedings are dealt with separately in this volume.[1]

MHPs often play important roles in juvenile court. They assess the needs of children; determine whether those needs are being met; design, implement, and evaluate treatment programs and services; and evaluate the child's potential for danger to the public and the needs for supervision arising from that danger.

---

1. Proceedings governing adoption are dealt with in chapter 5A.14; those dealing with guardianship, in chapter 5A.11; those with conservatorship, in chapter 5A.12; those with abused and neglected children, in chapter 5A.9; those with mental health treatment for juveniles, in chapter 5A.19.

General Policies Underlying Juvenile Court Intervention

Juvenile court intervention operates in a tension between important and sometimes conflicting societal values. On the one hand, our society values the privacy of the family unit and the right of parents to raise their children as they see fit. Equally, we recognize an interest in liberty, shared by adults and children. Sometimes in tension with these two values are the society's rights to protect its vulnerable members—including children—and to protect itself. The law governing juvenile courts is designed to respect, where possible, all of these fundamental values.

Where a child is under the jurisdiction of the court because the child is in need of protection or services, the court must ensure that reasonable efforts (including culturally appropriate services by the social service agency) are made to prevent placement out of the home. Where removal is necessary, the court must assure that reasonable efforts are made to eliminate the need for removal and to reunite the child with the child's family at the earliest possible time, consistent with the best interests, safety, and protection of the child.[2] In all circumstances, the services must be culturally appropriate. Where the child is before the court on a delinquency petition, the court has similar obligations, but they are tempered by its obligation to protect the safety of the public.[3]

Terms and Definitions[4]

Before considering how the law operates, it is important to understand the terms the law uses and their legal meanings:

1. *Child in need of protection or services* means a child who is in need of protection or services because the child

    a. is abandoned or without parent, guardian, or custodian;

    b. has been a victim of physical or sexual abuse; resides with a victim or perpetrator of domestic child abuse; or is the victim of emotional maltreatment;[5]

---

2. M.S.A. § 260.012(a) (West 1992). Where the child is an American Indian child, the court must document its compliance with the Indian Child Welfare Act of 1978, 25 U.S.C. § 1901 et seq. *See* discussion below.
3. M.S.A. § 260.012(a) (West 1992).
4. M.S.A. § 260.015 (West 1992).
5. *Emotional maltreatment* means "consistent, deliberate infliction of mental harm on a child" that has an "observable, sustained, and adverse effect on the child's physical, mental, or emotional development." M.S.A. § 260.015, subd. 5a (West 1992).

c. is without necessary food, clothing, shelter, or other required care for the child's physical or mental health or morals because the child's parent is unable or unwilling to provide that care;

d. is without the special care made necessary by a physical, mental, or emotional condition because the child's parent is unable or unwilling to provide that care;

e. is medically neglected;[6]

f. is one whose parent for good cause desires to be relieved of the child's care and custody;

g. has been placed for adoption or care in violation of law;

h. is without proper parental care because of the emotional, mental, or physical disability or state of immaturity of the child's parent;

i. is one whose occupation, behavior, condition, environment, or associations are such as to be injurious or dangerous to the child or others;

j. has committed a delinquent act before age 10;

k. is a runaway; or

l. is a habitual truant.

2. A child who is *neglected and in foster care* means a child who has been placed in foster care by court order, who cannot be returned to his or her parent, and whose parents, despite the availability of appropriate services, have failed to adjust their circumstances so that the child can be returned to them, or have willfully failed to visit the child or provide financial support for the child.[7]

3. *Delinquent child* means a child who

a. has violated any state or local law, not including runaways, habitual truants, or juvenile alcohol or controlled substance offenders;

b. has violated a federal law or law of another state if the violation would be an act of delinquency if committed in this state or a crime if committed by an adult; or

---

6. The term "medically neglected" includes the withholding of medically indicated treatment from a disabled infant with a life-threatening condition. Where the child is irreversibly comatose, the treatment would be inhumane and futile, or it would merely prolong the dying of the infant without ameliorating the life-threatening conditions, the definition is limited to the failure to provide nutrition, hydration, and medication. M.S.A. § 260.015, subd. 2a(5) (West 1992).

7. M.S.A. § 260.015, subd. 18 (West 1992).

c. has escaped from confinement to a state juvenile correctional facility.

Judicial Procedures

Petition[8]

Juvenile court proceedings are commenced by petition. In theory, any "reputable person" may bring the petition. In practice, petitions are most often brought by social service workers. Once the petition is filed with the court and the court exercises jurisdiction over the matter, a hearing will be scheduled. The court will issue a summons and notice to the child and to the parents to appear before the court as stated. The court may also subpoena any other person who may be needed to appear at the hearing. The court may continue or adjourn the hearings and may make any orders it deems to be in the best interests of the child.

Rights[9]

The child who is the subject of the petition and the child's parents have a right to participate in all proceedings and have the right to legal counsel, paid for by the government if necessary. The court will appoint a "guardian *ad litem*" to protect the child's interests if it appears that the child is without a parent or guardian, the parent is incompetent, or the parent is indifferent or hostile to the child's interests, or if any of the conditions under the definition of a "child in need of protection or services" are present. Appointment of a guardian *ad litem* may be waived by the court if an attorney is appointed or retained for the child.[10] Often, guardians *ad litem* undertake an independent investigation of the child's circumstances and make a recommendation to the court concerning the disposition of the matter.[11]

Detention Hearings[12]

A detention hearing must be held within 36 or 72 hours (depending on the circumstances under which the child was taken into custody) of a child being taken into custody to determine whether the child should remain in custody. Unless there is reason to believe that the child would endanger self or others or would run away from the parent or guardian or that the child's health or welfare would be immediately endangered, the child will be released to the custody of the parent or other suitable person.

---

8. M.S.A. § 260.131 (West 1992).
9. M.S.A. § 260.155, subds. 2, 4 (West 1992).
10. M.S.A. § 260.155, subd. 4(b) (West 1992).
11. Minn. R. P. Juv. Ct. 39.04.
12. M.S.A. § 260.172, subd. 1 (West 1992).

Dispositional Phase[13]

Final disposition will depend on whether the child is found to be delinquent or in need of protection or services.[14] Before making a disposition in a case, the court may consider any report and recommendations made by the county welfare board, probation officer, licensed child-placing agency, or guardian *ad litem*, or any other information deemed material by the court. At any stage of the juvenile court process, the court may request that the county welfare board or probation officer investigate the personal and family history and environment of the child. The court may also order the child under its jurisdiction to be examined by a qualified physician, psychiatrist, or psychologist appointed by the court.[15]

Delinquent Child

If the court finds the child to be delinquent, it may order any of the following that are deemed necessary to rehabilitate the child:[16]

1. counsel the child or parents;

2. place the child under the supervision of a probation officer under conditions including reasonable rules for conduct designed for the physical, mental, and moral well-being and behavior of the child;

3. transfer legal custody of the child to a child-placing agency, the county welfare board, a reputable individual of good moral character, a county home school, or a probation officer for placement in a group foster home;[17]

4. order the child to make reasonable restitution for any property damage;

5. impose a fine of up to $700;

---

13. M.S.A. § 260.181, subd. 2 (West 1992).
14. Disposition where the child is found to be neglected in foster care is discussed in chapter 5A.13.
15. M.S.A. § 260.151, subd. 1 (West 1992).
16. M.S.A. § 260.185, subd. 1 (West 1992).
17. In transferring custody of a child and in placing the child in foster care, the juvenile court and social service agencies are governed by a set of preferences designed to protect racial, ethnic, and religious heritage. Due, but not sole, consideration must be given to the child's race or ethnic heritage. The child must be placed in the following order of preference: with family members or relatives, a person of the same racial or ethnic heritage as the child, or someone who is knowledgeable and appreciative of the child's racial or ethnic heritage. M.S.A. § 260.181, subd. 3 (West 1993). The child's parents may request that the child be placed in a way that preserves his or her religious affiliation or that none of the preferences listed be followed. If it is consistent with the child's best interests, the court must honor that request.

6. order the child's parents to provide special treatment and care for reasons of physical or mental health;

7. cancel the child's driver's license until his or her 18th birthday, if it would be in the best interests of the child and of public safety; or

8. order, in cases involving sexual offenses, a professional assessment of the child's need for sex offender treatment, and, if indicated in the report, order that the child undergo such treatment.

Child in Need of Protection or Services

If the court finds that the child is in need of protection or services, it may order any of the following:[18]

1. place the child under the protective supervision of the county welfare board or child-placing agency under conditions prescribed by the court;

2. transfer legal custody to a child-placing agency or county welfare board;[19]

3. order the child's parents to provide special treatment and care for reasons of physical or mental health; or, if the parents do not provide it, the court may order it provided; or

4. order that the child 16 years or older be allowed to live independently if the child has sufficient maturity and judgment and if the court believes it is in the child's best interests.

If the child is adjudicated in need of protection or services because the child is a runaway or habitual truant, the court may also order any of the following:[20]

1. counsel the child or parents;

2. place the child under the supervision of a probation officer or other suitable person in the child's home under conditions prescribed by the court, including reasonable rules for the child's conduct and the conduct of the parents, designed for the physical, mental, and moral well-being and behavior of the child;

3. transfer legal custody of the child to a reputable person of good moral character, or a county probation officer for placement in a group foster home;

---

18. M.S.A. § 260.191, subd. 1 (West 1992). The standard of proof is "clear and convincing evidence." M.S.A. § 260.155, subd. 1 (West Supp. 1993).

19. In placing a child whose legal custody has been transferred, the agency or board must follow the principles of protection of racial or ethnic heritage and religious affiliation. *See supra* note 17.

20. M.S.A. § 260.191, subd. 1(b) (West 1992).

4. require the child to pay a fine of up to $100;

5. require the child to participate in a community service project;

6. order the child to undergo a chemical dependency evaluation and, if warranted by the evaluation, order participation by the child in a drug awareness program or an inpatient or outpatient chemical dependency treatment program;

7. cancel the child's driver's license for any period up to the child's 18th birthday, if the court believes it is in the best interests of the child and of public safety; or

8. require the child to perform any other activities or participate in any other treatment programs deemed appropriate by the court.

In any of the above circumstances, the order must also include reasons to support why the best interests of the child are being served by the disposition ordered, and what alternatives were considered by the court and why they were not appropriate in the case at hand. For each disposition ordered, the court will also order the appropriate agency to prepare a written case plan developed with the child and the child's parent that will specify the actions to be taken by the child and parent.[21] If the court places the child in a residential facility, the court must review the placement at least once every six months.[22]

Permanency Planning Determination

If a child is placed by the court in a residential facility, the court must conduct a hearing to determine what permanent placement is consistent with the child's best interests.[23] Generally, the hearing must be held no more than 12 months after the child has been removed from the home, but the time can be extended under certain circumstances. At the hearing, the court determines whether the child is to be returned home. If not, then the court must determine what permanent placement is consistent with the child's best interests. Dispositions available if the child is not to be returned home are permanent legal and physical custody to a relative, adoption,[24] or permanent foster care.[25] Permanent foster care may be ordered only if the court finds that other dispositions are not possible.

21. M.S.A. § 260.191, subd. 1(e) (West 1992).
22. M.S.A. § 260.191, subd. 3a (West Supp. 1993).
23. M.S.A. § 260.191, subd. 3b (West Supp. 1993).
24. See chapter 5A.14.
25. See chapter 5A.13.

Termination and Continuation of Jurisdiction

The court may terminate its jurisdiction at any time. Unless terminated by the court, the jurisdiction of the court continues until the child becomes 19 years of age.[26]

The Indian Child Welfare Act of 1978

The Indian Child Welfare Act of 1978[27] is a federal law that controls the removal of American Indian children from their homes and their placement in foster and adoptive homes.[28] Its terms are briefly described here.

In the late 1970s, Congress became increasingly concerned about the rate at which Indian children were being removed from their families and placed with non-Indian families. The Congressional response was the Indian Child Welfare Act of 1978. Congressional findings indicated that states "often failed to recognize the essential tribal relations of Indian people and the cultural and social standards prevailing in Indian communities and families" and that an "alarmingly high percentage of Indian families are broken up by the removal, often unwarranted, of their children from them by nontribal public and private agencies."[29] The act creates federal standards for the removal of Indian children from their families and the placement of such children in foster or adoptive homes.[30]

The act applies to "child custody" proceedings, which include foster care,[31] preadoptive and adoptive placements,[32] and termination of parental rights.[33] It governs proceedings concerning "Indian children," which means any unmarried person, under age 18, who either is a member of an Indian tribe or is eligible for membership in an Indian tribe and is the biological child of a member of an Indian tribe.[34]

The act works to protect the Indian heritage of Indian tribes and their children in a number of ways, three of which will be discussed here. First, the act controls which court may take jurisdiction of child custody proceedings involving Indian children.

---

26. M.S.A. § 260.181, subd. 4 (West 1992). Jurisdiction for habitual truancy may not continue beyond the child's 17th birthday.
27. 25 U.S.C. § 1901 et seq.
28. Minnesota law must be construed consistently with the act. M.S.A. § 260.157 (West Supp. 1993).
29. 25 U.S.C. § 1901(4), (5).
30. 25 U.S.C. § 1902.
31. See chapter 5A.13.
32. See chapter 5A.14.
33. See chapter 5A.10.
34. 25 U.S.C. § 1903(1), (4).

Indian tribal courts have exclusive jurisdiction over such proceedings involving an Indian child who resides on or is domiciled within the reservation of the tribe.[35] State courts have concurrent jurisdiction of child custody cases involving Indian children who are not residing or domiciled on the reservation. However, the state courts must transfer jurisdiction over such proceedings to the jurisdiction of the tribe upon request and absent the objection of the parents of the child. The court may decline to transfer jurisdiction for other "good cause."[36]

Second, the act establishes certain standards that any court must use in custody proceedings. The court must find that "active efforts" have been made to provide services and programs designed to prevent the breakup of the family. It may not order foster care unless it finds by "clear and convincing" evidence that the child is likely to suffer "serious emotional or physical" harm. It may not terminate parental rights unless it makes the same finding "beyond a reasonable doubt."[37] The act sets standards for giving and withdrawing consent to foster placement, termination of parental rights, and adoptive placement.[38]

Third, the act establishes a set of preferences for adoptive and foster placements of Indian children. In foster care or preadoptive placements, preference is to be given, in order, to members of the child's extended family,[39] a foster home approved by the tribe, an Indian foster home licensed by a non-Indian licensing authority, or an institution for children approved by an Indian tribe. Preference in adoptive placements goes, in order, to the child's extended family, other members of the child's tribe, or other Indian families.[40] Individual tribes can set different orders of preference. In meeting the preference requirements, courts and agencies are to use the prevailing social and cultural standards of the Indian community.

---

35. 25 U.S.C. § 1911(a). In emergencies, state officials and courts can remove Indian children from their homes, if they are temporarily located off of the reservation, to prevent imminent physical harm to the child. However, the state authorities must take immediate steps to comply with the jurisdictional requirements of the act. 25 U.S.C. § 1922.
36. 25 U.S.C. § 1911(b).
37. 25 U.S.C. § 1912.
38. 25 U.S.C. § 1913. Compare with chapters 5A.13 and 5A.14.
39. *Extended family* has the definition established by "law or custom" of the child's tribe. 25 U.S.C. § 1903(2).
40. 25 U.S.C. § 1915.

5A.16

Competency of Juveniles to Stand Trial

The right not to be tried or convicted of a crime while incompetent is a fundamental constitutional right, applicable in the juvenile court context as well as in the criminal courts.[1] Competency, in this context, entails the ability to understand the proceeding and participate in one's own defense.

The Rules of Juvenile Court provide that no child may be subjected to a trial or a reference hearing[2] while "mentally ill or mentally deficient so as to be incapable of understanding the proceedings or participating in the child's defense."[3] The rules provide no definition of "mentally ill" or "mentally deficient," and one may assume that the emphasis in the rule is on the functional part of the rule—incapacity to understand or participate—rather than on the source of the lack of capacity.

Note that the rule applies only to trials and reference hearings for delinquent acts or petty matters. Competency to stand trial is not an issue in other types of juvenile proceedings, such as those dealing with children allegedly in need of protection or services.

The issue of incompetence can be raised at any time by an attorney, the child's guardian, or the judge. The court has a continuing obligation to inquire further when there is reason to doubt the juvenile defendant's competency.[4] Upon such a motion, the court suspends the proceeding and schedules a hearing to determine the child's competency.[5] The hearing is conducted in an informal manner so that all participants may have a chance to

---

1. In re S.W.T., 277 N.W.2d 507 (Minn. 1979). *See* chapters 5D.5, 5D.14, 5D.19.
2. *See* chapter 5A.18.
3. Minn. R. P. Juv. Ct. 33.01.
4. In re S.W.T., 277 N.W.2d 507 (Minn. 1979).
5. Minn. R. P. Juv. Ct. 33.02, subd. 1.

comment on the child's mental state.[6] If the court finds that the child is incompetent, it is to dismiss the petition without prejudice (so that it may be refiled after the child regains competency) unless jeopardy has attached.[7]

---

6. Minn. R. P. Juv. Ct. 33.02, subd. 2.
7. *Id.*, subd. 4. Jeopardy attaches when the court begins to hear evidence. Breed v. Jones, 421 U.S. 519, 533 (1975).

5A.17

Nonresponsibility Defense for Juveniles

The Minnesota Supreme Court has determined that the right to raise the defense of not guilty by reason of mental illness is protected by the constitution.[1] Although the court decided the case in the context of a criminal prosecution,[2] rather than in a juvenile delinquency proceeding, it is reasonable to assume that the right extends to the latter proceedings as well. Indeed, the Minnesota Juvenile Court Rules acknowledge that mental illness or mental deficiency may be a defense.[3]

As a matter of practice, mental illness is rarely presented as a *defense* in juvenile delinquency proceedings.[4] Because, in theory, juvenile court proceedings are aimed at treatment and rehabilitation rather than punishment, the child's mental status is relevant and important in determining the disposition of the matter, rather than in assessing "blameworthiness." A child who was mentally ill when the offense was committed may thus be adjudicated delinquent, but the disposition should take any continuing mental illness into account and include treatment suited to the child's individual needs.

---

1. State v. Hoffman, 328 N.W.2d 709 (Minn. 1982).
2. *See* chapter 5D.9.
3. "The child's counsel shall inform the county attorney in writing of any defense, other than that of denial, which the child intends to rely at the trial, including but not limited to the defenses of self-defense, entrapment, *mental illness or deficiency*, duress, alibi . . ." (emphasis added), Minn R. P. Juv. Ct. 24.02, subd. 1(C)(1).
4. Compare mental illness that renders the child incompetent to participate in the trial. *See* chapter 5A.16.

5A.18

Transfer of Juveniles to Stand Trial as Adults

The juvenile court has "original and exclusive" jurisdiction over juveniles alleged to be delinquent, except where the child is "referred" for prosecution as an adult.[1] Because "delinquency" includes violations of state and local criminal laws (certain petty and traffic offenses excluded),[2] it follows that prosecutions against juveniles for criminal violations must commence in juvenile court. A violation of a state or local law by a juvenile is not a crime unless the juvenile court refers the matter to the appropriate adult prosecuting authority. This chapter describes the process of making such a reference, thereby certifying a juvenile to stand trial for a crime as an adult.

There are several differences between trial as a juvenile and trial as an adult: There is no right to a jury trial in juvenile court, whereas there is in adult court.[3] Juvenile court has a wider range of dispositions available than does adult criminal court.[4] Juvenile court jurisdiction over juveniles extends only to their 19th birthdays.[5] Court-imposed dispositional orders end with the termination of the court's jurisdiction. Juvenile court delinquency adjudication does not impose on the child any of the civil disabilities imposed by conviction, and such an adjudication is not deemed to be criminal or a conviction of a crime.[6]

---

1. M.S.A. § 260.111 (West 1992).
2. M.S.A. § 260.015, subd. 5 (West 1992). *See* chapter 5A.15.
3. *See* chapter 5C.1.
4. M.S.A. § 260.185 (West 1992). *See* chapters 5A.15 and 5D.15.
5. M.S.A. § 260.181, subd. 4 (West 1992).
6. M.S.A. § 260.211 (West 1992).

At the request of the court or one of the parties, MHPs may make an evaluation of the child to be used as evidence in the transfer hearing.

Initiation of Transfer Proceedings

When a child is alleged to have violated a criminal law after becoming 14 years of age, the juvenile court may refer the violation to the local prosecuting authority for action under laws governing adult criminals.[7]

The Transfer Hearing

Before referring the juvenile, the court must conduct a hearing.[8] At the hearing, the burden is on the prosecutor to demonstrate probable cause to believe that the child committed the offense alleged.[9] After meeting this burden, the prosecutor must then show through clear and convincing evidence that

1. the child is not suitable for treatment, or
2. the public safety is not served under the provisions of laws governing juvenile courts.

A "prima facie" case that one or both of these conditions applies is made if the child is 16 years of age or older and has committed one or more of a number of serious felonies.[10] A prima facie case means one that meets the prosecutor's burden but that can be rebutted by evidence presented by the child. Unless the prosecutor's prima facie case is substantially unrebutted, the court considers the "totality of circumstances" in deciding whether to refer the juvenile.[11] The court takes into account the following factors:

1. the seriousness of the offense in terms of community protection;
2. the circumstances surrounding the offense;

---

7. M.S.A. § 260.125. subd. 1 (West 1992).
8. M.S.A. § 260.155, subd. 1 (West 1992).
9. M.S.A. § 260.125, subd. 2 (West 1992).
10. M.S.A. § 260.125, subd. 3 (West 1992). The list includes first-degree murder; a serious felony while escaping from a juvenile correctional facility; two or more serious offenses, within two years, such as second- or third-degree murder, manslaughter, arson, criminal sexual conduct, robbery, burglary, or assault; and an aggravated felony against a person in furtherance of criminal activity by an organized gang.
11. Minn. R. P. Juv. Ct. 32.05.

3. whether the offense was committed in an aggressive, violent, premeditated, or willful manner;

4. whether personal injury resulted;

5. the reasonably foreseeable consequences of the offense;

6. the sophistication and maturity of the child as determined by consideration of the child's home, environmental situation, emotional attitude, and pattern of living;

7. the record and previous history of the child;

8. whether the child acted with particular cruelty or disregard for life or the safety of others;

9. the absence of adequate protective and security facilities available to the juvenile treatment system;

10. whether the offense involved a high degree of sophistication or planning by the child; and

11. whether there is sufficient time available before the child reaches the age of 19 to provide appropriate treatment and control.

The court may order a social, psychiatric, or psychological study concerning the child to be used as evidence.[12] MHPs may be asked to testify on whether the child is amenable to treatment or a threat to public safety. The final decision by the judge to certify the child for adult prosecution is based on the totality of the evidence and need not be based solely on the recommendations of MHPs.[13]

---

12. Minn. R. P. Juv. Ct. 32.03.
13. In re Welfare of S.R.J., 293 N.W.2d 32 (Minn. 1980).

5A.19

Informal Admission and Judicial Commitment of Minors

As a general matter, the admission of minors to facilities for mental health treatment follows the same basic rule as the admission of adults: Admission must be either accompanied by valid consent (informal admission)[1] or ordered by a court after a hearing satisfying the requirements of due process.[2] The admission of minors is made complicated by questions surrounding the giving of consent. Normally, minors are incompetent (by reason of their minority) to give consent.[3] Their parents, as their natural guardians, can give competent consent on their behalves. These normal rules of consent are partially modified by statute in the context of admission for mental health services. Unfortunately, the statutory modifications are not in all circumstances models of clarity. This chapter summarizes the law and notes its areas of ambiguity.

General Rules: Minors 16 Years of Age or Older

A minor 16 years of age or older may give consent for his or her own informal admission to a facility for mental health, mental retardation, or chemical dependency treatment.[4] Although the law is not entirely clear on this point, it appears that parental

---

1. See chapter 5E.3.
2. Zinermon v. Burch, 110 S.Ct. 975 (1990). Parham v. J.R. et al., 442 U.S. 607 (1979) (informal admission of children meets constitutional standards under certain circumstances). See chapter 5E.4.
3. See chapter 5A.21.
4. M.S.A. § 253B.03, subd. 6(d); § 253B.04, subd. 1 (West Supp. 1992).

consent for such a minor is not legally sufficient for informal admission.[5] In other words, if such a minor refuses consent, or is unable (because of his or her mental disorder) to give competent consent, he or she may be admitted only as an involuntary patient under the rules governing civil commitment.[6]

General Rules: Minors Under 16 Years of Age

Parents of a minor under 16 years of age are competent to give consent for the "informal" admission of their child if it is determined by "independent examination" that there is reasonable evidence that the child is mentally ill, mentally retarded, or chemically dependent and that the child is "suitable for treatment."[7] In the absence of parental consent, a child can be held for treatment only upon an order of commitment or, perhaps, pursuant to an order issued by the juvenile court.[8] It is unclear whether parental consent is sufficient to hold and treat a minor who is not compliant and does not acquiesce to the treatment.

Other Provisions: Emancipated Minors, Emergency Treatment, Drug Abuse Evaluation and Treatment

Minors who are emancipated, that is, who are living separate and apart from parents or legal guardians and managing their own personal financial affairs, may give effective consent for mental health services. Minors who have married or who have borne a child may also give effective consent for mental health services. No other consent is required.[9] It is unclear from the law whether

---

5. M.S.A. § 253B.04, subd. 1 (West Supp. 1992). The law does not explicitly foreclose the sufficiency of parental consent for 16-year-olds. The statement in the text is drawn by negative inference from the fact that such consent is explicitly made sufficient for those under 16.

6. See chapters 5E.4, 5E.5, 5E.6, 5E.7.

7. M.S.A. § 253B.04, subd. 1 (West Supp. 1992). The terms in the text are used without definition in the law. For additional discussion, see Janus, E. S. (1991). Civil commitment in Minnesota (2nd ed., pp. 126–129). St. Paul, MN: Butterworth.

8. See chapter 5A.15. The juvenile court can transfer legal custody to the county welfare board and can order the provision of special treatment and care for reasons of mental health. M.S.A. § 260.191 (West 1992).

9. M.S.A. § 14.341 (West 1989).

parental consent would be sufficient to authorize the treatment of an incompetent emancipated minor.

Minors of any age may give effective consent for medical, mental, or other health services to determine the presence of or to treat alcohol or other drug abuse.[10]

In emergency situations, mental (and other) health services may be legally furnished to minors of any age without consent of the parent or guardian.[11]

The consent of a minor for mental or other health services is effective if the person rendering the service relied in good faith on the representations of the minor.[12]

Rights of Minors Informally Admitted for Severe Emotional Disturbance

Minors admitted informally for treatment for severe emotional disturbance have certain rights that are set out in the Minnesota Comprehensive Children's Mental Health Act.[13] Pursuant to law, counties must conduct screenings of each child who is informally admitted to determine whether the admission "(1) is necessary; (2) is appropriate to the child's individual treatment needs; (3) cannot be effectively provided in the child's home; and (4) provides a length of stay as short as possible consistent with the individual child's need."[14] Services provided to children must be "based on individual clinical, cultural, and ethnic needs, and other special needs of the children being served; . . . delivered in a manner that improves family functioning when clinically appropriate; . . . provided in the most appropriate, least restrictive setting available; . . . and . . . provided in a manner and setting most likely to facilitate progress toward treatment goals."[15]

---

10. M.S.A. § 144.343, subd. 1 (West 1989).
11. M.S.A. § 144.344 (West 1989).
12. M.S.A. § 144.345 (West 1989).
13. M.S.A. § 245.487 et seq.
14. M.S.A. § 245.4885 (West Supp. 1992).
15. M.S.A. § 245.4876 (West Supp. 1992).

5A.20

Education for Handicapped Children

Minnesota and federal laws provide that all children, regardless of their mental, physical, or emotional disability, must be afforded an education that meets their individual needs. MHPs may become involved in this process through evaluations of the children and consultation with special education personnel and as part of the teams providing services to qualifying children.

Terms and Definitions

Before discussing the process by which a child may be deemed eligible for special education services, it is helpful to understand the terms in the law.[1]

1. *Special education* means any specially designed instruction and related services or support services to meet the unique cognitive, affective, or psychomotor needs of a pupil as stated in the individual education program (IEP).[2]

2. *Related services* means any specially designed services not provided by regular education or special education instruction to meet the unique needs of a pupil to benefit from the educational program. This includes psychological services, social worker services, occupational therapy, physical therapy, audiology, orientation and mobility training, health services,

---

1. M.S.A. § 120.17 (West Supp. 1992); Minn. R. 3525.0200 (1991).
2. Minn. R. 3525.0200, subp. 20a (1991).

medical services for diagnostic purposes, music therapy, and other similar services.[3]

3. *Individual education program* or *IEP* means a written individualized educational plan developed for a pupil. It is based on an assessment of the pupil's needs in a team process, an indication of appropriate goals and objectives, a selection of teaching strategies designed to enhance learning, delivery of services in an environment conducive to learning, and a periodic review and evaluation of the pupil's performance.[4]

4. *Handicapped child* means any child who has a hearing impairment, physical handicap, other health impairment, mental handicap, emotional/behavioral disorder, specific learning disability, or deaf/blind handicap and needs special instruction and services, as determined by the standards of the state board of education. In addition, every child under age 5 who needs special instruction and services, as determined by the standards of the state board, because the child has a substantial delay or has an identifiable physical or mental condition known to hinder normal development, is a handicapped child.[5]

Federal law contains more detailed definitions of the conditions that may constitute a handicap and entitle a child to special education services.[6] Among the definitions provided are the following:

1. *Mentally retarded* means significantly subaverage general intellectual functioning, existing concurrently with deficits in adaptive behavior and manifested during the developmental period, that adversely affects a child's educational performance.

2. *Multihandicapped* means a combination of impairments that causes severe educational problems that cannot be accommodated in a special education program solely for one of the impairments.

3. *Other health impaired* includes children with an autistic condition or having limited strength, vitality, or alertness because of health problems.

4. *Seriously emotionally disturbed* means a condition that exhibits one or more of a list of characteristics over a long period of time and to a marked degree. Included in the characteristics

---

3. Minn. R. 3525.0200, subp. 18b (1991).
4. Minn. R. 3525.0200, subp. 6a (1991).
5. M.S.A. § 120.03, subd. 1 (West Supp. 1992).
6. 34 CFR § 300.5 (1991).

are an inability to learn that cannot be explained by intellectual, sensory, or health factors; an inability to build or maintain satisfactory interpersonal relationships; inappropriate types of behavior or feelings; a general pervasive mood of unhappiness or depression; and a tendency to develop physical symptoms or fears associated with personal or school problems. The term includes children who are schizophrenic.

5. *Specific learning disability* means a disorder in one or more of the basic psychological processes involved in understanding or in using language. It may manifest itself in an imperfect ability to listen, think, speak, read, write, spell, or do math. It includes conditions such as perceptual handicaps, brain injury, minimal brain dysfunction, dyslexia, and developmental aphasia. It does not include learning problems that are primarily the result of visual, hearing, or motor handicaps; mental retardation; emotional disturbance; or environmental, cultural, or economic disadvantage.

Referral and Special Education Evaluation[7]

To secure special education services, the child must first be evaluated to determine his or her need for it. Although each district may vary in its referral process and evaluation procedures, the general guidelines have been established in Minnesota rules and statutes.

School districts are required to have systems in place to identify children who are handicapped and in need of special education.[8] Most referrals for special education assessments arise from these identification systems. In addition, parents, students, and other agencies can request referral for assessment.[9] When a referral is received, a multidisciplinary team determines whether an assessment is warranted. This determination by the team should take account of the person's intellectual functioning, academic performance, communicative status, motor ability, vocational potential, sensory status, physical status, emotional and social development, and behavior and functional skills.[10] The district must conduct an assessment when the student's needs are interfering with or affecting the student's academic or functional

---

7. *See generally* M.S.A. § 120.17 (West Supp. 1992); Minn. R. 3525.2500–2800 (1991).
8. Minn. R. 3525.2500 (1991).
9. Minn. R. 3525.2750 (1991).
10. Minn. R. 3525.2550, subp. 1 (1991).

skill acquisition in the present educational placement.[11] The assessment is conducted by an interdisciplinary team.[12]

Once the team determines that the assessment should be conducted, the school district must serve written notice and obtain written parental consent before the assessment can proceed. The assessment must then be conducted within 30 days from the time the district received parental permission.[13] The nature of the assessment will depend on the person's current level of performance and must be appropriate to the presenting problem. The assessment may include a review of a person's functioning in current and anticipated environments. The environmental review must address classroom performance, performance in other daily routine environments, and information reported by parents, teachers, and anyone else involved with the person.[14] This will also include a review of the person's learning environment and learning modes and will be administered in the person's primary language or mode of communication.[15] The assessment will be conducted by licensed special education personnel in accordance with recognized professional standards.[16]

Federal regulations[17] provide additional requirements for evaluations. Tests must have been validated for the specific purpose for which they are used and must be administered by trained personnel. Evaluation materials must include those tailored to assess the specific areas of educational need and not rely on merely a single general intelligence quotient. Tests must be selected and administered to ensure that they accurately reflect the child's aptitude or achievement level, rather than reflecting the child's impaired sensory, manual, or speaking skills (except if that is what the tests purport to measure). No single procedure or criterion may be used for determining the child's needs. The child must be assessed in all areas related to the suspected disability.

Federal regulations provide special criteria for determining the existence of a specific learning disability. The multidisciplinary team may determine that a child has a specific learning disability if the child does not achieve commensurate with his or her age and ability when provided with learning experiences appropriate for the child's age and ability levels. The team must also find that the child has a severe discrepancy between achievement and intellectual ability in one or more of the basic areas of

---

11. Minn. R. 3525.2750, subp. 1 (1991).
12. *Id.* at subp. 2.
13. Minn. R. 3525.2650, subp. 2 (1991).
14. Minn. R. 3525.2650, subp. 2(B) (1991).
15. *Id.,* subp. 2(D).
16. Minn. R. 3525.0200, subp. 1b (1991).
17. 34 CFR § 300.532 (1991).

academics. The child may not be identified as having a specific learning disability if the discrepancy is primarily the result of a visual, hearing, or motor handicap; mental retardation; emotional disturbance; or environmental, cultural, or economic disadvantage.[18]

Federal regulations also require that services to handicapped children be provided in accordance with the principle of the "least restrictive alternative."[19] Under this principle, handicapped children must be educated, to the maximum extent appropriate, with children who are not handicapped. Special classes, separate schooling, or other removal of handicapped children from the regular educational environment may occur only when, on the basis of the nature or severity of the handicap, and with the use of supplementary aids and services, education in the regular environment cannot be satisfactorily achieved. Generally, handicapped children should be educated in the schools they would attend if not handicapped.[20]

Evaluation Team Report and Individual Educational Plan[21]

Following the assessment, the designated team will organize the assessment data and other relevant information and reports and will review that data and develop a statement of the student's educational needs. The team must include a school administrator or designee, the student's regular classroom teacher, appropriate special education personnel, other support personnel, the parent, and, when appropriate, the student.[22]

A conference will be scheduled at a time and place that is mutually acceptable to the school and parents.

An IEP will then be developed for the child. This plan must be in writing and be based on the assessment data and other relevant reports and information. The plan must not be discriminatory,[23] must recognize professional standards, and must be based on the principle of the least restrictive alternative,[24] which states that a handicapped person will remain in the regular education pro-

---

18. 34 CFR § 300.541 (1991).
19. 34 CFR §§ 300.550 to 300.556 (1991).
20. 34 CFR § 300.552 (1991).
21. Minn. R. 3525.2900 to 3100 (1991).
22. Minn. R. 3525.2900, subp. 1 (1991).
23. Minn. R. 3525.0200, subp. 10 (1991) (districts shall not discriminate on the basis of race, color, creed, religion, national origin, sex, marital status, status with regard to public assistance, or disability).
24. Minn. R. 3525.0400 (1991).

gram to the extent possible and will be removed only when his or her needs cannot be met satisfactorily in the regular education setting. The IEP must include[25]

1. a description of the student's special education needs as determined by the members of the team;
2. a statement of annual goals and periodic review objectives, including criteria for attainment;
3. the plan for, location of, and frequency of review of the program in reaching the goals and objectives;
4. the reasons for the type of education placement and program, including the type of special education services to be provided, location, amount of time, starting date, anticipated duration, and names of personnel responsible for providing services, as well as a statement of why the proposed action is the most appropriate in terms of the person's educational needs;
5. the changes in staffing, transportation, facilities, curriculum, methods, materials, and equipment that will be made; and
6. in special cases where the student's primary placement will be in a special education program, a description of the educational program.

Parental Rights[26]

Parents must be given written notice of each step in the special education evaluation and placement process. The district may not proceed with the initial formal assessment of a child, the initial placement of a child in a special education program, or the initial provision of special education services for a child without the prior written consent of the child's parent or guardian.[27] If a parent objects to the district's proposed action, the district may initiate an impartial due process hearing, described below, but only after the parent has been given the opportunity to meet with the district in a conciliation conference. The conference must be held within 10 school days after receipt of the written objection. Its purpose is to review the reasons for the proposed action and to conciliate the matter. Within 7 days of the final conciliation conference, the district must serve the parents with a written memorandum informing them of the school district's proposed action following the conference and that if they continue to object they

---

25. Minn. R. 3525.2850, subp. 3 (1991).
26. M.S.A. § 120.17, subd. 3b (West Supp. 1992); Minn R. 3525.3200 to 4700 (1991).
27. M.S.A. § 120.17, subd. 3b (West Supp. 1992). The parents' refusal to give consent may be overridden after an appropriate hearing.

have a right to do so at an impartial due process hearing. The parents have the right to proceed directly to the hearing and can bypass the conciliation conference. The parents also have the right to be represented by counsel or another person of their choosing at the conciliation conference or the impartial due process hearing.[28]

Impartial Due Process Hearing

A hearing must be held upon the written request of the parents or school. A hearing may be requested to consider a range of issues, such as the assessment of a child; placement in or provision of special education services; or the proposed change or denial of an assessment, placement, or service.[29] Upon receipt of a request, the school district must inform the parent that the hearing will take place within 30 days, before an impartial hearing officer mutually agreed to by the school board and the parent.[30]

The hearing officer cannot be a school board member, an employee of the school district, an employee of any other public agency involved in the education or care of the child, or any person with a personal or professional interest that would conflict with the person's objectivity at the hearing. The hearing officer may request an independent educational assessment of the child at the district's expense.[31] Prior to the hearing, the hearing officer is given copies of the notices sent to parents; tests, evaluations, and other written reports relating to the assessment or proposed action; the student's current and proposed IEP; and any other information relevant to the hearing.[32] The hearing officer then reviews the information and may require the school district to perform additional assessments, propose an alternative IEP, or take other necessary action to comply with the notice and consent requirements within the law.[33] The hearing will be closed unless the parents request an open hearing. The parents or their representative must be given access to all of the records pertaining to the child prior to the hearing.[34]

Within 45 days after receipt of the request for a hearing, the hearing officer must prepare a written decision based on the evidence introduced at the hearing. The decision shall be in writ-

---

28. Minn. R. 3525.3300, subps. F, G, H (1991).
29. M.S.A. § 120.17, subd. 3b (West Supp. 1992).
30. Minn. R. 3525.3900 (1991). If the school board and parent are unable to agree on a hearing officer, the school board requests the commissioner to appoint an officer.
31. Minn. R. 3525.4000 (1991).
32. Minn. R. 3525.4100, subp. 1 (1991).
33. Minn. R. 3525.4100, subp. 2 (1991).
34. Minn. R. 3525.4200 (1991).

ing, state the controlling facts on which the decision is made, state whether the special education services appropriate to the child's needs can be reasonably provided within the resources available to the responsible district, state the amount and source of any additional district expenditure necessary to implement the decision, and be based on the standards set forth in the law.[35]

The decision of the hearing officer is binding on all parties unless appealed to the commissioner of education by the parent or school board within 15 days. The commissioner will make an impartial review of the hearing and issue a final decision within 30 days of the filing of the appeal. The commissioner's decision can be appealed to either state or federal court.

Gifted Education

There is no state mandate for gifted education in Minnesota law. However, the rules of the State Board of Education contain the following provision: "The educational program shall provide a general education for all pupils and suitable special education for exceptional children handicapped, gifted and talented. It shall meet the needs and interests of all pupils and the needs of the community served."[36] School districts receive a small percentage of state aid funding that they may use for gifted and talented education.[37]

Standards for services to gifted and talented students were adopted by the Minnesota State Advisory Council for the Gifted and Talented in 1988. These standards define gifted and talented children as those who by virtue of outstanding abilities are capable of high performance. They include those with demonstrated achievement or potential in general intellectual ability, specific academic areas, creative or productive thinking, leadership ability, or visual or performing arts. The standards contain guidelines for minimum service and standards for excellence in services to gifted and talented children.

The Minnesota Department of Education employs a gifted and talented education specialist who can provide additional information and resources.[38]

---

35. M.S.A. § 120.17, subd. 3b(f) (West Supp. 1992).
36. Minn. R. 3500.0500 (1991).
37. M.S.A. § 124A.27 (West Supp. 1992).
38. The Department also has a publication titled "Success for Every Learner: Connections in Concept and Practice: Gifted and Talented Learners and Outcome-Based Education in Minnesota" (Minnesota Department of Education, 1992).

5A.21

Consent, Confidentiality, and Services for Minors

In general, the parent of a child, as his or her natural guardian, has the authority to give or withhold consent on the minor's behalf. However, because of the intensely personal nature of health and mental health services, the law authorizes the minor him- or herself to give or withhold consent in a variety of circumstances. MHPs must be familiar with these guidelines in order to avoid liability for providing services or disclosing information on the basis of inadequate consent.[1] In addition, where MHPs provide services to minors without their parents' knowledge or consent, the MHPs' obligations to maintain client confidences, and to disclose information appropriately, is further complicated.

Consent

Minors who are "emancipated," that is, living apart and separate from their parents or legal guardians and managing their own personal financial affairs, may give effective consent to personal medical, dental, mental, and other health services.[2] The same is true for minors who have been married or have borne a child.[3]

Any minor can give effective consent for medical, mental, and other health services to treat or evaluate alcohol or drug abuse or pregnancy. No other consent is required.[4]

---

1. *See* chapters 4.1, 4.2, 6.5, 6.6.
2. M.S.A. §§ 144.341, 144.342 (West 1989).
3. *Id.*
4. M.S.A. § 144.343 (West 1989).

The consent of a minor for mental or other health services is effective if the person rendering the service relied in good faith on the representations of the minor.[5] In other words, an MHP who relies in good faith on a minor's statements, concluding therefrom that the minor's consent is valid, is protected from liability, even if it turns out that the minor did not have legal authority to give consent.

Medical, dental, mental, and other health services may be given to minors of any age without the consent of a parent or guardian when, in the MHP's judgment, the treatment must be given without delay in view of the risk to the minor's life or health.[6]

The authority of a minor to consent to informal admission to a mental health facility is discussed in chapter 5A.19.

Confidentiality

In general, MHPs are obligated to maintain the confidentiality of patient/client information.[7] Generally, this means that MHPs are constrained from releasing information except upon request of the patient and are required to release information and records upon the patient's request. As a general rule, parents of minors have the same rights to information as do their children. In other words, parents are authorized to have access to the records and information regarding their children and may consent to the release of such records to third parties.[8] However, this rule does not apply to parents of minors who have received health care services based on the minors' own consent, as described above. In such cases, information may be released to the parents only upon the consent of the child.[9] However, the MHP may inform the parent or guardian of the minor patient of any treatment given or needed where, in the judgment of the MHP, failure to inform the parent or guardian would seriously jeopardize the health of the minor.[10]

---

5. M.S.A. § 144.345 (West Supp. 1992).
6. M.S.A. § 144.344 (West Supp. 1992).
7. *See* chapters 4.1, 4.2, 4.3.
8. M.S.A. § 144.335 (West Supp. 1992).
9. *Id.*
10. M.S.A. § 144.346 (West Supp. 1992).

5A.22

Consent for Abortion

The state of Minnesota does not require a minor to have a parent's consent for an abortion. The law does impose a waivable notification requirement where a minor seeks an abortion. MHPs may become involved in the process of evaluating and testifying as to whether the minor woman is mature enough to make the decision without parental notification.

The law[1] provides that a physician cannot perform an abortion on an unmarried or unemancipated minor woman unless both parents or a guardian have been notified in writing. The abortion may not be performed until at least 48 hours after the notification has been delivered.[2] Notification is not required when[3]

1. the attending physician certifies that the abortion is necessary to prevent the woman's death and there is insufficient time to provide notice;
2. the abortion is authorized in writing by the person or persons who are entitled to notice;
3. the minor woman declares she is a victim of sexual abuse, neglect, or physical abuse;[4] or
4. after a confidential hearing, a judge determines that the woman is mature and capable of giving informed consent to

---

1. M.S.A. § 144.343 (West 1989).
2. Delivery must be made personally to the parent by the physician or an agent or may be made by certified mail. M.S.A. § 144.343, subd. 2 (West 1989).
3. M.S.A. § 144.343, subd. 4 (West 1989).
4. As defined in M.S.A. § 626.556 (West Supp. 1992). A report of such abuse must also be made to the proper authorities, as required by law. *See* chapter 5A.8.

the abortion, or that it would be in her best interests, even if she is not mature, to authorize the abortion without parental notification.[5]

MHPs may be involved in the last exception, which requires evidence that the woman is mature or that it would be in her best interests to waive the notification.

---

5. M.S.A. § 144.343, subd. 6 (West 1989).

5A.23

Evaluation and Treatment of Children at the Request of a Noncustodial Parent

MHPs may be asked to provide services to children whose parents are separated or divorced. In responding to such requests, the MHP must determine whether the parent making the request is authorized to give any consent that may be required.[1]

Minnesota law[2] provides that where one parent has legal custody, that person exercises the right to determine the child's upbringing, including education, health care, and religious training. If the parties have joint legal custody, both parents have equal rights and responsibilities to "participate in major decisions determining the child's upbringing, including education, health care, and religious training."[3]

Thus, in the absence of joint custody, the noncustodial parent generally lacks the authority to "determine" the health care of the child. In the case of joint legal custody, the law gives both parties the right to "participate" in determining health care issues. The law is ambiguous as to whether the consent of one joint legal custodian is sufficient to authorize medical or mental health care.[4]

The right of the custodial parent to determine these issues is limited by the noncustodial parent's right to ask the court to

---

1. Under certain circumstances, parental consent is not required for the treatment of minors. *See* chapters 5A.19, 5A.21, 5A.22.
2. M.S.A. § 518.003 (West Supp. 1992).
3. M.S.A. § 518.003, subd. 3 (West Supp. 1992).
4. The ambiguity is heightened by an inconsistency in the law. Although purporting to give those with "joint legal custody" the right to "determine" the child's upbringing, the law also appears to give the person with "physical custody" this same right. This clearly poses a problem where physical and legal custody are separated. *See* M.S.A. § 518.003, subd. 3; § 518.176. The ambiguity is of concern only where the parents disagree about consent.

override the former's decision.[5] In the absence of joint custody, the court apparently is to override the custodial parent's decision only if the child's physical or emotional health is likely to be endangered or the child's emotional development impaired by that decision. If parents who have joint legal custody cannot agree, however, the court is to apply a "best interests of the child" standard in deciding the question.[6]

MHPs who provide services at the request of a noncustodial parent without first obtaining the permission of the custodial parent are vulnerable to a malpractice claim on the basis that proper consent to the services was not given.[7] However, in an emergency, services can be provided to a minor even without proper consent.[8]

---

5. M.S.A. § 518.176 (West 1990).
6. Novak v. Novak, 446 N.W.2d 422 (Minn. Ct. App. 1989).
7. See chapter 6.1.
8. M.S.A. § 144.344 (West Supp. 1992). See chapter 5A.19.

Other Civil Matters

5B.1

Mental Status of Licensed/Certified Professionals

The mental status of a licensed or certified professional may be relevant to his or her ability to perform safely and competently. As such, it is generally at least implicitly relevant both to application for licensure or certification and to the ongoing oversight of the professional's performance. In many cases, mental condition is made an explicit subject for concern by the applicable law or rules. In some cases, special provisions are made for ascertaining and evaluating the mental condition of a professional, and some professions provide a special category of licensure for persons who are temporarily disabled from performing because of a mental disability. This chapter discusses such provisions.

Attorneys

To be admitted to the practice of law in Minnesota, applicants must be of good character and fitness.[1] The burden of proving good character is on the applicant.[2] In determining good character and fitness, the Minnesota Board of Law Examiners considers evidence of mental or emotional instability.[3] If evidence of prior mental or emotional instability is shown, the Board takes into

---

1. Rules of the Supreme Court and of the State Board of Law Examiners for Admission to the Bar of Minnesota, Rule II (West 1993).
2. *Id.*
3. Character and Fitness Standards, Rules of the Supreme Court and of the State Board of Law Examiners for Admission to the Bar of Minnesota (West 1993).

account a variety of factors in determining what weight and significance to give that prior condition.[4]

An attorney whose mental illness or deficiency prevents him or her from practicing competently will be transferred to *disability inactive status*.[5] The lawyer will be immediately transferred to disability inactive status if found in a judicial proceeding to be mentally ill, mentally deficient, incapacitated, or an "inebriate person."[6] An attorney who raises the defense of mental illness or deficiency in a disciplinary hearing may also be transferred to disability inactive status.[7] The state Supreme Court, which is the ultimate arbiter of attorney discipline, has additional options that include ordering examinations. The court itself can transfer an attorney to disability inactive status following a proceeding initiated by the director of the Board of Professional Responsibility.

An attorney transferred to disability inactive status can be reinstated by the Supreme Court.[8] A petition for reinstatement is deemed to constitute a waiver of any "doctor–patient privilege" with respect to any treatment of the lawyer during the period of disability.[9]

Dentists

The law[10] provides that a dentist's license may be denied, suspended, revoked, limited, or modified on the ground of any mental or emotional disability that adversely affects his or her ability to perform services. For good cause, the Board of Dentistry may order a licensee or applicant to submit to an appropriate examination.[11] Dental licensees and applicants are deemed to have given consent to a mental or physical examination when directed by the Board and to have waived any objection to the introduction of testimony or reports resulting from such an examination. The dentist or applicant will be allowed, at reasonable

---

4. *Id*. Factors include the recency and seriousness of the condition, evidence of rehabilitation, and the applicant's candor in the application process.
5. Rules on Lawyers Professional Responsibility, Rule 28, subd. a (West 1993).
6. *Id*. Presumably, the rules here are referring to findings made in civil commitment, guardianship, and conservatorship proceedings. "Inebriate person" is not a term used in any of these contexts, although one may assume that commitment as a "chemically dependent person" would trigger the transfer to disability status. *See generally* chapters 5A.2, 5A.3, 5E.4, 5E.5.
7. *Id*.
8. *Id*.
9. Presumably, this includes the psychologist–client privilege. *See* chapter 4.3.
10. M.S.A. § 150A.08, subd. 1(8) (West 1989). The statute covers dentists, dental hygienists, and registered dental assistants.
11. *Id*., subd. 5.

intervals, to demonstrate the ability to start or resume a competent practice.

Pharmacists

The law[12] provides that the Board of Pharmacy may deny, suspend, revoke, or refuse to renew any registration or license of a pharmacist if a mental disability is found that could cause incompetency in the practice of pharmacy. The law does not specify a definition or specific procedures pertaining to mental disability.

Physical Therapists

Applicants for licensure as physical therapists must supply to the Board of Medical Examiners "an accounting by the applicant of any disease, illness, or injury that impairs the applicant's ability to practice physical therapy."[13] The rule provides no further definition. Note that this rule, by its terms, applies only to the application process.

Physicians

Applicants for a medical license must be of good moral character and must not have engaged in conduct warranting disciplinary action against the licensee.[14] The definition of such "conduct" includes adjudication as mentally incompetent, mentally ill or mentally retarded, or chemically dependent, or as a person who has a psychopathic personality.[15] Such an adjudication automatically suspends a medical license for the duration of the adjudication, unless the Board of Medical Examiners orders otherwise. Presumably, such an adjudication would also bar issuance of a license in the first place. Also included in the list of conduct warranting disciplinary action is the inability to practice medicine with reasonable skill and safety to patients by reason of drunken-

---

12. M.S.A. § 151.06 (1988).
13. Minn. R. 5601.0300 (1991).
14. M.S.A. § 147.02, subds. 1(a), (h) (West Supp. 1993). *See* chapter 1.1.
15. M.S.A. § 147.091, subd. 1(j) (West 1989). The terms used in the statute correspond to the categories used in the civil commitment act. *See* chapters 5D.25, 5E.4, 5E.5, 5E.6.

ness or use of drugs or as a result of any mental condition, including deterioration through the aging process.[16]

Nurses

Applicants for a nurse's license must be of good moral character and mental health.[17] A nurse's license may be suspended, revoked, denied, or limited if the nurse is adjudicated incompetent, mentally ill, chemically dependent, or dangerous to the public.[18] Additionally, actual or potential inability to practice nursing with reasonable skill and safety because of illness, use of drugs, or any mental condition is grounds for disciplinary action or denial of license.[19]

Marriage and Family Counselors

To apply for a license in marriage and family therapy, the applicant must be of good moral character.[20] The rules do not note any requirements for physical or mental health.

Psychologists

A psychologist must not provide psychological services to a client when his or her objectivity is impaired. Note that objectivity is impaired when the psychologist is dysfunctional as a "result of a severe physical or mental health problem including chemical abuse or dependence."[21]

---

16. M.S.A. § 147.091, subd. 1(l) (West 1989).
17. Minn. R. 6315.0400, subp. 4; 6315.0500, subp. 4 (1991). *See* chapter 1.2.
18. M.S.A. § 148.261, subd. 1(8) (West Supp. 1993). Presumably, the rules here are referring to findings made in civil commitment, guardianship, and conservatorship proceedings. *See generally* chapters 5A.2, 5A.3, 5E.4, 5E.5, 5E.6.
19. M.S.A. § 148.261, subd. 1(8) (West Supp. 1992).
20. M.S.A. § 148B.33, subd. 1(2)(4) (West Supp. 1992). *See* chapter 1.8.
21. Minn. R. 7200.4810, subp. 2(D) (1991). *See* chapter 1.3.

5B.2

Workers' Compensation

Workers' compensation law provides employees with protection against the treatment costs and income losses resulting from work-related personal injuries or occupational diseases. The employer purchases compensation insurance (or is self-insured) to provide benefits for its employees. The benefits are available regardless of the fault of either the employer or the employee, unless the injury was intentionally inflicted by the employee.[1]

MHPs may become involved in this process in a number of ways: providing treatment to injured workers,[2] writing a medical report in support of a claim petition,[3] doing an examination and report for the employer,[4] attending the employer's examination in behalf of the employee,[5] doing an examination and report as a neutral physician,[6] and testifying at a hearing.[7]

Scope of Coverage

To be compensated for a personal injury, the employee must show that the injury or disease arises out of and in the course of

---

1. M.S.A. § 176.021, subd. 1 (West Supp. 1992). The law also excludes injuries caused by the employee's own intoxication and injuries, not related to the employment, caused by others. *Id.*
2. M.S.A. § 176.135 (West Supp. 1992).
3. M.S.A. § 176.291(5) (West Supp. 1992).
4. M.S.A. § 176.155, subd. 1 (West Supp. 1992).
5. M.S.A. § 176.155, subd. 1 (West Supp. 1992).
6. M.S.A. § 176.155, subd. 2 (West Supp. 1992).
7. M.S.A. § 176.155, subd. 5 (West Supp. 1992) (allowed only in limited circumstances).

employment.[8] For an occupational disease to be compensable, it must be shown that the disease (a) is peculiar to the occupation in which the employee is engaged, (b) is due to causes in excess of the ordinary hazards of employment, and (c) can be traced to the employment as a direct causal connection.[9] Personal injuries are compensable if they occur while the employee is serving the employer and if they result from the employment, except for certain conditions such as self-inflicted injuries, injuries from attacks by others for reasons not related to employment, or injuries resulting from the intoxication of the injured employee.[10]

Workers' Compensation and Mental Stress/Disorder

Minnesota law places workers' compensation claims involving mental problems into three categories.[11] Only two of the categories, physical injury caused by mental stimulus and mental injury caused by physical stimulus, are recognized as compensable.[12] Minnesota courts do not provide compensation when a mental stimulus produces a mental injury.[13]

Processing the Claim

For the employer to be liable for compensating an employee, the employer must have written notice or actual knowledge of the occurrence of the injury or disease.[14] A variety of consequences flow from the timing of the notice or knowledge.[15] In general,

---

8. M.S.A. § 176.021, subd. 1 (West Supp. 1992).
9. M.S.A. § 176.011, subd. 15(a) (West Supp. 1992).
10. M.S.A. § 176.021, subd. 1; § 176.011, subd. 15 (West Supp. 1992).
11. Johnson v. Paul's Auto & Truck Sales, 409 N.W.2d 506, 508 (Minn. 1987).
12. Aker v. State Department of Natural Resources, 282 N.W.2d 533 (Minn. 1979) (heart attack produced by work-related mental stress compensable); Dotolo v. FMC Corp., 375 N.W.2d 25 (Minn. 1985) (depression resulting from work-related tinnitus held compensable). *See also* Hartman v. Cold Spring Granite Co., 243 Minn. 264, 67 N.W.2d 656 (Minn. 1954) (disabling psychological problems caused by work-related back injury compensable).
13. Lockwood v. Independent School Dist. No. 877, 312 N.W.2d 924 (Minn. 1981) (manic–depressive disorder from stressful experiences at work not compensable). *See* Johnson v. Paul's Auto & Truck Sales, 409 N.W.2d 506 (Minn. 1987) (no compensation for tics, tremors, and stomach cramps that are symptoms of and not treatable separately from employee's work-induced emotional condition).
14. M.S.A. § 176.141 (West 1966).
15. *Id.*

immediate notice to the employer will best protect the employee.[16]

An MHP who is aware that an injury may be compensable must report the injury to the commissioner of labor and industry within 10 days after the MHP has received written request for the information from the commissioner.[17] Failure to do so may result in a fine.[18]

There are three steps to a compensation claim. First, the employee must notify the employer. The employee's doctor sends a Workers' Compensation Physicians Report Form to either the employer's insurer or the Department of Labor Workers' Compensation Division.[19]

Second, the employer or its insurance company must send a First Report of Injury to the Department of Labor and Industry.[20] The employer or insurance company has 14 days from the date of notice of an injury either to accept the claim and begin paying benefits or to deny the claim.[21] If the employee is dissatisfied with the denial of a claim, the employee first informs the insurer why he or she disagrees.[22] If that does not resolve the difference, the employee should contact a compensation specialist at the Workers' Compensation Division.[23]

If the matter is not resolved, the employee may have to file a claim petition, which will be referred for a settlement conference, an administrative conference, or a hearing before a compensation judge.[24] The compensation judge is not bound by any statutory or common law rules of evidence, and hearsay evidence, if reliable, is admissible.[25] MHPs are likely to become involved at this point to help show the need for compensation. The commissioner or compensation judge may appoint a neutral expert witness to testify.[26] Compensation for the witness may be paid by either or both parties as the judge directs.[27]

---

16. *Id.*
17. M.S.A. § 176.231, subd. 3 (West 1966).
18. M.S.A. § 176.231, subd. 10 (West 1966).
19. Minnesota Department of Labor and Industry, *What Employees Need To Know About Workers' Compensation* (1991).
20. *Id.*
21. M.S.A. § 176.221, subd. 1 (West Supp. 1992).
22. Minnesota Department of Labor and Industry, *supra* note 19 at 3.
23. *Id.*
24. M.S.A. § 176.291; § 176.305, subd. 1 (West Supp. 1992). *See also* Minnesota Department of Labor and Industry, *What Employees Need to Know About Workers' Compensation* (1991).
25. M.S.A. § 176.411 (West Supp. 1992).
26. M.S.A. § 176.391, subd. 2 (West Supp. 1992).
27. M.S.A. § 176.391, subd. 4 (West Supp. 1992).

Workers' Compensation Benefits

There are five types of benefits that may be awarded in a compensation claim: medical, disability, death, rehabilitation, and remodeling.

Medical care benefits are covered in full and include immediate and long-term expenses.[28]

Disability payments cover the loss of income during recuperation and are classified according to the seriousness of the injury and its duration. The law in Minnesota provides for calculation of these benefits on the basis of standardized tables according to the percentage of disability and length of disability.[29] The percentage of injury is calculated by tables that compare the percentage of injury to the whole body.[30]

Benefits upon death are set to cover burial expenses[31] and payments to dependents.[32]

Rehabilitation benefits are intended to restore the injured employee, through physical and vocational rehabilitation, so that the employee may return to a job related to his or her former employment or to a job that produces an economic status as close as possible to that which the employee would have had without the disability. Employers or insurers must provide rehabilitation consultation by qualified rehabilitation consultants to injured employees if the employees have lost a set period of work because of the personal injury. The consultants develop rehabilitation plans for the employees.[33]

Remodeling benefits allow injured employees to alter or remodel their homes to enable them to accommodate their work-related disabilities. These benefits are available only when the Compensation Court of Appeals determines that the injury substantially prevents the employee from functioning in his or her home.[34]

---

28. M.S.A. § 176.135 (West Supp. 1992).
29. M.S.A. §§ 176.101, 176.105 (West Supp. 1992).
30. Minn. R. 5223.0010 (1991).
31. M.S.A. § 176.111, subd. 18 (West Supp. 1992).
32. M.S.A. § 176.101, subd. 3r; § 176.111 (West Supp. 1992). *See* M.S.A. § 176.102, subd. 1a (West Supp. 1992) (rehabilitation of surviving spouse).
33. M.S.A. § 176.102 (West Supp. 1992).
34. M.S.A. § 176.137 (West Supp. 1992).

Limitation on Fees

Minnesota limits workers' compensation reimbursement of psychologists',[35] psychiatrists',[36] and social workers'[37] fees. The purpose of the limitations is to discourage excessive fees and prevent professionals from taking undue advantage of the workers' compensation system.[38]

35. Minn. R. 5221.3150 (1991).
36. Minn. R. 5221.1300 (1991).
37. Minn. R. 5221.3160 (1991).
38. Minn. R. 5221.0300 (1991).

5B.3

Vocational and Independent Living Rehabilitation Services

The Department of Jobs and Training administers programs of vocational and independent living rehabilitation services for persons with disabilities. The programs are funded jointly by the state and federal governments. Eligible persons can receive a wide range of services, including mental health diagnostic, evaluative, and therapeutic services. MHPs are involved in the programs at the eligibility determination stage, at the service-design stage, and as providers of rehabilitation services. By law, the commissioner of jobs and training is to promulgate rules governing eligibility for services. As of the date of this writing, those rules had not been published. Detailed federal regulations govern provision of these services. These regulations are referred to throughout this chapter.

Vocational Rehabilitation Services

Definition

The vocational rehabilitation (VR) services available to eligible individuals include the following:[1]

1. evaluation of vocational rehabilitation potential;

2. counseling and guidance, including personal adjustment counseling, and referral to necessary services;

---

1. M.S.A. § 268A.03 (West Supp. 1992); 34 CFR § 361.42 (1991)

3. physical and mental restoration services necessary to correct or substantially modify a physical or mental condition that is stable or slowly progressive;
4. vocational and other training services, including personal and vocational adjustment;
5. maintenance, including payments;
6. transportation;
7. services to members of the handicapped individual's family;
8. interpreter and reader services;
9. placement in suitable employment;
10. postemployment services necessary to maintain or regain other suitable employment; and
11. rehabilitation engineering services.

Eligibility

To be eligible for VR services, an individual must meet the following criteria:[2]

1. The individual must have a physical or mental disability that for that individual constitutes or results in a substantial handicap to employment; and
2. vocational rehabilitation services are reasonably expected to benefit the individual in terms of employability.

Eligibility Determination Process

The eligibility determination process proceeds through three stages:

1. The *preliminary diagnostic study*[3] determines whether the individual has a physical or mental disability that, for that individual, constitutes or results in a substantial handicap to employment; whether vocational rehabilitation services may reasonably be expected to benefit the individual in terms of employability; and whether an extended evaluation of vocational rehabilitation potential is necessary to make this determination. In all cases of mental or emotional disorder, an examination must be provided by a physician skilled in the diagnosis and treatment of such disorders or by a licensed psychologist.
2. The *thorough diagnostic study*.[4] Once an individual's eligibility for VR services has been determined, the Department must undertake a thorough diagnostic study to determine the na-

---

2. 34 C.F.R. § 361.1(c) (1991).
3. 34 C.F.R. § 361.32 (1991).
4. 34 C.F.R. § 361.33 (1991).

ture and scope of services needed by the individual. This study consists of a comprehensive evaluation of the individual's handicap to employment and rehabilitation needs. It includes a review of pertinent medical, psychological, vocational, educational, recreational, and other factors. The study must include an appraisal of the individual's employability; personality; intelligence level; educational achievement; work experience; personal, vocational, and social adjustment; employment opportunities; and other pertinent data helpful in determining the nature and scope of services needed.

3. *Extended evaluation to determine vocational rehabilitation potential.*[5] If the evaluations determine that the individual has a disability that substantially handicaps him or her in employment, but if it is unclear that VR services might benefit the individual in terms of employability, the Department may undertake an extended evaluation to determine vocational rehabilitation potential. This evaluation may last up to 18 months, during which time the individual will receive services necessary for the determination of rehabilitation potential.

Provision of Services

Each individual being provided VR services must have a written rehabilitation program.[6] Services must be provided in accordance with the written program. The program must be developed jointly by the VR counselor or coordinator and the individual.[7] The program must be based on a determination of employability designed to achieve the vocational objective of the individual and must be developed through assessments of the individual's particular rehabilitation needs. It must include the basis on which eligibility has been determined, the long-range and intermediate rehabilitation objectives, the specific rehabilitation services to be provided, an assessment of the expected need for postemployment services, a procedure for periodic review, and the terms and conditions for the provision of vocational rehabilitation services.

---

5. 34 C.F.R. § 361.34 (1991).
6. 34 C.F.R. § 361.40 (1991).
7. *Cf.* In re Wegner, 417 N.W.2d 97 (Minn. Ct. App. 1993) (the Department of Jobs and Training could properly refuse to include in the program plan a vocational goal that would not lead to gainful employment).

Independent Living Rehabilitation Services

Definition

Independent living rehabilitation services are those services designed to materially improve opportunities for persons with disabilities to live and function more independently in their home, family, and community.[8] They include[9]

1. counseling services, including psychological counseling, psychotherapeutic counseling, and peer counseling;
2. referral and counseling services with respect to attendant care;
3. counseling and advocacy with respect to legal and economic rights and benefits;
4. independent living skills training and counseling;
5. housing and transportation referral and assistance;
6. assistance in identifying appropriate housing and other support services;
7. education and training necessary for living in the community;
8. social and recreational activities;
9. attendant care and training of personnel to provide the care;
10. therapeutic treatment, such as speech, occupational, physical, recreational, drama, music, dance, and art therapies;
11. vocational and other training services, including personal and vocational adjustment; and
12. job placement services.

Eligibility

Eligibility for independent living rehabilitation services is based on the presence of three factors: (a) a severe physical or mental disability, (b) a severe limitation in ability to function independently in the family or community or to engage or continue in employment, and (c) a reasonable expectation that the independent living rehabilitation services will significantly assist the individual to improve his or her ability to function independently in the family or community or to engage or continue in employment.[10]

---

8. M.S.A. § 268A.11 (West Supp. 1992).
9. Id.; 34 CFR § 365.37 (1991).
10. 34 CFR § 365.31 (1991).

Procedures

Eligibility determinations are based on evaluations of applicants. The evaluation must be sufficient in scope to determine which services will best meet the current and future needs of the individual.[11] An individualized rehabilitation program must be written for each person who is provided services. It must be developed jointly by the staff and the program recipient.[12]

---

11. 34 CFR § 364.32 (1991).
12. 34 CFR § 365.36 (1991).

5B.4

Emotional Distress as a Basis for Civil Liability

The law of Minnesota recognizes the right to recover compensatory damages for emotional or mental suffering or distress.[1] The infliction of emotional distress is actionable in its own right under some circumstances. In addition, emotional suffering can appropriately be taken into account in calculating damages for other torts.

In cases involving claims based on emotional distress, MHPs often evaluate the origins, nature, severity, and prognosis of the plaintiff's emotional condition.

Emotional Distress as an Element of Damages

Traditionally, where a defendant has committed an actionable tort against the plaintiff, the jury, in measuring the amount of damages to award to the plaintiff, has been permitted to take into account any emotional or mental suffering caused by the defendant's tortious actions.[2] For example, in a suit to recover for injuries caused to the plaintiff by the defendant's negligent operation of a motor vehicle, the jury could properly consider the plaintiff's physical injuries, property damage, medical expenses, and mental suffering accompanying those injuries. Considered as an element of damages, the emotional injury is neither a neces-

---

1. *See generally* Steenson, *Civil Actions for Emotional Distress and R.A.V. v. City of St. Paul,* 18 Wm. Mitchell L. Rev. 983 (1992).
2. Minnesota Jury Instruction Guide III 155.

sary nor a sufficient element of the plaintiff's claim. Rather, the emotional suffering is compensable only if the plaintiff has an otherwise valid claim against the defendant. Put another way, there has traditionally existed no separate and independent claim for damages for emotional distress. On the other hand, where an independent basis for liability existed, recovery could be had for the associated emotional distress.[3]

In many cases, the "underlying" tort involved some physical injury. However, in the case of certain torts, recovery for resultant emotional distress has been allowed even if there was no accompanying physical injury. These torts consisted of conduct of the defendant that constituted a "direct invasion of the plaintiff's rights." Examples are slander, libel, malicious prosecution, seduction, and other similar willful, wanton, or malicious misconduct.[4] In addition, emotional distress damages have been allowed for harassment and discrimination claims under the Minnesota Human Rights Act, even though such violations involve no physical injury.[5]

Negligent Infliction of Emotional Distress

As long ago as 1892, Minnesota courts began to recognize a claim for damages for the negligent infliction of emotional distress.[6] In its modern formulation, recovery under this theory is governed by the following rules: The claimed emotional distress is compensable only if it was accompanied by a physical injury or manifestation. That is, the defendant's negligence must have caused a contemporaneous physical injury to the plaintiff, or if there was no such contemporaneous physical injury, the plaintiff must have been in the "zone of danger" and the emotional distress must have produced physical symptoms. The zone of danger rule requires that the plaintiff have been in some personal physical danger caused by the defendant's negligence.[7] The physical

---

3. Lee v. Metropolitan Airports Commission, 428 N.W.2d 815 (Minn. Ct. App. 1988); Johnson v. Miera, 433 N.W.2d 926 (Minn. Ct. App. 1989).
4. Hubbard v. UPI, Inc., 330 N.W.2d 428, 438 (Minn. 1983); see State Farm Mutual Automobile Ins. Co. v. Village of Isle, 122 N.W.2d 36 (Minn. 1963).
5. State v. Mower County, 434 N.W.2d 494 (Minn. Ct. App. 1989). See chapter 5B.12.
6. Purcell v. St. Paul City Railway, 48 Minn. 134, 50 N.W. 1034 (1892); Okrina v. Midwestern Corp., 282 Minn. 400, 165 N.W.2d 259 (Minn. 1969); Stadler v. Cross, 295 N.W.2d 552 (Minn. 1980).
7. Langeland v. Farmers State Bank of Trimont, 319 N.W.2d 26 (Minn. 1982); Quill v. TWA, 361 N.W.2d 438 (Minn. Ct. App. 1985), pet. for rev. denied (1985).

manifestation requirement is designed to ensure that the plaintiff's claim is real. Understandably, there is no clear line defining how severe the physical manifestation of the distress must be to allow compensation under the zone of danger theory. In one case involving the sudden, violent tailspin of a commercial airliner, the court found sufficient the plaintiff's sweaty hands, elevated blood pressure, and adrenaline surges that reoccurred on subsequent airplane flights.

Intentional Infliction of Emotional Distress

The two legal theories described above left a significant area of emotional distress noncompensable: intentional action on the part of the defendant that causes emotional–but not physical–injury to the plaintiff. This hole was partially closed in 1983 when the Minnesota Supreme Court approved recovery for the intentional infliction of emotional distress.[8] Still fearful of the possibility of frivolous or exaggerated claims for such mental suffering, the court limited this new tort to cases involving "particularly egregious facts." The court established the following elements for this tort: that the defendant's actions were extreme and outrageous, that the conduct was intentional or reckless, that the conduct caused emotional distress, and that the distress was severe.

The first element requires a societal judgment of the defendant's actions. The actions must be so atrocious that they pass the boundaries of decency and are utterly intolerable to a civilized community.[9] The second element involves the intent or knowledge of the defendant and is a factual determination. The third and fourth elements require that the plaintiff must have suffered severe emotional distress. Severe distress is distress that no reasonable person could be expected to endure.[10]

---

8. Hubbard v. UPI, Inc., 330 N.W.2d 428 (Minn. 1983).
9. *Id.*; Hagenson v. National Farmers Union Property and Casualty Co., 277 N.W.2d 648, 652 (Minn. 1979).
10. Hubbard v. UPI, Inc., 330 N.W.2d 428 (Minn. 1983).

5B.5

Mental Disabilities in Civil Tort Litigation

A person's mental condition may be significant in several ways in litigation concerning civil injuries. Mental condition may determine whether an individual is legally liable for his or her acts.[1] The mental status of the wrongdoer may be critical in determining whether the acts for which he or she is liable are covered by insurance. Furthermore, some mental disabilities will trigger special protections and procedures in court proceedings.

The Liability of a Person With Mental Deficiency

Minnesota has not addressed directly the question of tort liability for persons with mental deficiencies. Minnesota cases suggest that in general, a tort-feasor's cognitive capacities are presumed to be sufficient to form the requisite intent. In certain circumstances, however, the court has allowed the actor's mental condition to be taken into account. In particular, in determining whether an act was intentional for purposes of insurance coverage, testimony about mental condition is relevant and allowed.[2] It is unclear whether Minnesota will allow similar testimony in connection with the determination of the standard of care in negligence cases.

---

1. This chapter deals with liability for torts. Mental status is also of central importance in determining contract liability. *See* chapter 5B.6.
2. State Farm Fire & Cas. Co. v. Wicka, 474 N.W.2d 324, 330-31 (Minn. 1991).

Nationally, the generally accepted statement of tort law does not take the defendant's mental deficiency into account in determining liability for injuries caused to others. Under this statement of the law, a person's inability to see the consequences of his or her actions, to know they were wrong or dangerous, or to conform to generally acceptable standards would not excuse the person from liability.[3] Care should be taken in applying this statement of the law too broadly. Some courts have held, for example, that an individual's *physical* disabilities may be taken into account in determining the standard of care by which that person's actions should be judged.[4] Furthermore, some courts have held that the mental status of an injured party may be relevant in determining contributory or comparative fault, especially where the defendant's duty was to care for the disabled plaintiff.[5] These decisions may portend a more widespread willingness of courts to take specific mental disabilities into account in judging tort liability.

Mental Illness and Liability Insurance

Insurance policies routinely contain exclusionary clauses that deny coverage for personal injuries or property damage caused by the intentional actions of the insured. The exclusion reflects the basic idea that insurance is meant to protect against contingencies beyond the control of the insured. The Minnesota Supreme Court has adopted a two-pronged test to determine whether an insured's acts are to be deemed unintentional by reason of mental illness or defect. The test has a "cognitive" and a "volitional" component. The intentional-act exclusion is inapplicable where either component is satisfied. The cognitive component is satisfied where, because of a mental illness or defect, the insured does not know the nature or wrongfulness of an act. The volitional component is satisfied where, because of mental illness or defect, the insured is deprived of the ability to control his or her conduct regardless of any understanding of the nature of the act or its wrongfulness.[6] Note that this test is significantly broader than the test applicable in criminal law. See chapter 5D.9.

---

3. Restatement (Second) of Torts § 283(B).
4. *See* W. Page Keeton et al., Prosser and Keeton on the Law of Torts § 32, at 175–176 (5th ed. 1984).
5. *Id.*
6. State Farm Fire & Cas. Co. v. Wicka, 474 N.W.2d 324, 331 (Minn. 1991).

Procedural Rights of Mentally Incompetent Persons

To protect the rights of an incompetent person or minor who is a party to civil litigation, Minnesota law requires the person to have a personal representative sue or defend on his or her behalf. The representative–either a guardian[7] or a conservator[8]–makes litigation decisions on behalf of the disabled individual. The representative is not the person's lawyer, but rather stands in for the disabled person or minor as the client in the lawyer–client relationship.

If a person has a conservator or guardian, that representative may sue or defend on behalf of the individual.[9] If there is no such representative, the court in which an action is pending or is to be brought may appoint a guardian *ad litem*.[10] A guardian *ad litem* acts as the guardian of the individual only with respect to the litigation. A guardian *ad litem*, working with legal counsel, determines whether suit is advisable, authorizes suit, makes fundamental decisions about the direction of the litigation, and authorizes settlements and appeals.[11]

The law does not define incompetency in this specific context. However, at the very least, an individual who lacks the ability to enter into contracts would be considered incompetent for litigation purposes, because much of litigation, from retaining a lawyer to entering into settlements, requires contractual consent.

Once appointed, the guardian *ad litem* is treated just like a party to the action. To avoid conflict of interest, the lawyer for a party cannot serve as that party's guardian *ad litem*.[12]

Special rules govern the distribution of damages or settlement funds in personal injury actions. Where the funds are recovered on behalf of a minor or incompetent person, no funds may be paid to any person except under written petition to the court and written order of the court. This rule applies whether the funds are to be paid under a settlement, a jury verdict or court finding, or a judgment.[13] The court, upon receiving a petition, evaluates the proposed settlement, determines what expenses may be paid

---

7. *See* chapter 5A.2.
8. *See* chapter 5A.3.
9. Minn. R. Civ. Proc. 17.02.
10. *Id.* Guardians *ad litem* are sometimes appointed for minors in family and juvenile court proceedings. *See* chapters 5A.6, 5A.14, 5A.15.
11. Blacque v. Kalman, 30 N.W.2d 599 (Minn. 1948) (the guardian *ad litem* has a duty to examine the case and determine the most successful course of action).
12. General Rules of Practice for the District Courts, Rule 108.
13. General Rules of Practice for the District Courts, Rule 145.

from the proceeds, and specifies what disposition is to be made from the balance of the proceeds.

Competency to Contract

Capacity or *competency* is the legal label used to describe whether a person has the legal power to enter into a contract. Incapacity or incompetency can arise from a number of grounds.[1] This chapter discusses incapacity that arises from a deficiency in mental functioning.

Generally, the question of capacity arises only after a purported contract has been entered into. Lack of capacity may be raised by an individual (or by his or her guardian or conservator) in an effort to resist enforcement of the contract or undo its effects. The question may also arise at the time the contract is being contemplated. In either case, the role of the MHP will be to evaluate the individual's mental capacity in light of the legal standard for competency. Where an individual's capacity is questionable, prudent prospective contractors may demand that a guardian or conservator be sought for the individual. Depending on the powers granted to such a legal representative, she or he may have the capacity to enter into contracts that validly bind the incompetent individual.[2]

Legal Test of Competency to Contract

The test of whether a person was competent to enter into a contract is whether the person had, at the time the contract was

---

1. For example, minors are generally considered to lack the capacity to enter into contracts. *See* chapter 5A.11.
2. M.S.A. § 525.56, subd. 3(5) (West Supp. 1992). *See* chapters 5A.2 and 5A.3.

entered into, the capacity or ability to understand to a reasonable extent the nature and effect of what she or he was doing.[3]

The Minnesota courts are in some conflict over the effect of a legal adjudication of incompetency. Such an adjudication could be made by a court in connection with a guardianship or conservatorship proceeding. The question is whether a person who has been adjudicated incompetent in such a proceeding ever has the capacity to enter into a contract.[4] The guardianship law states that appointment of a guardian is "evidence of the incompetency of the ward," whereas appointment of a conservator, by itself, is not.[5] However, a guardian (and a conservator, if the court so orders) has the power to "approve or withhold approval of any contract, except for necessities, which the ward or conservatee may make or wish to make."[6] The Minnesota Supreme Court, interpreting prior guardianship law, has at times stated that the placement of a person under guardianship is "prima facie" evidence of incompetency,[7] that a person under guardianship is "conclusively presumed to be incompetent to make a valid contract of disposition of his property,"[8] and that an adjudication of incompetency is "evidence, but not conclusive, in any litigation to prove the mental condition of the alleged incompetent at the time the judgment was rendered or at any past time during which the judgment finds the person to be incompetent."[9]

Commitment under the civil commitment laws is not a judicial determination of legal incapacity, and commitment does not, in and of itself, deprive any person of the right to dispose of property, execute instruments, make purchases, or enter into contractual relationships.[10]

The fact that a person had not, at the time of the contract, been adjudicated incompetent and had no guardian is not conclusive on the issue of capacity to contract.[11] Incapacity to contract is in general a factual question. The fact that the person was placed under guardianship subsequent to entering into the contract is relevant to that determination.[12]

---

3. Krueger v. Zoch, 285 Minn. 332, 173 N.W.2d 18, 20 (Minn. 1969).
4. Wards in general have the capacity to enter into contracts for necessaries. M.S.A. § 525.56, subd. 3(5) (West Supp. 1992). *See* chapter 5A.2.
5. M.S.A. § 525.54, subd. 5 (West Supp. 1992). *See* chapters 5A.2 and 5A.3.
6. M.S.A. § 525.56, subd. 1(5) (West Supp. 1992).
7. Long v. Campion, 250 Minn. 196, 84 N.W.2d 686 (Minn. 1957).
8. Johnson v. Johnson, 8 N.W.2d 620, 622 (1943).
9. Schultz v. Oldenburg, 202 Minn. 247, 277 N.W. 918 (1938).
10. M.S.A. § 253B.23, subd. 2 (West Supp. 1992). *See* chapter 5E.4.
11. M.S.A. § 525.543; § 525.56, subd. 5 (West Supp. 1992).
12. Krueger v. Zoch, 285 Minn. 332, 173 N.W.2d 18 (1969).

Determination of Competency to Contract

An individual's capacity to contract is a question for the trier of fact, unless the evidence is conclusive.[13] Parties attacking the validity of the contract may bring in evidence of the individual's business acts, declarations, and conversations at the time of contract. Evidence will be liberally allowed on the issue of competency.[14]

Effect of Determination of Incapacity

Minnesota courts have held that contracts entered into by persons without capacity to contract are voidable rather than void.[15] In other words, the contract is enforceable unless the incompetent person asserts grounds to void it. Furthermore, the actions of the incompetent person, if taken after regaining competency, may be deemed an affirmance of the contract.[16]

---

13. Dunnell's Minnesota Digest, Vol. 4A, § 1.04 (4th ed. 1990).
14. Wheeler v. Mckeon, 137 Minn. 92, 162 N.W. 1070 (1917).
15. Dunnell's Minnesota Digest, Vol. 4A, § 1.04 (4th ed. 1990). Whitcomb v. Hardy, 73 Minn. 285, 76 N.W. 29 (1898); Ham v. Potter, 101 Minn. 439, 112 N.W. 1015 (1907). But see M.S.A. § 525.543 (West Supp. 1992), which uses the term *void*.
16. Dunnell's Minnesota Digest, Vol. 4A, § 1.04 (4th ed. 1990); Matz v. Martinson, 127 Minn. 262, 149 N.W. 370 (1914).

5B.7

Competency to Sign a Will

Persons (referred to as testators) who make wills or amend existing ones must meet minimum mental status requirements. If it is later shown that the person did not have the requisite testamentary capacity, the testator's estate will be distributed according to the terms of a previous valid will, if any, or by the intestacy (i.e., without a will) statutes of Minnesota.

Mental health consultation or testimony may be utilized where an MHP treated or evaluated the testator.[1] Alternatively, an MHP may be asked to provide an opinion concerning the person's mental status at the time the will was signed, on the basis of reports of other witnesses and any other relevant information.[2]

Test of Testamentary Capacity

Minnesota law defines *testamentary capacity* as follows: "Any person eighteen or more years of age who is of sound mind may make a will."[3] The test of whether the testator was of "sound mind" at the time the will was signed requires proof that the testator had the capacity to know and understand the nature, situation, and extent of his or her property and claims of others on his or her bounty or remembrance, and that he or she was able to hold these things in his or her mind long enough to form a

---

1. The doctor–patient privilege survives death and can be waived by the heirs who contest the will as well as by the one nominated as executor. Koenig v. Barrett, 247 Minn. 580, 78 N.W.2d 364 (1956). *See* chapters 4.2 and 4.3 for limitations on use of such information.
2. *See* chapter 5C.5.
3. M.S.A. § 524.2-501 (West 1975).

rational judgment concerning them.[4] The courts stress that only the capacity to have this knowledge is required; testamentary capacity does not require that the testator have actual knowledge of his or her property.[5] Testamentary capacity is less stringent than capacity to contract.[6] Thus, it is possible for a court to find that a person under guardianship[7] or conservatorship[8] at the time the will was made had the requisite testamentary capacity.[9]

Proving Testamentary Incapacity

When a will is being contested in court, the people supporting the will must initially prove that the will was properly executed.[10] The party opposing the will has the burden to prove lack of capacity.[11] The determination of whether the decedent lacked capacity is a factual issue for the trier of fact,[12] and its decision will not be reversed absent significant error.[13] Expert testimony is admissible on the issue of capacity. The court, however, is not bound by expert testimony, even if it is unrebutted by other expert testimony on the issue of capacity. Expert opinion is not conclusive of mental capacity but is merely evidence to be weighed along with the rest of the evidence by the trier of fact.[14]

---

4. In re Estate of Congdon, 309 N.W.2d 261 (Minn. 1981); In re Estate of Jenks, 291 Minn. 138, 189 N.W.2d 695 (1971).
5. Id.
6. See chapter 5B.6.
7. See chapter 5A.2.
8. See chapter 5A.3.
9. In re Estate of Congdon, 309 N.W.2d 261 (Minn. 1981).
10. M.S.A. § 524.3-407 (West 1975).
11. Id.
12. In re Rasmussens's Estate, 69 N.W.2d 630, 635 (Minn. 1955).
13. Id. at 636.
14. In re Estate of Congdon, 309 N.W.2d 261 (Minn. 1981).

5B.8

Competency to Vote

The right to vote may be denied or revoked on the basis of a judicial determination of mental incompetency. MHPs play a central role in such determinations.

To be eligible to vote in Minnesota, an individual must be 18 years of age or older, a citizen of the United States, and a resident of Minnesota for 20 days immediately preceding the election.[1]

The law specifies three disqualifying conditions. Two of these relate to mental competency: Persons who are under guardianship of the person[2] and persons who have been found by a court of law to be "legally incompetent" are ineligible to vote.[3] Note that both disqualifying conditions require a formal, judicial adjudication.

Minnesota law specifically provides that civil commitment[4] is not an adjudication of incompetency[5] and does not deprive the committed individual of the right to vote.[6] Thus, the only venues for the adjudication of legal incompetency are guardianship and

---

1. M.S.A. § 201.013, subd. 1 (West Supp. 1992); Minn. Const. Art. VII, § 1.
2. See chapter 5A.2.
3. M.S.A. § 201.013, subd. 2 (West Supp. 1992). The Minnesota Constitution states that persons who are "insane or not mentally competent" are ineligible. The third condition of ineligibility is conviction of treason or a felony.
4. See chapters 5E.4, 5E.5, 5E.7.
5. M.S.A. § 253B.23, subd. 2 (West 1992).
6. M.S.A. § 253B.23, subd. 2 (West 1992). This section applies to persons committed as mentally ill, mentally ill and dangerous, mentally retarded, or chemically dependent. It probably also covers people committed as psychopathic personalities. See M.S.A. § 526.10, subd. 1 (West 1992) (provisions of commitment law apply with "like force and effect to persons having a psychopathic personality. . . .").

conservatorship proceedings.[7] A person placed under guardianship of the person is, by that placement, disqualified from voting. Appointment of a conservator would be disqualifying only if the court specifically made a finding that the person was "legally incompetent."

There is some inconsistency in the law governing this area. There is a provision of law that requires probate judges to report to the county auditor the names of persons "adjudged legally incompetent by reason of mental illness, mental deficiency, or inebriation" and those of persons adjudged psychopathic personalities.[8] The auditors are to attach notices to voter registration cards informing election judges that these individuals are not eligible to reregister or vote.[9] These provisions appear to be potentially inconsistent with the provisions of the law stating that civil commitment is not a finding of incompetency. These provisions of the law are implemented at the county level. Thus, there may be some inconsistency in application around the state.

---

7. *See* chapters 5A.2 and 5A.3. In general, civil commitment courts do not make competency decisions. However, commitment courts may make competency decisions in connection with nonconsensual administration of intrusive treatment. *See* M.S.A. § 253B.03, subds. 6a, 6b, 6c (West 1992), and chapter 6.2. These are not findings of "legal incompetency" in any broad sense, but rather competency "to consent" to the treatment. Arguably, then, these findings of incompetency would not deprive a person of the right to vote.

8. M.S.A. § 201.15, subd. 1 (West 1992).

9. *Id.*

5B.9

Competency to Obtain a Driver's License

The law provides that a person who has been adjudged legally incompetent by reason of mental illness or deficiency will not be issued a driver's license unless the Department of Motor Vehicles is satisfied that the person is competent to drive safely.[1]

The commissioner of public safety of Minnesota also has discretion to determine if a person suffering from a mental disability or disease is competent to exercise the care needed for driving.[2] The commissioner has the power to cancel a driver's license if, at the time of cancellation, the driver would not be entitled to receive a license because of mental illness or deficiency.[3]

1. M.S.A. § 171.04, subd. 1(5) (West Supp. 1992).
2. M.S.A. § 171.04, subd. 1(9) (West Supp. 1992).
3. M.S.A. § 171.14 (West Supp. 1992).

5B.10

Product Liability

Product liability litigation seeks compensation for personal injuries or property damages arising out of the use of a product. Although a product liability claim may be based on principles of negligence[1] or warranty,[2] this chapter is limited to the third basis, strict tort liability. The central element of this claim is that the product was unreasonably dangerous for its intended use. MHPs who have special expertise in "human factors," the interaction of people and machines, may be asked to evaluate the dangerousness of a product and testify in court as to the results.

Elements of a Product Liability Claim[3]

The law provides that a manufacturer or seller[4] is subject to liability for physical harm to the user or the user's property if the product is in a defective condition and unreasonably dangerous.[5]

---

1. *Negligence* means that the wrongdoer's conduct fell below what would be expected of the reasonably prudent person in the particular circumstances.
2. A warranty claim alleges that the product did not work as promised or represented by the seller or manufacturer.
3. *See generally* Arthur, L. G. (1991). *Minnesota products liability.* Minneapolis: Minnesota Institute of Legal Education.
4. A *seller* means any person engaged in the business of selling products for use or consumption. It applies to manufacturers, wholesalers, distributors, or retailers. Restatement (Second) of Torts § 402A, comment f.
5. For the most part, Minnesota follows Restatement (Second) of Torts § 402A. McCormack v. Hankscraft Co., 278 Minn. 322, 154 N.W.2d 488 (1967).

"Defective condition" refers to its state at the time it left the seller.[6] Whether a product is "unreasonably dangerous" is measured by various tests. Under some circumstances, courts use the "reasonable care balancing test." This test considers all of the facts and circumstances, including the "likelihood and seriousness of harm [and] the feasibility and burden of any precautions which would be effective to avoid the harm." The manufacturer is obligated to keep informed of scientific knowledge in its field.[7] Under other circumstances, the courts use the "consumer expectation standard." Under this standard, a product is in unreasonably dangerous condition if it is more dangerous than would be contemplated by the ordinary consumer who purchases it, with the ordinary knowledge common to the community as to its characteristics.[8] Furthermore, a product may be unreasonably dangerous because of the absence of adequate instructions for use and warnings as to misuse.[9] The basic issue is whether the product, taken with available instructions and warnings, is likely to be more dangerous than expected.[10]

Defenses to a Product Liability Claim

Minnesota provides four basic defenses to a product liability claim: (a) misuse and alteration, (b) open and obvious hazard, (c) assumption of the risk, and (d) state of the art defense.[11]

The defense of misuse and alteration is available when the product in question is used or altered in a way that makes it dangerous or harmful.[12]

The next defense involves the design of the product. The purpose of the product may mean that some dangers are inevitable.[13] If such a danger is open and obvious, the jury may take its obviousness into account in determining whether the plaintiff acted with reasonable care.[14]

The "assumption of the risk" defense is a total bar to recovery.[15] The defense, which is closely related to the open and obvi-

---

6. Restatement (Second) of Torts § 402A(h).
7. Minnesota Jury Instruction Guide (JIG) III 117.
8. Bilotta v. Kelly Co., Inc., 346 N.W.2d 616 (Minn. 1984). Restatement (Second) of Torts § 402A(i).
9. Minn. JIG III 119; Restatement (Second) of Torts § 402(A)(j).
10. Id.
11. Arthur, Minnesota products liability, supra note 3.
12. Magnuson v. Rupp Mfg., 285 Minn. 32, 171 N.W.2d 201 (1969).
13. Arthur, Minnesota products liability, supra note 3, p. 50.
14. Holm v. Sponco Mfg., Inc., 324 N.W.2d 207, 212 (Minn. 1982).
15. Arthur, Minnesota products liability, supra note 3, p. 55.

ous hazard defense, arises if the plaintiff has voluntarily entered into a situation where the defendant's negligence is obvious.[16]

Finally, the "state of the art" defense refers to the principle that the manufacturer's liability is determined in reference to the level of knowledge and practice at the time of manufacture.[17] This evidence may be considered in determining whether the product was defective and unreasonably dangerous.[18]

16. Andrew v. White-Rodgers, 465 N.W.2d 102 (Minn. Ct. App. 1991), rev. denied.
17. Arthur, *Minnesota products liability, supra* note 3, p. 55; Minn. JIG III, 119.
18. Employers Mutual Insurance Co. v. Oakes Mfg. Co., 356 N.W.2d 719 (Minn. Ct. App. 1984).

5B.11

Unfair Competition

The regulation of unfair trade practices operates against a background of laissez-faire competition.[1] Vigorous competition, by definition, may result in one business prevailing to the detriment of another. Such interference, when pursued for self-interest, is generally legal. However, certain categories of competition have been made unlawful, either because their methods are deemed unfair to competitors or because their effects are considered harmful to the public. A bevy of statutory schemes and common law doctrines allows victims of such practices to sue for damages or to seek to enjoin the practices from continuing.[2] In addition, many statutory schemes provide for governmental involvement through the issuance of regulations and guidelines for competition, the registration of distinctive marks, the imposition of fines, and the issuance of orders to cease and desist.[3]

Of principal interest to MHPs are those trade laws that make competitive practices actionable on the grounds that the practices deceive or engender confusion in the minds of the consuming public. Legal liability for such practices falls under two main headings. First, deceptive practices are actionable when they falsely represent the quality or other attributes of a product or

---

1. Dunnell's Minnesota Digest, Unfair Competition, § 100; Restatement of the Law: Unfair Competition (Tentative Draft No. 1) (1988) § 1.
2. *See, e.g.,* 15 U.S.C. § 1051 et seq. (trademarks); 15 U.S.C. § 41 et seq. (Federal Trade Commission); M.S.A. § 325D.43 et seq. (Minnesota Uniform Deceptive Trade Practices Act); Scott v. Mego Int'l, Inc., 519 F. Supp. 1118, 1126 (D. Minn. 1989) (suit for common law trademark infringement); Mayo Clinic v. Mayo's Drug and Cosmetic, Inc., 262 Minn. 101, 113 N.W.2d 852 (1962); Sheffield-King Milling Co. v. Sheffield Mill & Elevator Co., 105 Minn. 315, 117 N.W. 447 (1908).
3. *See, e.g.,* authorities cited in note 2.

service.[4] Conduct of this type is generally described as "false advertising." Second, confusion is actionable when advertising or packaging has created the false impression that two goods, actually made by different manufacturers, share a common source, origin, or sponsorship. Conduct of this latter type falls within the general heading of trademark or service mark infringement.

MHPs are sometimes employed in unfair competition litigation to help develop evidence of whether advertising or packaging has deceived or confused the typical relevant consumer.[5] Anything that affects the perception of the relevant consumers is pertinent to these inquiries.[6] Thus, factors that a court will take into consideration in determining whether the public is confused are the names of the products,[7] the use of color and design in packaging,[8] the precautions the defendant has taken to distinguish its product from that of the plaintiff,[9] channels of trade, and characteristics of the relevant consumers.[10]

There is a significant separate body of law governing the use of trademarks and service marks.[11] Marks can be registered and protected under either federal[12] or state law.[13] Although marks can be registered, registration is not determinative of whether the mark is protectable.[14] Rather, the degree of protection of the trademark depends on the nature of the mark and how it has been used. Courts have developed four categories to classify the validity and strength of a purported trademark. Protection is afforded only to valid trademarks in a degree proportionate to their

---

4. See M.S.A. § 325D.44, subd. 1 (West Supp. 1992).
5. See, e.g., Mayo Clinic v. Mayo's Drug and Cosmetic, Inc., 262 Minn. 101, 113 N.W.2d 852 (1962). Some cases are decided without the use of such evidence, the court making a decision "of law" that the confusion, if any exists, is not legally actionable. Team Central, Inc. v. Xerox Corp., 606 F. Supp. 1408, 1413 (D. Minn. 1985) (use of term "Team Xerox" did not violate rights of "Team Electronics" because word "team" was used generically, and thus evidence of public understanding was not relevant).
6. Restatement of the Law: Unfair Competition, § 21, comment (a).
7. Winston & Newell Co. v. Piggly Wiggly Norwest, Inc., 221 Minn. 287, 22 N.W.2d 61 (1946) (use of names that are highly descriptive of the product tends to negate a claim of unfairness).
8. Color or a color combination may be protectable where the coloring has acquired a "secondary meaning so that the color indicates the source of the product." Id.
9. Id. (Despite "strikingly similar" products and packaging, defendant did not "palm off" its product because it took reasonable steps to identify the source of its product.)
10. See Restatement of the Law: Unfair Competition (Tentative Draft No. 1) (1988) § 2.
11. McCarthy, J. T. (1984). Trademarks and Unfair Competition. Rochester, NY: Lawyers Co-operative.
12. 15 U.S.C. § 1051. There is also a body of common law protecting trademarks. Scott v. Mego Int'l, Inc., 519 F. Supp. 1118, 1126 (D. Minn. 1989).
13. M.S.A. § 325D.43 et seq.
14. Scott v. Mego Int'l, Inc., 519 F. Supp. 1118, 1127 (D. Minn. 1989).

"strength."[15] The categories, in order of increasing strength, are (a) generic, (b) descriptive, (c) suggestive, and (d) arbitrary or fanciful.[16] Generic terms (those commonly used as the name or description of a kind of goods) cannot be trademarks and are therefore afforded no trademark protection. Descriptive terms are given protection only if they have been used so extensively as to have acquired "secondary meaning."[17] Suggestive terms, which are conceptually between descriptive terms and fanciful and arbitrary terms, are entitled to trademark protection upon initial use, without proof of secondary meaning. Arbitrary and fanciful terms are afforded the strongest trademark protection.[18] They are also protected upon first use and require no secondary meaning.

Much of the litigation surrounding marks is concerned with determining whether the mark is valid and what its strength is. If the mark is held to be valid and thus entitled to protection, the issue becomes whether the defendant has "infringed" the plaintiff's mark. The test for infringement is whether "consumers are likely to be confused or deceived by" the defendant's use of the mark such that "the consuming public is likely to be confused as to the origin or sponsorship of goods."[19]

---

15. *Id.* at 1126.
16. *Id.*
17. *Id.* Secondary meaning "exists when the public interprets a mark to be not only an identification of the product, but also a representation of the product's origin." In essence, secondary meaning is achieved when the relevant public learns to use the trademark primarily as a source identifier for the trademark owner's goods, thereby displacing the preexisting, descriptive meaning of the term.
18. *Id.* at 1127.
19. *Id.* at 1128-299 (listing factors to be considered by the court in determining whether there has been such confusion).

5B.12

Discrimination

The law prohibits discrimination on a wide variety of personal characteristics in a variety of settings. MHPs are affected by these laws as employers and service providers, as consultants in testing and evaluation, and as expert witnesses when discrimination has been alleged.

The law of discrimination is complex and has many sources. The state of Minnesota has a comprehensive Human Rights Act.[1] Many municipalities have ordinances defining and prohibiting discrimination.[2] Finally, there are extensive federal laws and regulations governing discrimination.[3] This chapter provides only a basic summary of the law of discrimination. We focus on the law of the state of Minnesota, on the newly enacted Americans with Disabilities Act, and, in those contexts, on the forms of discrimination likely to be of most relevance to MHPs.

The law prohibits discrimination on the basis of a list of characteristics with respect to a specified list of circumstances. Under Minnesota law, for example, discrimination is prohibited with respect to the following characteristics: age, disability,[4] familial status, marital status, national origin, race, color, creed,

---

1. M.S.A. § 363.01 et seq.
2. See, e.g., Minneapolis, MN, Civil Rights Ordinance, Chapter 139, §§ 139.10 to 142.70 (1992).
3. See, e.g., Americans with Disabilities Act of 1990, 42 U.S.C. 12101 et seq.; Section 504 of the Rehabilitation Act of 1973, 29 U.S.C. § 701 et seq.; Title VII of the Civil Rights Act of 1964, 42 U.S.C. § 2000a et seq.
4. *Disability* means "any condition or characteristic that renders a person a disabled person. A disabled person is any person who (1) has a physical, sensory, or mental impairment which materially limits one or more major life activities; (2) has a record of such an impairment; or (3) is regarded as having such an impairment." M.S.A. § 363.01, subd. 13. (West 1991).

religion, sex, sexual orientation, and status with regard to public assistance.[5] Discrimination is prohibited in the following contexts: employment, real property, public accommodations,[6] public services, and educational institutions.

As expert witnesses, MHPs may be involved in several ways. MHPs may be asked to evaluate psychological damage suffered by a plaintiff in a discrimination case.[7] MHPs may also be asked to evaluate an employment or other setting to assess whether it poses a hostile or otherwise discriminatory environment.[8] In the context of disability discrimination, MHPs will be centrally involved in assessing the capabilities of plaintiffs and the bona fides of asserted job qualifications. They may also be asked to describe modifications or accommodations that would make a workplace or other setting accessible to a disabled plaintiff.

Minnesota Law

Employment

Employers and labor organizations are covered by the employment discrimination prohibition. Employers are prohibited from discriminating with respect to hiring, tenure, compensation, and terms of employment, on the basis of race, color, creed, religion, national origin, sex, marital status, status with regard to public assistance, disability, sexual orientation, or age. Actions taken on the basis of a "bona fide occupational qualification" are not prohibited.

Employers, employment agencies, and labor organizations may not, before a person is employed or admitted, require or request the person to furnish information pertaining to any of the protected characteristics.[9]

Employers with 50 or more permanent, full-time employees must make "reasonable accommodations" to the known disability of a qualified disabled person or job applicant, unless the employer can demonstrate that the accommodation would impose an undue hardship on the business.[10] A "qualified disabled person" is a person who, with reasonable accommodations, can

---

5. M.S.A. § 363.01 (West Supp. 1993).
6. *See* below for a definition of this term.
7. Kresko v. Rulli, 432 N.W.2d 764 (Minn. Ct. App. 1988), rev. denied (Minn. 1989).
8. Jensen v. Eveleth Taconite Co., 824 F. Supp. 847 (D.Minn. 1993) (expert testimony on sex stereotyping, sexualized work environment, "priming" effect).
9. There are some exceptions. For example, a law enforcement agency may request certain information for purposes of doing a background check. M.S.A. § 363.03, subd. 1 (West Supp. 1993).
10. M.S.A. § 363.03, subd. 1 (West Supp. 1993).

perform the essential functions required of all applicants for the job. "Disability," in this context, excludes any condition resulting from alcohol or drug abuse that prevents a person from performing the essential functions of the job in question or that constitutes a direct threat to the property or safety of others.[11] "Reasonable accommodation" includes such steps as making facilities accessible and usable by the disabled person, job restructuring, modified work schedules, acquisition or modification of equipment or devices, and the provision of aides. In determining whether an accommodation would impose an undue hardship on a business, a number of factors are considered, including the overall size of the business, the nature and cost of the accommodations, the ability of the business to finance the accommodations, and good faith efforts to explore less restrictive or less expensive alternatives, including consultation with the disabled person or with knowledgeable disabled persons or organizations. It is a defense to an action that the person complaining has a disability that, under the particular circumstances and even with reasonable accommodation, poses a serious threat to the health or safety of the disabled person or others.[12]

Discrimination laws are often held to prohibit practices that have the effect of discrimination, even though they were not specifically intended to discriminate. Employment tests are evaluated to determine whether they have discriminatory or disparate impact on protected groups. Minnesota law specifically permits the administration of pre-employment tests, provided that the tests measure only essential job-related abilities, are required of all applicants for the same position (regardless of disability), and accurately measure the applicants' aptitude, achievement level, or whatever factors they purport to measure, rather than reflecting the applicants' impaired sensory, manual, or speaking skills (except when those are the skills that the tests purport to measure).[13]

Public Accommodations

Under Minnesota Law, it is unlawful to discriminate in the provision of public accommodations on the basis of race, color, creed, religion, disability, national origin, sexual orientation, or sex.[14] "Public accommodation" means any "business, accommodation ... of any kind, whether licensed or not, whose goods, services, facilities ... are extended, offered, sold, or otherwise made

---

11. M.S.A. § 363.01, subd. 35 (West 1991).
12. M.S.A. § 363.02, subd. 5 (West 1991).
13. M.S.A. § 363.02, subd. 1 (West Supp. 1993).
14. M.S.A. § 363.03, subd. 3 (West Supp. 1993).

available to the public."[15] Thus, the practice of MHPs would be included in this definition and covered by the law.

Providers of public accommodations must make "reasonable accommodations" to the known physical disability of a disabled person.

Public Services

Under Minnesota law, it is unlawful to discriminate in the provision of public services because of race, color, creed, religion, national origin, disability, sex, sexual orientation, or status with regard to public assistance.[16] Public services are those facilities or governmental operations owned, operated, or managed by or on behalf of the state or any subdivision of the state.[17] Providers of public services must ensure that they provide physical and program access for disabled persons, unless they can demonstrate that the provision of this access would impose an undue hardship on the program. "Physical access" means the absence of physical obstacles that limit a disabled person's opportunity for full and equal use of or benefit from the services.[18] "Program access" means the use of auxiliary aids or services to ensure full and equal use of or benefit from goods and services, and the absence of criteria or methods of administration that directly or indirectly subject qualified disabled persons to discrimination on the basis of disability or that defeat or impair the objectives of the program.[19] A "qualified disabled person" is a person who meets the "essential eligibility criteria required of all applicants for the program or service in question."[20]

Sexual Harassment

One common form of sex discrimination is sexual harassment. Although most commonly associated with employment settings, sexual harassment is actionable in public accommodations, public services, and educational and housing settings as well.

The law defines two types of sexual harassment.[21] Both involve some form of unwelcome sexual behavior. *Quid pro quo* harassment is present when submission to that conduct is made a condition or term of obtaining or keeping employment, public accommodations, public services, education, or housing. It is also present when the individual's response to the unwelcome con-

15. M.S.A. § 363.01, subd. 3 (West 1991).
16. M.S.A. § 363.03, subd. 4 (West Supp. 1993).
17. M.S.A. § 363.01, subd. 19 (West 1991).
18. M.S.A. § 363.01, subd. 33 (West 1991).
19. M.S.A. § 363.01, subd. 34 (West 1991).
20. *Id.*, subd. 25a(2).
21. M.S.A. § 363.01, subd. 10a (West Supp. 1993).

duct is used as a factor affecting the individual's employment, public accommodations, public services, education, or housing.

Hostile environment harassment occurs when the conduct has the purpose or effect of substantially interfering with the individual's employment, public accommodations, public services, education, or housing, or creates an intimidating, hostile, or offensive environment. Hostile environment employment harassment is actionable only if the employer knew, or should have known, of the conduct and failed to take timely and appropriate action.

Disability Discrimination Under the Americans With Disabilities Act

The Americans with Disabilities Act (ADA) of 1990[22] prohibits discrimination on the basis of disability in employment,[23] public services,[24] and public accommodations and services operated by private entities.[25]

Employment

The ADA prohibits employment discrimination against a "qualified individual with a disability" in regard to all aspects of employment.[26] A person is a "qualified individual with a disability" if he or she can, with our without reasonable accommodation, perform the essential functions of the employment position. In determining what functions of a job are "essential," consideration is given to the employer's judgment and to any written job description, but neither is conclusive on the issue.[27] The term "reasonable accommodation" includes making existing facilities readily accessible to and usable by people with disabilities, and such changes as job restructuring; modified work schedules; reassignment; use of equipment; and adjustment or modification of examinations, training materials, or policies.[28]

It is unlawful for an employer to refuse to make reasonable accommodations to the known physical or mental limitations of an otherwise qualified individual with a disability, unless the employer can demonstrate that the accommodation would impose an undue hardship on the business. The ADA prohibits using standards, tests, or selection criteria that screen out or tend

---

22. 42 U.S.C. § 12101 et seq.
23. 42 U.S.C. §§ 12111 to 12117.
24. 42 U.S.C. §§ 12131 to 12165.
25. 42 U.S.C. §§ 12181 to 12189.
26. 42 U.S.C. § 12112.
27. 42 U.S.C. § 12111(8).
28. 42 U.S.C. § 12111(9).

to screen out disabled persons, unless the standards are shown to be job-related for the position in question and are consistent with business necessity. The ADA requires that tests used in the employment situation accurately reflect the tested skills or aptitude, rather than impaired sensory, manual, or speaking skills (except where those skills are the factors the test purports to measure).[29] The law prohibits pre-employment inquiries or examinations regarding disabilities unless the inquiries relate to the ability of an applicant to perform job-related functions.[30] Employers are allowed to use standards, tests, and selection criteria, even if they tend to screen out individuals with a disability, if they have been shown to be job-related and consistent with business necessity and if adequate performance cannot be accomplished by reasonable accommodation.[31] In addition, an employer may set qualification standards to exclude those who pose a direct threat to the health or safety of other individuals in the workplace.

Public Accommodation and Public Services

The ADA prohibits governmental agencies from excluding qualified individuals with disabilities from the benefits of their services, programs, and activities.[32] A person with a disability is "qualified" if he or she meets the "essential eligibility requirements" for the services or programs. "Reasonable modifications" of rules, policies, practices, architecture, transportation, and communication must be considered in determining whether the person meets the eligibility requirements.[33]

Discrimination on the basis of disability in public accommodations is unlawful.[34] The rules applicable to public accommodation discrimination are complex and vary to some extent from context to context. In general, it is unlawful to deny participation to, to separate, or to provide unequal participation opportunities to disabled persons.[35] Services must be provided in the most integrated setting appropriate to the needs of the individual with a disability. Reasonable accommodations must be made unless the provider of services can demonstrate that the modifications would fundamentally alter the nature of the services.[36] Architectural and communication barriers must be removed where the removal is readily achievable.[37]

---

29. 42 U.S.C. § 12112(b).
30. 42 U.S.C. § 12112(d).
31. 42 U.S.C. § 12113(a).
32. 42 U.S.C. § 12132.
33. 42 U.S.C. § 12131(2).
34. 42 U.S.C. § 12182.
35. 42 U.S.C. § 12182(a).
36. 42 U.S.C. § 12182(a)(2).
37. *Id.*

Section **5C**

Civil/Criminal Matters

5C.1

Jury Selection

Parties in civil and criminal cases exercise control over the make-up of the jury through *peremptory* and *for-cause* challenges to potential jurors. MHPs may be involved in this process by conducting pretrial surveys, constructing questions to ask the potential jurors, and evaluating jurors on the basis of the results of pretrial surveys and/or of in-court observations.

Juror Qualifications

The jury selection process begins by a random selection of names from a source list that reflects registered voters in a county.[1] This source list may be supplemented with names from other lists.[2] These selected persons are then required to complete a juror eligibility questionnaire.[3] Eligible jurors must be U.S. citizens, at least 18 years of age, residents of the county, able to communicate in English, and physically and mentally capable of rendering satisfactory jury service. A prospective juror is automatically disqualified if he or she is a judge, is a person convicted of a felony whose civil rights have not been restored, or has served as a state

---

1. General Rules of Practice, Rule 806; Minn. R. Crim. P. 26.02, subd. 1.
2. General Rules of Practice, Rule 806.
3. General Rules of Practice, Rule 807. The questionnaire requests information to determine whether the person meets the criteria for eligibility and whether there is a mental or physical disability that would prevent the person from rendering satisfactory jury service. The questionnaire also requests basic background information including age, race, gender, occupation, educational level, address, marital status, prior jury service, occupation of spouse, and ages of any children.

or federal grand or petit juror within the past four years.[4] After the disqualification determination, each prospective juror is served with a summons requiring the prospective juror to report for jury service at a specified time and place.[5] Those summoned may request to be excused on a number of grounds: impairment of their ability to handle the information, hardship of jury service, or membership in or employment at the legislature while in session.[6] Panels of potential jurors for a particular trial are then selected from the pool of eligible jurors called on the day of the trial.

Criminal Trials

Defendant's Right to a Jury

A defendant is entitled to a jury trial in any prosecution for an offense punishable by incarceration. In any prosecution for the violation of a misdemeanor not punishable by incarceration, trial is before a judge without a jury.[7] A defendant may waive the right to trial by jury if the court approves and if the waiver is made after the defendant has been advised of his or her rights by the court and has had an opportunity to consult with his or her counsel.[8]

Jury Size

In a criminal action where the offense charged is a felony, the jury must consist of 12 persons. In all other cases, only 6 jurors are required to be impaneled.[9] The parties, however, may stipulate any time before the verdict that the jury may consist of a lesser number than that provided by law.[10]

Unanimity Requirement

Verdicts require a unanimous decision of the jury unless the parties and court stipulate a lesser percentage.[11]

---

4. General Rules of Practice, Rule 808.
5. General Rules of Practice, Rule 801; Minn. R. Crim. P. 26.02, subd. 1.
6. General Rules of Practice, Rule 810.
7. Minn. R. Crim. P. 26.01, subds. 1(a), (b).
8. Minn. R. Crim. P. 26.01, subd. 2(a). *See* chapter 5D.2 for a discussion of the issue of competency to waive the right to a jury trial.
9. Minn. Const. of 1857, Art. 1, § 6 (amended 1988).
10. Minn. R. Crim. P. 26.01, subd. 4.
11. Minn. R. Crim. P. 26.01, subd. 6.

Change of Venue

In general, criminal trials are tried in the county in which the offense is alleged to have taken place.[12] The place of trial (venue) may be changed to another county within the state if the court is satisfied that a fair and impartial trial cannot be had in the county in which the case is pending.[13] If the request for a change of venue is based on prejudicial pretrial publicity, the party must show that the dissemination of potentially prejudicial material creates a likelihood that, in the absence of the trial being moved, a fair trial cannot be had. The party requesting the move does not have to show actual prejudice.[14] The moving party may support the motion to change venue by presenting the court with testimony or affidavits of individuals in the community, qualified public opinion surveys, or other materials having probative value.[15] MHPs may be involved in designing and conducting a survey of a sample of potential jurors within a county to determine the level of prejudice or bias toward the particular parties, attorneys, or issues in the case. The results may then be used in a pretrial motion for a change of venue. In addition, MHPs may be called to testify in a pretrial hearing on the matter.

Voir Dire

After a determination on venue is made, the process of selecting the jurors who will serve in the case begins. First, the court administrators select a panel of potential jurors. Then, through a process called *voir dire*, the lawyers and judge select the actual jurors and alternates from that panel.

From the potential juror pool assembled that day, the court randomly selects the panel from which the jury and its alternates will be chosen. The panel is larger than the number of jurors and alternates because each of the parties has a right to strike a given number of panelists by use of *peremptory challenges*. The number of panel members equals the number needed to serve on the jury itself, plus the number of alternates, plus the number of peremptory challenges allowed the parties.[16]

The number of peremptory challenges granted to each party is specified by law. If the offense charged is punishable by life imprisonment, the defendant is allowed 15 peremptory challenges, and the state is allowed 9. For any other offense, the defendant is entitled to 5 and the state to 3 peremptory challenges. In cases where there is more than one defendant, the court

---

12. Minn. R. Crim. P. 24.01.
13. Minn. R. Crim. P. 24.03, subd. 1(a)(d); Minn. R. Crim. P. 25.02, subd. 3.
14. Minn. R. Crim. P. 25.02, subd. 3.
15. Minn. R. Crim. P. 25.02, subd. 2.
16. Minn. R. Crim. P. 26.02, subd. 4(3)(a)(1).

may allow the defendants additional peremptory challenges and permit them to be exercised separately or jointly, and in that event the state's peremptory challenges are correspondingly increased.[17]

Prior to the commencement of the voir dire process, the parties and the court are furnished with information, previously collected by the clerk of court, about the members of the panel of potential jurors.[18] Then the process of voir dire examination begins. Voir dire examination is conducted for the purpose of discovering the prospective jurors' qualifications to serve as jurors in the case. The information gathered is used as a basis for exercising two types of challenges to potential jurors: *for-cause* and *peremptory* challenges.[19]

The court initiates the voir dire examination of the potential jurors by identifying the parties and their respective counsel and by briefly outlining the nature of the case. The judge then asks each prospective juror, or all of the jurors collectively, any questions that he or she thinks necessary, touching on their qualifications to serve as jurors in the case. Either party, commencing with the defendant, may make reasonable inquiries of the qualifications of prospective jurors.[20]

Each party may make an unlimited number of for-cause challenges during or at the close of the voir dire. A for-cause challenge alleges that a potential juror is unqualified. The following are among the grounds on which a for-cause challenge may be made:[21]

1. the existence of a state of mind that satisfies the court that the juror cannot try the case impartially and without prejudice;

2. a felony conviction, unless the juror's civil rights have been restored;

3. the lack of any of the qualifications prescribed by law to render a person a competent juror;[22]

4. a physical or mental defect that renders him or her incapable of performing the duties of a juror;

5. a familial relationship (consanguinity or affinity within the ninth degree) to a person involved in the case;

6. a family, business, or fiduciary relationship to a person involved in the case;

---

17. Minn. R. Crim. P. 26.02, subd. 6.
18. Minn. R. Crim. P. 26.02.
19. Minn. R. Crim. P. 26.02, subd. 4(1).
20. Minn. R. Crim. P. 26.02, subd. 4(1); 26.02, subd. 4(3)(a)(3). In federal courts, voir dire questioning is generally conducted solely by the judge.
21. Minn. R. Crim. P. 26.02, subd. 5(1).
22. *See* above.

7. being a party adverse to the defendant in a civil action; or having complained against, or been accused by, the defendant in a criminal prosecution; and/or

8. having been involved with the defendant in some other court case (either criminal or civil).

The attorneys make their for-cause challenges known to the court by stating the grounds on which they are based. If the court sustains the challenge, the potential juror is excused.[23]

After both parties have had an opportunity to challenge for cause, each, starting with the defendant, may alternately strike potential jurors by exercising their peremptory challenges. Traditionally, the exercise of peremptory challenges has been considered to be totally discretionary with each party and his or her attorney. These challenges are often used to eliminate from the jury persons whose answers to voir dire questions or other personal characteristics suggest a lack of sympathy toward the party. MHPs are often involved in helping to evaluate potential jurors or in developing "profiles" for the attorneys and parties to use in exercising peremptory challenges. Recent Supreme Court cases have held that parties cannot exercise peremptory challenges on the basis of the race of the prospective juror.[24] Lower court cases have split on the propriety of using other factors, such as gender or religion.[25] After both parties have exercised their challenges, the jury is constituted by the remaining panel members.[26]

Civil Trials

Right to a Jury Trial

Complex rules govern a party's right to a jury trial in civil cases. In general, a party has a right to have a jury determine factual issues in claims for money only or for the recovery of specific real or personal property.[27] These claims are labeled claims *at law*.

---

23. Minn. R. Crim. P. 26.02, subd. 5(2).
24. Bateson v. Kentucky, 476 U.S. 79 (1986); Hernandez v. New York, 500 U.S. ____, 111 S.Ct. 1859 (1991); Power v. Ohio, 499 U.S. 400, 111 S.Ct. 1364 (1991).
25. United States v. DeGross, 960 F.2d 1433 (9th Cir. 1992) (gender an inappropriate factor); United States v. Broussard, 987 F.2d 215 (5th Cir. 1993) (not improper to use gender). The United States Supreme Court has agreed to review the issue in J.E.B. v. State of Alabama *ex rel*. T.B., 606 So.2d 156 (1992), cert. granted ____ U.S. ____, 113 S.Ct. 2330 (1993). The Minnesota Supreme Court has held that peremptory strikes based on religious affiliation are not improper. State v. Davis, 504 N.W.2d 767 (Minn. 1993), pet. for cert. pending.
26. Minn. R. Crim. P. 26.02, subds. 4(3)(a)(6), (7).
27. Rules of Civ. P. 38.01.

Parties do not have the right to have juries determine facts in claims in *equity*. These claims generally seek nonpecuniary, coercive relief such as injunctions (where a party seeks to force another party to stop doing something like polluting a river) or restitution (where the defendant is ordered to return the injured party to his or her original condition). For example, a malpractice claim seeking monetary damages would be a claim "at law" for which a party would have a right to a jury trial. On the other hand, a lawsuit seeking to prohibit the state from releasing certain confidential information would be a suit "in equity" for which the parties would have no right to a jury. The rules governing the right to a jury are complex: Many arise from accidents of history, and there may be variations in the rules from jurisdiction to jurisdiction. In cases where a party has a right to a jury, the judge must abide by the factual determinations of the jury but may set the jury's verdict aside under extraordinary conditions.[28]

Jury Size

A jury for trial in a civil case consists of six persons.[29]

Unanimity Required; Exception

As in criminal trials, civil verdicts require unanimity. However, after six hours of deliberation, a civil jury may return a verdict that is concurred in by five sixths of its members.[30]

Change of Venue

A party in a civil suit may request a change in the place of the trial if an impartial trial cannot be had in the present location or when the convenience of witnesses and the ends of justice would be promoted by the change.[31] The parties may jointly agree to such a change in writing. MHPs may be involved in this process by providing information to be used in motions to the court for a change of venue or by testifying as expert witnesses on this issue. MHPs may be involved in conducting pretrial surveys, construct-

---

28. There are a number of ways in which a judge may properly usurp the jury's fact-finding role. If, during the trial, the judge decides that it would be irrational for the jury to decide in favor of one of the parties, the judge may terminate the trial prior to its submission to the jury by rendering a "directed verdict" or a "judgment as a matter of law." If the case is decided by the jury, but the judge decides that the jury's verdict seems to be the result of some error in the trial or to be against the "great weight" of the evidence, the judge may order a new trial. If the judge concludes that the jury's verdict is irrational, the judge may enter a judgment for the party who had been the verdict loser. This is called a judgment "notwithstanding the verdict," sometimes referred to by its Latin abbreviation, JNOV.
29. Minn. Const. of 1857, Art. I, § 4 (amended 1988).
30. M.S.A. § 546.17 (West 1988).
31. M.S.A. § 542.11 (West 1988).

ing questions to ask the potential jurors, and evaluating jurors on the basis of the results of pretrial surveys and/or of in-court observations.

Voir Dire

Jury selection in civil trials proceeds in much the same way as it does in criminal trials.[32] Basic information about each prospective juror (age, race, gender, occupation, educational level, address, marital status, occupation of spouse, ages of any children) is collected from the prospective jurors and made available to the parties.[33] The parties may question the jurors to gather additional information to allow the exercise of challenges.[34] The grounds for excluding a person from a civil jury are the same as those listed as disqualifying potential criminal jurors.[35]

The attorneys make their for-cause challenges known to the court, which decides whether the jurors must be dismissed. After these challenges are completed, each side is entitled to a number of peremptory challenges.[36] Generally, each side is entitled to two such challenges. Under certain circumstances, the number can be increased.[37] Peremptory challenges are made by alternate strikes (i.e., first one side and then the other), beginning with the defendant.[38] When the peremptory challenges have been exhausted, the first six of the remaining panel members constitute the jury.[39]

---

32. M.S.A. § 546.10 (West 1988).
33. General Rules of Practice, Rule 807.
34. M.S.A. § 546.10 (West 1988).
35. *See* above, text accompanying note 21.
36. M.S.A. § 546.10 (West 1988). Peremptory challenges are exercised at the discretion of the parties and their attorneys. However, the race of the prospective juror may not be used as a factor in exercising the challenges. Edmonson v. Leesville Concrete Co., 500 U.S. ____, 111 S.Ct. 2077 (1991). Lower courts are split on the propriety of using other factors, such as gender, in make peremptory strikes. United States v. DeGross, 960 F.2d 1433 (9th Cir. 1992) (gender an inappropriate factor); United States v. Broussard, 987 F.2d 215 (5th Cir. 1993) (not improper to use gender). The United States Supreme Court has agreed to review the issue in J.E.B. v. State of Alabama *ex rel.* T.B., 606 So.2d 156 (1992), cert. granted ____ U.S. ____, 113 S.Ct. 2330 (1993). The Minnesota Supreme Court has held that peremptory strikes based on religious affiliation are not improper. State v. Davis, 504 N.W.2d 767 (Minn. 1993), pet. for cert. pending.
37. *Id. See also* Rules of Civ. P. 46.02.
38. M.S.A. § 546.10 (West 1988).
39. *Id.*

5C.2

Expert Witnesses

A person may testify as an expert witness if he or she can provide testimony that is based on specialized knowledge that will assist the trier of fact[1] to understand the evidence or decide an issue of fact.[2] MHPs testify as expert witnesses on a variety of issues. The key distinction between lay and expert testimony is that whereas experts are allowed to frame their testimony in the form of opinions and inferences drawn with the help of their expertise, lay witnesses may give opinion or inference testimony only where the opinion or inference is "rationally based on the perception of the witness" and is helpful to the trier of fact.[3]

Qualifying as an Expert Witness

A witness will be "qualified" (allowed by the court to testify) as an expert if he or she has knowledge, skill, experience, training, or education regarding the subject that would be helpful to the trier.[4] This rule requires only that the expert have some specialized knowledge or training that will be of some assistance to the trier; it is not necessary that the expert be the most qualified person in his or her field.[5] If, however, the court determines that the demonstrative value of the information provided by the ex-

---

1. The trier of fact could be the jury or, if it is a trial without a jury, the judge.
2. Minn. R. Evid. 702.
3. Minn. R. Evid. 701.
4. Minn. R. Evid. 702.
5. Hueper v. Goodrich, 263 N.W.2d 408 (Minn. 1978).

pert is outweighed by its prejudicial effect, the court may refuse the testimony.[6]

In general, expert testimony is limited to those areas that are outside of the trier's experience or common knowledge.[7] For instance, in a homicide case[8] involving a self-defense claim, the defense attempted to introduce a clinical psychologist's opinion that the defendant was motivated by fear for his personal safety when he shot the victim. The trial court refused to allow the testimony on the basis that the subject matter of the expert's proposed opinion was within the range of common knowledge. That is, the court felt that whether the defendant was indeed motivated by such fear was a question the jury could appropriately determine simply by choosing which version of the facts to believe.

When an Expert Witness May Be Called to Testify

As a general rule, expert testimony is admissible only when it is based on specialized knowledge. For instance, the courts have held that the unreliability of eyewitness identification testimony is not a proper subject for expert witness testimony.[9] On the other hand, courts have allowed expert witnesses to testify on the standard of care for health service providers[10] and the mental status of criminal defendants.[11] The determination of whether to allow expert testimony on a particular subject is generally within the discretion of the trial court.[12]

---

6. U.S. v. Green, 525 F.2d 386 (8th Cir. 1975).
7. Although the rules of evidence do not explicitly rule out "common knowledge" expert testimony, such testimony is excludable on the grounds that it is not based on "specialized knowledge." It may also be excluded because framing common knowledge as expert knowledge might confuse or prejudice the jury.
8. State v. Matthews, 301 Minn. 133, 221 N.W.2d 563 (1974).
9. State v. Helterbridle, 301 N.W.2d 545 (Minn. 1980) (refusing to reverse a trial court's exclusion of expert testimony on the reliability of eyewitness identification).
10. Horju v. Allen, 146 Minn. 23, 177 N.W. 1015 (1920); Kanter v. Metropolitan Medical Center, 384 N.W.2d 914 (Minn. Ct. App. 1986). *See* chapter 6.5.
11. State v. Eubanks, 277 Minn. 257, 152 N.W.2d 453 (1967), cert. denied, 88 S.Ct. 1070, 390 U.S. 964 (1967). *See* chapters 5D.5 and 5D.9. Note that there are significant limitations placed on expert testimony on defendants' mental status. *See* chapter 5D.8.
12. State v. Helterbridle, 301 N.W.2d 545 (Minn. 1980).

Form and Content of Testimony

An expert witness may testify in the form of an opinion or inference.[13] The expert may base his or her testimony on facts or data presented at trial, or the testimony may be based on material reviewed by the expert prior to the trial.[14] The expert may testify as to his or her opinion without initially disclosing in testimony the facts underlying the opinion.[15] However, the opposing party may force disclosure of the underlying facts on cross-examination.[16] The facts underlying the expert's testimony need not be admissible as evidence as long as they are of a type reasonably relied on by experts in the field.[17] The primary reason for this rule is to avoid problems with hearsay testimony.[18] Thus, a health service provider/expert witness could base her testimony on a patient's history or statements, even though the patient's statements might be inadmissible hearsay.[19] Similarly, an expert could base his opinion on social science data, even though that data might not be in a form that would be admissible in court.[20]

In cross-examining an expert witness, a lawyer may, under certain circumstances, refer to statements in "learned treatises" that contradict or are inconsistent with the expert's testimony. A passage in a learned treatise may be referred to if it is called to the expert's attention and is established or accepted as reliable.[21]

The expert's opinion or inference may touch on the ultimate issue to be decided at trial so long as it assists the trier to understand the evidence. Generally, opinions from qualified experts as to factual matters will be admitted, whereas opinions that involve a legal analysis or the application of law to fact would not be deemed to be of use to the trier and thus would not be admissible.[22]

---

13. Minn. R. Evid. 703.
14. Minn. R. Evid. 703.
15. Minn. R. Evid. 705. However, the basis for the opinion is, in civil cases, discoverable in pretrial proceedings. Minn. R. Civ. P. 26.02(d).
16. Minn. R. Evid. 705.
17. Minn. R. Evid. 703.
18. Hearsay is a statement or an assertion of another person that is repeated by a witness to prove the truth of the matter stated. For instance, a witness to an auto accident generally cannot testify as to what another person said at the accident scene. Minn. R. Evid. 801(c).
19. Simchuck v. Fullerton, 299 Minn. 91, 216 N.W.2d 683 (1974).
20. Busch v. Busch Const., Inc., 262 N.W.2d 377 (Minn 1977).
21. Minn. R. Evid. 803(18). Its reliability may be established by the admission of the testifying expert, by the testimony of another expert, or by the judge's action without any testimony.
22. Minn. R. Evid. 704 (Committee Comment–1977).

Polygraph Evidence

Minnesota law prohibits polygraphic tests both in the workplace and as evidence in a court of law. MHPs may thus be affected both in their capacity as consultants to employers and as expert witnesses at trial.

Polygraph Tests in the Workplace

No employer may require a polygraph test, a voice stress test, or any other test that purports to measure the honesty of an employee or prospective employee.[1] Furthermore, no person may sell or interpret any test for an employer that the person knows is being used to test the honesty of an employee or prospective employee.[2] Any person knowingly selling, administering, or interpreting such tests is guilty of a misdemeanor.[3]

An employee may voluntarily request a polygraph test.[4] An employer or its agent administering a polygraph or "honesty" test to such a volunteer must inform the employee that taking the test is voluntary. The result of such a test may be disclosed only to the individual tested or to persons authorized by the individual to receive the results.[5]

---

1. M.S.A. § 181.75, subd. 1 (West Supp. 1992).
2. *Id.*
3. *Id.*
4. *Id.*
5. M.S.A. § 181.76 (West Supp. 1992).

Liability for Violation

Persons found to be violating the provisions of the statute are liable to criminal proceedings, injunctive relief, and the payment of civil penalties.[6] Furthermore, any person injured by a violation of the statute may bring a civil action to recover damages, including trial costs, investigative costs, reasonable attorney's fees, and other equitable relief (e.g., injunctions) as determined by the court.[7]

Note that the prohibitions of the statute can apply to persons who sell or interpret a test for an employer.[8] Because the penalties for violation are so severe, MHPs who routinely conduct polygraph, voice stress analysis, or any other test purporting to measure honesty should use great care. If the client is an employer (or prospective employer) of the test subject or an employer's agent, the prohibitions of this law apply to the MHP. The test should not be given unless the employee or prospective employee is truly volunteering to take the test. The MHP must inform the subject that the test is voluntary.

If the MHP does administer a test (no matter what the circumstances), the results may not be disclosed except to the individual tested (or, in the case of an employee, to persons authorized by the employee to receive the results).

Polygraph Tests as Evidence in a Court of Law

As a general rule, polygraph tests are inadmissible as evidence in Minnesota in both civil and criminal actions because of insufficient evidence of their reliability.[9] References to the taking of or refusal to take such a test are also excluded from evidence because of the prejudicial impact such evidence could have on a jury.[10] The inadmissibility of polygraph results does not deny a litigant his or her rights to due process.[11] The judicial prohibition against the admission of evidence related to a litigant's taking or refusing to take a polygraph test is so strong that convictions

---

6. M.S.A. § 181.75, subds. 2, 3 (West Supp. 1992).
7. M.S.A. § 181.75, subd. 4 (West Supp. 1992).
8. *See* above.
9. State v. Sullivan, 360 N.W.2d 418, 422 (Minn. Ct. App. 1985); M.N.D. v. B.M.D., 356 N.W.2d 813, 819 (Minn. Ct. App. 1984).
10. State v. Schaeffer, 425 N.W.2d 719, 722 (Minn. Ct. App. 1990).
11. United States v. Gordon, 688 F.2d 42, 44 (8th Cir. 1984), citing United States v. Bohr, 581 F.2d 1294, 1303 (8th Cir.), cert. denied, 439 U.S. 958 (1978).

where such evidence is admitted are uniformly reversed by appellate courts.[12] Thus, taking or refusing to take a polygraph test should not affect the outcome of any civil or criminal action.

One caveat should be noted. The Minnesota Supreme Court has found that a defendant's confession following a polygraph test was voluntary, even though police told the defendant that the test indicated he was lying.[13] The confession was admitted because the police did not misrepresent the results of the test or imply that the results would be admissible in evidence.[14] Thus, where a confession follows a polygraph test and an adequate Miranda warning (regarding the individual's right to remain silent, that anything she/he says may be used against her/him, etc.),[15] the confession may be introduced into evidence.[16]

---

12. State v. Schaeffer, 425 N.W.2d at 722.
13. State v. Schaeffer, 425 N.W.2d at 724, citing State v. Jungbauer, 348 N.W.2d 344 (Minn. 1984).
14. *Id.*
15. *See* chapter 5D.2.
16. State v. Schaeffer, 425 N.W.2d at 725.

5C.4

Competency to Testify

A witness in a civil or criminal trial must have the mental capacity to testify accurately and truthfully. This capacity is known as *competency*. Competency determinations must be distinguished from judgments concerning witness *credibility*. Whereas the former relate to the witness's ability to remember and tell the truth, the latter are determinations of whether, in fact, the witness has done so in his or her testimony. Competency determinations are made by the judge, whereas credibility is judged by the jury.[1] The law concerning the competency of witnesses applies to both criminal and civil matters.[2]

Only those persons who are competent are allowed to testify. Thus, the competency determination is a preliminary determination, made by the judge, out of the hearing of the jury. In general, it is assumed that a witness is competent to testify unless the court or a party suggests otherwise.[3] The competency determination is often made by the judge solely on the basis of her or his questioning of the witness. However, MHPs are sometimes asked to aid in this assessment and to testify as to their findings.[4]

---

1. In cases tried without a jury, the judge would make both determinations.
2. M.S.A. § 595.02, subd. 1 (West 1992).
3. Until 1987, Minnesota law provided that a child under 10 years of age was incompetent unless the court, after an examination, held that the child was competent. State v. Lau, 409 N.W.2d 275 (Minn. Ct. App. 1987). In 1987, the law was changed, removing the presumption of incompetence. Under current law, a child under 10 years of age is competent to testify "unless the court finds that the child lacks the capacity to remember or to relate truthfully facts respecting which the child is examined." M.S.A. § 595.02, subd. 1(l) (West 1988). It is unclear whether the court must hold a hearing respecting all under-10 witnesses, or only with respect to those whose competency has been sufficiently brought into question.
4. State v. Johnson, 256 N.W.2d 280 (Minn. 1977).

Legal Test of Competency to Testify

The test for mental competency to testify depends on the age of the prospective witness. A child under 10 is competent unless the court finds that the child "lacks the capacity to remember or to relate truthfully facts respecting which the child is examined."[5] Other witnesses are incompetent if they are "of unsound mind" or "intoxicated" at the time of the testimony and if they "lack the capacity to remember or to relate truthfully facts respecting which they are examined."[6]

The definition of "unsound mind" does not simply refer to a mental disorder. Rather, the test for someone whose mental competency is challenged is whether that person understands the obligation of an oath and is capable of correctly narrating the facts to which his or her testimony relates.[7]

Capacity to remember and tell the truth is distinguished from actual accuracy and truthfulness. Thus, merely because a child is mistaken about some details of past events does not mean that he or she lacks the *ability* to remember. Moreover, the inability to remember certain types of information (such as chronological relationships) does not render the witness incompetent with respect to other types of information (for example, details of an alleged sexual assault).[8]

A person's ability to testify is determined at the time of the legal proceeding, not at the time the person witnessed the event in question.[9] Legal proceedings are not limited to trials. Witnesses are frequently first questioned by the attorneys while under oath at depositions (pretrial meetings in which witnesses are questioned under oath in the same manner as they would be questioned at trial). If the witness is later unable to testify at trial, the competency issue will rest on whether the person was competent at the deposition. Likewise, the validity of a pretrial element such as a grand jury indictment might depend on the competency of the witnesses upon whose testimony it was based.[10]

5. M.S.A. § 595.02, subd. 1(l) (West 1988).
6. M.S.A. § 595.02, subd. 1(f) (West 1988).
7. State v. Johnson, 256 N.W.2d 280 (Minn. 1977).
8. State v. Struss, 404 N.W.2d 811 (Minn. Ct. App. 1987).
9. State v. Kahner, 217 Minn. 574, 15 N.W.2d 105 (1944).
10. *Id.*

Determination of Witness Competency

The determination of whether a witness is competent is not a jury matter but is within the discretion of the court.[11] The decision process may be broken down into three parts, each of which is within the court's broad discretion. First, once the competency issue has been raised, it is the court's responsibility to determine whether it should conduct a preliminary interrogation of the witness.[12] Second, if there is a reasonable doubt regarding the witness's competency, the court may request an examination by an MHP.[13] However, the court may forego a mental status evaluation if it feels that such a procedure will not help.[14] Finally, on the basis of its own questioning and any evaluations conducted, the court determines whether the witness is competent. The trial court has broad discretion, and its decision will not be overturned on appeal unless the court clearly abuses that discretion.[15]

---

11. State v. Struss, 404 N.W.2d 811 (Minn. Ct. App. 1987).
12. State v. Magee, 413 N.W.2d 230 (Minn. Ct. App. 1987).
13. State v. Johnson, 256 N.W.2d 280 (Minn. 1977).
14. State v. Shotley, 305 Minn. 384, 233 N.W.2d 755 (1975).
15. State v. Struss, 404 N.W.2d 811 (Minn. Ct. App. 1987).

5C.5

Psychological Autopsy

The motivations and mental state of a person prior to death are frequently critical issues in subsequent litigation. For instance, a finding that a person committed suicide rather than died accidentally may determine whether there is insurance coverage.[1] Similarly, liability for an injury caused by an insured may be excluded from insurance coverage if the injury was "intentional." Under Minnesota law, the mental illness of the insured can be taken into account in determining whether the act was intentional.[2] In each of these circumstances, a retrospective psychological profile may be a central piece of postdeath litigation.

Courts in Minnesota have held that a nonexamining psychiatrist is qualified to give expert testimony regarding a deceased's mental condition.[3] The Minnesota Supreme Court has held that such an opinion may be based on a hypothetical question that presents sufficient facts to enable the expert to give a reasonable opinion not based on speculation or conjecture. Admissibility does not require the expert to have actually examined the deceased.[4] Whether the expert has actually examined the individual goes to the "weight" of the expert's opinion, not to its admissibility.

In making its ruling, the Minnesota Supreme Court discussed the standards of the American Psychiatric Association. The court

---

1. *See* R. I. Simon, *You Only Die Once—But Did You Intend It? Psychiatric Assessment of Suicide Intent in Insurance Litigation*, 25 Tort and Insurance L.J. 650 (1990).
2. *See* chapter 5B.5.
3. State Farm Fire & Cas. Co. v. Wicka, 474 N.W.2d 324 (Minn. 1991); Anderson v. Armour & Co., 257 Minn. 281, 287–88, 101 N.W.2d 435, 439–40 (1960). *See* chapter 5C.2.
4. State Farm Fire & Cas. Co. v. Wicka, 474 N.W.2d 324, 332 (Minn. 1991).

distinguished the Association's prohibition on psychiatrists' offering professional opinions on the basis of information about individuals "in the light of public attention."[5] The relevant standard, according to the court, allows psychiatric testimony without examination. However, ethical guidelines promulgated by the American Academy of Psychiatry and the Law put some limits on non-examination-based testimony. As stated by the Minnesota Supreme Court,

> Honesty, objectivity and the adequacy of the clinical evaluation may be called into question when an expert opinion is offered without a personal examination. While there are authorities who would bar an expert opinion in regard to an individual who has not been personally examined, it is the position of the Academy that if, after earnest effort, it is not possible to conduct a personal examination, an opinion may be rendered on the basis of other information. However, under such circumstances, it is the responsibility of the forensic psychiatrist to assure that the statement of his opinion and any reports or testimony based on this opinion clearly indicate that there was no personal examination and that the opinion expressed is thereby limited.[6]

---

5. *Id.*, citing American Psychiatric Association, *Principles of Medical Ethics With Annotations Especially Applicable to Psychiatry*, §§ 7(3) to 9 (1989 ed.).
6. *Id.*, quoting from American Academy of Psychiatry and the Law, *Ethical Guidelines for the Practice of Forensic Psychiatry IV & Commentary* (rev. 1989).

Criminal Matters

5D.1

Screening of Police Officers

Prior to being appointed permanently as a peace officer or part-time peace officer, which in Minnesota includes state and local police, state patrol, and conservation officers,[1] a person must first be licensed by the Board of Peace Officers Standards and Training.[2] MHPs do not have any mandated role in the process, although mental fitness is one of the qualifications governing the recruitment and licensing of peace officers.[3]

Minnesota Board of Peace Officers Standards and Training

The Minnesota Board of Peace Officers Standards and Training consists of 15 members, 14 of whom are appointed by the governor. The superintendent of the Minnesota Bureau of Criminal Apprehension or his or her designee is the 15th member.[4] Ten of the 14 members selected by the governor must have experience or education in law enforcement, 2 must be members of the general public, and 2 must be selected from among elected city officials outside of the metropolitan areas.[5] The Board must adopt rules with respect to minimum standards of physical, mental, and

---

1. M.S.A. § 626.84(1)(c).
2. M.S.A. § 626.846..
3. M.S.A. § 626.843(d).
4. M.S.A. § 626.841.
5. *Id.*

educational fitness and prescribe minimum courses of training and minimum standards for training facilities.[6]

Powers and Duties

The Board has the power and duty to certify peace officer training schools or programs and monitor their compliance with Board regulations, to certify and license peace officers and peace officer instructors, and to obtain criminal conviction data for persons seeking a license. The Board also assists political subdivisions or state law enforcement agencies with the investigation and resolution of allegations of misconduct of persons licensed by the Board.[7] The Board must prepare a training course to assist officers in identifying and responding to crimes motivated by bias.[8]

---

6. M.S.A. § 626.843.
7. M.S.A. § 626.845.
8. M.S.A. § 626.8451 (West Supp. 1992). Individuals who have not completed such a course may not be licensed after August 1, 1990.

5D.2

Competency to Waive the Rights to Silence, Counsel, and a Jury

The U.S. and Minnesota Constitutions guarantee the right against self-incrimination and the right to counsel in criminal proceedings. These rights may be waived during a criminal investigation when police are interrogating a person suspected of a crime. In addition, these rights, along with the right to a jury trial, may be waived during the criminal proceedings themselves.

Right to Silence

The right against self-incrimination, also known as the right to remain silent, attaches as soon as a person is taken into custody by a police officer. An individual is under *custodial interrogation* when the individual is restrained and questioned in a police-dominated environment with the expectation of more than just a brief delay to the individual's freedom of movement.[1] The prosecution may not use statements stemming from custodial interrogation of any defendant unless the defendant has been warned that he or she has the right to remain silent and the right to counsel.[2] The principle function of this *Miranda* warning is to ensure that the accused is aware of his or her constitutional rights, for one cannot legally waive the right unless one knows he or she has it.[3] If, after being informed of his or her rights, the individual knowingly, intelligently, and freely waives the right to remain silent, any subsequent incriminating statements may be admitted

---

1. State v. Harem, 384 N.W.2d 880 (Minn. 1986).
2. Miranda v. Arizona, 348 U.S. 436 (1966).
3. State v. Merrill, 274 N.W.2d 99 (Minn. 1978).

into court.[4] The prosecution has the burden of proving that the constitutional rights to counsel and to remain silent were not violated while the individual was under custodial interrogation.[5]

There are two separate aspects that must be evaluated in determining whether a person's waiver of the right to remain silent is effective. One aspect focuses on the conduct of the police. The second focuses on the capacity of the individual. To determine whether a confession is voluntary (i.e., was freely given), or whether the conduct by police has improperly induced a confession, a court must look at both of these aspects (i.e., at the totality of the circumstances).[6] If the circumstances indicate that the accused's will was overcome, then the accused's confession was not voluntary.[7] The immaturity, mental subnormality, illness, and intoxication of a suspect have all been recognized as factors by the court that might render a confession invalid.[8]

The law is somewhat unclear as to whether the constitution protects criminal defendants from their own incompetent confessions in the absence of police misconduct. The United States Supreme Court has ruled that "coercive police activity is a necessary predicate to the finding that a confession is not 'voluntary' within the meaning of the [Constitution]."[9] However, in several cases, the Minnesota Supreme Court has treated the questions of police coercion and mental capacity as separate and independent grounds in the analysis of the validity of a confession.[10] However, these cases predated the U.S. Supreme Court's analysis. Thus, the state of the law under the Minnesota Constitution is unclear.[11]

---

4. *Id.*
5. State v. Heidelberger, 353 N.W.2d 582 (Minn. Ct. App. 1984).
6. State v. Merrill, 274 N.W.2d 99 (Minn. 1978).
7. *Id.*
8. State v. Brown, 345 N.W.2d 233, 238 (Minn. 1984).
9. Colorado v. Connelly, 479 U.S. 157, 107 S.Ct. 515, 93 L.Ed.2d 473 (1986).
10. State v. Hoffman, 328 N.W.2d 709, 714 (Minn. 1982); State v. Merrill, 274 N.W.2d 99 (Minn. 1978); State v. Kinn, 178 N.W.2d 888 (Minn. 1970). *But compare* State v. Erickson, 449 N.W.2d 707 (Minn. 1989), in which the Minnesota Supreme Court cited Colorado v. Connelly with apparent approval. The court's analysis suggested that it was in accord with the U.S. Supreme Court's analysis. (The fact that the defendant was young and had previously had psychological problems provides "no indication that defendant was coerced into confessing involuntarily.")
11. The Minnesota Supreme Court may interpret the Minnesota Constitution as being more protective of the right to remain silent than the U.S. Constitution.

Right to Counsel

A criminal defendant is entitled, under the Sixth Amendment, to be represented by counsel in any criminal proceeding. The right attaches when the person is formally charged.

The right to counsel may be waived if the defendant makes a knowing, intelligent, and voluntary relinquishment of the right.[12] To be able to validly waive the right to counsel, a defendant must have sufficient ability to appreciate the consequences of the decision, the nature of the charges and proceedings, the range of applicable punishments, and any additional matters essential to a general understanding of the case.[13] Competency to waive the right to counsel and competency to proceed[14] are separate, although related, issues.[15] It is possible that a defendant would be held incompetent to waive the right to counsel yet competent to proceed with trial.[16]

Right to Waive a Jury Trial

A defendant is entitled to a jury trial in any prosecution for an offense punishable by incarceration.[17] A defendant may waive the right to trial by jury if the court approves and if the waiver is made after the defendant has been advised of his or her rights by the court and has had an opportunity to consult with his or her counsel.[18] An individual's right to waive a jury trial is subject to the same scrutiny as the right to waive counsel. The person must be capable of making an intelligent and informed choice.[19]

---

12. State v. Heidelberger, 353 N.W.2d 583, 587 (Minn. Ct. App. 1984).
13. Minn. R. Crim. P. 20.01, subd. 1.
14. *See* chapter 5A.2.
15. State v. Hoffman, 328 N.W.2d 709, 713 (Minn. 1982).
16. Note, however, that as a matter of U.S. Constitutional analysis, the two levels of competency are the same. Godinez v. Moran, ____ U.S. ____, 113 S.Ct. 2680 (1993).
17. Minn. Const. Art. 1, § 4; Minn. R. Crim. P. 26.01, subds. 1(a), (b). In any prosecution for the violation of a misdemeanor not punishable by incarceration, trial is before a judge without a jury. *See* chapter 5C.1.
18. Minn. R. Crim. P. 26.01, subd. 2(a).
19. Adams v. United States, 317 U.S. 269, 87 L. Ed. 268, 63 S. Ct. 236, 143 A.L.R. 435 (1942), reh. denied 317 U.S. 713, 87 L. Ed. 568 (1943).

5D.3

Precharging and Pretrial Evaluations

In some states, the prosecutor may request a mental health evaluation to determine whether to charge a person with a criminal offense or to divert him or her to the mental health system or some other social services program. Minnesota does not have any statutory provisions specifically authorizing such a precharging evaluation. In its place, prosecutors can, in appropriate circumstances, turn to the civil commitment system for evaluation[1] or make use of the postcharging process for evaluating a criminal defendant's competency.[2]

Diversion of criminal defendants after charging but prior to trial is permitted.[3] However, such diversion requires notification of the victim, consideration of the victim's views, and approval of the court.[4] In certain circumstances involving domestic abuse, prosecutors must keep a written record of the reasons for failure to prosecute.[5]

---

1. *See* chapter 5E.4.
2. *See* chapter 5D.5.
3. Minn. R. Crim. P. 27.05.
4. *Id.*
5. M.S.A. § 611A.0315 (West Supp. 1992). *See* chapter 5D.26.

5D.4

Bail Determinations

The Minnesota Constitution provides that all criminal defendants have the right to post bail to secure their release from custody. The primary purpose of bail is to secure the defendant's return to court for trial. Bail may also be used as a tool to protect the safety of the public or of particular individuals.

MHPs may contribute to the setting of bail by evaluating the defendant.

Determining Whether Bail is Appropriate

The Minnesota Constitution guarantees that all persons "shall before conviction be bailable by sufficient sureties. . . ."[1] The Constitution prohibits the imposition of "excessive" bail[2] but provides few guarantees to defendants beyond that. Under the Minnesota Rules of Criminal Procedure, the court is required to set a monetary amount as bail for each criminal defendant.[3]

---

1. Minn. Const. Art. 1, § 7. The Constitution exempts "capital offenses"–those in which the death penalty may be imposed. Because Minnesota has abolished the death penalty, this exception is moot.
2. Minn. Const. Art. 1, § 5.
3. Minn. R. Crim. P. 6.02, subd. 1.

Determining the Amount and Conditions of Bail

The Minnesota Rules of Criminal Procedure establish a hierarchical list of release conditions for criminal defendants. The court is to release a defendant on the first of the conditions (or combinations) that will "assure the appearance of the person for trial or hearing."[4] The list, in order of increasing severity, is as follows:

1. release without bail;
2. release on personal recognizance;
3. release on an order to appear;
4. release on execution of an unsecured appearance bond in a specified amount;
5. place the person in the care and supervision of a designated person or organization;
6. place restrictions on travel, association, or place of abode;
7. require the execution of an appearance bond in an amount set by the court, or the deposit of cash or other security;
8. impose any other conditions, including the condition that the person return to custody after specified hours.

If the court sets nonmonetary conditions for release, it must also fix an amount of monetary bail, without other conditions, upon which the defendant may obtain release.

In determining which conditions of release to impose, the judge takes into account the following factors:[5]

1. the nature and circumstances of the offense charged;
2. the weight of the evidence against the defendant;
3. the defendant's family ties, employment, financial resources, character and mental condition, length of residence in the community, record of convictions, and record of appearance at court proceedings or of flight to avoid prosecution; and
4. the safety of any other persons or of the community.

The court may order the court's probation service or other qualified facility to gather information for determining the conditions of release. Information obtained from the defendant in response to an inquiry during the course of this investigation and

---

4. *Id.*
5. *Id.*, subd. 2.

any evidence derived from such information may not be used against the defendant at trial.[6]

If the defendant violates the conditions imposed on release, the judge, after a hearing, may impose different or additional conditions for release.[7]

---

6. *Id.*, subd. 3.
7. Minn. R. Crim. P. 6.03, subd. 3.

5D.5

Competency to Stand Trial

Mental competency is required in both adult prosecution[1] and juvenile court proceedings[2] to ensure the right to a fair trial guaranteed under the U.S. Constitution.[3] A defendant cannot enter a plea, be tried, or be sentenced if he or she lacks sufficient mental ability to consult rationally with counsel, understand the proceedings, or participate in the defense. MHPs may participate in the competency evaluation as court appointees or as experts retained by the defendant or prosecuting attorney.

This chapter discusses three aspects of competency-to-proceed law. First, the definition of *mental competency*, as used in this context, is discussed. Second, we discuss the manner in which the competency of the defendant is put in issue in a criminal proceeding. Third, the procedures used to determine competency are summarized.

Definition of Competency to Proceed

Defendants in criminal proceedings must be competent to proceed with each critical step in the criminal process. A defendant is not permitted to waive counsel if he or she lacks sufficient ability to knowingly, voluntarily, and intelligently waive the constitutional right to counsel, to appreciate the consequences of the decision to proceed without representation by counsel, or to

---

1. Minn. R. Crim. P. 20.01, subd. 1.
2. Minn R. P. Juv. Ct. 33.01. *See* chapter 5A.16.
3. Pate v. Robinson, 383 U.S. 375, 86 S.Ct. 836; State v. Swain, 269 N.W.2d 707 (Minn. 1978).

comprehend the nature of the charge and proceedings, the range of applicable punishments, and any additional matters essential to a general understanding of the case.[4] A defendant may not be permitted to enter a plea, be tried, or be sentenced if he or she (a) lacks sufficient ability to consult with a reasonable degree of rational understanding with defense counsel or (b) is mentally ill or mentally deficient so as to be incapable of understanding the proceedings or participating in the defense.[5]

The terms *mentally ill* and *mentally deficient* are not defined in this context. It is likely that they will not be given a restrictive, technical meaning because the main focus of inquiry is on the defendant's functional abilities.

Raising the Issue

The issue of competency can be raised at any point during the proceeding if any of the participants has doubts about the defendant's competency to proceed. The defense counsel or prosecuting attorney may raise the issue by motion, setting out the grounds for their doubts. The court may raise the issue on its own motion, as well.

Because the issue involves the defendant's mental competency, the procedural rules governing raising the issue are somewhat unique. A criminal defendant can waive most procedural rights by failing to raise them in a timely manner. However, an incompetent defendant cannot be held to have waived fundamental rights. Thus, the law puts an obligation on all participants, including the judge, to raise the issue of competency when there is reason to doubt the defendant's ability to proceed.[6] Furthermore, the defense counsel is obligated to raise the issue even over her or his own client's objections, although the lawyer may not reveal privileged information in the process.

Because the court is responsible for considering a defendant's competency throughout the proceedings, the competency issue may be raised several times. Regardless of a determination of competency before the trial or at the beginning of the trial, the court can and should reconsider the issue whenever there is reason to believe the defendant is incompetent.[7]

---

4. Minn. R. Crim. P. 20.01, subd. 1. *See* chapter 5D.2.
5. Minn. R. Crim. P. 20.01, subd. 1; Godinez v. Moran, ____ U.S. ____, 113 S.Ct. 2680 (1993).
6. Minn. R. Crim. P. 20.01, subd. 1; Drope v. Missouri, 420 U.S. 162, 180, 95 S.Ct. 896, 908 (1975); State v. Bauer, 245 N.W.2d 848, 857 (Minn. 1976).
7. Drope v. Missouri, 95 S.Ct. 896, 908 (1975); State v. Bauer, 245 N.W.2d 848, 857 (Minn. 1976).

Procedures in the Determination of Incompetency

If the court determines that there is reason to doubt the defendant's competency, the court suspends the criminal proceedings. If the case is a misdemeanor, the court may cause civil commitment proceedings[8] to be instituted against the defendant, dismiss the case, or proceed according to the rules governing competency in felony and gross misdemeanor cases.[9]

In felony and gross misdemeanor cases, the court first determines whether there is sufficient probable cause stated on the face of the criminal complaint, dismissing the complaint if there is not. The court then appoints an examiner[10] to examine the defendant and report to the court on his or her mental condition. The examination may be done on an outpatient basis or at a state mental hospital or other suitable hospital or facility. It may not exceed 60 days.[11] A psychiatrist, psychologist, or physician retained by the defendant or prosecution can observe the examination.[12]

The court-appointed examiner must submit a detailed report of the exam to the judge who ordered it. When a defendant makes it impossible to conduct an exam because of his or her refusal to participate, the examiner should indicate whether mental illness or deficiency caused the unwillingness. The report should include a diagnosis of the defendant's mental condition and the factual basis for the examiner's findings. If the examiner finds the defendant mentally ill or mentally deficient, the report should state the examiner's opinion regarding

1. the defendant's capacity to understand the proceedings and participate in the defense;

2. whether the defendant poses an imminent risk of serious danger to another person, is imminently suicidal, or otherwise needs emergency intervention (if so, the examiner must promptly notify the court, prosecuting attorney, and defense attorney);

---

8. See chapters 5E.4, 5E.5, 5E.7.
9. Minn. R. Crim. P. 20.01, subd. 2.
10. The rule adopts the definition of "examiner" from the Minnesota Commitment Act: "a licensed physician or a licensed consulting psychologist, knowledgeable, trained and practicing in the diagnosis and treatment of the alleged impairment." M.S.A. § 253B.02, subd. 7 (West Supp. 1992).
11. Minn. R. Crim. P. 20.01, subd. 2. If the court subsequently decides that the defendant is competent, and convicts the defendant of the charge, any time spent confined in a mental health facility for a competency examination will be credited toward jail time.
12. Minn. R. Crim. P. 20.01, subd. 2.

3. treatments required to attain competency, including possible treatments that do not entail institutionalization; and

4. the probability of the defendant's regaining competency, the treatments available, and the time required to do so.[13]

If either party files objections to the examiner's report, the court must hold a hearing to determine competency. At the hearing, additional evidence can be submitted, including testimony from the court-appointed examiner and from any other MHPs retained by the parties.[14] If no objection is filed, the court may determine the defendant's competency on the basis of the examiner's report alone, without conducting any hearing.[15]

Effect of Finding on Issue of Competency

If the court finds that the defendant is competent to proceed, the criminal proceedings are to be resumed. In misdemeanor cases, if the defendant is found incompetent, the court will dismiss the case. If the defendant is found incompetent in felony or gross misdemeanor cases, the criminal proceedings continue to be suspended. Upon request or at the court's own initiative, additional competency hearings may be held. If the defendant is found competent at one of these subsequent hearings, the court will resume the criminal proceedings. However, unless the case involves murder charges, the court will dismiss the case if the defendant remains incompetent for three years.[16]

Incompetent defendants already committed as a result of prior civil commitment proceedings continue to be committed. If the incompetent defendant is not under commitment, the court will order the institution of civil commitment proceedings against the defendant. In either case, the commitment of an incompetent defendant is under the supervision of the criminal court.[17] At least once every six months, the institution or individual responsible for the defendant must submit a report to the trial court on the defendant's mental condition.[18]

---

13. *Id.*
14. *Id.*, subd. 3.
15. *Id.*
16. *Id.*, subds. 5, 6.
17. The criminal court and the prosecuting attorney must be notified of any proposed change in the status of such committed patients, such as transfer, partial institutionalization, discharge, or provisional discharge. Minn. R. Crim. P. 20.01, subd. 5.
18. Minn. R. Crim. P. 20.01, subd. 4.

Confidentiality and Privileged Communications

When a defendant is examined by an MHP to determine competency to proceed, any statements made by the defendant and any evidence derived from the examination are admissible in evidence at the proceedings to determine competency. In addition, when defendants raise the defense of mental illness or deficiency,[19] the court may require disclosure of any information concerning the defendant's mental condition that is relevant to that defense.[20] Moreover, in such mental-deficiency-defense cases, MHPs who participated in the competency proceedings may be called as witnesses in the trial to provide information about the defendant's mental illness or deficiency.[21]

---

19. *See* chapter 5D.9.
20. Minn. R. Crim. P. 20.03, subds. 1, 2. *See* chapter 5D.9.
21. State v. Dodis, 314 N.W.2d 233, 240 (Minn. 1982).

5D.6

Provocation

Under the law, an intentional killing may be mitigated to first-degree manslaughter if the killing was done in the heat of passion and the passion was provoked by words and acts of another sufficient to provoke a person of ordinary self-control under similar circumstances.[1] The test for this mitigation has two elements. The first element—that the defendant acted in the "heat of passion"—is a subjective test. That is, it refers to the defendant's actual emotional state. The second element is an objective test: whether a person of "ordinary self-control" would be provoked under similar circumstances.

Provocation is not a complete excuse for killing, but rather an extenuating circumstance that reduces criminal culpability.[2] Provocation is similar to the defense of "self-defense" but differs in significant respects. Whereas provocation reduces but does not eliminate criminal culpability, self-defense is a complete exoneration of criminal liability. Provocation focuses on the state of the defendant's emotions at the time of the killing. Self-defense looks at the quality of the defendant's judgment with respect to the danger presented by others, and alternate methods to avoid the danger.[3]

It is not likely that Minnesota courts would allow MHP testimony on the issue of provocation. Minnesota courts rely on the

---

1. M.S.A. § 609.20; State v. Buchanan, 431 N.W.2d 542 (Minn. 1988).
2. State v. Boyce, 284 Minn. 242, 170 N.W.2d 104 (1969).
3. *Id.*

lay judgment of juries to evaluate matters of criminal motivation and intent.[4]

---

4. *See* State v. Bouwman, 328 N.W.2d 703 (Minn. 1982). *See* chapters 5D.7 (mens rea) and 5C.2 (expert witnesses). Such testimony is allowed, however, to assist a defense of self-defense in certain circumstances. *See* chapter 5D.10 (battered woman syndrome).

5D.7

Mens Rea

In general, the minimum requirement for criminal liability is a voluntary act or omission, causing a particular result, accompanied by a culpable mental state. This culpable mental state is traditionally referred to by the term *mens rea*. In general, the criminal law is designed to punish those who acted with a "guilty mind," rather than inadvertently or accidentally. Degrees of criminal liability—our notions of how "bad" an act was and hence how severely it should be punished—are also closely tied to the defendant's mental state. Thus, the mental state of the defendant is often of central importance in criminal prosecutions.

Whether a defendant had a particular mental state is to be judged by the jury on the basis of the defendant's conduct and the circumstances. Minnesota courts use an objective standard for determining whether the defendant had the requisite criminal intent. As explained by the Minnesota Supreme Court,

> Direct evidence as to the fact of intent is usually impossible because of the subjective nature of this element of the crime. What a person intends lies within the recesses of that individual person's mind. Yet, in determining this question, inquiry is made under an objective standard, namely, the standard that people operate within the broad boundaries of what is deemed normal or sane. To put it another way, the law presumes people, including the defendant standing trial, are responsible for their acts, i.e., that they have the capacity to intend what they do. Minn. Stat. § 611.025 (1982).[1]

---

1. State v. Bouwman, 328 N.W.2d 703 (Minn. 1982).

Thus, Minnesota courts do not allow testimony by MHPs on the question of whether a defendant had, or had the "capacity" to have, a particular mental state.[2]

Minnesota law[3] contains definitions of a number of different culpable mental states:

1. To *know* requires only that the actor believes that the specified fact exists.

2. *Intentionally* means that the actor either has a purpose to do the thing or cause the result, or believes that the act performed, if successful, will cause the result. In general, the actor must have knowledge of the facts that are necessary to make the actor's conduct criminal.

3. *With intent* means that the actor either has a purpose to do the thing or cause the result, or believes that the act, if successful, will cause the result.

Some crimes are based on the terms *recklessly* or *culpable negligence*. For example, manslaughter in the second degree is based on the culpable negligence of the defendant, which is defined as creating "an unreasonable risk, and consciously tak[ing] chances of causing death or great bodily harm to another."[4] Culpable negligence is more than ordinary or gross negligence. It is gross negligence coupled with recklessness. It is intentional conduct that actually may not be intended to be harmful but that ordinary and reasonably prudent people would recognize as involving a strong probability of injuries to others.[5]

Some crimes are based on conduct that is negligent or grossly negligent. Gross negligence is a very high degree of negligence. However, it requires no conscious and intentional action that the actor knows or should know creates an unreasonable risk of harm to others.[6]

First-degree murder can be supported by a showing that the defendant acted "with premeditation."[7] Extensive planning and deliberation are not needed to establish premeditation. Rather, the requisite "plan" can be formulated almost instantaneously.[8]

Criminal intent does not require knowledge of the existence of the criminal statute.[9]

---

2. *Id.*; State v. Brom, 463 N.W.2d 758 (Minn. 1990), cert. denied, _____ U.S. _____, 111 S.Ct. 1398, 113 L.Ed.2d 453 (1991). *See* chapter 5D.8.
3. M.S.A. § 609.02, subd. 9 (West 1987).
4. M.S.A. § 609.20 (West Supp. 1992).
5. State v. Beilke, 267 Minn. 526, 127 N.W.2d 516 (1964).
6. State v. Brehmer, 281 Minn. 156, 160 N.W.2d 669, 673 (1968).
7. M.S.A. § 609.185 (West Supp. 1992).
8. State v. Alton, 432 N.W.2d 754 (Minn. 1988).
9. M.S.A. § 609.02, subd. 9 (West 1987).

5D.8

Diminished Capacity

The defense of *diminished capacity* (also referred to as *diminished responsibility*) is one in which the defendant asserts that although he or she may have had the requisite mens rea,[1] or guilty mind, it was severely diminished as a result of a mental disease or defect and that because of this the offense should be lessened. Minnesota does not recognize this defense.[2]

---

1. *See* chapter 5D.7.
2. State v. Bouwman, 328 N.W.2d 703 (Minn. 1982). In *Bouwman*, the court refused to allow psychiatric testimony about the defendant's capacity to form the requisite intent. The court distinguished between evidence of mental illness, which it rejected, and evidence of intoxication, which it allowed on issues of intent.

Criminal Responsibility

At the foundation of criminal law is the concept of moral agency or responsibility. The defense of insanity (referred to in Minnesota as mental illness or mental deficiency) is the device by which the criminal law incorporates this foundational idea. The Minnesota Supreme Court has held that the defense is so inherent in our notions of fundamental fairness that it is constitutionally required.[1] MHPs play a central role in the application of this defense. Although the question of nonresponsibility is ultimately a question to be decided by the jury, psychological and psychiatric expertise provides the basis for these decisions.

Legal Determination of the Mental Illness or Mental Deficiency Defense

Minnesota's statute regarding criminal responsibility reads as follows:

> No person shall be tried, sentenced, or punished for any crime while mentally ill or mentally deficient so as to be incapable of understanding the proceedings or making a defense; but the person shall not be excused from criminal liability except upon proof that at the time of committing the alleged criminal act the person was laboring under such a defect of reason, from one of these causes, as not to know the nature of the act, or that it was wrong.[2]

---

1. State v. Hoffman, 328 N.W.2d 709 (Minn. 1982).
2. M.S.A. § 611.026 (West 1987).

Minnesota uses the M'Naghten rule as the test for criminal insanity.[3] The rule is as follows: To be found not guilty by reason of insanity, the defendant must not have known the nature and quality of his or her acts or that those acts were wrong.[4] An example of a defendant who fulfills these two criteria is one who believed the killing of her grandson was necessary to purge the victim of internal demons and assure his everlasting salvation. Because she was convinced of the rightness of her act and could not appreciate the nature of it, she was acquitted under the M'Naghten rule.[5]

The test of mental illness or mental deficiency in the M'Naghten test is a severely limited one, much narrower than the test in the civil commitment or incompetency-to-proceed contexts.[6] The criminal defense test is limited to defects in perception or cognition. However, evidence as to "volition" and "capacity to control" behavior may be considered by the jury in determining whether the M'Naghten test has been met (State v. Rawland, 294 Minn. 17, 32, 199 N.W.2d 774, 782 [1972]). Minnesota has rejected several tests for excusing criminal responsibility that take into account affective and volitional disorders. These include the American Law Institute (ALI) and the irresistible impulse tests. The ALI test provides the insanity defense for a defendant who, as a result of mental disease or defect, lacks the capacity to appreciate the criminality (wrongfulness) of his or her conduct or to conform his or her conduct to the requirements of law.[7] This test has been adopted by a substantial number of states. The irresistible impulse test excuses a defendant whose "will . . . has been otherwise than voluntarily so completely destroyed that his actions are not subject to it, but are beyond his control."[8]

The defense of voluntary intoxication is recognized as a partial defense by Minnesota if the intoxication renders the person unable to form the requisite intent essential to the crime.[9] Involuntary intoxication is a defense to criminal activities if the defendant is found to be temporarily "insane" as defined by the M'Naghten test. There are four types of involuntary intoxication: coerced intoxication, pathological intoxication, intoxication by

3. State v. Hoffman, 328 N.W.2d 709 (Minn. 1982).
4. State v. Bouwman, 328 N.W.2d 703 (Minn. 1982).
5. State v. Sheppo, No. 76566 (Minn. Dist. Ct., Jan. 14, 1981).
6. *E.g.*, State v. Knox, 311 Minn. 314, 250 N.W.2d 147 (1976) (mental illness alone does not excuse criminal liability). *See* chapters 5E.4 and 5D.5 for further discussion of civil commitment and incompetency to proceed.
7. Model Penal Code, 4.01.
8. Rathke, *Abolition of the Mental Illness Defense*, 8 Wm. Mitchell L. Rev. 143, 149 n.30 (1982) (quoting Davis v. United States, 165 U.S. 373, 378 [1897], citing State v. Eubanks, 277 Minn. 257, 152 N.W.2d 453 [1967]); State v. Finn, 257 Minn. 138, 100 N.W.2d 508 (1960).
9. M.S.A. § 609.075 (West 1987).

innocent mistake, and unexpected intoxication resulting from the ingestion of a medically prescribed drug.[10]

The defendant has the burden of proof in the defense of mental illness or mental deficiency.[11] The standard of proof on this issue is not the criminal "beyond a reasonable doubt" standard, but the more lenient, civil standard, "preponderance of the evidence."[12]

Procedures Upon Assertion of Defense of Mental Illness or Mental Deficiency[13]

The court may order a mental examination of the defendant when the defense notifies the prosecuting attorney of an intention to assert a defense of mental illness or deficiency, or when the defendant pleads not guilty by reason of mental illness or deficiency. If the court orders an examination, it appoints an "examiner"[14] experienced in the field of mental illness or mental deficiency to examine the defendant and report his or her findings.

The report of the examination must include a diagnosis of the defendant. It must also include the examiner's opinion as to whether, because of mental illness or deficiency at the time of the commission of the offense charged, the defendant was laboring under such a defect of reason as not to know the nature of the act constituting the offense, or that it was wrong. The report must contain the factual basis upon which the diagnosis and opinions are formed.

If the defendant does not participate in the examination so that the examiner is unable to make an adequate report, the court may take a number of steps, including prohibiting the defendant from introducing evidence of his or her mental condition at the trial.

For the purpose of the examination, the court may order the defendant confined to a hospital or other suitable facility for a

---

10. City of Minneapolis v. Altimus, 306 Minn. 462, 238 N.W.2d. 851 (1976).
11. State v. Linder, 304 N.W.2d 902 (Minn. 1981).
12. Minn. R. Crim. P. 20.02, subd. 6.
13. Minn. R. Crim. P. 20.02.
14. The person appointed must meet the definition of "examiner" under the Minnesota Commitment Act: An "examiner" means a licensed physician or licensed psychologist who is "knowledgeable, trained and practicing in the diagnosis and treatment of the alleged impairment." M.S.A. § 253B.02, subd. 7 (West Supp. 1992).

specified period not to exceed 60 days. This can only be done upon a special showing of need.

The prosecution and defense may retain independent experts, who may observe the court-ordered mental examination and conduct their own if they so chose.

Expert testimony regarding a defendant's mental condition is relevant but not conclusive in establishing the defendant's criminal responsibility. The jury may ignore all expert testimony and rely on lay testimony if that is more persuasive.[15]

Confidentiality and Privileged Communications

Under normal circumstances, communications between therapist and patient, made for the purposes of treatment, are confidential and privileged unless the protections are waived.[16] These protections are not fully available to the defendant who asserts the defense of mental illness or deficiency. By asserting the defense, the defendant effectively waives the protections. Furthermore, examinations done at the court's direction or otherwise for the purpose of evaluating the applicability of the defense are not for the purpose of treatment and thus may not qualify for the privilege.

When a defendant is ordered by the court to undergo a mental examination, a written report of the examination will be sent to the judge, who then sends a copy to both parties.[17] Unless the defendant makes her or his mental condition an issue at trial, no evidence derived from the mental examination is admissible at trial. If the defendant does raise the issue of her or his mental condition, any party may call the person who examined the defendant at the direction of the court to testify as a witness at the trial. The examiner's report may also be received as evidence.

When a defendant raises the mental illness or deficiency defense, the court orders the defendant to furnish all medical reports and hospital or medical records concerning the mental condition of the defendant and relevant to the issue of the defense. The court may inspect the records for relevancy, forwarding relevant records to the prosecution. This information, and any evidence obtained from the records, may be admitted in

---

15. State v. Schnider, 402 N.W.2d 779 (Minn. 1987).
16. See chapters 4.2 and 4.3.
17. Minn. R. Crim. P. 20.02, subd. 4.

evidence only on the issue of the defense of mental illness or deficiency.[18]

If the defendant chooses to rely solely on the defense of mental illness or mental deficiency, statements made by the defendant for the purposes of the mental examination and evidence obtained as a result of those statements are admissible at trial on that issue.[19] However, if the defendant relies not only on that defense but also on the defense of not guilty, then the trial is bifurcated, or split in two. Both parts of the trial are tried to the same jury. In the first part of the trial, the issue of the defendant's guilt is tried. Evidence of the defendant's mental impairment is generally not admissible at this stage.[20] If the jury finds the defendant guilty, the same jury hears the second or mental illness/deficiency phase of the trial. During that phase, the statements made by the defendant for the purpose of the mental examination and any evidence obtained as a result of such statements are admissible against the defendant. After the second phase of the trial, the jury or the court finds the defendant either not guilty by reason of mental illness or deficiency, or guilty.

Commitment of Defendants Found Not Guilty by Reason of Insanity

When a defendant is found not guilty by reason of mental illness or deficiency, the court orders that civil commitment proceedings be instituted and that the defendant be detained in a state hospital pending completion of the commitment proceedings.[21] Where the defendant has been found not guilty of felony or gross misdemeanor charges by reason of mental illness or deficiency, the criminal court retains supervision over the commitment. The court and the prosecuting attorney must be notified of any proposed institutional transfer, partial hospitalization status, or termination, discharge, or provisional discharge of the civil commitment. The prosecuting attorney has the right to participate as a party in any proceeding concerning proposed changes in the defendant's civil commitment status.

---

18. Minn. R. Crim. P. 20.03.
19. Minn. R. Crim. P. 20.02, subd. 6(1).
20. State v. Bouwman, 328 N.W.2d 703 (Minn. 1982) (expert testimony not admissible on question of capacity to form specific intent required for crime).
21. Minn. R. Crim. P. 20.02, subd. 8 (West 1979 & Supp. 1992). If the defendant is already committed, the court orders that the commitment be continued. *Id.* *See* chapters 5E.4 (mental illness commitment) and 5E.7 (mental retardation commitment).

Civil commitment proceedings for persons referred after a mental illness or deficiency acquittal follow the same procedures as are generally used,[22] with some exceptions. The continuing supervision of the criminal court, mentioned above, is one such exception. In addition, the law modifies the procedures to make it somewhat less likely that an acquittee will be released without a commitment. Applications for prepetition screening are not required in such cases if the same information already exists in the criminal proceeding.[23] Generally, the civil commitment petition should be heard by the judge before whom the acquittal took place.[24] In connection with the preliminary hearing, at which the commitment court is to decide whether there is sufficient evidence to continue to confine a proposed patient, the fact that the proposed patient was acquitted of a crime of violence immediately preceding the filing of the commitment petition "constitutes evidence that serious imminent physical harm" is likely if the proposed patient is not confined.[25] At the hearing on the commitment petition, the court may take "judicial notice" of the record of the criminal proceeding.[26] In other words, the commitment court may refer to and make use of the evidence and findings of the criminal court. Finally, in a proceeding where the defendant is alleged to be mentally ill and dangerous to the public, the acquittal constitutes evidence that the proposed patient is mentally ill and dangerous and shifts the burden of going forward in the presentation of evidence to the proposed patient. However, the burden of proof remains on the petitioner to prove by clear and convincing evidence that the proposed patient is mentally ill and dangerous.[27]

---

22. *See* chapters 5E.4, 5E.5, 5E.7.
23. M.S.A. § 253B.07, subd. 1 (West 1982 & Supp. 1992).
24. M.S.A. § 253B.07, subd. 2a (West Supp. 1992).
25. M.S.A. § 253B.07, subd. 7 (West 1982 & Supp. 1992). *See* chapter 5E.4.
26. M.S.A. § 253B.08, subd. 7 (West 1982 & Supp. 1992).
27. M.S.A. § 253B.18, subd. 1 (West 1982 & Supp. 1992). *See* chapter 5E.4.

5D.10

Battered Woman Syndrome

Battered woman syndrome describes a relationship wherein a man controls a woman by the use of physical violence, sexual abuse, verbal abuse, economic control, social isolation, and threats of future violence.[1] In addition, the woman blames herself for the partner's abusive behavior, feels she deserves it, or considers it to be his right.[2] The woman also hopes her partner will stop the abuse, because the battering partner often promises to do so.[3] Thus, the couple is engaged in an ongoing cycle of violence.

Historically, when a battered woman killed or seriously injured her abuser, the woman would rely on a mental illness defense.[4] More recently, however, many battered women pleaded self-defense when charged with the assault or murder of the battering partner.[5] Although "no jurisdictions have held that the existence of battered woman syndrome in and of itself operates as a defense to murder,"[6] a recent Minnesota case has held that expert testimony on battered woman syndrome is admissible to assist in the defense of self-defense.[7]

---

1. Mather, *The Skeleton in the Closet: The Battered Woman Syndrome, Self Defense, and Expert Testimony*, 39 Mercer L. Rev. 545, 555–56 (1988). *See also* Walker, *Battered Women Syndrome and Self-Defense*, 6 Notre Dame J.L., Ethics & Pub. Policy 321 (1992); Allard, *Rethinking Battered Woman Syndrome: A Black Feminist Perspective*, 1 UCLA Women's L.J. 191 (1991). Although the syndrome is often described in terms of male–female abuse, it may have applicability in other relationships as well.
2. Mather, *supra*, note 1 at 552.
3. *Id.*
4. *Id.* at 560.
5. *Id.*
6. State v. Steward, 243 Kan. 639, 763 P.2d 572, 577 (1988).
7. State v. Hennum, 441 N.W.2d 793 (Minn. 1989).

To justify the use of deadly force in self-defense, one must show that (a) the deadly force was undertaken in the belief that it was necessary to avert death or grievous bodily harm, (b) the belief was reasonable under the circumstances, and (c) the defendant's action was such as a reasonable person would have done under the circumstances.[8] Furthermore, in Minnesota, "it is well settled that there is a duty to retreat and avoid danger if reasonably possible."[9]

Expert testimony is admissible when specialized knowledge will assist the judge or jury to understand the evidence.[10] The Minnesota Supreme Court has ruled that expert testimony regarding battered woman syndrome is admissible "since it would help to explain a phenomenon not within the understanding of an ordinary lay person."[11] Courts have admitted expert testimony on battered woman syndrome for the following reasons:

1. to dispel the common misconception that a normal or reasonable person would not remain in such an abusive relationship;

2. for the specific purpose of bolstering the defendant's position and lending credibility to her version of the facts; and

3. to show the reasonableness of the defendant's fear that she was in imminent peril of death or serious bodily injury.[12]

In Minnesota, the expert's testimony is limited to a description of the general syndrome and the characteristics that are present in an individual suffering from the syndrome.[13] The expert may not testify to the ultimate fact, that is, whether the defendant suffers from battered woman syndrome. Rather, the jury must determine this from the evidence presented by both the prosecution and the defense.[14]

The rule limiting the role of expert testimony regarding battered woman syndrome serves two purposes. First, by preventing the defense from presenting expert testimony regarding whether the defendant suffers from the syndrome, the prosecution will not be denied a fair chance to rebut the defense expert.[15] Second, by preventing the prosecution's expert from examining the defendant, the defendant is spared an adverse examination

---

8. State v. Austin, 332 N.W.2d 21, 24 (Minn. 1983). *See* M.S.A. §§ 609.06, 609.065 (West Supp. 1994).
9. *Austin* at 24, citing State v. Johnson, 277 Minn. 368, 373, 152 N.W.2d 529, 532 (1967).
10. Minn. R. Evid. 702. *See* chapter 5C.2.
11. *Hennum* at 798. *See also id.* at n.2 (listing decisions from numerous states on battered woman syndrome).
12. *Hennum* at 798.
13. *Id.* at 799.
14. *Id.*
15. *Id.* at 800.

and the possible violation of her constitutional rights.[16] Thus, fairness is ensured for both parties.

---

16. *Id.*

5D.11

Rape Trauma Syndrome

Rape trauma syndrome describes the stages that a victim typically experiences following a rape. One commentator described the syndrome as being characterized by two phases:

> Phase I or the "acute phase," [is] a period of disorganization in which the victim is either emotionally out of control . . . or extraordinarily controlled. Headaches, fatigue, sleep problems, and gastrointestinal and genitourinary disturbances are common during this period. Phase II or the "long term reorganization process" is a period of nightmares, phobic reactions, sexual fears, and changes in routine.[1]

The presence of rape trauma syndrome tends to negate a defendant's claim that the sexual act was consensual. Some states allow expert testimony on this subject.[2]

The Minnesota Supreme Court has held that it is an error to admit expert testimony on rape trauma syndrome in a rape case.[3] Expert testimony is only admissible when the subject matter is beyond the knowledge and experience of a lay jury.[4] The expert's testimony should not be admitted if the jury is in as good a position to reach a decision as an expert.[5] The Minnesota Supreme Court stated that testimony about rape trauma syndrome has not reached the level of scientific reliability necessary to surpass the quality of common sense evaluation present in a jury deliberation.[6] The court felt that rape trauma syndrome testi-

---

1. Bartlett, K. T. (1993). *Gender and law* (pp. 702–703). Boston: Little, Brown.
2. *E.g.*, State v. Marks, 647 P.2d 1292 (Kan. 1982).
3. State v. Salandana, 324 N.W.2d 227 (Minn. 1982).
4. *See* chapter 5C.2.
5. Minn. R. Evid. 702.
6. State v. Salandana, 324 N.W.2d at 230.

mony unfairly prejudiced the defendant by creating around the victim an aura of special reliability and trustworthiness.[7] The court held that ordinary jurors are competent to consider the evidence and determine whether a rape occurred, and thus denied the admission of the expert testimony.[8]

7. *Id.*
8. *Id.* at 231.

5D.12

Hypnosis of Witnesses

Hypnosis is increasingly used in criminal investigations and proceedings. Because hypnosis touches the normal processes of memory, the admissibility of hypnotically influenced testimony raises important legal questions.

Hypnotically influenced information can be used in the investigatory phase[1] of criminal cases, as well as in the trial phase. Because the Minnesota courts have not ruled on issues surrounding its use in investigation,[2] this chapter focuses on the admissibility of the testimony of witnesses who have been hypnotized.

Testimony at a trial of a previously hypnotized witness has given rise to much scholarly and judicial controversy. It has been found that a hypnotized subject is highly susceptible to suggestion, even that which is subtle and not intended. It is difficult to determine which parts of the subject's "memory" are accurate and which are fabrication. Hypnosis also tends to solidify the subject's memory. A subject who is ambivalent about his or her story before hypnosis can become convinced of its accuracy after hypnosis.[3]

---

1. Hypnosis has frequently been used by police departments as an investigative tool and as a technique to produce evidence for criminal prosecutions. State v. Mack, 292 N.W.2d 764 (Minn. 1980). A witness under hypnosis may, for instance, bring forth information previously unknown to the police, such as a license plate number, that subsequently aids the police in their investigation. *Id.* at 771.
2. In State v. Mack, 292 N.W.2d 764 (Minn. 1980), the Minnesota Supreme Court noted, without adopting, a set of "safeguards" for using hypnosis in the investigatory interview. The safeguards are similar to the standards adopted by the court for admission of hypnotically influenced testimony. *See* below.
3. *Id.* at 768, 769.

Because hypnotically induced testimony "does not meet ordinary standards of reliability for admission," the Minnesota Supreme Court has ruled that testimony of a "previously hypnotized witness concerning the subject matter adduced at the pretrial hypnotic interview may not be admitted in a criminal proceeding."[4]

However, the Minnesota courts recognize that hypnosis can be a valuable tool in criminal investigations. Because prehypnotic memories may be untainted by the influence of the hypnosis, the automatic exclusion of testimony applies only to those recollections that are recalled during hypnosis.[5]

A party seeking to introduce prehypnotic recall testimony must prove that[6]

1. the hypnosis was performed by a psychiatrist or psychologist with special training in its use;
2. the psychiatrist or psychologist was not an investigator or witness or otherwise involved in the case;
3. the hypnosis and all contact with the psychiatrist or psychologist was videotaped;
4. a detailed description of the facts as the witness remembered them was obtained by the psychiatrist or psychologist prior to the hypnosis;
5. no other person besides the psychiatrist or psychologist was present during the initial interview or the hypnosis of the witness; and
6. the psychiatrist or psychologist avoided adding any new elements to the witness's description of his or her experiences, including those the witness had in his or her waking state, lest the hypnotist inadvertently alter the witness's memory.

The trial court determines whether the witness's memory is reliable and not the product of unnecessary suggestiveness. It then determines the scope of the witness's testimony to be permitted at trial. The witness's testimony is limited to the witness's prehypnotic recollections. If the witness is allowed to testify, the opposing party may introduce proof with respect to the hypnotic procedures followed and expert testimony concerning the potential effects of hypnosis on the witness's recollection. The psychiatrist or psychologist who performed the hypnosis may not testify about his or her beliefs regarding the truthfulness of the witness's statements or the state of the witness's mind at the time of the crime.

---

4. *Id.* at 772.
5. Rodriguez v. State, 345 N.W.2d 781 (Minn. Ct. App. 1984).
6. *Id.*

5D.13

Eyewitness Identification

Eyewitness identification testimony plays a central role in some forms of litigation. Its reliability is an important question. There is a body of scientific knowledge about the reliability of such identification.[1] Although the courts in some states have allowed expert testimony on the subject of eyewitness identification reliability,[2] Minnesota's appellate courts have not followed their lead. In Minnesota, the admission of such testimony is at the discretion of the trial court.

Expert testimony on the reliability of eyewitness identification is treated like other expert testimony.[3] To be admissible, the witness must have specialized knowledge, and the knowledge must be of assistance to the trier of fact (judge or jury) in understanding the evidence or determining an issue of fact. It is on the second requirement (helpfulness) rather than on the first (specialized knowledge) that the admissibility of identification-reliability testimony falters. Trial courts may exclude expert testimony if it will not add precision or depth to the jury's ability to reach conclusions, or if the court concludes that it will confuse the jury. Trial courts have broad discretion in making those determinations.[4] When the issue has arisen in Minnesota's appellate courts, they have uniformly refused to reverse trial court decisions not to

---

1. *See, e.g.,* Loftus, E. (1979). *Eyewitness testimony.* Cambridge, MA: Harvard University Press.
2. *See, e.g.,* State v. Happle, 135 Ariz. 281, 660 P.2d 1208. *See also* State v. Helterbridle, 301 N.W.2d 545 (Minn. 1980) (referring to trial courts "around the country" that have admitted such testimony).
3. *See* chapter 5C.2.
4. State v. Helterbridle, 301 N.W.2d 545 (Minn. 1980).

allow such expert testimony.[5] Although the basis for these decisions has not been extensively spelled out, it is clear that the courts are not convinced that juries need help in carrying out what is considered to be their central task, judging witness credibility.

The courts have left the door open for the admission of such testimony in a proper case. To support the admission of such testimony, the proponent should attempt to establish its helpfulness to the jury deliberation process. Admission is most likely in areas where the average juror's life experiences are unlikely to provide the "common knowledge" necessary to judge witness credibility adequately.[6]

---

5. *Id. See* Cummings v. State, 1989 WL 109377 (Minn. Ct. App. 1989), rev. denied Sept. 26, 1989 (unpublished opinion); State v. St. John, 299 N.W.2d 737 (Minn. 1980).

6. For example, Minnesota courts allow expert testimony on battered woman syndrome, in part on the theory that the average juror's life experience will not produce an appropriate evaluation of the abused woman's response to her partner's violence. *See* chapter 5D.10.

5D.14

Competency to Be Sentenced

Minnesota law provides that "no person shall be tried or sentenced for any offense while mentally ill or mentally deficient so as to be incapable of understanding the proceedings or participating in his defense."[1] This rule and its application are discussed in detail in chapter 5D.5.

---

1. Minn. R. Crim. P. 20.01, subd. 1; M.S.A. § 611.026 (West 1987).

5D.15

Sentencing

After a conviction of a crime, the court sentences the defendant. Presentence investigations are used to provide the court with additional information about the defendant to be used in setting the sentence. Because sentences serve a number of functions (rehabilitation and treatment as well as punishment), presentence investigations cover a wide range of types of information. MHPs may be involved in providing a variety of assessment information as part of the investigation.

Presentence Investigations: When Ordered, Contents

Presentence investigations are required where the defendant has been convicted of a felony. They are optional where the conviction is for a misdemeanor or gross misdemeanor. The investigations examine the defendant's individual characteristics, circumstances, needs, potentialities, criminal record, and social history; the circumstances of the offense; and the harm caused to others and to the community.[1] As part of the investigation, the court may order a mental or physical examination of the defendant.[2] This mental examination should be distinguished from a mental examination ordered by the court regarding the defendant's competency. Defendants may not be sentenced if they are not "com-

---

1. M.S.A. § 609.115, subd. 1 (West Supp. 1992).
2. Minn. R. Crim. P. 27.03, subd. 1(A). The rule provides no further information about the circumstances or content of the examination.

petent."[3] A court with doubts about competency must order an examination to evaluate competency to proceed.[4]

The presentence investigation is conducted by a probation officer of the court or by agents of the commissioner of corrections.[5] The investigation and subsequent report must contain, if the court directs, an estimate of the prospects of the defendant's rehabilitation, as well as recommendations as to the sentence that should be imposed. The defendant may be committed to the commissioner of corrections while the report is being prepared.

If the defendant is convicted of a felony, the investigator must determine whether alcohol or drug use contributed to the commission of the offense. If so, the report must contain the results of a chemical use assessment.[6] The chemical use assessment must include a recommended level of care and must be conducted by an assessor qualified under the rules adopted by the commissioner of human services.[7]

If the defendant was convicted of one of a variety of economic crimes,[8] the investigator must determine whether or not compulsive gambling contributed to the commission of the crime. If so, the report must contain the results of a compulsive gambling assessment. The assessment must include a recommended level of care if the assessor concludes that the defendant is in need of compulsive gambling treatment.[9] The assessment must be conducted by an assessor qualified by law.[10]

Disclosure of Presentence Investigation Reports

Written presentence investigation reports must be provided to counsel for all parties before the sentence.[11] Written reports are not to disclose confidential sources of information unless the court otherwise directs.[12] If the report contains some confidential information, that portion is normally withheld from the defendant and counsel. However, the court advises counsel that the

---

3. *See* chapter 5D.14.
4. *See* chapter 5D.5.
5. M.S.A. § 609.115, subd. 1 (West Supp. 1992).
6. M.S.A. § 609.115, subd. 8 (West Supp. 1992).
7. *See* chapter 5E.5.
8. For example, theft, embezzlement of public funds, or forgery.
9. M.S.A. § 609.115, subd. 9 (West Supp. 1992).
10. M.S.A. § 245.98, subd. 2a provides the qualification criteria.
11. The 1987 Advisory Committee Comment suggested that psychiatric reports should be given to the defendant's lawyer, who would then exercise discretion as to whether to share the report with the client.
12. M.S.A. § 609.115, subd. 4 (West Supp. 1992).

information is available for inspection.[13] Neither the law nor the rules define what information is considered confidential.

---

13. Minn. R. Crim. P. 27.03, subd. 1(C).

5D.16

Probation

In Minnesota, unless a term of imprisonment is mandated, the sentencing court may stay the sentence and either order noninstitutional sanctions without probation or place the defendant on probation, with or without supervision.[1] A court staying a sentence without imposing a term of incarceration must order noninstitutional sanctions wherever practicable.[2] Noninstitutional sanctions include, but are not limited to, reinstitution, fines, and community service work.[3] The presentence investigation report (PSI) may include an estimate of the defendant's prospects for rehabilitation, as well as recommendations as to the appropriate sentence to be imposed.[4] If MHPs are involved in preparing the PSI, their recommendations will be considered.

When a defendant violates any term of his or her probation or noninstitutional sanction, the court may revoke the stay and order the defendant taken into custody.[5] Conversely, a defendant may refuse probation and demand execution of the sentence "if the conditions of probation make probation more onerous than prison and if it cannot be demonstrated that society's interests suffer."[6]

The court must notify the defendant, in writing, of each condition of probation.[7]

---

1. M.S.A. § 609.135, subd. 1 (West Supp. 1992).
2. *Id.* at subd. 6.
3. *Id.* at subd. 1.
4. M.S.A. § 609.115, subd. 1 (West Supp. 1992).
5. M.S.A. § 609.14, subd. 1 (West Supp. 1992).
6. State v. Randolf, 316 N.W.2d 508, 510 (Minn. 1982).
7. Minn. R. Crim. P. 27.03, subd. 4(E)(1–3).

5D.17

Dangerous Offenders

Under certain circumstances, the sentencing judge may take into account the defendant's dangerous propensities in setting the duration of the sentence. In addition, sex offenders who pose a future danger may be committed under the psychopathic personality law. The opinions of MHPs may play a role in assisting the court in assessing the defendant's dangerousness.

Minnesota uses a complex system of sentencing guidelines as a means of achieving some degree of uniformity in criminal sentences.[1] Where the defendant has been convicted of a violent crime,[2] the judge may impose a sentence that is higher than the "presumptive imprisonment sentence" in the guidelines, under the following conditions: The offender was at least 18 years old at the time the offense was committed, the offender has two or more prior convictions for violent crimes, and the court finds that the offender is a danger to public safety.[3] If the court finds that the offender is a danger to public safety, it must specify the basis for the finding, which may include references to the offender's past criminal behavior and any aggravating factors involved in the present offense.[4]

Minnesota law provides for the civil commitment of persons who have a "psychopathic personality." Included within that term are persons whose lack of sexual control renders them dangerous to others.[5]

---

1. See M.S.A. § 244.01 et seq.
2. As defined in M.S.A. § 609.152, subd. 1(d) (West Supp. 1992).
3. Id., subd. 2.
4. Id.
5. M.S.A. § 526.09 (West 1989). See chapter 5D.25 for a more detailed discussion of this law.

5D.18

Habitual Offenders

Under certain circumstances, a sentencing judge can increase the sentence of a convicted offender who has substantial prior criminal activity. Because the criteria for such increases depend on the nature of the past criminal record and the present offense, rather than on a prediction of future dangerous behavior, it is doubtful that assessments by MHPs would play a major role in determining whether such increases are appropriate.

Minnesota uses a complex system of sentencing guidelines as a means of achieving some degree of uniformity in criminal sentences.[1] Where the defendant has been convicted of a felony, the judge may impose a sentence that is higher than the "presumptive imprisonment sentence" in the guidelines if the offender has more than four prior felony convictions and the present offense is a felony that was committed as part of a pattern of criminal conduct from which a substantial portion of the offender's income was derived.[2]

---

1. *See* generally M.S.A. Chapter 244.
2. M.S.A. § 609.152, subd. 3 (West Supp. 1992).

5D.19

Competency to Serve a Sentence

Minnesota law provides that "no person shall be . . . punished for any crime while mentally ill or mentally deficient so as to be incapable of understanding the proceedings or making a defense."[1] If the incompetency is discovered prior to sentencing, the trial court will order a competency examination and hold a hearing to determine whether the defendant can proceed to be sentenced.[2]

The concern prior to sentencing is whether the defendant has the capacity to understand the proceeding and participate in the defense. After the imposition of the sentence, the law becomes concerned with the treatment needs of the inmate.

Any time a person confined in an adult correctional facility is alleged to be mentally ill,[3] the person in charge of the institution is to arrange to have the allegedly mentally ill person examined by a licensed physician or licensed consulting psychologist.[4] If the examiner finds the person mentally ill and in need of short-term treatment, the examiner may recommend transfer to the psychiatric unit at the Minnesota Correctional Facility–Oak Park Heights. If the examiner finds the person in need of long-term treatment, or the person refuses to participate in the treatment program, judicial commitment proceedings will be started.[5] The court may

---

1. M.S.A. § 611.026 (West Supp. 1992).
2. *See* chapter 5D.5 for a more detailed discussion of the procedures to be followed under those circumstances.
3. The term "mentally ill" has the same meaning in this context as it has in the civil commitment context. *See* chapter 5E.4. M.S.A. § 241.69, subd. 8 (West 1992).
4. M.S.A. § 241.69 (West 1992).
5. *See* chapter 5E.4 for detailed information about the civil commitment process.

commit the person either to the correctional facility psychiatric unit at Oak Park Heights or to some other hospital. The chief medical officer of the psychiatric unit may provisionally discharge the person back to the general population of the correctional facility subject to return for further treatment. When the person is no longer in need of mental health hospitalization, he or she will be discharged back to the correctional facility and the commitment will be discharged. If the sentence of a person who is committed to a psychiatric hospital expires before the person recovers and is discharged, and he or she still requires hospitalization, he or she will be transferred to a state hospital and be detained as any other person under judicial commitment.

5D.20

Mental Health Services in Jails and Prisons

Mental Health Services in Minnesota Jails

Rules of the State Department of Corrections govern the provision of mental health services in jails.[1] Jails must have policies for the management of mentally ill prisoners. The policies must include procedures for diagnosing mental illness and for managing mentally ill prisoners who pose a danger to themselves or others. A physician or licensed psychologist must be consulted in the diagnosis. If the prisoner is separated and/or restrained because of mental illness, a licensed physician must be contacted within eight hours to approve a written plan for managing the prisoner's behavior. Jails must develop criteria and procedures for transferring mentally ill prisoners to a licensed medical facility.[2] The criteria must be approved by a licensed physician.

Mental Health Services in Minnesota Prisons

By law, the commissioner of corrections is to provide appropriate mental health programs for prison inmates who desire to volun-

---

1. Minn. R. 2910.6200 (1991).
2. *See* chapter 5D.21.

tarily participate in such programs.[3] The design and implementation of the programs is at the sole discretion of the commissioner, acting within limitations imposed by appropriate funds.

The commissioner of corrections is required to establish a psychiatric unit for the care and treatment of inmates of state correctional institutions who become mentally ill.[4] This unit has been established at the Oak Park Heights facility. Inmates may be transferred voluntarily to that unit if, after examination, it appears that they are in need of short-term treatment. Inmates who need longer-term treatment, or who refuse needed voluntary treatment, may be referred to the civil commitment process for involuntary transfer to the mental health unit.[5]

---

3. M.S.A. § 244.03 (West 1992).
4. M.S.A. § 241.69, subd. 1 (West 1992).
5. *Id.* at subds. 3, 4. *See* chapter 5D.21.

5D.21

Transfer From Penal to Mental Health Facilities

Inmates of adult correctional facilities who are in need of mental health services may be transferred to a mental health facility either within or outside of the correctional institution.

Procedures in State Prisons

By law, the commissioner of corrections is to establish a psychiatric unit at one of the state correctional facilities.[1] A mentally ill prison inmate may be transferred to that unit or, if the inmate needs treatment or care not available at any state correctional facility, to another state institution under the control of the commissioner of human services or to a private medical facility.[2]

The person in charge of the correctional institution may cause any inmate alleged to be mentally ill to be examined by a physician especially qualified in the diagnosis of mental illness or, if none is available, by any licensed physician or licensed consulting psychologist.[3] If the examination determines that the inmate needs short-term treatment, he or she is transferred to the department of corrections psychiatric unit on a voluntary basis. If the inmate refuses or if the examiner determines that long-term treatment is necessary, the inmate is referred for civil commitment proceedings.[4] If the person is committed, the commitment may be to the correctional psychiatric unit or to another hospital. If the

---

1. M.S.A. § 241.69 (West 1992). Such a facility has been established at the Oak Park Heights facility.
2. M.S.A. § 241.07 (West 1992).
3. M.S.A. § 241.69, subd. 2 (West 1992).
4. *See* chapter 5E.4.

commitment is to the correctional psychiatric unit, the inmate is held there until the head of that unit determines that he or she can be discharged, at which time the inmate is returned to the general institutional population. If the person's sentence expires before his or her recovery and, in the judgment of the chief medical officer of the unit, the person requires further hospitalization for mental illness, the commissioner of corrections will transfer the person to a state hospital.[5]

Procedures in Jails[6]

Jails must have policies for the management of mentally ill prisoners. The policies must include procedures for diagnosing mental illness and for managing mentally ill prisoners. A physician or licensed psychologist must be consulted in the diagnosis. If the prisoner is separated and/or restrained because of mental illness, a licensed physician must be contacted within eight hours to approve a written plan for managing the prisoner's behavior.

Each jail must have a policy for transferring mentally ill prisoners to a licensed medical facility. The transfers must be done in accordance with the emergency hold provisions of the civil commitment act.[7]

In general, mentally ill prisoners held in jail while awaiting trial will be transferred to and held in mental health facilities under the procedures for determining competency to stand trial.[8] Mentally ill jail prisoners who have been convicted will be transferred to and held at mental health facilities under the civil commitment act procedures.[9]

---

5. M.S.A. § 241.69, subd. 6 (West 1992).
6. Minn. R. 2910.6200 (1991).
7. M.S.A. § 253B.05. *See* chapter 5E.4.
8. *See* chapter 5D.5.
9. *See* chapter 5E.4.

Parole Determinations and Supervised Release

In 1980, Minnesota reformed its criminal sentencing structure. The reform replaced a system of indeterminate sentencing with a system of determinate sentencing. The change reflected at least two important policy goals: First, determinate sentencing aims to produce sentences that are more uniform, hence less discriminatory. Second, the new system de-emphasizes rehabilitation as a sentencing goal and is frankly more retributive.[1]

The reform is implemented at both the sentencing and the release stages of the criminal justice process. Under an indeterminate sentencing scheme, convicts received sentences of indeterminate length, perhaps bounded by a minimum and a maximum term. The actual release of the inmate was determined by a parole board whose task was to determine whether there was a reasonable probability that a prisoner could be released and remain at liberty without violating the law.[2] Thus, the parole determination was a highly discretionary function involving predictions of future inmate behavior. The underlying philosophy was one of rehabilitation. The parole board judged whether the inmate's "treatment" had progressed adequately to justify release.[3] MHPs were frequently involved in evaluating inmates' fitness for parole.

Prisoners whose sentences arose from crimes committed prior to April 30, 1980, remain subject to the older, indeterminate sentencing/parole system. However, the law directs the commis-

---

1. See generally W. Stockman, *Parole and Good Time*, 5 Hamline L. Rev. 355 (1982).
2. See id., citing Black's Law Dictionary 1006 (rev. 5th ed. 1979).
3. *Parole and Good Time, supra* note 1, at 356.

sioner of corrections to "take into consideration, but not be bound by," the new sentencing guidelines in determining their parole.[4]

Under Minnesota's determinate sentencing scheme, each person convicted of a crime is sentenced to a definite term. The term is determined by reference to a complex set of sentencing guidelines established by the Sentencing Guidelines Commission.[5] While serving his or her sentence, an inmate earns "good time" at the rate of one day of good time for each two days during which the inmate violates none of the disciplinary rules of the commissioner of corrections.[6] Good time, once earned, is "vested." However, disciplinary offenses can result in the prospective loss of good time, up to a limit of 90 days.[7]

Under the determinate sentencing scheme, parole is replaced by "supervised release."[8] An inmate's sentence is reduced for each day of good time earned. When an inmate has served the sentence, as so reduced, he or she is released into the community to serve the remainder of the original sentence under supervised release.[9] This release is not discretionary. Thus, under the current system, MHPs play little or no role in the release decision.[10]

The commissioner of corrections establishes rules governing behavior during supervised release. If the released inmate violates the rules, the commissioner may revoke the supervised release and re-imprison the inmate for an appropriate period of time. However, the period of time for which the release may be revoked may not exceed the period of time remaining in the inmate's original sentence.[11]

---

4. M.S.A. § 244.08, subd. 1 (West 1992).
5. M.S.A. § 244.09 (West 1992). The guidelines establish a "presumptive fixed sentence" and may provide for an increase or decrease of up to 15% by the sentencing judge. *Id.*, subd. 5.
6. M.S.A. § 244.04, subd. 1 (West Supp. 1992).
7. M.S.A. § 244.04, subds. 1, 2 (West Supp. 1992).
8. M.S.A. § 244.05 (West Supp. 1992).
9. M.S.A. § 244.05, subd. 1 (West Supp. 1992). A separate rule governs persons sentenced to life in prison. *See* M.S.A. § 244.05, subds. 4, 5 (West Supp. 1992).
10. However, before the commissioner releases a convicted sex offender, the commissioner is required to make a preliminary determination whether a petition under the psychopathic personality laws may be appropriate. M.S.A. § 244.05, subd. 7 (West Supp. 1992). MHPs will be involved in this determination, which requires a judgment as to whether the individual has uncontrollable sexual urges. *See* chapter 5D.25. If the commissioner determines that the petition would be appropriate, the determination is forwarded to the appropriate county attorney for further action.
11. M.S.A. § 244.05, subds. 2, 3 (West Supp. 1992). However, the rules are different for certain sex offenders. *Id.*

5D.23

Competency to Be Executed

Minnesota does not have a death penalty. In states that have a death penalty, executions of incompetent persons are generally prohibited.

5D.24

Pornography

The law prohibits knowing involvement in the sale, exhibition, or circulation of obscene materials.[1] MHPs who are knowledgeable about the effects of sexually oriented materials may be asked to evaluate and testify on these issues. Violation of the obscenity law is a gross misdemeanor. Second and subsequent violations of the law are felonies.

A work is "obscene" if, taken as a whole, it appeals to the prurient interest in sex, depicts or describes in a patently offensive manner sexual conduct, and does not have serious literary, artistic, political, or scientific value. The trier of fact must find that the "average person, applying contemporary community standards would find that the work, taken as a whole, appeals to the prurient interest in sex." The act defines, in some detail, the meaning of "sexual conduct." "Community" means the political subdivision from which persons properly qualified to serve as jurors in a criminal proceeding are chosen.

---

1. M.S.A. § 617.241 (West Supp. 1992).

5D.25

Services for and Civil Commitment of Sex Offenders

A range of services is available for sex offenders in Minnesota. These services fall into three broad categories: programs in correctional facilities, programs in state mental health facilities, and programs in the community. This chapter summarizes the programs available in state-run correctional and mental health facilities. The chapter then describes the legal procedures for civilly committing sex offenders as "psychopathic personalities."

Services for Sex Offenders in State Correctional Facilities

The state Department of Corrections operates a number of programs for sex offenders in state correctional institutions. Rules for the certification of sex offender treatment programs in correctional facilities are being developed but have not been, as of this writing, promulgated.[1] Sex offenders are evaluated upon admission to a state correctional facility by a program review team. The team determines what type of programming will be developed for the offender and recommends placement in a treatment program.

The sex offender programs and services operated by the Department are summarized as follows:[2]

---

1. Minnesota Department of Corrections, Backgrounder, Sex Offender Facts, February 1992.
2. Minnesota Department of Corrections, Programs for Sex Offenders, February 1992.

The *sex offender/chemical dependency program at Oak Park Heights* is designed to reach inmates early in their incarceration period and focuses on the treatment of recidivist, chemically dependent sex offenders in need of long-term programming.

The *sex offender program, Stillwater,* is a six-month program that is intensive and predominately educational and evaluative. It is designed to reach inmates who would benefit from this approach as a first step to other programs.

Transitions, Lino Lakes, is designed for inmates in their last 10 to 12 months of incarceration. Treatment continues into the community through contracted service providers, with four to six months of aftercare.

Sex offender services, St. Cloud, include assessment and individual psychotherapy, preliminary to more intensive programs at other facilities.

The *sex offender program for women, Shakopee,* has been temporarily suspended but could be reinstated as necessary. It is structured in a group format.

Programming for juvenile sex offenders, Red Wing, includes assessment, incorporation of goals in release planning, aftercare recommendations, peer group counseling sessions, and individual counseling.

Programming for juvenile sex offenders, Sauk Centre, uses individual counseling and group sessions, assessment, release planning, and aftercare recommendations.

Services at St. Peter Regional Treatment Center. The St. Peter Regional Treatment Center Forensic Division operates a Sex Offender Program. As of July 1993, the Center states the mission of the program as follows:

> [Its] mission is the comprehensive evaluation, management, and rehabilitation of individuals committed under the Psychopathic Personality Statute or admitted as voluntary participants on condition of probation (COP) from state district courts. Relapse prevention is the guiding principle of treatment but eclectic treatment delivered in a psycho-educational format will be employed to treat individuals in a humane and secure environment.

Civil Commitment of Sex Offenders as Psychopathic Personalities

Minnesota law provides for the civil commitment of persons with "psychopathic personalities."[3] The term is defined as follows: "the existence in any person of such conditions of emotional

---

3. M.S.A. § 526.09 (West Supp. 1992). For a fuller discussion, see Janus, E. S. (1991). *Civil commitment in Minnesota* (2nd ed.). St. Paul, MN: Butterworth.

instability, or impulsiveness of behavior, or lack of customary standards of good judgment, or failure to appreciate the consequences of his acts, or a combination of any such conditions, as to render such person irresponsible for his conduct with respect to sexual matters and thereby dangerous to other persons." The Minnesota Supreme Court has construed this language "to include those persons who, by a habitual course of misconduct in sexual matters, have evidenced an utter lack of power to control their sexual impulses and who, as a result, are likely to attack or otherwise inflict injury, loss, pain or other evil on the objects of their uncontrolled and uncontrollable desire."[4]

In general, the procedures applicable to psychopathic personality commitments are the same as those applicable to commitments as mentally ill and dangerous (MID).[5] Persons committed as psychopathic personalities also apparently have the same rights as those committed as MID, including a right to appropriate treatment.[6]

---

4. State *ex rel.* Pearson v. Probate Court, 205 Minn. 545, 287 N.W. 297 (1939), aff'd 309 U.S. 270 (1949). See also In re Blodgelt, _____ N.W.2d _____ (Minn. 1994) (requiring proof of a "volitional dysfunction which grossly impairs judgment and behavior").

5. M.S.A. § 526.10 (West Supp. 1992). *See* chapter 5E.4.

6. *See, e.g.,* In re Joelson, 385 N.W.2d 810 (Minn. 1986); In re Martenies, 350 N.W.2d 470 (Minn. Ct. App. 1984), pet. for rev. denied (Minn. Sept. 12, 1984).

5D.26

Rights of and Services for Victims of Crimes

Minnesota has enacted a series of laws defining the rights of victims of crimes. These rights are summarized in this chapter.

Notification of Victim Services and Victims' Rights

The commissioner of corrections is required to develop a plan to provide crime victims with information concerning victim services in their geographic area.[1] Victims are to be notified of the following types of services: victim crisis centers, programs for victims of sexual assault, victim witness programs, elderly victims projects, victim assistance hotlines, incest abuse programs, and domestic violence shelters and programs.[2] The commissioner must also develop a notice of the rights of crime victims. The notice must include a form for the preparation of a preliminary written victim impact summary, which is a concise statement of the immediate and expected damage to the victim as a result of the crime. The notice, which is to be distributed to crime victims by police officers, must notify the victim of the right to request restitution, the right to be notified of any plea negotiation, the right to be present at sentencing, and the right to be notified of the final disposition.[3]

---

1. M.S.A. § 611A.02 (West Supp. 1992).
2. *See* chapter 5A.7A for a discussion of domestic abuse protection proceedings.
3. M.S.A. § 611A.02 (West Supp. 1992).

Victim Input Prior to Pretrial Diversion

In certain circumstances, the prosecutor must make reasonable efforts to notify and seek input from the victim prior to referring a person into a pretrial diversion program.[4]

Victim Notification: Domestic Assault

Prosecutors must make every reasonable effort to notify a domestic assault victim if the prosecutor has decided not to prosecute the assault.[5] The prosecutor must keep a written record of the reasons for failure to prosecute such an assault.

Presentence Investigation: Victim Impact

Presentence investigation reports[6] must contain information from and about the victim, including a summary of the harm done to the victim and a statement of what disposition the victim deems appropriate.[7]

Minor Victim Witnesses

Minors who are prosecuting witnesses in cases of child abuse or crimes of violence may be accompanied by a parent, guardian, or other supportive person when they testify.[8]

Restitution

A crime victim has the right to request that the offender be ordered to pay restitution as part of the disposition of a criminal charge or juvenile delinquency proceeding.[9] A request for restitu-

---

4. M.S.A. § 611A.031 (West Supp. 1992).
5. M.S.A. § 611A.0315 (West Supp. 1992).
6. See chapter 5D.15.
7. M.S.A. § 611A.037 (West Supp. 1992).
8. M.S.A. § 631.046, subd. 1 (West Supp. 1993). The right may be limited in some circumstances.
9. M.S.A. § 611A.04 (West Supp. 1992); § 260.013 (West Supp. 1993). See chapters 5D.15 (sentencing) and 5A.15 (delinquency proceedings). Victims of domestic abuse may seek restitution from their abusers. See chapter 5A.7A.

tion may include, but is not limited to, any out-of-pocket losses resulting from the crime, including medical and therapy costs, replacement of wages and services, and funeral expenses. In determining whether to order restitution, the court considers the amount of economic loss sustained by the victim and the income, resources, and obligations of the defendant.[10]

Notice of Risk of Sexually Transmitted Disease

Hospitals treating a victim of a sexual assault must give written notice to the victim, or the parent or guardian, of the risk of sexually transmitted diseases.[11]

Programs for Victims of Sexual Assault

The commissioner of corrections is to appoint a 12-member advisory council on sexual assault.[12] The commissioner of corrections is to award grants to programs that provide emergency shelter services and support services to battered women and their children.[13] At least one of the programs is to serve American Indian women.

Crime Victim Crisis Centers

The commissioner of corrections is to establish crime victim crisis centers to provide services to victims of crime.[14] Centers provide direct crisis intervention to crime victims, transportation to assist victims in obtaining necessary emergency services, investigation into the availability of insurance or other financial resources, referral to public and private agencies, encouragement in the development of services, coordination of existing services, and public education.[15]

---

10. M.S.A. § 611A.045 (West 1987).
11. M.S.A. § 611A.20 (West Supp. 1992).
12. M.S.A. § 611A.20 (West Supp. 1992).
13. M.S.A. § 611A.32 (West Supp. 1992). Grantees must comply with rules promulgated by the commissioner.
14. M.S.A. § 611A.41 (West 1991).
15. M.S.A. § 611A.20 (West 1987).

Crime Victim Reparations

Minnesota law establishes a Crime Victims Reparations Board that is authorized to pay crime victims reparations for certain losses suffered as a result of crime.[16] Generally, to be eligible for reparations, a person must be a crime victim, or a dependent or the estate of a crime victim, who has suffered economic loss as a result of the crime, or any other person who has incurred economic loss by purchasing services or products for the victim.[17] Certain limitations on eligibility are set forth in the law.[18] Reparations equal the amount of economic loss suffered, although they are to be reduced to the extent that the loss was recouped from some other source[19] or that the claimant had some contributory misconduct. Reparations may not exceed $50,000.[20]

Recoverable economic loss includes reasonable expenses for medical care, loss of income, and child care or household services. Also included are reasonable expenses incurred for psychological or psychiatric services, where the nature of the injury or the circumstances of the crime are such that the treatment is necessary to the rehabilitation of the victim. If the treatment is lengthy or expensive, the provider may be required to submit to the Board a plan that includes measurable treatment goals, the estimated cost of treatment, and the estimated date of completion of treatment.[21]

In connection with a claim for reparations, the law provides no privilege for information relevant to the issue of the physical, mental, or emotion condition of the claimant or victim. However, the attorney–client privilege is not abridged.[22]

---

16. M.S.A. § 611A.55 and § 611A.56 (West Supp. 1992). *See generally* M.S.A. §§ 611A.51 to 611A.68. The Board has the authority to promulgate rules governing its operations. M.S.A. § 611A.56 (West Supp. 1992).
17. M.S.A. § 611A.53 (West Supp. 1992). There are limitations on eligibility for health care providers who are not individuals. *Id.*, subd. 1a.
18. *Id.*, subd. 2. For example, with certain limitations, no reparations are payable unless the crime was reported to the police within five days. Claimants who have refused to cooperate, who were offenders or accomplices, or who file claims more than one year after the injury may, with some exceptions, be barred from recovery. *Id.*, subd. 2.
19. M.S.A. § 611A.52, subd. 5 (West Supp. 1992).
20. M.S.A. § 611A.54 (West Supp. 1992).
21. M.S.A. § 611A.52, subd. 8 (West Supp. 1992).
22. M.S.A. § 611A.62 (West 1991).

Section **5E**

Voluntary or Involuntary Receipt of State Services

5E.1

Medical Assistance for Needy Persons

Minnesota has two main programs for funding medical services to low-income persons. This chapter discusses the Medical Assistance (MA) program. This is a joint federal–state program operating under the federal Medicaid law.[1] Chapter 5E.2 discusses the General Assistance Medical Care program, which is a state-funded program serving low-income people who are not eligible for MA.[2] Both programs provide direct payments to suppliers of medical care and services.

The law governing these medical assistance programs is complex. In basic outline, the applicable law and rules for the programs govern the following areas:

1. Financial eligibility: Both programs have income and asset limits on eligibility.

2. Categorical eligibility: Both programs impose nonfinancial criteria on eligibility.

3. Definition of covered services.

This chapter briefly summarizes the law relating to categorical eligibility and covered services for the MA program.

General Provisions

All payments under the MA program are made to the vendor of medical services. Maximum payments are based on the usual and

---

1. *See generally* 42 U.S.C.A. § 1395 et seq.
2. *See generally* M.S.A. § 256D.03 et seq.

customary charge for the rendered services.[3] The commissioner of human services is permitted to contract with prepaid health plans to provide medical services to MA recipients.[4]

Eligibility Categories

The following categories of individuals or families are eligible for MA[5] if they meet the financial criteria:[6]

1. children eligible for subsidized adoption assistance;[7]
2. foster children receiving foster care maintenance payments;
3. families receiving Aid to Families With Dependant Children (AFDC);
4. recipients of Minnesota Supplemental Aid (generally, low-income elderly and disabled persons);
5. pregnant women and dependent or needy unborn children;
6. aged, blind, and disabled persons;
7. children and infants;
8. elderly hospital inpatients; and
9. disabled children.

Covered Services

The following services are, or may be, covered by MA[8] (in some cases, coverage is limited or conditional): inpatient hospital services; mental illness and mental retardation case management;[9] hospice care;[10] community mental health center services; alternate care programs to provide funding for and access to home and community-based services for frail elderly persons;[11] skilled and intermediate nursing care; physicians' services; outpatient and physician-directed clinic services; home health services; private duty nursing; physical therapy; occupational therapy; dental services; laboratory and X-ray services; nurse anesthetist services; eyeglasses, dentures, and prosthetic devices; drugs; diagnostic,

---

3. M.S.A. § 256B.03, subd. 1 (West 1992).
4. M.S.A. § 256B.031, subd. 1 (West 1992).
5. M.S.A. § 256B.055 (West 1992).
6. M.S.A. § 256B.056 et seq. (West 1992).
7. See chapter 5A.14.
8. M.S.A. § 256B.0625 (West 1992).
9. See chapters 5E.6 and 5E.7.
10. See chapter 5E.8.
11. M.S.A. § 256B.0913 (West 1992).

screening, and preventive services; health plan premiums; abortion services; transportation costs; personal care services; nutritional products; and home care services.[12]

---

12. M.S.A. § 256B.0627 (West 1992).

5E.2

General Assistance Medical Care

Minnesota has two main programs for funding medical services to low-income persons. Both programs provide direct payments to suppliers of medical care and services. This chapter discusses the General Assistance Medical Care (GAMC) program,[1] which is a state-funded program serving low-income people who are not eligible for Medical Assistance (MA). The MA program is a joint federal–state program operating under the federal Medicaid law.[2] Chapter 5E.1 discusses the MA program.

The law governing these programs is complex. In basic outline, the applicable law and rules for the programs govern the following areas:

1. Financial eligibility: Both programs have income and asset limits on eligibility.

2. Categorical eligibility: Both programs impose nonfinancial criteria on eligibility.

3. Definition of covered services.

This chapter briefly summarizes the law relating to categorical eligibility and covered services for the GAMC program.

The GAMC program is funded from state and county funds. It is intended to provide access to medical care for individuals who are ineligible for MA on categorical (rather than financial) grounds.[3] Eligibility categories for GAMC include the following:

---

1. *See generally* M.S.A. § 256D.03 et seq.
2. *See generally* 42 U.S.C.A. § 1395 et seq.
3. M.S.A. § 256D.03, subd. 3 (West 1992).

1. those who are receiving benefits under the General Assistance or the Work Readiness programs;[4]

2. persons who are residents of Minnesota and whose equity in assets is less than $1,000 per assistance unit; and

3. persons who would be eligible for MA except that they are in a facility that is determined to be an institution for mental diseases, and are for that reason ineligible for MA.

Covered services include inpatient and outpatient hospital services, rehabilitation services, prescription drugs, eyeglasses, hearing aids, prosthetic devices, laboratory and X-ray services, physicians' services, medical transportation, chiropractic and podiatric services, dental services, outpatient mental health center or clinic services, day treatment services for mental illness, prescribed medications for persons who have been diagnosed as mentally ill as necessary to prevent more restrictive institutionalization, case management services for persons who have serious and persistent mental illness,[5] psychological services, and medical equipment.[6]

---

4. Eligibility categories for General Assistance include persons suffering from a professionally certified permanent or temporary illness, injury, or incapacity that prevents the person from obtaining or retaining employment; persons who reside in a licensed or certified facility for purposes of physical or mental health or rehabilitation, or in an approved chemical dependency domiciliary facility; persons residing in battered women's shelters; persons who have been diagnosed by a qualified professional as mentally retarded or mentally ill, where that condition prevents them from working; persons who are unable to obtain or retain employment because of advanced age; persons who are not employable; persons who are learning disabled; children under age 18 not living with parents; women in the last trimester of pregnancy; persons eligible for displaced homemaker services or programs; families that are ineligible for Aid to Families With Dependant Children (AFDC); and persons whose primary language is not English who are enrolled in high school at least half-time. M.S.A. § 256D.05 (West 1992).

5. Persons who meet the financial eligibility requirements for General Assistance, but who do not fall into one of the eligibility categories, are eligible for the Work Readiness Program for a maximum period of 5 consecutive calendar months during any consecutive 12-calendar-month period. M.S.A. § 256D.051 (West 1992). *See* chapter 5E.6.

6. M.S.A. § 256D.03, subd. 4 (West 1992).

5E.3

Voluntary Admission of Mentally Ill Adults to Treatment Facilities

The law provides that informal admission by consent to mental health treatment facilities is preferred over involuntary commitment.[1] Informal admission of minors is treated elsewhere in this volume.[2] This chapter summarizes the law applicable to the informal admission of adults.

As used in the law, the term *informal admission* is synonymous with voluntary admission. Any adult may request to be admitted to a treatment facility. The head of the facility may not arbitrarily refuse any person as an informal patient.[3] The Minnesota courts have emphasized the importance of voluntary admissions.[4] However, the U.S. Supreme Court has issued a cautionary note about the overuse of informal admission. The Court's ruling in Zinermon v. Burch suggests that the state must have procedures in place to ensure that persons who are incompetent to consent are not admitted as voluntary patients.[5] Because *Zinermon* was based on the due process clause of the U.S. Constitution, which is only applicable to "state action," it is not clear how the Court's holding would apply to voluntary admissions of incompetent persons to private hospitals.

Informal patients have the right to leave the facility within 12 hours of making a written request, unless they are held under

---

1. M.S.A. § 253B.04, subd. 1 (West Supp. 1992). *See* chapter 5E.3 (involuntary admission).
2. Chapter 5A.19.
3. Counties are required to "screen" all adults before they may be admitted as informal patients to residential treatment centers. *See* chapter 5E.6.
4. Hennepin County v. Levine, 345 N.W.2d 217 (Minn. 1984).
5. Zinermon v. Burch, 449 U.S. 113, 110 S.Ct. 975, 108 L.Ed.2d 100 (1990).

some provision of the law, such as an emergency hold.[6] Patients must be informed in writing at the time of admission of these release rights.

Informal patients are entitled to all of the rights accorded to committed patients.[7] Services for persons who are mentally ill are discussed in chapter 5E.6.

---

6. M.S.A. § 253B.04, subd. 2 (West Supp. 1992). The time period is 72 hours for persons admitted for chemical dependency. *See* chapter 5E.4 for a discussion of emergency hold provisions.
7. *See* chapter 5E.4.

5E.4

Involuntary Civil Commitment of Mentally Ill Adults

Involuntary civil commitment is among the most intrusive tools the state has for dealing with mental illness. Civil commitment laws are based on two fundamental powers of government: first, the *parens patria* power, which is the right (and duty) of government to act as "parent" for those of its citizens who cannot care for themselves; second, the police power, the power of the government to protect the health and safety of the public.

The law governing civil commitment covers three main areas: (a) a set of standards defining the criteria for commitment, (b) a set of procedures guaranteeing due process for those individuals subject to civil commitment, and (c) a set of rules governing the rights of those committed.

MHPs play central roles in the civil commitment process. They assist in identifying those who meet the criteria for commitment, and they have charge of the treatment of individuals who have been committed. The law governing civil commitment is complex. Its treatment in this volume is necessarily brief.[1]

Standards for Committing Adults as Mentally Ill

Minnesota law defines two levels of commitment for persons who are mentally ill. Most common is commitment as a "mentally ill person," which requires a showing of a substantial psychiatric

---

1. For a more detailed treatment of the subject, *see* Janus, E. S. (1991). *Civil commitment in Minnesota* (2nd ed.). St. Paul, MN: Butterworth.

illness coupled with some demonstrated risk of harm to self or others. Where there is a more serious risk of harm to others, the law allows commitment as a person who is mentally ill and "dangerous to the public" (MID). Stringent controls are placed on the transfer and release of persons committed as MID.

The definition[2] of "mentally ill person" has three components: mental status, past conduct, and prediction.

To satisfy the mental status component, a person must have an organic disorder of the brain, or a substantial psychiatric disorder of thought, mood, perception, orientation, or memory, that grossly impairs judgment, behavior, or capacity to recognize reality, to reason, or to understand. The disorder must be manifested by instances of grossly disturbed behavior or faulty perceptions. The following do not satisfy the mental status component: epilepsy, mental retardation,[3] brief periods of intoxication caused by alcohol or drugs, or dependence on or addiction to any alcohol or drug.[4]

The predictive and past conduct elements are linked to the mental status element. The disorder must pose a substantial likelihood of physical harm to self or others. This likelihood of harm must be demonstrated by either a recent attempt or threat to physically harm self or others, or a failure to provide necessary food, clothing, shelter, or medical care for oneself.

Once it is determined that a person meets the definition of "mentally ill person," the court must determine whether involuntary commitment is the least restrictive alternative. The person may be involuntarily committed only if the court finds that reasonable alternative dispositions—including, but not limited to, dismissal of the petition, voluntary outpatient care, informal admission to a treatment facility,[5] appointment of a guardian or conservator,[6] or release before commitment[7]—are not suitable.[8]

---

2. M.S.A. § 253B.02, subd. 13 (West Supp. 1992).
3. *See* chapter 5E.7.
4. *See* chapter 5E.5.
5. *See* chapter 5E.3.
6. *See* chapters 5A.2 and 5A.3.
7. *See* below.
8. M.S.A. § 253B.09, subd. 1 (West 1982 & Supp. 1992).

Standards for Committing Adults as Mentally Ill and Dangerous to the Public

As is clear from the discussion above, no adult may be committed as a mentally ill person unless his or her behavior poses some sort of danger to self or others. Minnesota law provides an additional category of commitment for mentally ill persons who pose a particularly severe danger to the public. This category, "person mentally ill and dangerous to the public" (sometimes shortened to "mentally ill and dangerous" or MID), imposes additional procedures and standards to control the discharge of such persons. The definition is based on the definition of mentally ill person, plus the following elements: that, as a result of the mental illness, the person presents a "clear danger to the safety of others" in that the person has engaged in an "overt act" causing or attempting to cause "serious physical harm to another'; and that there is a "substantial likelihood" that the person will engage in acts capable of inflicting "serious physical harm on another."[9]

Procedures for Involuntary Commitment of Adults

Emergency Admission

The law provides three methods by which an individual who is mentally ill may be held in a treatment facility involuntarily on an emergency basis: an examiner's emergency hold, a peace or health officer hold, and an apprehend and hold order from a court.

Examiner's emergency hold. A person may be held in a treatment facility for emergency care and treatment, with the consent of the head of the facility, upon a written statement by an "examiner" that the examiner has examined the person not more than 15 days previously; that the person is mentally ill, mentally retarded, or chemically dependent; that the person is in "imminent danger" of causing injury to self or others if not "immediately" restrained; and that an order of the court cannot be obtained quickly enough to prevent the injury. An "examiner" means a licensed physician, or a licensed psychologist with a doctoral degree, who is knowledgeable, trained, and practicing in the diagnosis and treatment

---

9. M.S.A. § 253B.02, subd. 17 (West 1982 & Supp. 1992).

of the alleged impairment.[10] "Emergency treatment" means treatment that is necessary to protect the patient or others from immediate harm.[11] The examiner's statement must state the basis for the confinement. To justify an emergency hold, there must have been an "overt act, attempt or threat of harm."[12]

Peace or health officer hold. If the individual is not in a treatment facility and will not voluntarily go to a treatment facility, a peace or health officer may take the person into custody and transport him or her to a treatment facility or a licensed physician.[13] The hold may be executed if the officer has reason to believe that the person is mentally ill or mentally retarded[14] and is in imminent danger of injuring self or others if not immediately restrained. The person may be admitted to a treatment facility upon application of the officer if the medical officer on duty at the facility determines, after a preliminary examination, that the person has symptoms of mental illness or mental retardation and appears to be in imminent danger of harming self or others, and if the medical officer makes a written statement to that effect.

Duration of emergency and peace officer hold, notice, and examination. Persons under emergency or peace officer holds may be held involuntarily up to 72 hours, exclusive of Saturdays, Sundays, and legal holidays, without court intervention. After that period of time, the person may be held only if a petition for commitment has been filed and the court has issued an order directing that the person be held. If the person requests and the head of the facility consents, the person may remain at the facility as an "informal" or voluntary patient.[15] Persons held under these emergency provisions must be given a notice of their rights and must be examined by a qualified physician no later than 48 hours following their admission.[16]

Apprehend and hold order. The court may issue an order to apprehend and hold a person without a hearing in several circumstances: (a) There has been a "particularized showing" that serious imminent physical harm is likely; (b) the person has not voluntarily appeared for examination or hearing, although summoned to do so; or (3) the person is currently held under an

---

10. M.S.A. § 253B.02, subd. 7 (West 1982 & Supp. 1992). (If licensed before July 1, 1975, a consulting psychologist can also serve.)
11. M.S.A. § 253B.02, subd. 6 (West 1982).
12. Enberg v. Bonde, 331 N.W.2d 731 (Minn. 1983).
13. M.S.A. § 253B.05, subd. 2 (West 1982 & Supp. 1992).
14. The provisions for persons who are chemically dependent are slightly different. *See* chapters 5E.5 and 5E.6.
15. M.S.A. § 253B.05, subd. 4 (West 1982 & Supp. 1992). *See* chapter 5E.3.
16. M.S.A. § 253B.05, subd. 5 (West 1982 & Supp. 1992); § 253B.06, subd. 1 (West Supp. 1992).

emergency or officer hold (see above).[17] The apprehend and hold order is normally issued only when a petition for commitment has been filed (see below).

Preliminary hearing. No person may be held pursuant to such an order for longer than 72 hours, exclusive of Saturdays, Sundays, and legal holidays, unless the court holds a preliminary hearing and determines that probable cause exists to continue to hold the person. The proposed patient, his or her legal counsel, and the petitioner must be given at least 24 hours notice of the preliminary hearing, including the alleged grounds for confinement. The court may order the continued holding of the proposed patient if it finds that serious imminent physical harm is likely if the proposed patient is not confined. If, immediately preceding the filing of the petition, the proposed patient was acquitted, on the basis of a mental illness defense,[18] of a "crime against the person," the burden of going forward shifts to the proposed patient to present evidence that he or she is not dangerous.[19] Proposed patients may waive the preliminary hearing.[20]

Judicial Commitment

Emergency confinement, as described above, is often the first step in the commitment process. These emergency procedures allow health officials to act promptly in the face of imminent danger, but they are extremely time-limited because they do not provide for a due-process opportunity for the patient to be heard in opposition. Any long-term involuntary treatment and hospitalization must proceed pursuant to the judicial commitment procedure. The major elements of this procedure are prepetition screening, petition, apprehend and hold order, preliminary hearing, examination, commitment hearing, disposition, treatment facility report, continuation hearing, and discharge. These are discussed in this section.

Prepetition screening. Involuntary civil commitment is extremely intrusive on personal liberty and ought to be used only when no other alternative is available. To ensure that the commitment process is invoked only when necessary, the law provides for a prepetition screening process.[21] Before a commitment petition is filed, the county social services agency must conduct an investigation including the following: a personal interview with

---

17. M.S.A. § 253B.07, subd. 6 (West 1982 & Supp. 1992).
18. *See* chapter 5D.9.
19. M.S.A. § 07, subd. 7 (West 1982 & Supp. 1992). A "crime against the person" is a violation of, or an attempt to violate, one of a specified list of violent crimes. *See* M.S.A. § 253B.02, subd. 4a (West Supp. 1992).
20. Minn. R. Civ. Comm. R. 6.05.
21. M.S.A. § 253B.07, subd. 1 (West 1982 & Supp. 1992).

the proposed patient and others who have knowledge of the patient's circumstances; investigation of the proposed patient's conduct; and identification, exploration, and listing of the reasons for rejecting or recommending alternatives to involuntary placement.[22] The screening is conducted by a team appointed by the county welfare agency. The team may have access to all relevant medical records of proposed patients who are currently in treatment facilities. The team makes a recommendation as to whether there is sufficient basis to proceed with a commitment petition. If the team recommends against commitment, the person seeking commitment may apply to the county attorney, who will determine whether or not to proceed with commitment nonetheless.[23]

The petition.[24] Any interested person may file a petition for commitment. The petition is to be filed in the probate court of the county of the proposed patient's residence or presence. It must contain factual descriptions of the proposed patient's recent behavior. Factual allegations must be supported by observations of witnesses named in the petition. The petition must be accompanied by a written statement of an examiner who has examined the proposed patient within the last 15 days (or by an explanation as to why that is impossible). Allegations in the petition must be factual and nonjudgmental.

Appointment of examiners and examination. After the petition is filed, the court appoints an examiner.[25] An examiner is either a licensed physician or a licensed psychologist[26]. The examiner must be knowledgeable, trained, and practicing in the diagnosis and treatment of the alleged impairment. At the request of the proposed patient, the court must appoint a second examiner of the patient's choosing to be paid for by the county at a rate of compensation set by the court. Each of the examiners then conducts an examination of the proposed patient.[27] The examinations are to be held at either a treatment facility or some other suitable place not likely to have a harmful effect on the health of the proposed patient. The county attorney and the patient's attorney

---

22. The screening may not be required if the proposed patient was acquitted of a crime by reason of mental illness. *See* chapter 5D.9.
23. Most commitment petitions are handled by the county attorney. Theoretically, a private individual could bring a petition without the county attorney's assistance. Such a private petition could be filed even contrary to the recommendation of the prepetition screening team.
24. M.S.A. § 253B.07, subd. 2 (West 1982 & Supp. 1992).
25. M.S.A. § 253B.07, subd. 3 (West 1982 & Supp. 1992).
26. M.S.A. § 253B.02, subd. 7 (West 1982 & Supp. 1992).
27. M.S.A. § 253B.07, subd. 5 (West 1982 & Supp. 1992). Either the proposed patient is summoned to appear at the examination, or the court issues an order to apprehend the proposed patient and bring him or her to the examination. Use of the summons is the statutorily preferred route, but it is rarely used. M.S.A. § 253B.07, subd. 4; Minn. R. Civ. Comm. R. 2.

may be present, although either party may waive this right. At least 48 hours prior to the commitment hearing, the examiner must file three copies of the report with the court. Examinations are to conform to the same standards that apply to other aspects of professional practice.[28] Each examiner must conduct an examination and prepare a separate report. The reports should address the following issues, stating facts to support each opinion:[29]

1. whether the proposed patient is mentally ill, mentally retarded, or chemically dependent;
2. whether the examiner recommends commitment;
3. the examiner's recommendation as to the form, location, and conditions of treatment; and
4. if the petition alleges that the proposed patient is MID, whether there is a substantial likelihood that the proposed patient will engage in acts capable of inflicting serious physical harm on another.

In making their reports, court-appointed examiners may receive access to all of the patient's medical records that are relevant and germane to the examination.[30] To procure the records, the petitioner secures a court order directed to the custodians of the records, directing them to send copies of the records to the court and to the proposed patient's counsel. Examiners may have access to the records before they perform their examinations.[31] No evidentiary privilege protects the report or opinions of court-appointed examiners.[32] The examiners testify in court, but their opinions are not binding on the court because the determination of mental illness is a mixed question of law and fact.[33]

The commitment hearing. The court must hold a full, evidentiary hearing on the petition within 14 days of the filing, although this time may be extended for good cause up to an additional 30 days.[34] The proposed patient may demand an immediate hearing, which must be held within 5 days of the demand, excluding weekends and legal holidays. However, the time may be extended an additional 10 days for good cause.

---

28. Minn. R. Civ. Comm. R. 8.
29. *Id.*
30. In re D.M.C., 331 N.W.2d 236 (Minn. 1983).
31. In re Niskanen, 385 N.W.2d 323 (Minn. Ct. App. 1986). Examiners may also have access to the prepetition screening report. In re Morton, 386 N.W.2d 832 (Minn. Ct. App. 1986).
32. In re Skarsten, 350 N.W.2d 455 (Minn. Ct. App. 1984).
33. In re Moll, 347 N.W.2d 67 (Minn. Ct. App. 1984).
34. M.S.A. § 253B.08, subd. 1 (West 1982 & Supp. 1992).

The proposed patient has a right to attend the hearing and to testify.[35] At the time of the hearing, the proposed patient may not be so under the influence of drugs, medication, or other treatment that he or she is hampered in participating in the proceedings.[36] The court may exclude persons not necessary for the conduct of the hearing. However, the court may not exclude persons whose presence the proposed patient has requested.

The hearing proceeds with the examination and cross-examination of witnesses, including court-appointed examiners, whose reports are not admissible unless they are present to testify in court.[37] The court admits all relevant evidence and makes its decision pursuant to the rules of evidence.[38]

Decision and disposition. The court must base its decision on clear and convincing evidence.[39] In addition to finding that the proposed patient has the requisite disability, the court must make two distinct but related findings regarding the "least restrictive alternative." First, it may not commit an individual unless commitment, rather than some form of voluntary treatment, is the only suitable alternative. In judging which alternative might be suitable, the court must consider a variety of alternatives, including release before commitment, which is described below.[40]

Second, having determined that involuntary commitment is the only suitable alternative, the court must commit the person to the least restrictive treatment program that can meet the person's treatment needs consistent with the patient's right to treatment.[41] In making this decision, the court must consider community-based treatment and partial hospitalization in addition to residential, inpatient treatment.[42] The court must also consider the proposed patient's treatment preferences and willingness to participate in treatment. The court may not commit a person to a facility or program that is not capable of meeting the person's needs. If the court orders commitment, it must specify the less restrictive alternatives considered and rejected.

---

35. M.S.A. § 253B.08, subd. 3. The court may permit the proposed patient to waive the right to be present, but only if the waiver is on the record and freely given. If the proposed patient is seriously disruptive or totally incapable of comprehending and participating in the proceedings, the court may exclude the proposed patient from the hearing. M.S.A. § 253B.08, subd. 5 (West 1982 & Supp. 1992).
36. If the patient's medication cannot be safely discontinued, the court must be presented with a record of the drugs that the patient has received in the 48 hours prior to the hearing.
37. The parties may, by agreement, waive this requirement.
38. M.S.A. § 253B.08, subd. 7 (West 1982 & Supp 1992).
39. M.S.A. § 253B.09, subd. 1 (West Supp. 1992).
40. M.S.A. § 253B.095 (West Supp. 1992).
41. *See* M.S.A. § 253B.03, subd. 7 (West 1982 & Supp. 1992). The right-to-treatment provision is discussed below.
42. Community-based treatment is discussed below.

The court's commitment order must specify the initial commitment period,[43] which may not exceed six months.[44] Between 60 and 90 days after the commencement of the commitment, the head of the treatment facility must file a written report with the court. The report should set forth the person's diagnosis, the anticipated discharge date, the treatment plan, a description of the discharge planning process, whether the patient is in need of further care and treatment and whether it must be provided in a treatment facility, and whether the patient must continue to be committed.

Community-based treatment. In proper circumstances, the court may commit a proposed patient to community-based treatment.[45] To do so, the court must include in its order of commitment

1. a written plan for services,
2. a finding that the proposed treatment is available and accessible to the patient,
3. conditions that the proposed patient must meet, and
4. consequences of the proposed patient's failure to follow the commitment order.

The order must appoint a case manager to provide case management services.[46] The case manager must report to the court at least every 90 days about compliance with conditions of commitment. If the patient or a service provider fails to comply with the terms of an order for community-based treatment, the case manager may petition for a reopening of the commitment hearing.[47]

Release before commitment. After the hearing and before a commitment order has been issued, the court may release a proposed patient to the custody of an individual or an agency, if it is

---

43. In re Abrahams, 394 N.W.2d 234 (Minn. Ct. App. 1986).
44. M.S.A. § 253B.09, subd. 5 (West 1982 & Supp. 1992). A different rule applies to MID commitments. *See* below.
45. M.S.A. § 253B.093 (West Supp. 1992). "Community-based treatment" means community support services such as medication monitoring, assistance in independent living skills, development of employability and work-related opportunities, psychosocial rehabilitation, help in applying for government benefits, day treatment services, outpatient services, and residential treatment services in a licensed community residential setting. M.S.A. § 253B.02, subd. 4b.
46. Case managers help clients "gain access to needed medical, social, educational, financial, and other services necessary to meet their mental health needs" and "coordinate and monitor the delivery" of those services. Minn. R. 9505.0477, subp. 4. *See generally* the Minnesota Comprehensive Mental Health Act, M.S.A. §§ 245.461 to 245.486, and the rules implementing the case management provisions of that act, Minn. R. 9505.0476 to 9505.0491. *See* chapter 5E.6.
47. Consequences for failure to comply with the conditions may include commitment to another setting for treatment.

satisfied that the care and treatment of the patient are guaranteed.[48] Generally, such a release would be accompanied by a "stay" of a commitment order. A stay postpones the imposition of the ordered commitment. If this stay is to extend beyond 14 days, the order must include

1. a written plan for services to which the patient has agreed,
2. a finding that the treatment is available and accessible to the patient, and
3. the conditions the patient must meet to avoid imposition of the stayed commitment order.

The court must appoint a case manager, who must report to the court at least every 90 days. The maximum duration of a stay order is six months. The order may be extended an additional 12 months if the court finds that the person continues to be mentally ill and that the extension is needed to protect the patient or others. The patient must be given notice and a hearing prior to an extension. Upon notice and hearing, the court may revoke the stay and commit the person.

Treatment report; review; and hearing. Prior to the expiration of the initial commitment order, the head of the treatment facility must file a treatment report with the court.[49] The contents of this report are identical to the interim report filed by the head of the facility, described above. If the report describes the patient as no longer in need of institutional care and treatment, the proceedings are terminated and the patient is to be discharged from the treatment facility. Otherwise, the court orders the patient examined by one or two appointed examiners, in the same manner as for the initial commitment. Then, a commitment continuation hearing is held. A patient may waive this continuation hearing. The court may continue the commitment beyond its initial period only if it finds by clear and convincing evidence that the person continues to be mentally ill, mentally retarded, or chemically dependent; that involuntary commitment is necessary for the protection of the patient or others; and that there is no alternative to involuntary commitment. If the court makes this finding, it determines the probable length of commitment necessary and commits the person for that period of time or 12 months, whichever is less.[50] At the end of this period, the commitment may not be continued unless a new petition is filed and the court finds, after following the judicial commitment proceedings described above,

48. M.S.A. § 253B.095 (West Supp. 1992).
49. M.S.A. § 253B.12 (West 1982 & Supp. 1992).
50. M.S.A. § 253B.13 (West 1982 & Supp. 1992).

that the commitment is justified. The maximum length of time for such renewal commitments is 12 months.[51]

Provisional discharge, discharge, partial institutionalization. Except for persons committed as MID, the authority to discharge or provisionally discharge committed persons rests with the head of the treatment facility.[52] A discharge terminates the facility's and the court's control over the person. A provisional discharge allows the patient to leave the facility, but continues some controls over the individual by setting conditions that will justify a revocation of the provisional discharge and a return to the facility. Partial hospitalization allows the patient to be absent from the facility for certain fixed periods.

Patients released on provisional discharge must have an aftercare plan that specifies the services and treatment to be provided, the expected period of provisional discharge, and the restrictions on the patient. A case manager must be appointed to ensure continuity of care by being involved with the treatment facility and the patient prior to the provisional discharge and by coordinating the aftercare program. The law provides detailed procedures that must be followed to revoke a provisional discharge in the event the patient has violated material conditions of the plan or poses a serious danger to the safety of self or others.[53] Revocation is to be viewed as a last resort, and efforts must be made to avoid unnecessary revocations. Under some circumstances, a provisional discharge may be extended, but no provisional discharge or extension may extend beyond the period provided in the commitment order. With the consent of the head of the treatment facility, the patient may voluntarily return to inpatient status from provisional discharge. The patient's status on return can be as an informal patient or as a committed patient, or the patient may be on a temporary return, which means that the patient's commitment and provisional discharge remain in effect.

The head of the treatment facility must discharge any patient (not committed as MID) when the patient is no longer in need of institutional care and treatment, or at the conclusion of any period of time specified in the commitment order, whichever occurs first.

Judicial determination of release.[54] Except for MID commitments, the committing court retains jurisdiction over every commitment. Upon the petition of a patient or an interested person,

---

51. Different rules apply for mentally retarded and chemically dependent persons. *See* chapters 5E.5 and 5E.7.
52. M.S.A. §§ 253B.15, 253B.16 (West 1982 & Supp. 1992).
53. The procedures need not be followed during the first 60 days of a provisional discharge. M.S.A. § 253B.15, subd. 6 (West 1982 & Supp. 1992).
54. M.S.A. § 253B.17 (West 1982 & Supp. 1992).

the court may discharge the person or issue any other relief required. The court must appoint examiners and hold a hearing.

Special Procedures Applicable to Persons Committed as Mentally Ill and Dangerous to the Public

In general, the procedures summarized above are applicable to all persons committed involuntarily. Procedures for those committed as MID diverge from those summarized in several respects.

Disposition, length of commitment. Commitments as MID are generally to the Minnesota Security Hospital at St. Peter, at least initially. Initial commitment as MID must be reviewed by the court at a hearing within 90 days of the initiation of the commitment.[55] At that time, the court may commit the person as mentally ill and dangerous or as mentally ill (but not dangerous to the public), or it may discharge the person. If the person's commitment as MID is continued, the court must order commitment for an indeterminate period.[56]

Passes, transfers, provisional discharge, discharge. In contrast with other commitments, neither the head of the treatment facility nor the committing court has the authority to release MID patients. Rather, before an MID patient may be released on a pass, a provisional discharge, or a final discharge, the matter must be reviewed at a hearing before the Special Review Board (a board consisting of a physician, an attorney, and one other member).[57] The same procedures apply to transfers of MID patients out of the Minnesota Security Hospital to another treatment facility.[58] Transfers and provisional and full discharges are issued by the commissioner of human services upon the recommendation of the Board. The law provides for judicial appeal to a three-judge appeal panel.[59]

Rights of Persons Under the Minnesota Commitment Act

There are many sources of rights applicable to persons subject to the Minnesota Commitment Act. These include the Patients' and Residents' Bill of Rights,[60] the Minnesota Data Practices Act,[61]

---

55. M.S.A. § 253B.18, subd. 2 (West 1982 & Supp. 1992).
56. *Id.*, subd. 3.
57. *Id.*, subd. 4.
58. *Id.*, subd. 6.
59. M.S.A. § 253B.19 (West 1982 & Supp. 1992).
60. M.S.A. § 144.651 (West 1989 & Supp. 1992).
61. M.S.A. §§ 13.42, 13.55 (West 1988 & Supp. 1992). *See* chapters 4.2 and 4.3 for a discussion of confidentiality rights.

rights associated with particular types of programs or facilities,[62] and rights applicable to handicapped persons in general.[63]

The Minnesota Commitment Act itself specifies a set of rights specifically applicable to "patients."[64] Those rights include the following:

1. *Restraints.* Restraints are not to be applied to a patient unless the head of the treatment facility or a medical staff member determines they are necessary for the safety of the patient or others. Special procedures and restrictions govern the use of restraints for persons who are mentally retarded or have related conditions[65] and for minors in residential treatment centers.[66]

2. *Correspondence, visitors, and phone calls* can be limited only for "medical reasons," which must be documented. A patient's right to meet with or call a personal physician, spiritual advisor, or legal counsel may not be curtailed.

3. *Periodic assessment.* Every patient must be assessed as frequently as necessary, but not less often than annually. For persons who are committed as mentally retarded, the assessment must include the annual interdisciplinary review of the person's individual service plan.[67]

4. *Consent for medical procedures.*[68] Patients have the right to give or refuse consent for medical treatment other than the treatment of mental illness or chemical dependency.[69] The patient's

---

62. Most facilities to which people are committed are licensed under detailed rules providing standards for staffing and programming. *See* Minn. R. Chapters 9520 (facilities for mentally ill persons), 9525 (facilities for mentally retarded persons), and 9530 (facilities for chemically dependent persons). *See* chapters 5E.5, 5E.6, 5E.7.

63. For example, the Minnesota Human Rights Act, M.S.A. Chapter 363, and the Americans with Disabilities Act of 1990, Pub. L. 101-336, July 26, 1990, 104 Stat. 327, prohibit discrimination on the basis of disability. Section 504 of the Rehabilitation Act of 1973 (42 U.S.C. § 794) and its implementing regulations (45 C.F.R., pt. 84) prohibit such discrimination in programs that receive federal funds. *See* chapter 5B.12. The Minnesota Comprehensive Children's Mental Health Act (M.S.A. §§ 245.487 to 245.4887) provides an enumeration of the rights of children who are receiving mental health services. *See* chapter 5A.19.

64. *See* M.S.A. § 253B.03 (West 1982 & Supp. 1992). The term "patient" includes any persons institutionalized or committed under the act. M.S.A. § 253B.02, subd. 15 (West 1982).

65. *See* chapter 6.3.

66. M.S.A. § 144.651, subd. 31. Restraints may be used only in emergency situations involving a likelihood of physical harm. They may not be used for discipline, to enforce rules, or for the convenience of staff.

67. *See* chapter 5E.7.

68. M.S.A. § 253B.03, subd. 6 (West 1982 & Supp. 1992).

69. *See* chapters 6.1 (informed consent) and 6.2 (right to refuse treatment). The right of informed consent applies to aversive or deprivation procedures and the administration of psychotropic medication for persons with mental retardation. *See* chapter 6.3.

informed consent is sufficient if the patient is competent to give consent. If the patient is not competent, the law provides for consent to be given by a guardian,[70] conservator,[71] or relative. In the absence of any of these, the court may give consent to medical treatment.[72]

5. *Right to treatment.*[73] Patients have the right to care and treatment "best adapted, according to contemporary professional standards, to rendering further custody, institutionalization, or other services unnecessary." Treatment facilities must produce a written program plan for each patient that describes the problems, goals, time periods, and specific treatment to be used. Plans must be reviewed at least quarterly to determine progress and make necessary modifications. Plans must be developed and reviewed with the patient and the appropriate social service agency.[74]

6. *Access to medical records.*[75] Patients have the right to complete access to their medical records that are relevant to the commitment.

7. *Right to counsel.*[76] Patients have the right to be represented by legal counsel at all commitment proceedings. The court is to appoint a lawyer if the patient does not have one. There is no financial or means test for the appointment of a publicly funded lawyer. Counsel is to be appointed when the petition is filed and is to continue to represent the patient throughout any proceedings. Lawyers for patients are instructed to be "vigorous advocates" for their clients. Proceedings under the Commitment Act are "adversarial," and counsel must act accordingly.

8. *Guardian ad litem.* A guardian *ad litem* is a guardian appointed by the court to look after the ward's interests with respect to a particular piece of litigation. Guardians *ad litem* are not appointed for commitment patients on a routine basis, but may be "if the interests of justice so require."[77]

---

70. *See* chapter 5A.2.
71. *See* chapter 5A.3.
72. *See* chapter 6.2 for a discussion of consent for intrusive psychiatric treatment.
73. M.S.A. § 253B.03, subd. 7 (West 1982 & Supp. 1992).
74. *See* chapters 5E.5, 5E.6, 5E.7.
75. M.S.A. § 253B.03, subd. 8 (West 1982 & Supp. 1992). *See* chapter 4.1.
76. M.S.A. § 253B.03, subd. 9 (West 1982 & Supp.1992). *See also* Minn. R. Civ. Comm. R. 3, 4 and the comments thereto that specify in some detail the duties of counsel for a civil commitment patient.
77. Minn. R. Civ. Comm. R. 13.

General Provisions

Involuntary commitment does not, in and of itself, deprive the patient of any legal right other than those rights, such as personal liberty, necessarily inherent in involuntary confinement. For example, the following rights are not affected by commitment: the rights to dispose of property, sue and be sued, execute instruments, make purchases, enter into contracts, vote, and hold a driver's license. Civil commitment is not a judicial determination of legal incompetency, except perhaps with respect to the right to refuse mental health treatment.[78]

Generally, persons acting in good faith, upon actual knowledge or information thought by them to be reliable, acting pursuant to the commitment laws to assist (procedurally or physically) in the commitment of any individual, are immune from any liability, civil or criminal.[79] However, persons who willfully make false reports, petitions, or representations in connection with a commitment proceeding are guilty of a gross misdemeanor.

The doctor/psychologist–patient privilege is waived with respect to any information provided pursuant to any provision of the commitment law.[80]

---

78. M.S.A. § 253B.23, subd. 2 (West 1982 & Supp. 1992). *See* chapter 6.2.
79. M.S.A. § 253B.23, subd. 4 (West 1982). *See* chapter 6.6.
80. M.S.A. § 253B.23, subd. 4. *See* chapters 4.2 and 4.3.

5E.5

Services for and Commitment of Chemically Dependent Persons

The law of Minnesota provides for the voluntary and involuntary treatment of individuals for chemical dependency. MHPs are centrally involved in evaluating persons for chemical dependency treatment and in designing and administering the treatment.

The law governing informal and involuntary admissions for treatment for chemical dependency can be divided into three main areas: (a) standards for admission, (b) procedures designed to protect the due process rights of individuals in the treatment system, and (c) rules setting forth the rights of individuals in treatment. In addition, Minnesota law and rules contain mandates for the provision of chemical dependency services for persons receiving public assistance, and govern the methods of providing those services.

Standards for Committing Adults as Chemically Dependent Persons

To be involuntarily committed as chemically dependent, a person must be found by the court to satisfy the definition of "chemically dependent person."[1] This definition has a mental status component, a past-conduct component, and a predictive-harm component. Under the mental status component, the court must determine that the individual is "incapable of self-management or management of personal affairs by reason of the habitual and

---

1. M.S.A. § 253B.02, subd. 2 (West Supp. 1992).

excessive use of alcohol or drugs." Under the past-conduct component, the court must find that there is evidence of a recent attempt or threat to physically harm self or others, evidence of a recent serious physical problem, or a failure to obtain necessary food, clothing, shelter, or medical care. The predictive-harm element is satisfied if the person's recent conduct shows a substantial likelihood of physical harm to self or others.

The definition also includes pregnant women who have engaged during the pregnancy in habitual or excessive use of a controlled substance.[2]

Procedures for Involuntary Commitment of Adults

The procedures for the commitment of adults as chemically dependent are nearly identical to those applicable to the commitment of persons as mentally ill. These procedures are described in chapter 5E.4.[3]

The procedures for peace- or health-officer hold differ from those applicable to mentally ill persons in a minor way. The officer may take a person who is believed to be chemically dependent or intoxicated in public into custody and transport the person to a treatment facility. If the person is not endangering him- or herself or any person or property, the officer may transport the person to his or her home. The law governing this area is somewhat ambiguous. It appears that a person who is intoxicated in public may be admitted involuntarily to a treatment facility even if he or she does not pose an imminent danger. However, a person who is not intoxicated in public can be held under the officer hold only if there is such a danger.[4]

Persons hospitalized informally as chemically dependent, or pursuant to emergency or officer holds, must be examined within 48 hours of admission. The examination must consist of a physical evaluation by facility staff according to procedures established by a physician, as well as an evaluation by staff knowledgeable and trained in the diagnosis of chemical dependency.

---

2. This provision is part of a series of provisions added to the law in 1989 directed at protecting the fetus from harm arising from the mother's use of drugs. Provisions in the Maltreatment of Minors Reporting Act require mandated reporters to report such use of controlled substances. M.S.A. §§ 626.5561, 626.5562 (West Supp. 1992). *See* chapter 5A.8.
3. There are differences in a few time periods. These differences are noted in chapter 5E.4.
4. *See* Carman v. City of Eden Prairie, 622 F.Supp. 963 (D. Minn. 1985).

Rights of Persons Committed or Hospitalized as Chemically Dependent

Persons receiving treatment for chemical dependency under the Minnesota Commitment Act are entitled to the rights discussed in chapter 5E.4 applicable to mentally ill persons.

Standards Governing the Provision of Chemical Dependency Care for Public Assistance Recipients

Counties in Minnesota are required to provide chemical dependency services to persons residing within their jurisdictions who meet criteria established by the commissioner of human services.[5] Eligibility criteria for these services include both financial and programmatic factors. Financially eligible persons include persons eligible for medical assistance and general assistance and those who meet certain other income standards.[6] Certain other persons are eligible to receive services if funds are available and/or if they pay for the services on a sliding fee basis.[7]

Counties must follow detailed rules to determine eligibility and the appropriate level of chemical dependency care for persons who meet the financial eligibility criteria.[8] The process begins with a chemical use assessment, which the county must provide for each person who seeks treatment or for whom treatment is sought. The assessment must precede placement in a chemical dependency treatment program. Assessments must be conducted by staff who meet qualification criteria set out in the rules.[9] Assessments must include a personal interview with the client, collateral contacts, and a review of relevant records and reports.[10] Collection of information must be in conformance with applicable confidentiality and data privacy provisions of Minnesota and federal law.[11]

---

5. M.S.A. § 254B.03 (West Supp. 1992).
6. M.S.A. § 254B.04, subd. 1 (West Supp. 1992). *See* chapters 5E.1 and 5E.2.
7. *Id.*
8. Minn. R. 9530.6600 et seq. (1991). The rules do not govern court placements pursuant to civil commitment proceedings. *Id.*
9. Minn. R. 9530.6615, subps. 1, 2 (1991).
10. *Id.*, subp. 3.
11. *See* M.S.A. §§ 144.343, 254A.09; 42 CFR §§ 2.1 to 2.67-1, which are discussed below. *See also* chapters 4.1 and 4.2 of this volume.

Using the information gathered in the assessment and any additional information deemed necessary, the county determines the appropriate level of care.[12] In making this determination, the county must consider the following factors: the client's chemical use, age, sex, cultural background, sexual preference, geographic location, specific behaviors exhibited when under the influence of chemicals, current family status, previous assessments or attempts at treatment for chemical abuse or dependency or mental illness, physical disorders, arrests or legal interventions related to chemical use, and the ability of the client to function in or be trained for work and educational settings.[13]

As part of the placement determination, the assessor must determine a rating level of chemical involvement. The levels are summarized as follows:

Level 0: no apparent problem.

Level 1: risk status. Although the individual demonstrates no current pattern of pathological use,[14] the individual's behavior suggests that he or she is at risk of developing a future problem associated with chemical use.

Level 2: chemical abuse. This is indicated where there is a pattern of inappropriate and harmful chemical use.

Level 3: chemical dependency. The individual has a pattern of pathological use accompanied by the physical manifestations of increased tolerance to the chemical or withdrawal syndrome.

The rules classify treatment levels and specify a set of placement criteria for each level. These are summarized as follows:

1. *Outplacement treatment* is appropriate where the client is capable of functioning in the usual community environment and either (a) is a chemical abuser who is experiencing legal intervention, employment problems, or family problems due to chemical use; or (b) is chemically dependent.[15]

---

12. The client is entitled to a second assessment by a different qualified assessor within five working days of a request. A client who is dissatisfied with the assessment, the second assessment, or the county's placement decision has a right to an administrative appeal. Minn. R. 9530.6655 (1991).
13. Minn. R. 9530.6620, subp. 1 (1991).
14. "Pathological use" means the compulsive use of a chemical characterized by a number of listed functional criteria. Minn. R. 9530.6605, subp. 20 (1991).
15. Minn. R. 9530.6625 (1991).

2. *Primary rehabilitation*[16] is appropriate when the client has been assessed as chemically dependent; is unable to abstain from chemical use when outside a facility; and is experiencing employment, family, or legal problems or has participated in a chemical dependency treatment program within the last year.[17] Adolescent clients who are chemical abusers or chemically dependent may be placed in primary rehabilitation if the client tried outpatient treatment within the past year and it proved insufficient or if the adolescent has a mental disorder that poses a serious threat in combination with chemical use.[18]

3. *Primary rehabilitation in a hospital setting* is appropriate if the client is a chemical abuser or chemically dependent and either (a) has a physical condition that requires more than brief or episodic nursing care or (b) has a mental disorder that does not prevent the client from participating in chemical dependency treatment.[19]

4. *Extended care* is appropriate if the client is chemically dependent and is experiencing four or more of the following: primary rehabilitation within the last two years, legal problems, physical deterioration due to chemical use, absence of family support, loss of employment, school troubles, lack of recognition of the need to change harmful behaviors, or a history of mental disorders.[20]

5. *Halfway house* placement is appropriate if the client is chemically dependent, either has been discharged from a chemical dependency program or is currently in one, and has experienced three or more of the following: inability to avoid chemical use, lack of family support, loss of employment or education, absence of friends and associates, or a history of mental disorders.[21]

The rules list a number of exceptions to the placement criteria. These relate to the need or desire for a culturally specific program, or a program that treats individuals of a specific age, sex, or sexual preference, and the absence of funding.[22] There are also

---

16. "Primary rehabilitation" means a licensed chemical rehabilitation program. The program can be located in a freestanding facility or in a hospital setting. In either case, it must provide intensive therapeutic services (at least 30 hours per week per individual). Minn. R. 9530.6605, subps. 22, 23 (1991). In a hospital setting, the program must have 24-hour nursing surveillance and physician availability. *Id.*, subp. 23.
17. Minn. R. 9530.6630 (1991).
18. Minn. R. 9530.6650, subp. 2 (1991).
19. Minn. R. 9530.6635 (1991).
20. Minn. R. 9530.6640 (1991).
21. Minn. R. 9530.6645 (1991).
22. Minn. R. 9530.6650, subp. 1 (1991).

specific exceptions listed for extended care and halfway house placements.[23]

Confidentiality of Patient Records

In addition to the general rules defining confidentiality of patient and client information,[24] specific federal and state law and regulations govern the confidentiality of information relating to alcohol or drug programs directly or indirectly assisted by the federal government.[25] In general, federal standards prohibit disclosure of patient information (whether recorded or not) without the prior written consent of the patient.[26] Information may be disclosed without consent in order to meet a bona fide medical emergency;[27] to qualified personnel for the purpose of conducting scientific research,[28] audits, or program evaluations;[29] and if authorized by an appropriate order of a court upon a showing of good cause.[30] In general, no information may be used to initiate or substantiate any criminal charges against a patient, although there are some exceptions.[31] These restrictions on disclosure do not apply to the reporting to appropriate authorities of incidents of suspected child abuse and neglect.[32] The law provides substantial penalties for violations of the confidentiality rules.

State law[33] requires that the Department of Human Services "assure confidentiality" to all recipients of alcohol or drug abuse information, assessment, or treatment from a licensed or approved program. The law authorizes the release of identifying or other confidential information by court order. In deciding whether to order the release of information, the court is to weigh the public interest and the need for disclosure against the injury to the patient and to the treatment relationship in the program affected and in other programs similarly situated, as well as the

---

23. *Id.*, subps. 3, 4.
24. *See* chapters 4.1 and 4.2. For rules applicable to committed patients, *see* chapter 5E.4.
25. *See* 42 U.S.C. §§ 290dd-3, 290ee-3. Regulations governing this subject are found at 42 CFR § 2.1 et seq. State law is found at M.S.A. § 254A.09 (West Supp. 1992).
26. 42 CFR § 2.31 et seq.
27. 42 CFR § 2.51 (1991).
28. 42 CFR § 2.52 (1991).
29. 42 CFR § 2.53 (1991).
30. 42 CFR § 2.61 et seq. (1991).
31. 42 CFR § 2.65. (1991).
32. 42 CFR § 2.12(c)(6) (1991). Restrictions do apply, however, to the use of the information in any civil or criminal proceedings that may arise out of the report. *Id.*
33. M.S.A. § 254A.09 (West Supp. 1992).

actual or potential harm to the ability of programs to attract and retain patients if disclosure occurs. This provision of the law does not modify reporting obligations regarding abuse and neglect of children.

5E.6

Services for Adults With Mental Illness

The state of Minnesota provides and funds an extensive network of services for persons with mental illness. These services range from relatively intrusive services such as civil commitment[1] to evaluation and coordination services, to habilitative and residential services in the community. The Minnesota Comprehensive Adult Mental Health Act is the centerpiece of the state's service program. This chapter describes the functioning of that act. In addition, this chapter summarizes the functioning of the state office of the ombudsman, which provides protection and advocacy for persons receiving services for mental illness.

Minnesota Comprehensive Adult Mental Health Act

The Minnesota Comprehensive Adult Mental Health Act[2] governs the provision of services to adults with mental illness. The purpose of the act is to create and ensure a unified, accountable, comprehensive adult mental health service system. The act provides a set of basic principles governing mental health services and regulates the provision of services by counties and private providers.

---

1. *See* chapter 5E.4.
2. M.S.A. §§ 245.461 to 245.486 (West Supp. 1992). Administrative rules governing the provision of case management services are found at Minn. R., pts. 9505.0476 to 9505.0491 (1991).

Basic Principles

The service system is to be governed by a number of principles. Among them are

1. the right of adults to control their own lives as fully as possible,
2. the promotion of independence and safety,
3. the reduction in chronicity of mental illness,
4. the elimination of abuse of adults with mental illness, and
5. the provision of housing services in settings that maximize community integration and opportunities for acceptance.

Services provided under the law must be

1. based on individual clinical needs, cultural and ethnic needs, and other special needs of the individuals being served;
2. provided in the most appropriate, least restrictive setting available;
3. accessible to all age groups;
4. delivered in a manner that provides accountability;
5. provided by qualified individuals;
6. coordinated with other services; and
7. provided in such a way as to protect the rights and dignity of the people being served.[3]

Service Requirements

The act regulates and prescribes services for mentally ill adults. All providers of residential and acute care services must complete a *diagnostic assessment* for each client within five days of admission. Outpatient and day treatment services must complete the assessment within 10 days of admission. Providers of outpatient services, day treatment, residential treatment, acute care inpatient treatment, and regional treatment center services must develop individual treatment plans for each of their adult clients. The plans must be based on the diagnostic assessments. Clients must be involved in the development of the plans, to the extent possible.[4]

The act provides for the availability of "case management and community support services."[5] *Case management services* are

---

3. M.S.A. § 245.467 (West Supp. 1992).
4. *Id.*
5. M.S.A. § 245.4711 (West Supp. 1992).

activities that are coordinated with community support services and are designed to help adults with serious and persistent mental illness gain access to medical, social, educational, vocational, and other necessary services. Included in case management services are the provision of a functional assessment,[6] the development of an individual community support plan,[7] referral and assistance in obtaining needed mental health and other services, and the monitoring and coordination of services. The case manager arranges for the diagnostic assessment, develops the individual community support plan, reviews the client's progress, and monitors the provision of services.[8]

Community support services include services under the clinical supervision of a mental health professional[9] designed to help adults with serious and persistent mental illness to function and remain in the community. They include outreach, medication monitoring, assistance in independent living skills, development of employability and work-related opportunities, crisis assistance, psychosocial rehabilitation, help in applying for government benefits, and the development, identification, and monitoring of living arrangements. County boards must provide or contract for sufficient community support services to meet the needs of adults with serious and persistent mental illness residing in the county. Clients may be required to pay a fee under certain circumstances.[10]

Counties are also required to provide *day treatment services* and assistance in applying for state and federal benefits. Day treatment services must be designed to provide a structured envi-

---

6. M.S.A. § 245.462, subd. 11a (West Supp. 1992).
7. M.S.A. § 245.462, subd. 12 (West Supp. 1992). This plan utilizes assessments and identifies specific services needed by a mentally ill adult to develop independence or improved functioning in a variety of daily living activities.
8. M.S.A. § 245.4711, subd. 3 (West Supp. 1992). For a definition of *case manager, see* chapter 5E.4.
9. A "mental health professional" is a person providing clinical services in the treatment of mental illness who is qualified as at least one of the following: a registered nurse, certified as a clinical specialist in adult psychiatric and mental health nursing by the American Nurses Association, or with a master's degree in nursing, behavioral science, or a related field, with 4,000 hours of post-master's supervised experience in the treatment of mental illness; a licensed independent social worker, or a person with a master's in social work with at least 4,000 hours of post-master's supervised experience; a licensed psychologist; a licensed physician certified by the American Board of Psychiatry and Neurology or eligible for board certification in psychiatry; or a person with a master's degree in one of the behavioral sciences or related fields, with at least 4,000 hours of post-master's supervised experience in the delivery of clinical services in the treatment of mental illness. M.S.A. § 245.462, subd. 18 (West Supp. 1992).
10. M.S.A. § 245.4712 (West Supp. 1992). *See* M.S.A. § 245.48 (West Supp. 1992) (counties may charge for services. Charges must be based on the person's ability to pay).

ronment for treatment, provide support for residing in the community, coordinate with a local education agency's special education program, and operate throughout the year. Under certain circumstances, counties may obtain waivers from these requirements.[11]

Case managers are responsible for developing the client's *individual community support plan,* which incorporates the client's *individual treatment plan.*[12] The case manager develops the community support plan within 30 days of client intake. It must be reviewed every 90 days.[13] The plan identifies specific services needed by the client to develop independence or improved functioning in a variety of areas including daily living, health and medication management, social functioning, interpersonal relationships, and financial management.

Counties are required to provide enough *residential treatment services* to meet the needs of all adults with mental illness residing in the county. Residential treatment must be designed to prevent placement in settings that are more intense, costly, or restrictive than necessary. Treatment must help clients achieve the highest level of independent living, gain skills to function in a less structured setting, and stabilize crisis admissions.[14] Residential treatment programs must help clients make the transition to other community-based services.[15] Counties are required to ensure that placement decisions for residential services are based on the clinical needs of the adult. Counties must ensure that service providers have appropriate planning criteria and that there is a coordination of services and planning.[16]

Counties are required to screen all adults before they may be admitted for treatment of mental illness to a residential treatment facility or an acute care hospital, or informally admitted to a regional treatment center, if public funds are used to pay for the services. The screening must ensure that the admission is necessary, that the length of stay is as short as possible consistent with client needs, and that the case manager, if assigned, is developing

11. M.S.A. § 245.4712, subds. 2, 3 (West Supp. 1992).
12. M.S.A. § 245.462, subd. 14 (West Supp. 1992). The individual treatment plan is a plan of intervention, treatment, and services developed by a service provider on the basis of a diagnostic assessment. It identifies goals and objectives of treatment, treatment strategies, and a schedule for accomplishing the goals and objectives of treatment.
13. M.S.A. § 245.4711, subd. 4 (West Supp. 1992).
14. M.S.A. § 245.472, subd. 1 (West Supp. 1992).
15. M.S.A. § 245.472, subd. 3 (West Supp. 1992).
16. M.S.A. § 245.472, subd. 4 (West Supp. 1992).

an individual community support plan.[17] Such screenings must be conducted by a mental health professional.[18]

Adults who require mental health services must be advised of services available and the right to appeal at the time of the request and when their plans are reviewed.[19] An adult whose request for services is denied, or whose services are reduced or terminated, may contest that action by an appeal before the Department of Human Services.[20]

Ombudsman Services

Minnesota law establishes an Office of the Ombudsman for persons receiving services or treatment for mental illness, mental retardation or a related condition, chemical dependency, or emotional disturbance. The purpose of the office is to promote the highest attainable standards of treatment, competence, efficiency, and justice.[21] The ombudsman may mediate or advocate on behalf of clients; investigate the quality of services; gather information about actions of agencies, facilities, or programs; and examine records, issue subpoenas, enter premises, and have access to agency, facility, and program data that are classified as private or confidential.[22] The ombudsman's office is instructed to give particular attention to unusual deaths or injures in a facility or program and to actions that may be contrary to law; that are unreasonable, unfair, or oppressive; that may result in abuse or neglect; or that may impede independence, community integration, and productivity.[23]

---

17. M.S.A. § 245.476 (West Supp. 1992).
18. M.S.A. § 245.476, subd. 2 (West Supp. 1992). *See* above, note 9, for a definition of "mental health professional."
19. M.S.A. § 245.477 (West Supp 1992).
20. *See* M.S.A. § 256.045 (West Supp. 1992) for a description of appeal procedures.
21. M.S.A. § 245.92 (West Supp. 1992).
22. M.S.A. § 245.94, subd. 1 (West Supp. 1992).
23. *Id.*, subd. 2.

5E.7

Services for Persons With Mental Retardation

The state of Minnesota provides and funds an extensive network of services for persons with mental retardation and related conditions. These services range from relatively intrusive services such as civil commitment and public guardianship and conservatorship to evaluative and coordination services and to residential and day habilitative services. MHPs play a central role in the provision of services and the assessment and design that go into the development of services.

Civil Commitment of Mentally Retarded Persons

Persons who are mentally retarded may be civilly committed for services and treatment. Civil commitment procedures are appropriate under two circumstances. First, if the person is to be placed in a regional treatment center (state hospital) for more than a 90-day period, the placement must be approved in a civil commitment proceeding.[1] Second, civil commitment is appropriate where the individual is considered a danger to self or others and will not remain in a suitable placement voluntarily. In other circumstances, voluntary, or informal, placements by parents or guardians are the norm, and no court involvement is necessary.

The procedures applicable to the commitment of mentally retarded persons are very similar to those applicable to the commitment of mentally ill persons. These procedures are discussed

---

1. M.S.A. § 252A.111, subd. 3 (West 1992).

in detail in chapter 5E.4. The major difference in procedure is that whereas continued commitments of mentally ill persons are limited to periods of no longer than 12 months, mentally retarded persons may be recommitted for an indeterminate period if they are found to be in continued need of commitment after the initial commitment period.[2] The commitment act requires that the commitment facility conduct annual reviews of the person's status and send the resultant reports to the person's attorney. There must be judicial review of the committed person's status at least once every three years.[3]

To be committed as a mentally retarded person, the statutory definition must be satisfied. Under the definition, a "mentally retarded person" is a person diagnosed as having significantly subaverage intellectual functioning existing concurrently with demonstrated deficits in adaptive behavior. In addition, the person's recent conduct, resulting from the mental retardation, must pose a substantial likelihood of physical harm to self or others. There must have been a recent attempt or threat to physically harm self or others, or a failure and inability to obtain necessary food, clothing, shelter, safety, or medical care.[4] To commit a person, the court must find by clear and convincing evidence that these criteria are satisfied and that there is no alternative less restrictive than commitment.[5]

Public Guardianship and Conservatorship for Persons With Mental Retardation

It is the policy of the state of Minnesota to provide a coordinated approach to the supervision, protection, and habilitation of adults who are mentally retarded. The mechanism of public guardianship and conservatorship serves the function for mentally retarded adults who cannot provide for their own needs when there is no qualified private guardian or conservator.[6] The purpose of public guardianship or conservatorship is twofold: first, to supervise mentally retarded citizens and, second, to protect those persons from violation of their human and civil rights by

---

2. M.S.A. § 253B.13, subd. 2 (West Supp. 1992).
3. M.S.A. § 253B.03, subd. 5 (West Supp. 1992). In re Harhut, 385 N.W.2d 305 (Minn. 1986).
4. M.S.A. § 253B.03, subd. 14 (West Supp. 1992).
5. M.S.A. § 253B.09, subd. 1 (West Supp. 1992).
6. M.S.A. § 252A.01 (West Supp. 1992). See chapters 5A.2 and 5A.3 for discussions of private guardianship and conservatorship law.

assuring that they receive all services to which they are entitled.[7] Public guardianship or conservatorship is viewed as the most restrictive form of guardianship and conservatorship, and thus may be imposed only when there is no other acceptable alternative. The commissioner of human services acts as guardian or conservator, although she or he may delegate those powers to local welfare agencies.[8]

Appointment Process

The appointment of a public guardian or conservator begins with a nomination, which is a sworn written request. The commissioner may accept or reject the nomination.[9] Whether the nomination is accepted or not, the commissioner must order the local welfare agency to arrange for a comprehensive evaluation of the proposed ward or conservatee.[10]

Next, a petition may be filed for the appointment of the commissioner as public guardian or conservator.[11] The law provides for notice and hearing, as well as an appointed attorney for the proposed ward or conservatee.[12] The court is to appoint the commissioner as guardian or conservator if it finds that (a) the person is a mentally retarded person,[13] (b) the person is incapable of exercising specific legal rights, (c) the person is in need of the supervision and protection of a guardian or conservator, and (d) no less restrictive appropriate alternative exists.[14]

Powers and Duties of Public Guardian or Conservator

In general, a public guardian or conservator has the same powers as a private guardian or conservator.[15] As in the private context, a public guardian has all of the possible powers, whereas a public

---

7. M.S.A. § 252A.01 (West Supp. 1992).
8. M.S.A. § 252A.02, subds. 7, 8; § 252A.111, subd. 5 (West Supp. 1992).
9. M.S.A. § 252A.03, subd. 2 (West Supp. 1992).
10. M.S.A. § 252A.04 (West Supp. 1992). The comprehensive evaluation consists of medical reports, reports on intellectual capacity and functional abilities prepared by a psychologist qualified in the diagnosis of mental retardation, and reports on individual service needs and service plans. M.S.A. § 252A.02, subd. 12 (West Supp. 1992).
11. M.S.A. §§ 252A.05, 252A.06 (West Supp. 1992). If the commissioner has accepted the nomination, he or she must file the petition. Otherwise, an interested person may file the petition.
12. M.S.A. §§ 252A.081, 252A.09, 252A.101 (West 1982 and Supp. 1992).
13. For purposes of this law, "mentally retarded person" means any person age 18 or older who has been diagnosed as having significantly subaverage intellectual functioning existing concurrently with demonstrated deficits in adaptive behavior such as to require supervision and protection for the person's welfare or the public welfare. M.S.A. § 252A.02, subd. 2 (West Supp. 1992).
14. M.S.A. § 252A.101 (West Supp. 1992).
15. M.S.A. § 252A.111, subd. 1 (West Supp. 1992). *See* chapter 5A.2.

conservator has only some. The court decides which specific powers the public conservator is to have.[16] Appointment of a conservator is not a finding of incompetency and does not deprive the conservatee of the right to vote.[17] In addition to the powers available in the private context, the power of public guardians and conservators may also include the following:

1. the power to permit or withhold permission to marry,
2. the power to begin and defend against legal action, and
3. the power to consent to the adoption of the ward.[18]

Although the guardian or conservator has in general the authority to consent to treatment and placement, that power is limited where the services or care are to be obtained from a regional treatment center (state hospital). For temporary care, the public guardian or conservator must obtain concurrence of the local social service agency. A ward may not receive services or care from a regional treatment center for a period exceeding 90 days in any calendar year unless committed under the civil commitment laws.[19]

Under certain circumstances, the commissioner may be appointed guardian or conservator of the mentally retarded person's estate.[20]

Duties of the Commissioner

As public guardian or conservator, the commissioner must maintain close contact with the ward, prohibit filming of the ward (unless it is in the ward's best interests), encourage and allow the maximum level of independent functioning in a manner least restrictive of the ward's personal freedom, and encourage maximum self-reliance on the part of the ward. The commissioner must permit input by the nearest relative in planning and decision making.[21] The commissioner must provide an annual review of the ward or conservatee, including an assessment of the need for continued public guardianship or conservatorship.[22]

---

16. M.S.A. § 252A.02, subds. 7, 8 (West Supp. 1992).
17. M.S.A. § 252A.12 (West 1982).
18. M.S.A. § 252A.111, subd. 2 (West Supp. 1992).
19. M.S.A. § 252A.111, subd. 3 (West Supp. 1992). *See* above for a description of civil commitment laws as they relate to persons with mental retardation.
20. M.S.A. § 252A.111, subd. 4 (West Supp. 1992).
21. M.S.A. § 252A.111, subd. 6 (West Supp. 1992).
22. M.S.A. § 252A.16 (West Supp. 1992).

Case Management Services

The provision of services to a person with mental retardation can be a complex task requiring sophisticated knowledge and coordination of resources and individual needs. This is the essential purpose of case management services.[23]

Before mental retardation services can be given to a person, the county must conduct a diagnostic evaluation to determine whether the person has or may have mental retardation or a related condition.[24] If the evaluation determines that the person has one of those conditions, the county is to conduct a needs assessment, develop an individual service plan, provide for ongoing case management services, and authorize the services identified in the person's individual service plan.

Case management administration consists of intake, diagnosis, screening, service authorization, and review. Case management services include developing the individual service plan (see below), informing the client of service options, assisting the client in identifying potential providers of services, helping the client get access to and coordinate services, evaluating and monitoring services, and reviewing service plans annually.[25]

The individual service plan must include assessment information on the person's needs; identify the client's preferences for services; set long- and short-term goals for the client; identify specific services and the amount and frequency of the services; identify the need for an individual program plan to be developed by the provider of services, as well as any additional assessments needed after service initiation; and identify what responsibilities service providers have. The client, or his or her legal representative, has the right to give or withhold consent to the plan.[26]

The case manager is charged with the coordination, evaluation, and monitoring of services specified in the individual service plan. Individual program plans are developed by providers of services. They must be developed to achieve goals of the service plan and must be consistent with the service plan. If, as is often the case, a number of providers are involved with a single

---

23. M.S.A. § 256B.092, subd. 1 (West Supp. 1992). Administrative rules governing the provision of case management services are found at Minn. R. 9525.0015 to 9525.0165 (1991).
24. "Related condition" is defined as "a severe chronic disability in which onset occurs before the person's twenty-second birthday and which is attributable to cerebral palsy, epilepsy, autism, or any other condition which is considered closely related to mental retardation because it results in the kind of functional impairment usually associated with mental retardation." Minn. R. 9525.0185, subp. 9 (1991).
25. M.S.A. § 256B.092, subd. 1a (West Supp. 1992).
26. *Id.*, subd. 1b (West Supp. 1992).

client, each must develop program plans that are consistent and coordinated with the others. In his or her monitoring function, the case manager must assure that the individual service plan is being followed, monitor the person's legal rights, and notify the person's legal guardian or conservator if the plan is not being followed or legal rights are not being respected.[27]

Other Services

Among the wide variety of services available for persons with mental retardation or related conditions are the following:

Day training and habilitation services include supervision, training, assistance, supported employment, work-related activities, and other community-integrated activities designed to help the client reach and maintain the highest possible level of independence, productivity, and integration into the community.[28]

Semi-independent living services provide support for people with mental retardation or related conditions to live as independently as possible in the community. They aim to reduce unnecessary use of intermediate care facilities. The services include training and assistance in managing money, preparing meals, and shopping and other activities needed to maintain and improve the client's ability to live in the community.[29]

Residential programs and services are services to residents of a supervised living facility, foster home,[30] or group home. Extensive state rules govern the operation of residential facilities for mentally retarded persons.[31]

Home and community-based services include case management, respite care, homemaker services, in-home family support services, supported living services, day training and habilitation, and adaptive aids.[32]

Screening services involve screening teams established to evaluate the need for the level of care provided by residential-based habilitation services, residential services, training and habilitation services, and nursing facility services. The evaluations must address home- and community-based services that are appropriate for persons who are at risk of placement in a more restrictive

---

27. *Id.*, subd. 1e (West Supp. 1992).
28. M.S.A. § 252.41 et seq. (West Supp. 1992).
29. M.S.A. § 252.275 (West Supp. 1992); Minn. R. 9525.0500 to 9525.0660 (1991).
30. *See* M.S.A. § 256B.0919 (West Supp. 1992) (adult foster care and family adult day care).
31. Minn. R. 9525.0210 et seq. The provision of habilitation services by residential facilities is governed by Minn. R. 9525.2000 et seq. (1991).
32. M.S.A. § 256B.092, subd. 4 (West Supp. 1992); Minn. R. 9525.2010, subp. 17 (1991).

intermediate care facility. Screening teams review diagnostic, health, social, and developmental assessment data; identify the level of services appropriate to maintain the person in the most normal and least restrictive setting consistent with the person's needs; assess whether the person needs long-term residential care; and make recommendations regarding placement and payment for social services, training and habilitation services, vocational rehabilitation and employment training, residential placement, and home- or community-based service alternatives to more restrictive placement options.[33]

Ombudsman services. Minnesota law establishes an Office of the Ombudsman for persons receiving services or treatment for mental illness, mental retardation or a related condition, chemical dependency, or emotional disturbance. The purpose of the office is to promote the highest attainable standards of treatment, competence, efficiency, and justice.[34] The ombudsman may mediate or advocate on behalf of clients; investigate the quality of services; gather information about actions of agencies, facilities, or programs; and examine records, issue subpoenas, enter premises, and have access to agency, facility, and program data that are classified as private or confidential.[35] The ombudsman's office is instructed to give particular attention to unusual deaths or injures in a facility or program and to actions that may be contrary to law; that are unreasonable, unfair, or oppressive; that may result in abuse or neglect; or that may impede independence, community integration, and productivity.[36]

---

33. M.S.A. § 256B.092, subds. 7, 8 (West Supp. 1992).
34. M.S.A. § 245.92 (West Supp. 1992).
35. M.S.A. § 245.94, subd. 1 (West Supp. 1992). *See* chapter 4.5.
36. M.S.A. § 245.95, subd. 2 (West Supp. 1992).

5E.8

Hospice Care

Hospice care programs strive to meet the various needs of terminally ill patients and their families during the final stages of illness, dying, and bereavement. Through a centrally coordinated interdisciplinary team, these programs address a wide variety of concerns: physical, emotional, spiritual, social, and other special needs.[1] MHPs are an integral part of a hospice care staff.

The Rights of Hospice Patients

Minnesota statutes include hospice programs in the general category of "home care services" subject to the Home Care Bill of Rights.[2] The list of rights is extensive and includes, but is not limited to, the right to

1. be notified in writing, before treatment, of rights and grievance procedures;
2. know, in advance, of services being provided, choices available, and consequences of refusing services;
3. be notified of changes in services, charges, or providers;
4. refuse services or treatment;
5. know the charges for services, no matter who is paying;
6. know, before receiving care, which charges the individual will have to pay and which are covered under health insurance, Medicare, and so forth;

---

1. M.S.A. § 144A.48 (West 1989).
2. M.S.A. § 144A.44 (West 1989 & Supp. 1992).

7. know about alternative providers and services and be able to choose freely among them within the limits of health insurance, medical assistance, or other health programs;

8. have personal, financial, and medical information kept private; and

9. receive service from trained, competent, respectful, courteous people.[3]

Regulation of Hospices

The commissioner of health is responsible for regulating hospice care programs. This task is accomplished through means such as license requirements, inspections, compliance orders, and legal action against violators.[4] Relevant rules were published in 1993.[5] The Office of Health Facility Complaints processes complaints against home care facilities and providers.[6]

3. Id.
4. M.S.A. §§ 144A.45, 144A.46 (West 1989 & Supp. 1992).
5. See Minn. R. 4668.002 to 4668.0250 and 4669.0001 to 4669.0050.
6. M.S.A. § 144A.53 (West 1989 & Supp. 1992).

Limitations on and Liability for Practice

6.0

Limitations on and Liability for Practice

There are a variety of theories under which legal responsibility or liability can be imposed on an MHP. Liability can be of two basic types: civil or criminal. The former is determined through a civil suit, which is generally brought by a private party alleging some wrongful conduct on the part of either the practitioner or someone whose actions the practitioner may be held responsible for. The latter is determined through a criminal proceeding brought by the government, alleging that the practitioner has violated a criminal statute.

Although the choice of practice entity[1] cannot insulate a practitioner from legal responsibility for her or his own actions, it can preclude a plaintiff from recovering from an MHP for the actions of another party associated with the MHP's practice. For example, the liability of one shareholder in a professional corporation may not normally be imputed to another,[2] whereas the liability of one partner in a partnership may often be imputed to the other partners.[3]

The role that the practitioner plays in the practice can also affect his or her exposure to liability arising from the actions of other parties. For example, a physician or an employer may be held liable, under the theory of *respondeat superior*,[4] for those

---

1. *See* chapters 2.1, 2.2, 2.3.
2. *See* chapter 2.2.
3. *See* chapter 2.3.
4. This term translates to "let the master answer." It is a long-standing legal construct under which a "master" or principal is held liable for the acts of her or his "servant" or agent. To establish responsibility under this theory, the plaintiff must show that the agent's negligent conduct was committed within the scope of the agency to further the interests of the principal. Edgewater Motels, Inc. v. Gatzker, 227 N.W.2d 11, 15 (Minn. 1979).

under his or her control and direction, such as nurses and employees.

Similarly, the practitioner's role in the practice may affect the scope of her or his legal duties, and thus her or his exposure to liability as a consequence of her or his own actions. For example, a member of the board of directors of a corporation assumes, as a function of acceptance of the position, certain legal responsibilities that he or she would not otherwise have. A member of the board of directors owes certain fiduciary duties to the corporation (the breach of which may result in liability) that nondirectors may not owe.[5] Likewise, a member of the board of directors may be held to have assumed certain responsibilities toward third parties, for example, to exercise appropriate care in the selection and retention of staff members.[6]

Prudent professionals should familiarize themselves with the responsibilities imposed by law in their various capacities. MHPs should also explore the variety of insurance products available and ascertain whether they have appropriate coverage, both in scope and as to limits. In some instances it may be wise, for example, to purchase a directors and officers policy as well as a policy covering professional liability. Practitioners should also explore and pursue such opportunities for indemnification from their employers as may exist.[7]

This section will briefly outline and explore the major areas of liability that are of concern to mental health professionals. In particular, with respect to civil liability, we will explore the parameters of professional liability (malpractice) and liability for certain sexual behavior between MHPs and their clients or former clients.[8] With respect to criminal liability, we will detail several criminal statutes specifically aimed at MHPs.[9] We will also intro-

---

5. See, e.g., M.S.A. § 302A.251 (West 1985 & Supp. 1992).
6. *See, e.g.*, Ponticas v. K.M.S. Invs., 331 N.W.2d 907 (Minn. 1983) (employer liable for "negligent retention" of employee). Under this theory, a director could be held liable for the actions of another shareholder, not because the liability is attributed to the director, but because the director him- or herself could be found to have been negligent in the selection of the shareholder as an agent of the practice.
7. *See, e.g.*, M.S.A. § 302A.521 (West 1985 & Supp. 1992).
8. The MHP should be aware that he or she remains exposed to the entire range of civil liability to which any member of the general public is exposed. For example, the MHP may be subjected to tort actions for negligent or intentional acts and omissions (e.g., assault and battery). Similarly, the MHP may be subject to suits alleging breach of contract. Depending on the facts of the case, it is possible that the complained-of conduct would not be professional (e.g., the plaintiff was not a patient but a business associate of the MHP). In such a case, the action would be governed by different statutes of limitation and procedural and evidentiary rules than those governing actions alleging professional negligence.
9. The MHP remains subject to all criminal statutes applicable to the general public.

duce the civil and criminal liability that can be incurred as a result of violating the laws dealing with unfair trade practices (i.e., the antitrust laws). Finally, this section will explore the exposure to liability that may be incurred as a result of participation in peer review and quality assurance or credentialing activities, and the various protections therefrom.

6.1

Informed Consent for Services

In most instances, an MHP must obtain his or her client's informed consent prior to starting treatment. This chapter discusses when informed consent must be obtained, what constitutes informed consent, and the consequences of failing to obtain adequate informed consent. Related issues are discussed in chapters 6.5 (malpractice claims), 6.7 (tort claims), 5A.21 (treatment of minors), and 5B.6 (competency to contract).

Generally

Except in certain exceptional circumstances, it is imperative that the MHP obtain his or her client's informed consent before beginning a course of treatment. The failure to obtain informed consent can serve as the basis of a claim of either negligent nondisclosure (a form of malpractice)[1] or battery. An action for negligent nondisclosure arises if the patient is not properly informed of a risk of the treatment, the undisclosed risk materializes and causes the patient harm, and the patient would not have consented to the treatment if the risk had been disclosed.[2] An action for battery arises when the "treatment consists of a touching that is of a substantially different nature and character than that to which the patient consented."[3]

Other forms of malpractice actions are premised on an allegation that the MHP has performed in a substandard manner. For

---

1. *See generally* chapter 6.5.
2. Cornfeldt v. Tongen, 262 N.W.2d 684, 699 (Minn. 1977).
3. *Id. See* chapter 6.7.

example, a malpractice action will typically allege that the services were performed in a negligent manner, that there was a failure to render an appropriate treatment, or that the patient was improperly diagnosed. However, an MHP may be held liable for the failure to obtain informed consent, even though the treatment rendered was not deficient.[4] The doctrine of informed consent is concerned with the patient's autonomy and his or her right to choose among the available courses of treatment, not with the standard of care.

Scope and Form of Required Disclosure

An MHP can avoid liability for negligent nondisclosure by obtaining an adequate written consent from each of his or her patients.[5] Written consent forms can and should be supplemented by careful and complete charting of discussions with the patient. Where the patient is not competent to give consent, consent should normally be obtained from the appropriate party.[6]

For a patient's consent to be considered informed, the consent must follow adequate disclosure of the relevant risks of the proposed treatment and a discussion of the availability of any viable treatment alternatives. The MHP need not disclose each and every risk or alternative. Rather, it is sufficient that the MHP disclose

> risks of a treatment or the existence of an alternative treatment . . . if a reasonable person in what the physician knows or should know to be the patient's position would likely attach significance to that risk or alternative in formulating his decision to consent to treatment. . . .[7]

Disclosure must be sufficient to allow the patient to knowingly and intelligently assess the risks and benefits of the treatment before giving or withholding consent. In particular, the MHP should

1. disclose the potential of death or serious harm and explain in lay terms any complications that might occur, and

---

4. Madsen v. Park Nicollet Medical Center, 431 N.W.2d 855, 861 (Minn. 1988).
5. Similarly, MHPs can avoid allegations of battery by obtaining clear written consent to any physical interaction they intend to undertake.
6. *See* chapters 5A.2, 5A.3, 5A.19, 5A.21, 5A.23.
7. *Cornfeldt*, 262 N.W.2d at 700.

2. supply the patient with such information as a skilled practitioner in good standing would provide under the circumstances.[8]

Exceptions to the Disclosure Requirement

There are limited instances in which an MHP may render treatment without first obtaining a patient's informed consent. Consent need not be obtained in an emergency where the patient's condition precludes the giving of consent. A discussion of commonly known risks is not required because in such circumstances the consent can be presumed to be informed. Informed consent is also not required in instances where the therapeutic privilege applies. This privilege excuses the withholding of information when disclosure would be unhealthy to the patient, but only if disclosure would complicate or hinder the treatment or cause such emotional distress as to preclude a rational decision or cause psychiatric harm to the patient.[9] Where the patient is a minor, incompetent, or committed, the law may set forth different requirements regarding the acquisition of informed consent.[10]

---

8. *Id.* at 702.
9. *Id.* at 700. Before undertaking to render care pursuant to this exception, it is advisable that you consult with your lawyer.
10. *See, e.g.,* chapters 5A.19, 5A.20, 5A.23, 6.2.

6.2

Right to Refuse Treatment

In general, informed consent is required for the administration of any form of medical or mental health treatment.[1] If a patient is incompetent to give informed consent, a guardian or properly authorized conservator can, in most circumstances, give valid consent.[2]

The Minnesota Supreme Court has held that the right to give or withhold consent for treatment is of constitutional origins. At least with respect to treatments that are "intrusive," the court has held that the state constitution's "right to privacy" guarantees to the patient the right to give or withhold consent.[3] However, this right is not absolute. Under proper circumstances, and with proper procedures, the state's interest in caring for its incompetent citizens outweighs the patient's interest and the state is allowed to force treatment on an individual without first obtaining consent.[4]

This chapter summarizes the standards and procedures that govern nonconsensual treatment. The subject is a complex one, and our treatment of it is necessarily simplified.[5]

MHPs play central roles in the administration of nonconsensual treatment. As treatment professionals, they evaluate

---

1. *See* chapter 6.1. *See also* M.S.A. § 144.651, subd. 12 (West Supp. 1994).
2. *See* chapters 5A.2 and 5A.3.
3. Price v. Sheppard, 307 Minn. 250, 239 N.W.2d 905 (1976); Jarvis v. Levine, 418 N.W.2d 139 (Minn. 1988).
4. *Id.* It is also possible that the state's interest in protecting the health and safety of other persons may, at least in emergencies, justify such nonconsensual treatment. *See* Jarvis v. Levine, 418 N.W.2d 139, 148 (Minn. 1988).
5. For more information, *see* Janus, E. S. (1991). *Civil commitment in Minnesota* (2nd ed.). St. Paul, MN: Butterworth.

their patients' needs for treatment and assess their patients' ability to give competent consent. Within the mental health system, MHPs may serve on institutional treatment review panels. In the context of judicial proceedings, MHPs function as court-appointed examiners, evaluating patients' needs and competency and testifying in court on those subjects. Finally, MHPs carry out nonconsensual treatment.

Scope of the Right to Refuse Treatment

Nothing in the law curtails the right of a competent voluntary patient to give or withhold consent to any particular aspect of the treatment offered. The right to intrude without consent on the patient's body and mind is reserved for the state and appears to be limited to those circumstances in which the patient has been committed involuntarily for treatment.[6] Committed patients retain the right to give or withhold consent for most medical or surgical treatment.[7] Competent patients, whether committed or not, may be subjected to "intrusive" mental health treatment only with their written, informed consent.[8] Finally, persons committed as mentally retarded retain the right to give or withhold consent to aversive and deprivation procedures (except in emergencies)[9] and to the administration of neuroleptic medication.[10]

The law does curtail the patient's right to refuse two categories of treatment. First, the law suggests, but does not explicitly state, that committed patients (whether competent or not) have no right to refuse chemical dependency treatment or "nonintrusive" treatment of mental illness.[11] Second, the law provides explicitly that the state may administer "intrusive" treatment for mental illness without the patient's consent, but only if the patient is incompetent to give consent and if certain standards and procedures are satisfied. The remainder of this chapter will discuss those circumstances and procedures.

---

6. M.S.A. § 253B.03, subd. 6c (West Supp. 1992).
7. M.S.A. § 253B.03, subd. 6 (West Supp. 1992).
8. M.S.A. § 253B.03, subd. 6b (West Supp. 1992). The term "intrusive" means treatment with electroconvulsive therapy and with neuroleptic medications.
9. See chapter 6.3.
10. M.S.A. § 253B.03, subd. 6a (West Supp. 1992). The person's guardian or conservator may exercise the person's right to give or withhold consent. However, the guardian's or conservator's powers to give and withhold consent may be subject, under some circumstances, to court review. In re Blilie, 494 N.W.2d 877 (Minn. 1993).
11. M.S.A. § 253B.03, subd. 6a (West Supp. 1992).

Nonconsensual, Intrusive Treatment

As stated above, The law permits intrusive mental health treatments to be administered without the patient's consent only if the patient is incompetent and if certain standards are met and procedures followed. The law provides separate rules for emergency administration of neuroleptic medication. Each of these elements is discussed below.

Intrusive Treatment

The law defines intrusive treatment as including electroconvulsive therapy and neuroleptic medication.[12] Minnesota statutory law governs the nonconsensual administration of neuroleptic medication. The procedures for administering nonconsensual electroconvulsive therapy (ECT) are not spelled out in the statute. Case law suggests that the ECT procedures are similar to the medication procedures.

Competency

The state may force intrusive treatment only on those patients who are not "competent." Competency is not defined by statute. The Department of Human Services has promulgated an internal policy defining competency.[13] This policy does not have the force of law but does represent the Department's understanding of the law's requirement. The Department's manual defines "incompetent" to mean either that the patient has been adjudicated legally incompetent by a court in a guardianship or conservatorship proceeding, or that the patient lacks any of the following:

1. the ability to comprehend relevant facts about the proposed medication, including both the expected benefits and possible risks of the treatment;

2. an appreciation or rational understanding of his or her mental disorder; or

3. acceptance or refusal of the proposed medication that is not based on delusional beliefs.

A panel of the Minnesota Court of Appeals stated the test of competency as follows:

---

12. M.S.A. § 253B.03, subd. 6b (West Supp. 1992). In addition, under case law and administrative rules, the following types of treatment would also probably be considered "intrusive': psychosurgery (Price v. Sheppard, 307 Minn. 250, 239 N.W.2d 905 [1976]), coma therapy (Minn. R. Chapter 9515), and aversive therapy involving the injection of any chemical substance (*id.*).

13. Department of Human Services, *Residential Facilities Manual, Policy Number: 6601* (July 25, 1990).

1. an awareness of having a mental disorder,
2. sufficient knowledge about medication and the mental disorder, and
3. a refusal that is not based on delusional beliefs.[14]

Procedures for Approving Nonconsensual Intrusive Treatment

The law provides three different procedures that can be followed to authorize treatment with intrusive therapy for a patient who is incompetent to consent:

1. *Judicial approval.* The medical director of the treatment facility may petition the court for approval of intrusive therapy.[15] The court appoints an examiner and, upon the patient's request, a second examiner. The court is also to appoint a guardian *ad litem* to "represent the interests of the patient."[16] The patient continues to be represented by his or her appointed counsel. The court holds an adversary hearing. The petitioner must prove the "necessity" for and "reasonableness" of the medication by clear and convincing evidence.[17] An order approving nonconsensual treatment must be based on present rather than possible future medical necessity.[18] If the court authorizes treatment, it must identify a reasonably specific time period during which a physician may treat the patient with a reasonably specific dosage of a particular medication.[19]

2. *Advanced declaration.* Neuroleptic medications may be administered without judicial approval to an incompetent patient who, while competent, prepared a declaration requesting treatment or authorizing a proxy to request treatment.[20] Such a declaration is effective only if it is signed by the declarant and two witnesses. The declaration becomes effective when delivered to the declarant's mental health treatment provider. The provider must comply with it to the fullest extent possible, consis-

---

14. In re Peterson, 446 N.W.2d 669 (Minn. Ct. App. 1989).
15. M.S.A. § 253B.03, subd. 6c(h) (West Supp. 1992) (neuroleptic medication); Price v. Sheppard, 307 Minn. 250, 239 N.W.2d 905 (1976). The medical director must notify the patient's attorney that the petition is being submitted. In re Schmidt, 443 N.W.2d 120 (Minn. Ct. App. 1989).
16. Price v. Sheppard, 307 Minn. 250, 239 N.W.2d 905 (1976); In re Schmidt, 443 N.W.2d 824, 828 n.4 (Minn. 1989). There is no need to appoint a guardian *ad litem* if the patient is under public guardianship. In re Blilie, 494 N.W.2d 877 (Minn. 1993).
17. In re Peterson, 446 N.W.2d 669 (Minn. Ct. App. 1989). *See* below for a discussion of the standard for approving involuntary treatment.
18. In re Kinzer, 375 N.W.2d 526 (Minn. Ct. App. 1985).
19. In re Sten, 437 N.W.2d 101 (Minn. Ct. App. 1989). The order may allow the physician to substitute equivalent dosages of other medication.
20. M.S.A. § 253B.03, subd. 6c (West Supp. 1992).

tent with reasonable medical practice.[21] If the patient has executed a declaration indicating a preference *not* to have neuroleptic medication, such treatment can be administered to the now-incompetent patient only by court order.[22] The declaration may be revoked at any time by a competent declarant.[23]

3. *Administrative approval for acquiescing patients.*[24] Nonconsensual treatment can be administered to incompetent patients without a court order if

   a. the patient does not object to or refuse the medication;

   b. a guardian *ad litem* gives written, informed consent to the administration;[25] and

   c. a multidisciplinary treatment review panel composed of persons who are not engaged in providing direct care to the patient gives written approval.[26]

Standards Governing Approval of Nonconsensual Treatment

Minnesota statutory law does not clearly define the standards to determine whether it is appropriate to approve the administration of intrusive treatment to an incompetent patient. Case law and Department of Human Services (DHS) policy provide some guidance.

The Minnesota Supreme Court has held that the decision is based on the following factors:

1. the extent and duration of changes in behavior patterns and mental activity effected by the treatment,

2. the risks of adverse side effects,

3. the experimental nature of the treatment,

4. its acceptance by the medical community, and

5. the extent of intrusion into the patient's body and the pain connected with the treatment.[27]

Current DHS policy indicates that the decision must be based on the "need" to treat the patient with neuroleptic medication. To

---

21. M.S.A. § 253B.03, subd. 6d (West Supp. 1992).
22. *Id.*
23. *Id.*
24. M.S.A. § 253B.03, subd. 6c(d) (West Supp. 1992).
25. Consent by the patient's public guardian is also effective. In re Blilie, 494 N.W.2d 877 (Minn. 1993).
26. There is some authority that a multidisciplinary treatment review team must be consulted in all cases of proposed nonconsensual administration of medication. Department of Human Services (DHS) policy makes consultation with such a team a prerequisite of submitting a court petition. DHS, *Residential Facilities Manual, Policy Number: 6601* (July 25, 1990), pt. 7.F.1. *See* Janus, E. S. (1991). *Civil commitment in Minnesota* (2nd ed., p. 90). St. Paul, MN: Butterworth.
27. Price v. Sheppard, 307 Minn. 250, 239 N.W.2d 905 (1976).

find need, the physician must conclude that the patient has a "major mental illness accompanied by a severe functional impairment for which the treatment of choice in prevailing medical practice is neuroleptic medication."[28]

Emergencies

Neuroleptic medication may be administered without judicial approval and without consent in an emergency situation for as long as the emergency continues to exist. The treating physician must determine that the medication is necessary to prevent serious, immediate physical harm to the patient or others.[29]

---

28. DHS, *Residential Facilities Manual, Policy Number: 6601* (July 25, 1990), pt. 5.A.1.
29. M.S.A. § 253B.02, subd. 6c(e) (West Supp. 1992). Statutory law suggests that competent patients may not be subjected to nonconsensual treatment, even in an emergency. M.S.A. § 253B.03, subd. 6b (West Supp. 1992). However, the DHS manual indicates that competent patients might be medicated without consent in "extraordinary circumstances." DHS, *Residential Facilities Manual, Policy Number: 6601* (July 25, 1990), pt. 5.B.2.

6.3

Regulation of Aversive and Deprivation Procedures

Because of their potential for abuse or well-intentioned misuse, aversive and deprivation procedures are heavily regulated by the state, particularly in programming for persons with mental retardation or related conditions.[1] MHPs are centrally involved in the use and regulation of aversive and deprivation procedures. MHPs evaluate the need for such procedures, design programs using them, and assess their efficacy. The highly regulated nature of the procedures, as well as the possibility of liability for their misuse,[2] suggests that MHPs must be familiar with the applicable laws and rules.

Minnesota law requires the commissioner of human services to promulgate rules governing the use of aversive and deprivation procedures in all licensed services and licensed facilities serving persons with mental retardation or related conditions. This law prohibits the following uses of aversive or deprivation procedures: procedures that restrict normal access to a nutritious diet, drinking water, adequate ventilation, necessary medical care, ordinary hygiene facilities, normal sleeping conditions, necessary clothing, counsel, and next of kin. Also prohibited is the use of faradic shock without a court order.[3]

---

1. A "related condition" is a severe chronic disability in which onset occurs before the person's 22nd birthday and that is attributable to cerebral palsy, epilepsy, autism, or any other condition that is considered closely related to mental retardation because it results in the kind of functional impairment usually associated with mental retardation. Minn. R. 9525.0185, subp. 9. (1991).
2. *See* below and chapter 6.6.
3. M.S.A. § 245.825, subd. 1 (West Supp. 1992).

The Reporting of Maltreatment of Vulnerable Adults Act[4] and the Reporting of Maltreatment of Minors Act[5] both include, as part of their definitions of "abuse," the use of any aversive or deprivation procedures that have not been "authorized" by the law.[6]

The law also requires that the State Board of Education adopt rules governing the use of aversive and deprivation procedures by school district employees or persons under contract with a school district. This law, and its implementing rules, is discussed below.

Use of Aversive and Deprivation Procedures at Mental Retardation Facilities

The commissioner of human services has promulgated extensive rules governing the use of aversive and deprivation procedures at facilities licensed by the commissioner and serving persons with mental retardation or related conditions.[7] The regulations define aversive procedures as the "planned application of an aversive stimulus."[8] An "aversive stimulus" is "typically . . . unpleasant and penalizes or confines."[9] A "deprivation procedure" is a "planned delay or withdrawal of goods, services, or activities to which the person is otherwise entitled . . . contingent on the oc- currence of a behavior that has been identified for reduction or elimination. . . ."[10]

In addition to the practices outlawed by the law itself, the rules prohibit certain procedures and actions. These include the

---

4. M.S.A. § 626.557 (West 1983 & Supp. 1992). *See* chapter 5A.7.
5. M.S.A. § 626.556 (West Supp. 1992). *See* chapter 5A.8.
6. These provisions of the reporting acts are somewhat ambiguous. Techni- cally, the aversive and deprivation procedures law does not "authorize" any procedures. Rather, it prohibits some procedures outright and requires the commissioner to promulgate rules governing their use in facilities for persons with mental retardation. Arguably, the use of procedures as autho- rized by those rules would be exempt from the reporting laws. However, neither the law nor the rules authorize the use of procedures with persons who are not mentally retarded. One reading of the reporting laws would classify all use of the procedures with non-mentally retarded persons as "abuse." However, another reading would hold that all procedures that are not forbidden are "authorized" by the law. Under this reading, all aversive and deprivation procedures used outside of mental retardation facilities would be exempt from the reporting laws.
7. Minn. R. 9525.2700 to 9525.2810 (1991).
8. Minn. R. 9525.2710, subp. 4. (1991).
9. Minn. R. 9525.2710, subp. 5. (1991).
10. Minn. R. 9525.2710, subd. 12. (1991).

use of corporal punishment; speaking to a person in a manner that ridicules, demeans, threatens, or is abusive; requiring the person to assume and maintain a specified physical position or posture; placing a person in seclusion; totally or partially restricting a person's senses (except in limited circumstances); the presentation of intense sensory stimuli; and the use of noxious smells or tastes as aversive stimuli.[11]

Certain procedures are permitted if they are implemented in accordance with the rules. These "controlled procedures" include time-out procedures, positive practice overcorrection, restitutional overcorrection, partially restricting a person's senses, manual restraint, and mechanical restraint.[12]

Certain procedures are exempted from the restrictions imposed by the rule. These include

1. the use of corrective feedback and prompts, including the use of physical assistance to facilitate a person's completion of a response where the person offers no physical resistance;
2. the use of physical contact to redirect a person's behavior under limited circumstances;
3. the use of positive reinforcement procedures alone or in combination with other permitted procedures;
4. temporary interruptions in instruction or activity in which the person is removed from the activity to a location where the person can observe the ongoing activity and see others receiving positive reinforcement for appropriate behavior;
5. temporary withdrawal or withholding of goods, services, or activities to which the person would otherwise have access, if it is a natural consequence of the person's inappropriate use of the good, service, or activity; and
6. the use of token fines or response cost procedures.[13]

Other procedures, not prohibited, may be used if approved by a "regional review committee."[14]

A controlled procedure may be used only as part of an individual habilitation plan. It must be part of a total methodology that has as its primary focus the development of adaptive behaviors. It must be the lowest level of intrusiveness required to influence the target behaviors and not excessively intrusive in relation to the behavior being addressed. There must be informed

---

11. Minn. R. 9525.2730, subp. 2. (1991).
12. Minn. R. 9525.2740. (1991).
13. Minn. R. 9525.2720 (1991). *See* Minn. R. 9525.2710 (1991) for definitions of the terms used in the text.
14. Minn. R. 9525.2740, subp. 2 (1991). The regional review committee is defined at Minn. R. 9525.2790. (1991).

consent for the procedure.[15] It must be approved by a facility review committee and an "expanded" interdisciplinary team. It must be implemented and monitored by trained staff members. Under certain circumstances, the person's primary care physician must be consulted prior to implementation.[16] The rules contain detailed requirements for individual habilitation plans that propose the use of controlled procedures.[17]

Emergency use of aversive and deprivation procedures is allowed only in limited circumstances if needed "to protect the person or others from physical injury or to prevent severe property damage which is an immediate threat to the physical safety or the person or others."[18] Facilities must have written policies on emergency use of aversive and deprivation procedures.[19]

Use of Aversive and Deprivation Procedures in Special Education Settings

Minnesota law requires the commissioner of education to promulgate rules governing the use of aversive and deprivation procedures in educational settings.[20] The commissioner has promulgated rules governing the use of such procedures in the special education setting (i.e., in the education of handicapped children).[21]

The purpose of these rules is to encourage the use of positive approaches to behavioral interventions. Behavioral intervention programs must focus on skills acquisition rather than merely behavior eradication or elimination. Behavioral intervention programs must be designed to enable students to benefit from their educational programs.

The rules govern the planned or emergency use of aversive or deprivation behavioral intervention techniques and procedures. Aversive procedures are planned applications of an aversive stimulus either as specified in the Individual Education Plan (IEP) or in an emergency. "Aversive stimulus" is defined as "an object

---

15. *See* Minn. R. 9525.2780 for a definition of and procedures for obtaining informed consent.
16. Minn. R. 9525.2750 (1991).
17. Minn. R. 9525.2760 (1991).
18. Minn. R. 9525.2770 (1991).
19. *Id.*
20. M.S.A. § 127.44 (West Supp. 1992). The rules are to govern employees of school districts and persons under contract to school districts.
21. Minn. R. 3525.2925 (1991).

that is used, or an event or a situation that occurs immediately after a specified behavior in order to suppress that behavior."[22] "Deprivation procedures" are planned delays or withdrawals of goods, services, or activities that the student would otherwise receive.[23]

The rules divide aversive and deprivation procedures into three categories:

Exempted procedures are those that are in common practice in regular education or that are consistent with the school district's discipline policy (if the policy is appropriate for the student), and are not subject to the restrictions established in the rule. Examples of exempted procedures are the use of corrective feedback or prompts; the use of physical assistance; the use of positive reinforcement; temporary interruptions in instruction or activity in which a pupil is directed to leave an activity for a brief period of time to a location where the pupil can observe the activity ("contingent observation"); and temporary withdrawal of goods, services, or activities as a natural consequence of the student's inappropriate use of them.

Regulated procedures are interventions used in a planned manner that are not exempted (as described above) or prohibited (as defined below.) Regulated procedures may be used only when they are part of the student's IEP or in an emergency situation. They include the use of manual restraints, mechanical or locked restraints, suspension or dismissal, time-out procedures, and temporary delay or withdrawal of regularly scheduled meals or water not exceeding 30 minutes (with certain exceptions). The rules contain criteria for the use of time-out procedures and isolation rooms.[24]

Prohibited procedures include corporal punishment; requiring a pupil to assume and maintain a specified physical position that induces physical pain; presentation of intense sounds, lights, or other sensory stimuli; use of a noxious smell, taste, substance, or spray; denying or restricting a student's access to equipment such as hearing aids and communication boards, except when the student is destroying or damaging the equipment; faradic skin shock; totally or partially restricting a pupil's auditory or visual sense (but not including use of a study carrel for academic intervention); withholding regularly scheduled meals or water; and denying access to toilet facilities.

---

22. *Id.*, subp. 3.
23. *Id.*
24. *Time-out* means exclusion procedures in which the pupil is completely removed from the regularly scheduled educational program. It includes "seclusion procedures" in which the student is placed in a specially designated isolation room.

School districts must have written policies describing their procedures for implementing the regulation of aversive and deprivation procedures.

School districts must conduct assessments before they recommend or initiate behavior intervention using regulated procedures. The assessments must include a description of the target behavior, baseline measurement, documentation of positive behavioral interventions, review of frequent use of exempted procedures, documentation that the team has ruled out other treatable causes for the behavior, and a description of alternative procedures that have been ruled out. The assessment team must include a professional whose background and expertise are in the use of positive behavioral interventions and the use of aversive and deprivation procedures. The IEP must contain similar information and a description of any discomforts, risks, or side effects likely to occur; conditions under which the intervention will be used or can or must be discontinued; the effects on the pupil if not implemented; names of persons responsible for implementing the program; and review and evaluation information.

Procedures may not be implemented without the informed consent of the parent(s). Parents have the right to withdraw consent at any time. Districts must immediately stop the procedure upon being notified of the withdrawal of consent.

The rules allow for the use of behavioral interventions in an emergency. An "emergency" is defined as a situation in which immediate intervention is necessary to protect a student or others from physical injury, emotional abuse due to verbal or nonverbal threats or gestures, or severe property damage. The intervention must be the least intrusive intervention possible. Staff persons may use reasonable force to protect themselves or others.[25] In emergencies, behavioral interventions may be used without the assessment and IEP planning described above. Regulated procedures may be used in emergencies, but only until the IEP team meets, which must be no later than three school days after the emergency procedures have commenced. If emergency intervention is used twice in a month, or if a pattern of behavior is emerging that interferes with the child's education, a team meeting must be called to determine if the IEP is adequate and if additional assessment is needed, and to amend the IEP to include the behavioral intervention plan, if necessary.

---

25. *See* M.S.A. § 609.379 (Supp. 1992).

6.4

Quality Assurance and Peer Review

MHPs may be involved in peer review activities in the context of credentialing, privileging,[1] utilization review, and quality assurance. Because these activities can result in significant adverse outcomes for the reviewed practitioner, they may spawn litigation. However, the law has developed to afford participants in the peer review process significant protection from liability. This chapter will provide a brief overview of the reviewer's legal obligations and privileges.

To promote quality assurance and cost containment, both federal and state law provide certain immunities to participants in and organizations constituted as review organizations.[2] Under state law, an organization will be considered to be a review organization (thus making it and the participants in the review process eligible to take advantage of the statutory protection) if it is organized by one of a number of specified sponsoring organizations, such as a hospital, clinic, or association of professionals;[3] concerned with the review of activities related to one of a number of specified professionals, including physicians, nurses, or psychologists;[4] and engaged in the performance of one of a number

---

1. *See* chapters 2.7 and 6.8.
2. The pertinent federal law is the Health Care Quality Improvement Act of 1986, codified at 42 U.S.C. § 1101 et seq., whereas the Minnesota law is M.S.A. § 145.61 et seq. (West 1989 & Supp. 1992). The discussion in this book is of the pertinent state law. However, any organization undertaking professional review activities of the sort outlined in the state statute should also consider organizing and operating in such a manner as to avail itself of the protection available under federal law.
3. A review organization may also be established by a variety of other organizations, including HMOs, PROs (peer review organizations), and health services plans. M.S.A. § 145.61, subd. 5 (West 1989 & Supp. 1992).
4. M.S.A. § 145.61, subd. 2 (West 1989).

of specified quality assurance activities.[5]

Among the activities that a review organization may be organized to engage in are

1. evaluating and improving the quality of health care rendered in the . . . medical institution;
2. developing and publishing guidelines showing the norms of health care in the . . . medical institution; and
3. determining what professional shall be granted staff privileges in a medical institution or whether a professional's staff privileges should be limited, suspended, or revoked.[6]

If the organization meets the statutory definition of a "review organization," the sponsoring organization, the members of the review organization, and persons supplying information to the review organization enjoy protection from certain liabilities.[7] For example, members of the review organization cannot be held liable for any act relating to the functioning of the review organization, premised on a "reasonable belief that the action or recommendation is warranted by facts known to the person . . . after reasonable efforts to ascertain the facts upon which the . . . action or recommendation is made. . . ."[8] Similarly, no person can be held liable for furnishing information to a review organization, unless the information is false and the person providing the information knew, or had reason to believe, the information is false.[9]

Except to the extent necessary to carry out the purposes of the review organization, data and information gathered by a peer review organization and the proceedings of the review organization must be kept confidential by all involved parties.[10] The proceedings and records of a review organization cannot be used as evidence against a professional in a civil action arising out of a matter that has been considered by the review organization.[11] However, information, documents, or records that originate elsewhere do not become immune from discovery merely because they have been presented to the review organization.[12] The provisions regarding confidentiality and immunity from discovery cannot be used by the review organization to withhold information from a professional if such information relates to "staff

---

5. M.S.A. § 145.61, subd. 5 (West 1989 & Supp. 1992).
6. M.S.A. § 145.62, subd. 5 (West 1989).
7. M.S.A. § 145.62 (West 1989); § 145.63 (West 1989 & Supp. 1992).
8. M.S.A. § 145.63, subd. 1 (West 1898).
9. M.S.A. § 145.62 (West 1989).
10. M.S.A. § 145.64 (West 1989 & Supp. 1992).
11. *Id.*
12. *Id.*

privileges or participation status."[13] Guidelines, such as practice parameters, developed by a review organization may not be used in a malpractice action to establish the adherence to or departure from a standard of care.[14]

---

13. M.S.A. § 145.64, subd. 2 (West 1989 & Supp. 1992).
14. M.S.A § 145.65 (West 1989). *But see* M.S.A. § 625.34, subd. 3 (West Supp. 1992) for exceptions to this rule. *See* chapter 6.5.

6.5

Malpractice

A patient's allegations of substandard professional care can result in a malpractice action[1] against the MHP. Whether the patient will prevail depends on a number of factors, including the ability of the patient to show that the care was indeed substandard, that he or she was harmed by the care, and that the action was brought within the legally specified time period. The financial effect of a malpractice action (in terms of both the cost of defending the action and any judgment that may be awarded) is greatly affected by the scope of the MHP's professional liability insurance coverage.

Legal liability incurred as a result of an act or omission committed in the course of rendering professional services is generally referred to as *malpractice*.[2] Malpractice occurs when professional services are performed in a manner that fails to meet the applicable standard of care and when the patient is damaged as a result of that failure. Typical claims include allegations that the MHP rendered professional services in a negligent manner, that he or she failed to render appropriate treatment, or that he or she reached an improper diagnosis.

An MHP fails to meet the standard of care if she or he fails to exercise the care and skill of an ordinary member of her or his profession in good standing in a similar locality.[3] Thus, the standard of care may differ between a rural and an urban area, if, for example, sophisticated diagnostic equipment available in all ur-

---

1. *See also* chapter 6.1 regarding informed consent and chapter 6.6 regarding other types of professional liability.
2. *See* chapter 6.8 for a discussion of the limits placed on malpractice liability by the doctrine of sovereign immunity.
3. Todd v. Eitel Hosp., 306 Minn. 254, 237 N.W.2d 357 (1975).

ban areas is not generally available in rural areas. Given the widespread availability of technologies and the ongoing development of national standards of practice, the "locality rule" is of diminishing importance.

Similarly, the standard of care may be different for specialists than for generalists. The former's conduct is measured against that of other specialists, whereas the latter's is measured against that of other generalists.[4] It is unwise to hold oneself out as a specialist unless one is prepared to be judged against this higher standard.

A recent change in the law provides that if a professional can establish that she or he adhered to a practice parameter that has been approved by the Minnesota commissioner of health, she or he has an absolute defense against a malpractice claim.[5] However, the failure to adhere to an approved practice parameter cannot be used to establish that the defendant departed from the standard of care.[6]

For the plaintiff to prevail, it is not sufficient to show that the professional departed from the applicable standard of care. Rather, the plaintiff must also show that he or she was being treated by the professional, that the departure from the standard of care caused the complained-of damage,[7] and that the damage is of a type recognized as compensable under the law.[8]

To discourage groundless malpractice claims, the law requires, with some limited exceptions, that a plaintiff first subject his or her claim to expert review.[9] The expert must review the case and conclude that at least one of the defendants breached the applicable standard of care and as a consequence injured the patient.[10]

---

4. McCormack v. Lindberg, 352 N.W.2d 30 (Minn. Ct. App. 1984).
5. M.S.A. § 625.34, subd. 3 (West Supp. 1992).
6. *Id.*
7. Christy v. Saliterman, 179 N.W.2d 288 (1970).
8. For example, certain injuries may be so tenuously related to the malpractice that the court will not recognize them as being proximately caused by the professional. Other types of injury, for example, certain emotional damage without accompanying physical symptoms, may simply not be compensable. *See* chapter 5B.4.
9. M.S.A. § 145.682 (West 1989).
10. M.S.A. § 145.682, subd. 3 (West 1989).

Statute of Limitations

An action alleging malpractice against a health care professional[11] must be brought, if at all, within a period of time specified by the statute of limitations.[12] The statute provides that all actions for malpractice, error, mistake, or failure to cure, whether based in contract or tort, be commenced within two years.[13] The two-year period generally begins from the date of the termination of the course of treatment out of which the complained-of damage arose.[14]

There are numerous circumstances, however, in which the running of the statute will be delayed or "tolled." For example, if the plaintiff is a minor, insane, or in prison at the time the action accrues, the statute is tolled until the curing of the applicable disability.[15] Similarly, fraud on the part of the provider will toll the running of the statute until the plaintiff discovers the fraud.[16]

There are also statutory exceptions to the two-year limit. The time for bringing an action is expanded to six years for actions seeking damages for sexual abuse.[17] This longer period applies both to actions alleging that the provider committed the abuse and to those alleging that the provider negligently permitted the abuse to occur.[18] The time for bringing an action is expanded to five years where the action alleges damages as a result of sexual exploitation by a psychotherapist.[19]

It should be noted that even professional conduct that falls short of malpractice can be grounds for disciplinary action by the applicable licensing board.[20] Thus, a provider who is exonerated in a court of law may still find her or his conduct subject to scrutiny and sanction.

---

11. A health care professional is a licensed physician, surgeon, or psychologist. M.S.A. § 145.61 (West 1989 & Supp. 1992). Other practitioners are subject to slightly different treatment under separate statutes of limitation. See, e.g., M.S.A. §§ 541.05, 541.07 (West 1988 & Supp. 1992).
12. M.S.A. § 541.07 (West 1988 & Supp. 1992).
13. M.S.A. § 541.07(1) (West 1988 & Supp. 1992).
14. Chimzmadia v. Simley's Point Clinic, 428 N.W.2d 459 (Minn. Ct. App. 1988).
15. M.S.A. § 541.15 (West 1988).
16. M.S.A. § 541.05, subd. 1(6) (West 1988).
17. M.S.A. § 541.073, subd. 2 (West 1988 & Supp. 1992).
18. M.S.A. § 609.345, subd. 1 (West 1988 & Supp. 1992).
19. M.S.A. § 148A.06 (West 1989). See chapter 6.6 for further discussion of this cause of action.
20. See, e.g., M.S.A. § 147.091 (West 1989 & Supp. 1992).

Malpractice Insurance

Although a full discourse on professional liability or malpractice insurance is beyond the scope of this book, there are a few major points of particular interest to MHPs:

1. Certain types of behavior are not generally covered by professional liability insurance. In particular, many actions alleging inappropriate sexual conduct are not covered.[21]

2. There are two general types of malpractice insurance: *claims made and occurrence.* Basically, the former covers claims that both arise and are made during the period in which the policy is in effect. Occurrence coverage generally covers claims that arise during the period for which the coverage is in effect, even if they are brought after the coverage lapses.[22]

An MHP may experience a gap in coverage whenever a claims-made policy is replaced by a new policy—for example, as a consequence of a change in employment. The first policy will not cover claims brought after its termination, and the second policy will not normally cover claims arising from conduct occurring prior to the time that the second policy becomes effective. In such a situation, the MHP should consider purchasing a "tail."

A tail is an insurance product that provides ongoing coverage for actions that arose during the period in which the first claims-made policy was in effect, but that are brought after the termination of that policy, thereby bridging the gap. Because a tail can be very expensive, an employee will often seek to have his or her employer agree, as part of an employment contract or termination agreement, to pay for the tail in the event of the termination of employment.

3. Policies may not provide coverage when a provider agrees to indemnify another party against certain damages or otherwise expands his or her exposure to liability from what it would be in the absence of such an agreement (for example, liability imposed as a result of a partnership or joint venture agreement).[23]

---

21. *See, e.g.,* Smith et al. v. St. Paul Fire & Marine, 353 N.W.2d 130 (Minn. 1984). But when the case alleges a mishandling of the transference phenomenon, insurance coverage may not be precluded. *See, e.g.,* St. Paul Fire & Marine v. D.H.L., 459 N.W.2d 704 (Minn. 1990); St. Paul Fire & Marine v. Love, 459 N.W.2d 698 (Minn. 1990).

22. This constitutes a very general discussion of professional liability insurance. The particulars of any given policy may differ from the general outline presented here. Providers should consult their insurance agent and policy to acquaint themselves with the provisions of their coverage.

23. *See* chapters 2.2 and 2.3 for further discussion of the attribution of liability in these contexts.

6.6

Other Forms of Professional Liability

An MHP may find him- or herself a defendant in a civil suit brought by a patient alleging something other than malpractice.[1] Possible causes of an action include breach of the duty of confidentiality,[2] unlawfully restraining a patient, and sexually exploiting a patient. This chapter will outline and discuss some of the most common of these causes of action.

Although most suits brought by clients against MHPs will be for malpractice,[3] there are several other civil theories under which an MHP might incur liability to a client. Actions alleging a failure to treat, an error in performing a treatment, or some other failure to adhere to the applicable standard of care in connection with the rendering of professional services is likely to be characterized as a malpractice action. Actions that allege damages that arise from activities wholly outside of the treatment relationship (e.g., from business transactions or car accidents) are unlikely to be considered malpractice actions. There is, however, much uncharted middle ground where it is unclear how the cause of action would be characterized.[4]

---

1. *See* chapter 6.5.
2. *See* chapter 4.3.
3. *See* chapter 6.5.
4. There are at least two Minnesota cases that touch on, but do not directly address, the question of where the lines of demarcation should be drawn. *See* St. Paul Fire & Marine v. Love, 459 N.W.2d 698, 700 (Minn. 1990) (holding that, for purposes of a malpractice insurance policy, a physician's sexual contact with his patients may in some contexts be unrelated to the rendition of professional services, whereas in other contexts amount to the mishandling of professional care); Stubbs v. North Memorial Medical Center, 448 N.W.2d 78, 83 (Minn. 1989) (holding that a patient may proceed against her physician under a theory of breach of an implied contract of confidentiality).

In some limited instances, it may be easier to sustain an action based on a theory other than malpractice than it would be to sustain a malpractice action. A suit that is characterized as a malpractice action is subject to a number of constraints that other types of actions may not be subject to. For example, if the plaintiff successfully avoids the characterization of the action as a malpractice action, the time during which a suit may be brought may be longer,[5] the periods for which the statue of limitations can be tolled may be shorter,[6] and the claim would not be subject to the requirement of expert review.[7]

The characterization of the action may also have other consequences. The availability of professional liability coverage may depend on a finding that the action relates to the performance of professional services.[8] Different actions require different elements of proof and allow for different defenses; thus, conduct that might not be actionable as malpractice may be actionable under some other theory. Finally, different actions allow for different measures of damages.

The behaviors of MHPs most likely to spawn additional causes of action include the following:

1. Breach of the duty of confidentiality: The breach of the duty of confidentiality might lead, among other things, to charges of defamation or breach of the implied contract of confidentiality.[9]

2. Unlawfully restraining a patient: Unlawfully restraining a patient or otherwise interfering with a patient's freedom of movement or choice might lead, among other things, to charges of unlawful imprisonment or assault and battery.[10]

3. Engaging in business transactions with a patient: The relationship between an MHP and his or her client is likely to be

---

5. It should be noted that *Stubbs* declines to recognize a number of causes of action against a physician, including the tort of invasion of privacy. *Cf.* M.S.A. § 541.05 (West 1988), which provides for a six-year period in which contract claims may be filed, with M.S.A. § 541.07(1) (West 1988 & Supp. 1992), which provides for a two-year statute of limitations on malpractice claims, whether in contract or in tort. *But cf.* M.S.A. § 541.07(1), which also provides that all tort actions resulting in personal injury be brought within two years, whether or not they are malpractice actions.

6. *See* M.S.A. § 541.15 (West 1988).

7. *See* M.S.A. § 145.682 (West 1989).

8. *See* chapter 6.5.

9. *See generally* chapters 4.2 and 4.3. *See Stubbs, supra* note 4, and the discussion therein. *See also* chapters 6.4 and 6.8 for a discussion of exposure to and protection from liability for libel and slander as a result of participation in credentialing, peer review, and quality assurance activities.

10. *See* section 5E and chapters 6.2 and 6.7 discussing the circumstances under which an individual may be lawfully restrained or required to accept treatment.

classified as a fiduciary relationship. A fiduciary is required to act with the best interests of his or her client in mind. The result is that transactions between MHPs and their clients are likely to be subjected to close scrutiny to determine whether the client has, in all respects, been treated fairly by the MHP.

4. Engaging in sexual activity with a patient: This last category of activity is explicitly addressed by a statute, outlined below.

Sexual exploitation is deemed to have occurred whenever a patient or former patient[11] is injured by sexual contact with a psychotherapist, if the sexual contact occurred during the period of psychotherapy, while the patient was emotionally dependent[12] on the psychotherapist, or through therapeutic deception.[13] The term "sexual contact" covers a wide range of sexual behavior, including the touching or kissing of, among other specified body parts, the genitals, breast, or buttocks by either the psychotherapist or the patient, provided, in the last instance, the psychotherapist consents to the touching. Requests to the patient by the psychotherapist to engage in sexual contact are also actionable under the statute.[14] The term "psychotherapist" is defined broadly to include any person purporting to perform or performing psychotherapy, regardless of whether the person is licensed.[15] "Psychotherapy" means the professional treatment, assessment, or counseling of a mental or emotional illness, symptom, or condition."[16]

The statute extends liability for the damages caused by the prohibited sexual contact to the psychotherapist's employer in certain specified instances. An employer may be held liable if it fails to either

> take reasonable action when the employer knows or has reason to know that the psychotherapist engaged in sexual contact with . . . a patient or former patient; or make inquiries of an employer or former employer . . . who employed the psychotherapist . . . within the past five years, concerning the occurrence of sexual contacts by the psychotherapist. . . .[17]

---

11. A former patient is a patient who has received psychotherapy from the psychotherapist within two years of the sexual contact. M.S.A. § 148A.01, subd. 3 (West 1989).
12. *Emotionally dependent* "means that the nature of the patient's or former patient's mental condition and the nature of the treatment performed by the psychotherapist are such that the psychotherapist knows or has reason to believe that the patient or former patient is unable to withhold consent to sexual contact by the psychotherapist." M.S.A. § 148A, subd. 2 (West 1989).
13. M.S.A. § 148A.02 (West 1989).
14. M.S.A. § 148A.02, subd. 7 (West 1989).
15. M.S.A. § 148A.02, subd. 5 (West 1989).
16. M.S.A. § 148A.02, subd. 6 (West 1989).
17. M.S.A. § 148A.03 (West 1989).

It should be noted that the statute can be read to mean that the failure to make inquiry of former employers will trigger liability, even in the absence of any evidence that the psychotherapist has previously engaged in prohibited sexual contact. In other words, it may be necessary to make inquiry as a routine part of the hiring process. An employer or former employer of a psychotherapist may be held liable for injuries for failing to disclose, in response to a written inquiry by another employer seeking to employ the psychotherapist as a psychotherapist, known instances of sexual misconduct.[18]

The allowable time for bringing such a suit is five years.[19]

---

18. M.S.A. § 148A.03(b) (West 1989).
19. M.S.A. § 148A.06 (West 1989).

6.7

Criminal Liability

Criminal charges can be brought against an MHP if she or he engages in legally proscribed behavior with a patient. These charges may stem from a variety of behaviors, including sexual contact with a patient, aiding a suicide, assaulting or restraining a patient,[1] or mistreatment of institutionalized patients. This chapter will detail some of the types of behavior that can result in criminal charges.

Criminal Sexual Conduct

Engaging in sexual conduct with a mentally impaired individual or with a patient or former patient can result in conviction of the crime of criminal sexual conduct. The proscribed conduct ranges from penetration, for first-degree criminal sexual conduct,[2] to a wide variety of sexual contact, including touching of the complainant's intimate parts, for fourth-degree criminal sexual conduct.[3] The statute precludes sexual contact between individuals with certain defined relationships. There are two such relationships that are of particular interest to MHPs:

1. The actor knows or has reason to know that the complainant is mentally impaired, mentally incapacitated, or physically helpless.[4]

---

1. *See* chapter 6.6 regarding civil liability for such behavior.
2. M.S.A. § 609.342, subd. 1 (West 1987).
3. M.S.A. § 609.345, subd. 1 (West 1987 & Supp. 1992).
4. *See, e.g.,* M.S.A. § 609.342, subd. 1(e)(ii) (West 1987).

2. The actor is a psychotherapist[5] and the complainant is

   a. a patient of the psychotherapist and the sexual conduct occurred during the psychotherapy session,

   b. a patient or former patient of the psychotherapist and is emotionally dependant[6] on the psychotherapist, or

   c. a patient or former patient of the psychotherapist and the sexual conduct is accomplished by means of therapeutic deception.[7]

   Consent by the patient is not generally available as a defense.[8]

Aiding Suicide

One who intentionally advises, encourages, or assists suicide commits the crime of aiding suicide.[9] Because of the absence of reported cases, it is unclear what type of behavior on the part of an MHP might be construed as encouragement or assistance of a suicide.

Assault and the Authorized Use of Force

An assault occurs when an act is committed with the intent to cause fear of immediate bodily harm or death, or constitutes the intentional infliction of or an attempt to inflict bodily harm.[10] However, one is entitled to use reasonable force "to restrain a mentally ill . . . person from self-injury or injury to another."[11] Reasonable force may also be used by one "with authority to do so to compel compliance with reasonable requirements for the [mentally ill] person's control, conduct or treatment."[12] Although the statute is not entirely clear on this point, it appears that one

---

5. A "psychotherapist" is defined broadly to include any person who "performs or purports to perform psychotherapy." M.S.A. § 609.341, subd. 17 (West 1987 & Supp. 1992).

6. A party is emotionally dependant if "the nature of the [complainant's] condition and the nature of the treatment . . . are such that the psychotherapist knows or has reason to know that the patient is unable to withhold consent to sexual [conduct]. . . ." M.S.A. § 609.341, subd. 18 (West 1987).

7. *See, e.g.*, M.S.A. § 609.344, subds. 1(d), (h)–(j) (West 1987 & Supp. 1992).

8. *Id.*

9. M.S.A. § 609.215 (West 1987).

10. M.S.A. § 609.02, subd. 10 (West 1987).

11. M.S.A. § 609.06(8) (West 1987). *See also* M.S.A. § 609.379 (West Supp. 1992) (use of reasonable force with children).

12. M.S.A. § 609.06(9) (West 1987).

would derive the requisite authority by virtue of a lawful commitment order[13] or pursuant to a lawful hold order.[14]

Mistreatment of Residents or Patients

An employee or manager of a nursing home or hospital who physically or mentally harms a patient of the facility by intentionally abusing, ill-treating, or culpably neglecting the patient is guilty of the crime of mistreatment of residents or patients.[15] The liability imposed by this statute is wholly distinct from that which an MHP may incur by virtue of his or her failure to comply with applicable reporting statutes.[16]

---

13. M.S.A. § 609.06(9) (West 1987).
14. M.S.A. § 253B.05 (West 1982 & Supp. 1992). *See* chapter 5E.4.
15. M.S.A. § 609.231 (West 1987).
16. *See* M.S.A. §§ 626.556, 626.557 (West 1983 & Supp. 1992). *See* chapters 5A.7 and 5A.8.

6.8

Liability Arising From Activities of Credentialing Boards

The state of Minnesota has established a number of credentialing boards and has vested them with broad authority over the licensure and regulation of the various mental health professions.[1] Members of these boards are often involved in activities, such as the restriction or suspension of an MHP's professional license, that can result in legal controversy. Similarly, persons reporting to or otherwise assisting or cooperating with such boards may become embroiled in legal disputes as a result of such involvement. Typical allegations include charges that the antitrust laws have been violated,[2] that the testimony offered to the board was libelous or slanderous, or that privileged information was illegally shared with the board.

There are, however, several sources of protection from liability for members of the credentialing boards. State law specifically provides a broad scope of immunity for members of the boards regulating physicians,[3] nurses,[4] and other MHPs.[5] This immunity extends to both civil and criminal liability for actions premised on violations of state law relating to the duties of members of the boards. Because these boards derive their authority from the state, protection from certain types of liability may also be avail-

---

1. For further discussion of the operations of these boards, *see* M.S.A. §§ 148B.01 to 148B.48 (West 1989 & Supp. 1992) and chapters 1.1 to 1.12.
2. *See, e.g.,* Patrick v. Burget, 800 F.2d 1498 (9th Cir. 1986), rev'd, 486 U.S. 94, 108 S.Ct. 1658 (1988). *See* chapter 6.9.
3. M.S.A. § 147.121, subd. 2 (West 1989).
4. M.S.A. § 148.103, subd. 2 (West 1989).
5. M.S.A. § 148B.08, subd. 2 (West 1989 & Supp. 1992). The statute regulating the board responsible for credentialing psychologists does not, however, provide for such immunity. *See* M.S.A. § 148.90 (West 1989 & Supp. 1992).

able under the common law doctrine of sovereign immunity,[6] the Minnesota Tort Claims Act,[7] the Minnesota law regulating peer review organizations,[8] and the Health Care Quality Improvement Act.[9] Although none of these laws provides complete insulation from all types of liability, together they constitute substantial protection from liability for members of the credentialing boards.

The laws detailed above, along with several other statutory provisions, also provide substantial insulation from liability to a person who reports a violation or alleged violation to one of the boards.[10]

---

6. Sovereign immunity grants the state and its agents immunity from liability for certain types of activities carried out in the name of the state. Although the scope of sovereign immunity has been greatly curtailed from what it once was, there are still a number of types of functions that remain protected by the doctrine. In particular, sovereign immunity remains a viable defense against claims attacking the exercise of discretionary, legislative, judicial, quasi-judicial, or quasi-legislative functions. Activities of members of a credentialing board may well be characterized as quasi-judicial, thus qualifying for immunity. *See* Nieting v. Blondell, 235 N.W.2d 597, 603 (Minn. 1975). This defense may also be available in certain negligence actions against MHPs who are state employees or agents. *See, e.g.,* Cairl v. State, 323 N.W.2d 20 (Minn. 1982) (decision of an MHP to grant holiday release to a patient of a psychiatric facility was a discretionary decision and thus immune from attack in a suit alleging negligence; the patient committed arson while on release); Engle v. Hennepin County, 412 N.W.2d 364 (Minn. Ct. App. 1987) (decision of an MHP not to impose a hold on a paranoid individual was discretionary and thus immune; the individual became acutely paranoid and drove into a wall, killing himself).

7. M.S.A. § 3.736 (West 1977 & Supp. 1992).

8. M.S.A. § 145.61 et seq.

9. 42 U.S.C. § 1112 et seq. The act provides for immunity from liability from "damages under any law of the United States or of any State (or political subdivision thereof)." 42 U.S.C. § 11111 (West 1992). However, no immunity is available for actions relating to "nurses, other licensed health care practitioners, or other health professionals who are not physicians." 42 U.S.C. § 11115.

10. *See, e.g.,* M.S.A. §§ 147.091, 147.121 (West 1989 & Supp. 1992).

6.9

Antitrust Limitations on Practice

There are both federal and state antitrust laws directed at eliminating anticompetitive behavior.[1] The goal of these laws is to ensure free competition on the basis of price, quality, and service. Violation of the antitrust laws can result in significant civil and criminal liability.

In both theory and application, the antitrust laws are highly complex, and a complete discourse on the topic is beyond the scope of this book. In this chapter we will briefly identify and describe those situations most likely to be encountered by an MHP that pose a high degree of risk of scrutiny or sanction under the antitrust laws.

1. *Restrictive covenants.* It is not uncommon for an MHP to enter into a restrictive covenant (or "no-compete" agreement), agreeing not to compete with his or her employer after the termination of employment. If properly drafted to protect legitimate business interests, these agreements may be legal and enforceable. If the agreement is overreaching, it may be

---

1. Federal antitrust laws include the Sherman Act, 15 U.S.C. § 1 et seq. (West 1973 & Supp. 1992) (*e.g.*, 15 U.S.C. § 1 prohibits conspiracies in restraint of trade, and § 2 proscribes monopolization, attempts to monopolize, and conspiracies to monopolize); the Federal Trade Commission Act, 15 U.S.C. § 41 et seq. (West 1973 & Supp. 1992) (*e.g.*, 15 U.S.C. § 45 precludes unfair competition and unfair deceptive practices); and the Clayton Act, including the Robinson–Patman Act, 15 U.S.C. § 13 (West 1973) (*e.g.*, 15 U.S.C. § 13 outlaws certain forms of price discrimination, and § 14 prohibits certain exclusive dealing and other arrangements where the effect is to substantially lessen competition). Minnesota antitrust laws are codified at M.S.A. § 325D.49 et seq. and incorporate many of the elements of the federal laws. *See, e.g.*, Hamilton, *Recent Developments in Minnesota Antitrust Law*, 8 Wm. Mitchell L. Rev. 741, n.68 (1982), and citations contained therein.

successfully challenged as an unfair restriction on trade, because an overbroad covenant restricts the public's access to the MHP laboring under the covenant and thus curtails competition. If found to be unreasonable, the covenant may be rewritten ("blue penciled") by the court or may be found to be unenforceable.

2. *Exclusive contracts.* Agreements giving a single MHP or single practice of MHPs exclusive rights to perform certain services in a provider are frequently challenged as being anticompetitive. Although exclusive agreements may be upheld as serving legitimate procompetitive interests, such as the enhancement of the quality of services at the facility, there are circumstances under which they may be held illegal.

3. *Denial of privileges.* Decisions by a group of MHPs to deny or curtail the privileges of another MHP may be challenged as anticompetitive, inasmuch as they can be characterized as an agreement among competitors to exclude another competitor from the market for services.[2]

4. *Contracting with third-party payers.* Efforts by MHPs to collectively bargain with third-party payers are subject to attack under the antitrust laws. These arrangements may be viewed as an attempt to eliminate competition on price or as a collective refusal to deal.

5. *Price fixing.* Because they eliminate competition, agreements among competitors to set prices for particular services are per se illegal under the antitrust laws. Guidelines setting minimum or maximum prices are considered to be a form of price fixing.

6. *Mergers and acquisitions.* The integration of two or more distinct and competitive practices may, depending on the conditions of the relevant market, violate the laws precluding the creation of a monopoly.

In addition to the practices outlined above, there are numerous other practices that may be challenged under the antitrust laws. Depending on the circumstances, there may or may not be successful defenses available to the MHP who has engaged in such behavior. Suffice it to say, however, that informed legal counsel should be sought prior to engaging in potentially suspect behavior.

---

2. *But see* chapter 6.4 discussing state and federal statutes providing immunity from liability for certain actions of peer review organizations.

Appendix

Table of Cases

Table of Statutes

Table of Rules of Court

Table of Administrative
Rules and Regulations

Table of Cases

References are to page numbers in this book

J

Jarvis v. Levine, 389
J.E.B. v. State of Alabama *ex rel.* T.B., 261, 263
Jensen v. Eveleth Taconite Co., 249
Johnson v. Johnson, 119, 235
Johnson v. Miera, 228
Johnson v. Paul's Auto & Truck Sales, 218

K

Kanter v. Metropolitan Medical Center, 265
Koenig v. Barrett, 237
Kresko v. Rulli, 249
Krueger v. Zoch, 235

L

Langeland v. Farmers State Bank of Trimont, 228
Lee v. Metropolitan Airports Commission, 228
Lockwood v. Independent School Dist. No. 877, 218
Long v. Campion, 235

M

Maas v. Laursen, 100, 101
Madsen v. Park Nicollet Medical Center, 387
Magnuson v. Rupp Mfg., 243
Matter of Welfare of K.T., 158, 159
Matz v. Martinson, 236
Mayo Clinic v. Mayo's Drug and Cosmetic, Inc., 245, 246
McCormack v. Hankscraft Co., 242
McCormack v. Lindberg, 405
McElwain v. Van Beek, 96
Metropolitan Life Ins. Co. v. Mass., 67
Mincy v. Arizona, 105
Miranda v. Arizona, 279

N

Nieting v. Blondell, 416
Northwest Residence, Inc. v. City of Brooklyn Center, 71
Novak v. Novak, 210

O

O'Conner v. Johnson, 106
Okrina v. Midwestern Corp., 228

P

Padilla v. Minnesota State Bd. of Medical Examiners, 30
Parham v. J.R. et al., 194
Pate v. Robinson, 286
Patrick v. Burget, 415
Ponticas v. K.M.S. Invs., 384
Power v. Ohio, 261
Price v. Sheppard, 389, 391, 392, 393
Purcell v. St. Paul City Railway, 228

Q

Quill v. TWA, 228

R

Rapp v. Travelers Ins. Co., 67
R.A.V. v. City of St. Paul, 227
Rodriguez v. State, 308
Roeder v. North Am. Life Ins. Co. of Chicago, 101

S

Saari v. Litman, 88
Schultz v. Oldenburg, 235
Scott County Lumber Co., Inc. v. City of Shakopee, 72
Scott v. Mego Int'l., Inc., 245, 246, 247
Sheffield-King Milling Co. v. Sheffield Mill & Elevator Co., 245
Simchuck v. Fullerton, 266
Smith et al. v. St. Paul Fire & Marine, 407
St. Paul Fire & Marine v. D.H.L., 407
St. Paul Fire & Marine v. Love, 407, 408
Staat v. Staat, 100, 102
Stadler v. Cross, 228
State *ex rel.* Pearson v. Probate Court, 330
State Farm Fire & Cas. Co. v. Wicka, 230, 231, 273
State Farm Mutual Automobile Ins. Co. v. Village of Isle, 228
State v. Alton, 294
State v. Andring, 101, 102, 143, 145
State v. Austin, 303
State v. Bauer, 287

Table of Statutes

Minnesota Statutes Annotated

Table of Rules of Court

References are to page numbers in this book

Minnesota Rules of Evidence

Minnesota Rules of Juvenile Procedure

Table of Administrative Rules and Regulations

References are to page numbers in this book

Index

References are to chapters

About the Authors

Eric S. Janus is professor of law at William Mitchell College of Law, St. Paul, Minnesota, where he has taught full-time since 1984. Professor Janus teaches mental health law, and his written work in this area includes *Civil Commitment in Minnesota* (2nd ed., Butterworth, 1991). He was a member of the Supreme Court Task Force on the Mentally Disabled and the Law, and chaired the committee that wrote the Civil Commitment Rules of Procedure. Professor Janus participated in drafting the Civil Commitment Act of 1982 and the Vulnerable Adults Protection Act. Prior to teaching, he practiced law for 11 years at the Legal Aid Society of Minneapolis, where he specialized in mental health law and served as the managing attorney for legal advocacy for developmentally disabled persons.

Professor Janus received his JD from Harvard Law School and his BA from Carleton College.

Ruth A. Mickelsen is senior corporate counsel for Medica, a nonprofit health maintenance organization serving over 500,000 members in Minnesota. She is an adjunct professor of health law at William Mitchell College of Law in St. Paul. She previously worked as a partner at the law firm of Popham, Haik, Schnobrich, and Kaufman, where she cochaired the national health law practice group. She is the past chair of the Minnesota State Bar Association Health Law Section.

Mickelsen received her BA from the University of Minnesota, her JD from William Mitchell College of Law, and her MPH from Harvard University. She is the author of numerous articles on health care law and is a frequent speaker on health law subjects. She resides in St. Paul with her husband, Bill Manning, and her daughter, Sonja.

Sheva J. Sanders is of counsel with the law firm of Lindquist & Vennum, representing health care providers and related ventures in business and regulatory matters. Her areas of concentration include health care business reorganizations, combinations, and affiliations; provider reimbursement; provider contracting; peer review; confidentiality issues; patients' rights; and professional corporations.

Sanders graduated from Northwestern University school of Law in 1984 and was elected to the Order of the Coif. She is also a member of the National Health Lawyers Association, has served as an adjunct professor in the area of health law, and has a number of publication credits in the field. She resides in Minneapolis with her husband, Tom, and three children, Noah, Mara, and Benjamin.